CONSERVATORSHIP

CONSERVATORSHIP

Inside California's System of
Coercion and Care for Mental Illness

_____

ALEX V. BARNARD

_____

Columbia University Press

New York

Columbia University Press
Publishers Since 1893
New York   Chichester, West Sussex
cup.columbia.edu

Library of Congress Cataloging-in-Publication Data
Names: Barnard, Alex V., 1987– author.
Title: Conservatorship : inside California's system of coercion and care for
    mental illness / Alex V. Barnard, Department of Sociology, New York University.
Description: 1. | New York : Columbia University Press, 2023. | Includes index.
Identifiers: LCCN 2023000881 (print) | LCCN 2023000882 (ebook) |
    ISBN 9780231210249 (hardback) | ISBN 9780231210256 (trade paperback) |
    ISBN 9780231558327 (ebook)
Subjects: LCSH: Conservatorship—California. | Guardian and ward—California. |
    Mentally ill—Care—California. | Mental health laws—California.
Classification: LCC KFC112 .B37 2023 (print) | LCC KFC112 (ebook) |
    DDC 344.04/409794—dc23/eng/20230712
LC record available at https://lccn.loc.gov/2023000881
LC ebook record available at https://lccn.loc.gov/2023000882

Printed and bound by CPI Group (UK) Ltd, Croydon, CR0 4YY

Cover design: Noah Arlow
Cover image: Getty Images

"The pressing problem with regard to the future of the insane in this country is: how can the chronic insane pauper be most cheaply cared for, consistently with a proper regard to humanity? And must this work be done by the state or the several counties?"

—Frederick Wines, Secretary, Illinois Board of
State Commissioners of Public Charities (1879)

For the moms, especially my own

CONTENTS

PART III: REFORM

PREFACE

I n 2015, I spent a year in France researching the mental health system there for my PhD dissertation at the University of California, Berkeley. I arrived during a dramatic rise in involuntary psychiatric hospitalizations (also known as civil commitments) that commentators saw as a symptom of a fracturing society and withering social safety net. The increasing frequency with which citizens' civil rights were being restricted in the name of their mental health provoked parliamentary inquiries and was treated as Exhibit A for a public psychiatric system in deep crisis.[1]

I returned to the United States wondering if the story was the same back home. Anecdotally, I heard that rates of involuntary hospitalization were increasing, but I could not find even the most basic data on the frequency of forced treatment in the United States or in New York, where I was living. In fact, I was discouraged from even looking. I spoke to a prominent academic psychiatrist who told me, no doubt concerned about my future prospects as a researcher, that "in the 1970s, civil commitments were a hot topic, and that spawned a large number of studies. . . . [But] we're on to new questions now." He was right. For decades, planning and oversight for the American mental health care system have treated involuntary hospitalization as an afterthought.

Despite having been warned away from the subject, I began conducting observations in courtrooms tucked away in psychiatric hospitals in New York City. There, people who had been hospitalized against their will requested to be released by a judge. I quickly realized that, unremarked though it may be, hospitalization remains the backbone of our response to the most serious mental illnesses. I saw people who had been hospitalized and discharged more than one hundred times. Others had been institutionalized for decades. Our mental health system spends more on psychiatric hospitals than it does for clinics or clinicians and about as much as it spends on medications.[2] A majority of people in America's psychiatric hospitals are there involuntarily.[3] As I saw in the courtrooms, many desperately want to get as far away from them as possible.

I returned to California in 2017. After two years' absence, the amalgam of disruptive behavior, drug use, and untreated suffering among unhoused individuals, which had been visible since I first moved to the Bay Area in 2011, seemed to have reached a new level of acuteness. As in France, involuntary treatment was on the agenda; unlike in France, the focus was on increasing its use. Legislators from San Francisco were pushing to ramp up the use of "conservatorships," a legal tool that allows a third party to force someone to take medication and to place them in a locked facility, sometimes for years at a time.

This was happening despite the lack of any real investigation from the legislature or state government into what was happening to the people who were already conserved. A quick internet search revealed that there was almost no recent academic research on conservatorship either. I embarked on a small side project on California's conservatorship system. Still, I feared the topic was too niche to appeal to readers beyond social service professionals or the parents of children tangled up in the system.

Enter Britney Spears. The explosive 2021 revelations of the wide range of abuses the pop star had experienced during a thirteen-year conservatorship in California meant that suddenly I was studying a hot topic. I circulated a draft of some of my findings to advocates working in the policy arena. Their positive response convinced me that there was real hunger for a comprehensive look at the system that many people, up to Governor Gavin Newsom, were talking about expanding and that others, like the Free Britney movement, were trying to tear down. When I told Eric Schwartz, the editor at Columbia University Press, to whom I owed an academic tome comparing the mental health systems in the United States and France, that I wanted to write a more accessible book focused on conservatorship in California specifically, he told me to go for it. So that's how we got here.

In some ways, I have conducted four years of research and hundreds of interviews only to confirm my initial intuitions. Conservatorship is being used to forcibly treat and institutionalize thousands of people per year in California. Yet I find an astonishing lack of government oversight and leadership, which means that the conservatorship system continues to fail the most visibly vulnerable people in the state. This book documents the myriad ways that government has abdicated authority, declining to ensure the accountable and coherent exercise of its own power. This makes coercive treatment haphazard, inconsistent, and rarely successful in transforming an individual's careening trajectory between hospitals, jails, shelters, and the street. More broadly, the book investigates what happens when "hypermarginalized" people become the targets of intervention from a mass of disjointed, privatized, and conflicting institutions of care and control.[4]

Even a long book cannot do everything. For one thing, this book is not an attempt to answer the perennial question of whether involuntary treatment "works." Proponents insist forced care is an indispensable "lifesaving" intervention.[5] Opponents counter that there is "little evidence" that coercion "confer[s] any clinical benefit."[6] The truth seems murkier. Many studies show that people subject to involuntary hospitalization demonstrate improvements in symptoms.[7] A significant minority of them will ultimately tell researchers that their hospitalization was justified.[8] Yet others finds that forced treatment leads to symptoms of post-traumatic stress[9] and increased risk of suicide.[10] There is a wealth of contradictory studies about whether involuntary treatment decreases people's subsequent willingness to engage with the mental health system in the longer term.[11] Yet these studies are plagued with methodological problems, and nearly all of them deal with hospitalizations that last days or weeks. There is almost no recent evidence showing the efficacy of longer-term institutionalization or conservatorship, which is what policy makers are proposing to expand.[12] This book does not seek to resolve this long-running debate. Rather, it shows how abdicated authority makes involuntary care crueler than it needs to be and voluntary services less effective alternatives than they could be.

This book is also not focused on the vitally important question of whether forced treatment is imposed equitably on different social groups. It almost certainly is not. A host of studies document that Black people are more likely to be misdiagnosed with schizophrenia,[13] more likely to be subjected to coercive hospitalization,[14] and more likely to be placed in low-quality facilities,[15] where they are more likely to be forcibly given medication and physically restrained.[16] Britney Spears's stifling conservatorship at the hands of her father reminded us that claims around who is "crazy" have all too frequently reinforced patriarchal domination.[17] And in interviews with LGBTQ people subject to forced hospitalization, I heard multiple times of the failure of the mental health system to ensure the basic dignity that comes from calling a patient by their chosen gender pronouns.

While this book nods to these disparities, it does not center on them. It highlights, instead, inequities that emerge from an underregulated and fragmented system. It reveals how some individuals are abandoned to the streets and others relegated to locked facilities not because of their clinical needs but because of which side of a county's border they live on, whether they see a cop or a clinician when in crisis, and whether they wind up in a private or a public hospital.

Before starting, a final note on terminology. The choice of words to describe the people subject to conservatorships is fraught. On the one hand, some advocates for expanding conservatorships (often parents) have called for relabeling conditions like schizophrenia as "neurobiological disorders." They are taking their cue from some reformers in the National Institute of Mental Health and have won over politicians such as Governor Newsom, who talks about "serious brain illnesses."[18] The assumption is that these labels reduce stigma (no one can be held responsible for their faulty genes or broken mental circuitry). They also imply that medical need should trump civil liberties ("you don't have to have the permission of a judge to treat someone for a brain disease like Alzheimer's," I have often been told).

In this book, I eschew terms like *brain disease* or *neurobiological disorder*. For one thing, they are potentially harmful. Describing people with schizophrenia as having damaged brains actually seems to increase stigma and fear.[19] They are also misleading. I am sympathetic to advocates' attempts to argue that conditions like schizophrenia are as "real" as diabetes or dementia. But the fact that psychiatric treatment can be imposed on people explicitly refusing it also makes conditions like schizophrenia unique in a way that terms like *brain illness* deliberately seek to elide.

On the other end of the spectrum are terms like *consumer, survivor,* or *ex-patient*, which are used by people on the receiving end of involuntary care. *Survivor* or *ex-patient* captures some people's lived experience of forced treatment but are rarely used among recipients of mental health services more generally.[20] *Consumer* harkens too much to the privatization of care that this book critiques. I do occasionally join activists and scholars who have reclaimed the otherwise pejorative term *mad* (much as LGBTQ activists have done for *queer*). I also talk about *clients* in clinics, *patients* in hospitals, and *residents* in board-and-care homes because those administrative labels are accurate shorthand for where someone is in the conservatorship system.

In the end, I have largely chosen the most banal route. In this book, I speak of "people living with serious mental illness" to describe individuals who are diagnosed with conditions such as schizophrenia, bipolar disorder, or major depression.[21] Studies have shown that such "person-first" language increases empathy toward those so labeled.[22] That said, this, too, is an imperfect moniker. While 4.5 percent of American adults had a "serious mental illness" in the past year,[23] this book is only about a tiny sliver of them. Even among the 0.4 percent of adults who live with schizophrenia,[24] many reside in the community without ever being considered for conservatorship. This book's focus is on those who have fallen through the cracks of the public mental health system. It offers less attention to those who have been well served and have thrived with its help.

Another drawback of talking about "people living with serious mental illness" is that the label *mentally ill* is precisely what some people subject to forced treatment are contesting. I'm tipping my hand here. As innumerable anthropologists have shown, "massive and lasting disturbances of reason, intellectual, and emotions" are "to be found in all known societies."[25] Whether and how we carve up those experiences into medical diagnoses varies enormously by social and cultural context.[26] Patients are right that these diagnoses are often applied in unfair and unhelpful ways. But the point is that "serious mental illness" captures experiences that are, in an important sense, "real." For some individuals, the suffering these conditions cause can be alleviated by biomedical treatments like pharmaceuticals, though too often our mental health system—and forced treatment in particular—exacerbates it.

Of course, the best option is to talk about people living with mental illnesses as, simply, people. Throughout this book, any person I interviewed who is introduced with a first and last name has given consent for their real name to be used. Other names are pseudonyms. I have let participants choose their preferred level of anonymity, which is why some people are introduced with a precise location and job title while others are referred to in vague terms. It is my hope that all these invaluable contributors to this study, whether or not they agree with my conclusions, find that I have accurately shed light on their experiences and given voice to their perspectives.

CONSERVATORSHIP

CONSERVATORSHIP

INTRODUCTION

The Other Magna Carta

Wally sits alone while California's mental health system swirls around him.

In July 2021, I drive to central Los Angles alongside Dr. Susan Partovi, the media-styled "Renegade Doctor of Skid Row."[1] We're on an outreach mission to one of her "super-dupers"—individuals who, as a result of a serious mental illness and substance use, are superfrequent users of public services, bouncing endlessly among emergency rooms, jails, shelters, and the street—and, for all that excess utilization, are at risk of imminent death.

As we pull into a gas station parking lot, Dr. Partovi points out Wally to me. He's easy to overlook. In a city where homelessness is visible not just in unhoused bodies but in makeshift shacks and overflowing shopping carts, Wally is sitting in a bus shelter without so much as a backpack. 'He's been there for weeks with absolutely nothing. That's the biggest sign to me that someone's really not doing well, really gravely disabled,'[2] Dr. Partovi tells me. Hold on to that term, *gravely disabled*. California's Welfare and Institutions Code defines it as someone who is, "as a result of a mental disorder, unable to provide for his or her basic personal needs for food, clothing, or shelter."[3] It's key to Wally's story.

Wally looks to be white and in his forties or fifties, although it's hard to tell. His face is grimy, and his gnarled hands are covered in sores. He's wearing a red heavy winter jacket, even though the temperature will soon plateau at one hundred degrees.

'Hi, do you remember me?' Dr. Partovi queries cheerily. She's been visiting him regularly for a year. Wally smiles, baring his two remaining teeth, but doesn't answer the question.

'Have you been eating?'

He responds slowly: 'Not really.'

'Are you drinking any water?'

He says 'yes.' But there are no bottles around him, so we have doubts about how recently.

'Can you take that jacket off if it keeps getting hot?' she asks.

He stares back.

Partovi proposes getting him a burrito, and we start crossing the street toward a nearby taqueria, although I circle back to ask him what kind.

Now he lights up: 'Carne asada.'

While we're waiting for the burrito, Dr. Partovi fills me in on a bit of Wally's back story. He had been in a shelter in Hollywood, where he was 'pretty happy' until it closed down. But the COVID-19 pandemic offered a potential upgrade: Project Roomkey, which gave him and thousands of "high-risk" homeless individuals converted hotel rooms. He left his room after one day, with no explanation. Shortly thereafter, he was hit by a car while inebriated and spent ten days in an intensive care unit. They released him to a nursing home, where Partovi hoped he would stay. But Wally walked out, cast still on his leg. Back to his bus stop.

We come back with the burrito, and Partovi continues quizzing him: 'Where have you been sleeping?'

'Here,' he tells us.

'You were at the hotel, why did you leave?'

He shrugs.

'We've been trying really hard to keep you indoors, you know.'

Wally smiles and nods.

Right then, I get a better sense of who 'we' is. Wally's case manager from his Full-Service Partnership team—the most intensive level of public outpatient mental health care in California—pulls up in a sedan. Dr. Partovi walks up to the car window and gives a quick rundown of our interaction so far. The caseworker starts ticking off the various shelters and supported housing programs she's been applying to on his behalf. 'We're just going to try everything and see if it sticks,' she announces.

They've had some successes. With Wally's agreement, one of Partovi's team members donned a hazmat suit and shaved off his lice-ridden hair. His case manager visited him daily until she convinced him to go onto a monthly antipsychotic injection. 'Do you see how he's making eye contact?' Partovi tells me, 'That's because we got him on Abilify [an antipsychotic].' Nonetheless, we presume he is still so delusional that we can stand right next to him talking about him, without expecting much of a response.

We leave Wally with his caseworker, but when we're pulling out of the parking lot, we hear 'Hey!' and see a staff member from his previous homeless shelter, who is driving up to check on him. Dr. Partovi will have a phone call this afternoon with a clinician from the LA Department of Mental Health's Homeless Outreach and Mobile Engagement team. They've picked Wally out of Los Angeles's 69,144 homeless individuals as one of a few dozen most "unable to live safely in the community."[4] With all those interventions swirling around him, he's still unhoused, barely fed, and wearing a winter jacket at a bus stop during a heat wave.

Partovi's credentials as someone who not only cares for but listens to and respects the poor and dispossessed are impeccable. Later that week, I join her at the Skid Row clinic where she treats homeless heroin users and sends them to pick up injection supplies at the needle exchange on the way out. She once took in a homeless woman's nine cats to get her to go into treatment. She tells me that, back when public insurance didn't cover the cost of antipsychotics, she'd buy them herself.

But when it comes to Wally, she's doesn't think we should be deferring to his decisions anymore. I ask her what she thinks you'd have to offer Wally to get him to agree to come off the street. She fires back: "Nothing. He's so paranoid that he doesn't want to go anywhere other than the bus stop that he's used to. And so you need to treat him." Wally is already on medication. "Treat" means forcing him into an institution where, in Partovi's words, he can "marinate" on his antipsychotic until he's capable of realizing he wants to stay indoors, properly fed and clothed.

In order to force him into an institution, Wally needs a conservatorship—a legal status under which a judge gives a third party the power to decide where a person lives, how to spend their money, and whether to consent to medical treatment on their behalf. And in order to get a conservatorship, not just a judge but a police officer, an emergency room clinician, a hospital psychiatrist, a county investigator, and the person deciding on admissions for a locked treatment facility all need to agree over the course of a months-long process that he is gravely disabled. Every time one of the many and varied actors serving Wally has tried to get him conserved, someone along that continuum has said, against all apparent indications, that Wally is not gravely disabled. And so he goes back to his bus stop.

This book follows the efforts of government officials, families, and medical professionals to get people like Wally onto conservatorship in California. It charts the simultaneous battles of civil liberties campaigners, survivors of forced treatment, and clinicians committed to voluntary care to keep people off of conservatorships.

Everyone agrees it's a life-or-death struggle. Governor Gavin Newsom claims that the state's strict laws governing conservatorship have "sentenced people" like Wally "to death."[5] In response, Newsom has supported a host of reforms to ramp up conservatorships to address disruptive behavior and substance abuse among people who are homeless. Many families of people with mental illness see conservatorship as their last hope to stabilize loved ones ricocheting among jails, hospitals, and the street. These efforts have been opposed by groups like the American Civil Liberties Union, which assert that conservatorships are "the greatest deprivation of civil rights aside from the death penalty."[6] There's no doubt where Dr. Partovi stands: "The idea that people 'just like being homeless, that's their choice, if they want to die, it's their right to die'—it's just bullshit," she tells me.

Most portrayals of this debate depict a titanic clash between people's civil rights and their well-being, between mental health clients who see conservatorship as coercion and family members who see it as compassionate care. Social scientists, too, have looked at debates over civil commitment as a battle between two powerful professions: law and medicine.

This book tells the story of conservatorship from a different angle. It focuses on how, for fifty years, the state of California has *abdicated authority* for the use of its own power. Government, which has the prerogative to organize, regulate, and direct the conservatorship system, doesn't. It has instead *delegated* responsibility for conservatorship to a welter of private and for-profit agencies and given them enormous *discretion* in using it. As a result, grave disability is being defined not by the courts or legislators but by the market forces that shape the availability of psychiatric hospital beds and the resources, constraints, and preferences of "street-level bureaucrats."[7]

The consequence of the state's abdication of authority is a paradoxical tragedy. People like Wally can be subjected to repeated, ineffectual bouts of coercive care. They are often the objects of exhaustive efforts of selfless clinicians. Yet their basic needs for shelter, dignity, and care are still unmet. When someone winds up conserved, it's more likely thanks to what one mother described as "luck and heroics"[8]—or what conservatees might think of as misfortune and abusive paternalism—than any coherent policy. The result is a triumph for neither law nor medicine but for privatization, fragmentation, and bureaucratization.

People under conservatorship in California and those potentially affected by the expansions of conservatorship number in the tens of thousands.[9] But this book is a broader cautionary tale. Nationwide, politicians want to address problems ranging from the overdose crisis to the mass incarceration of people living with severe mental illness by ramping up involuntary mental health care. But new laws will leave individuals like Wally at their bus stops until government assumes real authority over the mental health system and accountability to the people it serves.

A NEW BILL OF RIGHTS

To understand how Wally wound up at that bus stop, you need to go back to a landmark piece of legislation: the 1967 Lanterman-Petris-Short (LPS) Act. It is remembered as a "Bill of Rights" for people with mental illness that aimed to strictly limit involuntary psychiatric treatment.[10] Less visibly, it laid the groundwork for the state's departure from responsibility for providing care to people with the most serious mental illnesses.

By the mid-twentieth century, California's Department of Mental Hygiene was the second-largest agency in the state (after only the University of California).[11] It managed fourteen state psychiatric hospitals that, at their height, interned 37,000 people. In 1963, investigators discovered "shocking . . . brutality and neglect" at Fairview hospital, the state's newest facility.[12] Patients were shackled and left naked in unheated seclusion rooms for days on end.[13] The state hospital system was thus just the kind of bloated, underperforming government bureaucracy that was a ripe target for the likes of Frank Lanterman, an archconservative Republican state assembly member from Pasadena. So he, Nicholas Petris (a Democrat from Oakland), and a handful of other legislators launched an inquiry, trying to "ascertain whether we were getting our money's worth."[14]

They were not. State-run asylums had been set up in the nineteenth century on psychiatrists' promise that giving the "mad" a calm place cut off from society would restore them to sanity and productivity.[15] These institutions had become, in the words of these legislators, "a bin marked 'miscellaneous' to receive every personnel problem facing society."[16] Those abandoned inside included people diagnosed with schizophrenia as well as chronic alcoholism, dementia, and developmental disabilities. Few received anything resembling treatment. The legislators' survey found that 2 percent of "patients" went to individual or group therapy, 12 percent received drugs, 41 percent were getting "milieu therapy" (that is, "treatment" that comes from the mere fact of being in a hospital), and 40 percent had only custodial care (why they weren't even getting "milieu therapy" is unclear).[17]

Perhaps most alarming, though, was how people got there.[18] Petris recalled in a later interview: "A guy walking down the street, talking to himself . . . a policeman could pick him up, take him to the emergency hospital, and a judge would railroad him into a state hospital. . . . Senior citizens were being shoveled into hospitals by many thousands a year."[19] The people in state hospitals seemed to "suffer not from mental illness, but from contingencies"—the bad luck of lacking a family willing to keep them or the resources to go somewhere else.[20] They were subject to civil commitments: a very particular form of government power that allows the state to intern people deemed mentally ill, even when they are accused of no crime. The inquiry found that, in 1966, the court hearings approving commitments lasted an average of five minutes.[21] Commitment could be permanent.

In 1967, the legislature announced its intention to end the "inappropriate, indefinite, and involuntary commitment of mentally disordered persons." Lanterman and Petris characterized the bill that ultimately bore their names (and that of Senator Alan Short, a Democrat from Stockton) as the "Magna Carta" of the mentally ill.[22] There's a grain of grandiosity but also of truth to the analogy between the Lanterman-Petris-Short Act and the original Magna Carta, from 1215 CE: both protected people from unjust imprisonment at the hands of the state.

The first prong of the bill limited civil commitments to people who were deemed a danger to themselves or others or were gravely disabled as a result of a mental disorder. It replaced a single, never-ending court-ordered commitment with a series of time-limited hospitalization procedures subject to intensifying judicial scrutiny. It included a host of new legal protections, from guaranteed access to personal possessions or visitors to the right to refuse electroshocks or lobotomy. And, in the vein of the original Magna Carta, it extended to psychiatric patients the right to file a writ of habeas corpus asking to be released from hospitalization. The idea, to quote Art Bolton, a legislative aid involved in drafting the bill, was that "if we could lodge a huge boulder in the center of that over-used road to the [state] mental hospital, the patients would have to be sent somewhere else, to more appropriate facilities."[23]

A second prong of the bill would ensure those more appropriate facilities existed. The state pledged to pay for 90 percent of new county mental health programs.[24] The approach, the *Los Angeles Times* observed, was in line with the philosophy of "modern psychiatry" that "treating the mentally ill early and in the community environment is often more effective [than institutionalizing them]."[25] Indeed, Governor Ronald Reagan used the passage of LPS to announce that local mental health services "offer the most feasible and enlightened way to achieve the best results" and, as a result, "we can continue to reduce the size of our mental hospitals."[26] He delivered. By 1973, the state had already shuttered three of its hospitals—the first in the nation to do so.[27] The LPS Act put California at the leading edge of a movement to *deinstitutionalize* care for people with mental illness.

It is difficult to overstate the widespread enthusiasm for LPS when it went into effect. The *San Diego Union* celebrated in 1969 that it had already "advanced and improved the treatment of mental patients . . . and has restored their basic, civil rights as human beings."[28] Academics described California as a "trendsetter,"[29] the exemplar of how a "civil libertarian, legalistic approach"[30] could replace the abusive medical paternalism of the old commitment system. LPS became the "prototype for mental health laws" in many states and other Western countries.[31]

Fast-forward five decades, and the LPS Act remains largely unchanged. But depictions of it have been turned on their head. Heather Knight, a columnist for the *San Francisco Chronicle*, asserted in 2017 that LPS "lets the mentally ill choose to live on the streets"[32]—offering them not genuine freedom but the right to fester, untreated, in filth and feces. Politicians throughout the state blame LPS for homelessness, mass incarceration, homicides, and deaths from overdoses and untreated diseases.[33] Before he died in 1981, even Frank Lanterman purportedly confessed, "I wanted the LPS Act to help the mentally ill. I never meant for it to prevent those who need care from receiving it. The law has to be changed."[34]

Governor Newsom declared in 2020 that "California's behavioral health laws may have been ahead of their time but today call out for reform."[35] He has backed a flurry of bills to loosen legal protections against forced treatment. They are a particularly visible manifestation of a nationwide push to use coercive care to manage homelessness, curb substance abuse, and divert people from prisons and jails.[36] Prominent psychiatrists are calling for rebuilding the long-term care institutions LPS was intended to empty.[37] The Magna Carta is eight hundred years old. It's not clear if the Magna Carta of the mentally ill will make it to sixty.

THE "GRAVE DISABILITY" LOOPHOLE

These debates over expanding involuntary treatment overlook an inconvenient reality: forced treatment never went away. LPS's original boosters[38] as well as contemporary critics[39] seem to agree that the law made it nearly impossible to subject people to extended psychiatric internment. Social scientists, too, have depicted a system in which protracted institutionalization through civil commitments has largely disappeared.[40] Instead, researchers suggest, people with serious mental illness are either living in the community (where they are sometimes informally pressured into accepting treatment, but legally free to refuse it) or incarcerated in prisons and jails, not hospitals.[41]

But LPS, like most civil commitment laws around the United States, contains a loophole. Before LPS, the justification for civil commitments was *parens patriae*, or the state's obligation to serve as a substitute parent for subjects who are vulnerable and incapable of caring for themselves. LPS shifted the basis of commitments. Today, hospitalizations for danger to self or danger to others are based on the state's police power, its prerogative to protect citizens from physical harm.[42] Yet the law also contains a third criterion: *grave disability*, or an inability to provide for basic needs of food, clothing, or shelter as a result of a mental disorder.[43] Grave disability, psychiatrists observed after LPS went into effect, provided a fuzzy "catch-all for patients who did not meet specific criteria but for whom hospitalization appeared to be warranted on clinical grounds."[44] It was the escape clause that kept the spirit of *parens patriae* alive in the shadows of a reformed mental health system.

In California, someone who is a danger to themself or others can stay in the hospital for a few weeks (which can feel like an incredibly long time if you don't want to be there). But someone who is deemed gravely disabled by a court can be placed in a conservatorship, which lasts one year and can be renewed indefinitely.[45] A court-appointed conservator can be a family member or a private professional but is most frequently a county public guardian. This conservator becomes a heavy-handed parent in control of nearly every aspect of a person's life, from finances to medical care.

Conservatorship was designed to be the backstop that would catch people like Wally and keep them interned, in treatment, and alive.[46] Academics and policy makers have focused on how laws like LPS contributed to the deinstitutionalization of people with mental illness from hospitals onto the streets or their transinstitutionalization into prisons.[47] Conservatees are the ones stuck in the locked institutions that were supposed to have disappeared, the invisible population that stayed behind.[48]

They are so invisible, in fact, that it took a pop star with a hundred million record sales to bring conservatorship to light. In 2021, thanks to a *New York Times* documentary and the burgeoning "Free Britney Spears" movement, California's hidden conservatorship system burst into public view. Ms. Spears's father had been her conservator since 2008, when she suffered a breakdown exhaustively documented (and probably exacerbated) by the paparazzi, which spiraled into two psychiatric hospitalizations. Spears alleged that in the ensuing thirteen years, she faced a range of startling abuses, including being denied access to a phone, forced to perform, and de facto sterilized by an involuntarily implanted IUD. All this happened based on a ten-minute hearing during her hospitalization, which included a somewhat implausible allegation that the then twenty-six-year-old had dementia. The judge heard no testimony. Lawyers asked no questions.[49] It seemed California did it again: the parallels with the pre-LPS era—short sham hearings leading to indefinite rights restrictions by seemingly malevolent family members (usually men)—are striking.

Even if it brought conservatorship to the public's attention, Spears's case is not relevant to this book in an important sense. Although she was originally hospitalized through the procedures of the LPS Act, she was ultimately placed on a probate conservatorship, which is a separate legal tool (usually reserved for people with developmental disabilities or the elderly). LPS conservatorships are more potent: they grant the conservator the power not only to manage someone's money and personal affairs but also to place them in a locked facility and force them to take psychiatric medications. They are also harder to get. (It's almost inconceivable that Spears would qualify as gravely disabled.)

Spears's case is relevant, though, because civil liberties advocates seized on it to argue that, despite her stature and resources, it was "no exception."[50] According to Disability Rights California, "While Britney's fame may be unique, her experience in the current conservatorship system is not."[51] In the eyes of movements representing consumers, survivors, or ex-patients, conservatorships (usually referred to as guardianships in other states) are similarly toxic nationwide. In 2022, legislators suddenly began considering laws to get more people *out* of conservatorships rather than *into* them.[52]

So did LPS not go far enough in restoring the fundamental civil rights of people living with psychiatric disabilities?[53] Or have the restrictions imposed by LPS left people like Wally to die on the streets, by making lifesaving conservatorships excessively difficult to impose? It's hard to know because there has been barely any published research on conservatorship for decades.[54] The California state government provides no reliable data on conservatorships and conducts no regular evaluation of how the system is functioning.[55] This dearth of transparency is true of civil commitments around the United States, a situation that led Senator Elizabeth Warren to write the Departments of Justice and Health and Human Services to demand updated data on conservatorships after the Spears story broke.[56]

This book argues that the answer to the question of whether LPS went too far or not far enough in protecting people from forced treatment and institutionalization is "both." People who need intensive care are turned down for conservatorships and left to die in neglect. Others on conservatorship are locked in institutions despite having the potential to survive—and, in some cases, thrive—outside of them, if only society invested in the right supports. The culprit, I argue, is a joint failure of government authority and accountability over the conservatorship system.

LAW AND MEDICINE, CONFLICT AND COLLABORATION

Even for readers not riveted by the Spears case, debates about conservatorships speak to a bigger set of questions about our collective failure to address interlinked crises of homelessness, drug addiction, and untreated mental illness. Before getting to my own explanation, let's consider two existing diagnoses of the problem and the solutions each proposes.

One framing of laws like LPS is that they pit the professions of law and medicine against each other in *medicolegal conflict*. Lawyers and doctors have fought for centuries over who has primary jurisdiction over mad people.[57] When states began reforming civil commitment laws in the 1960s and '70s, social scientists portrayed them as provoking a "new collision between medical [and] legal . . .

concerns."[58] What was once "viewed as a basically psychiatric problem (the presence of mental illness and need for hospitalization)" would now have "superimposed upon it a legal qualification (constitutional liberties, a trial by jury, etc.)."[59] Battles between law and medicine are not just about competing professional prerogatives but about internal ethical conundrums.[60] As ethnographers embedded with clinical teams show, many providers today are torn between a desire to provide compassionate care and respect for their client's right to refuse it.[61]

This image of an intractable clash between law (as in "rights") and medicine (as in "care") has become the dominant popular lens for depicting disputes over LPS. To critics, the law is the paragon of civil liberties taken to excess, a power grab by disability rights advocates who have "succeeded in having the courts place so many roadblocks between patients and treatment that families wanting treatment . . . are forced to find a lawyer rather than a doctor."[62] As a 2012 proposal for reforming the law put it, California's system is "lengthy, multilayered, non-therapeutic, cumbersome . . . costly . . . complicated and 'Byzantine.'"[63] This book proves that this description is absolutely true. But if you believe that conservatorship is one step shy of the death penalty, you should want putting one into place to be as cumbersome and costly as possible.[64] From this conflict perspective, for people with severe mental illness, it's rights or care: you can't have both.

From the vantage point of a person subject to involuntary treatment (as well as many scholars studying the topic), a second perspective is probably more convincing. Law and medicine are not in conflict but instead collaborate in imposing forced treatment. The famed social theorist Michel Foucault examined how, in nineteenth-century France, the nascent discipline of psychiatry conspired with law in a "game of dual medical and judicial qualification" to label deviants as dangerously mad and requiring internment in asylums.[65] His insight was that law and medicine, acting in concert, have powers they do not have on their own. Doctors can typically treat people only with their consent.[66] Judges can normally imprison people only if they are accused of a crime. Together, though, law and medicine could declare someone to be insane and incarcerate them preemptively.

The authors of LPS imagined the legislation as an enormous break from the past, but theorists of what I'll call *medicolegal control* see surprising continuities. Foucault, for example, documented how a whole range of disadvantaged people were swept into asylums in a "Great Confinement" starting in the seventeenth century.[67] But according to the disability scholar Chris Chapman, "If one considers homeless shelters, group homes, supportive living centres [sic], retirement homes, jails, halfway houses, hospitals of various kinds, certain kinds of remedial schools, and so forth . . . [then the] 'great confinement'" of those same populations "lives on."[68] Deinstitutionalization from state hospitals did not end control of the mad; it simply dispersed (and, in many cases, privatized) it.[69]

Consistent with this perspective, there are myriad examples of how medicine and law in contemporary California intertwine to manage disadvantaged populations. On Skid Row, law enforcement engages in "therapeutic policing," writing an avalanche of citations to homeless people and offering participation in drug-recovery programs as a way out of paying them.[70] Police rely on ambulance crews to help clear out-of-place people without the hassle of arresting them.[71] Hospitals, for their part, depend on the police to cull overcrowded and unruly emergency department waiting rooms.[72] In drug or mental health courts, where people are mandated to accept services as an alternative to going to jail, the lines between punishment and treatment blur so much as to make the two indistinguishable.[73] "Care and control," according to the social theorist Nikolas Rose, "have become inextricably linked" in a common project of disciplining the mad.[74]

This is far from abstract theorizing. These perspectives prescribe distinctive solutions. From the vantage point of medicolegal conflict, LPS represented an attempt to use law to curb the excesses of medicine. The crisis on California's streets shows the need for the pendulum to swing back toward more forced treatment.[75] Those viewing the system through the lens of medicolegal control, on the other hand, see a never-ending excess of coercion that robs people with mental illness of autonomy and choice. The solution is a ramp-up of voluntary outpatient services and independent supported housing, with care offered not just by clinicians but by peers with lived experience of surviving psychiatric abuse.[76]

The problem with these perspectives is that, in contemporary California, neither law (in the sense of rights) nor medicine (as in care) nor medicolegal control (as in discipline of the disruptive or deviant) seems to be winning. For all the complaints that LPS created a system of civil libertarian excess, people living with mental illnesses in California are subjected to extensive restrictions of their rights—and not just in jails and prisons. The state's rate of seventy-two-hour emergency detentions (in which a police officer or clinician transports someone to the hospital for evaluation) is 50 percent higher than the U.S. average (figure 0.1).[77] The rate of people admitted for up to fourteen days in a hospital without their consent is above that of most European countries (figure 0.2).[78]

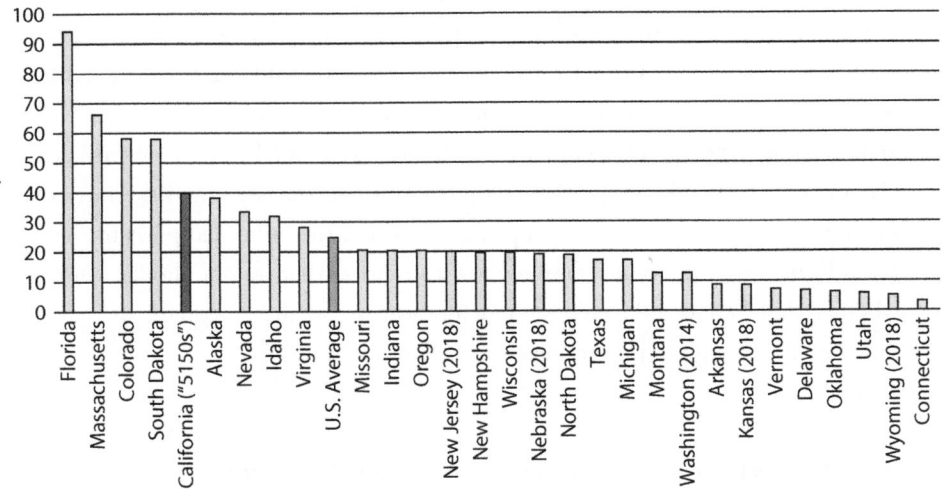

0.1 Involuntary holds and initial commitments in select states, 2016

Source: Lee and Cohen (2021); state Freedom of Information Act requests (by author)

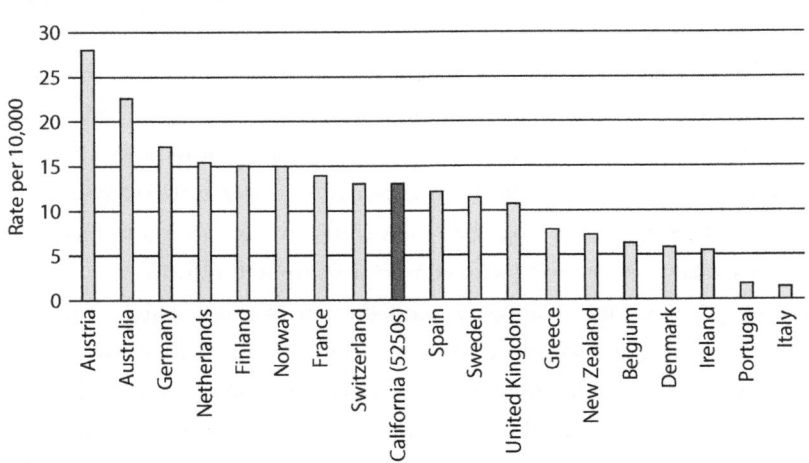

0.2 Involuntary hospitalizations in select countries and California, 2016

Source: Sheridan Rains et al. (2019); California involuntary detention reports

Far from serving as an insidiously effective tool of medicolegal control, though, this profusion of coercive interventions in California appears arbitrary, unpredictable, and ineffectual in calming crises and maintaining public order. Meanwhile, the state's expanding investment in community-based care and housing—the alternatives for which critics of medicolegal control are clamoring—has not kept up with rising overdose deaths, stemmed the rates of mental illness among homeless people, or answered the unheeded pleas for help by suffering individuals and families. It's a situation that no one should want—whether they believe LPS gave too much power to law over medicine or that it didn't go far enough in protecting citizens from both.

POWER OVER CONSERVATEES, AUTHORITY OVER CONSERVATORSHIP

To really understand the failings of California's conservatorship system, then, we need to move away from analyzing the clash (or collaboration) of two powerful forces, law and medicine. We should instead ask why both seem so impotent to effect real, enduring change in the lives of many people with serious mental illness. To do that, the reader will need to bear with me as we make three shifts: first, adding the role of government alongside law and medicine; second, moving from analyzing power in general to examining a specific type of power, authority; and third, looking at how authority is exercised not over conservatees but over the conservatorship system. Together, these shifts give us a clearer framework for explaining what's going wrong with conservatorship in California.

Conserving someone requires the cooperation of a psychiatrist (medicine) and a judge (law), but also a third party: a county public guardian (government), who investigates a conservatorship application from a hospital and files a petition with the courts. As you'll see, to go onto conservatorship, people often need to be on the edge of dying—so sick as to be unable to feed themselves or keep a roof over their head. It is not an exaggeration to say that LPS grants public guardians "sovereign power": what Foucault defines as the "the right to decide life and death."[79]

Yet a lifesaving conservatorship also imposes a kind of "social death" on conservatees. They are "expelled from normal participation in the community," potentially losing, for example, the right to vote, to make contracts, or to choose where they reside.[80] Although a conservatorship can be imposed without the use of force, the potential for violence lurks behind sovereign power. A conservatee lives with the threat of being cuffed by police, strapped to a bed, forcibly injected with medication, and confined behind locked doors for years at a time. One public guardian described his role in 1972 as "tak[ing] over most of the conservatee's civil rights. They [conservatees] have no powers, really, except to live and breathe."[81] Since public guardians can (and do) sign do-not-resuscitate orders for their wards, they can even take away that power to live and breathe.[82]

The second key to understanding the conservatorship system is to ask how government uses a specific kind of power: *authority*. Max Weber defined authority as the combination of a "power to command and duty to obey."[83] The political scientist Hannah Arendt went further, distinguishing authority from both "coercion by force" (like the sovereign power described above) and "persuasion through arguments."[84] Studies of physicians often describe their authority in this way: as power that cannot be physically imposed, but is not open to debate either. Doctors have authority because of their social prestige, claims to expertise grounded in science (symbolized by their white coats), and role as gatekeepers to things like badly needed prescriptions or qualification for receiving social security disability benefits. People feel compelled to follow their authority without being forced to.[85]

This brings us to the third shift I make in this book: from analyzing coercion over conservatees to examining government authority over the conservatorship system.[86] Obviously, no one in the conservatorship system (be it a judge, police officer, psychiatrist, or public guardian) has sovereign power—the power of life or death—over other professionals. But in order to get such a diverse range of actors to work together, someone does need to have authority over them. Here, I am using the clunky but useful elaboration of authority by legal theorist Joseph Raz. A person has authority when they are able to give "exclusionary reasons": commands that override whatever other reasons the person being commanded might have for acting or not acting a certain way.[87] Authority, in this sense, is the ability to ensure that actors in a system "engage in some common activity requiring a certain degree of coordinated action," even in the face of disagreements among them.[88]

Competing sides of debates over forced treatment would like to see law or medicine alone have this kind of authority over the conservatorship system. One mother who has tirelessly advocated for reforming LPS to make it easier to place people in conservatorship told me, "It [schizophrenia] is a medical illness. . . . You shouldn't have to go to lawyers, attorneys, jailors to get treatment for a medical disease." She was in effect arguing that medicine's diagnosis of a serious mental illness should be an exclusionary reason for law to help get someone conserved. But when Thatcher, a person who has been subjected to civil commitments, described conservatorship in an interview as a "human rights violation and . . . a form of torture," they were giving an exclusionary reason for abolishing it. This logic is also endorsed by the UN Convention on the Rights of People with Disabilities: that law should have authority to block medicine, because autonomy and freedom trump health and welfare.[89]

But neither law nor medicine has this authority in the conservatorship system created by LPS. Instead, the law reserved the authority to coordinate coercive care to government itself, in the guise of public guardians.[90] Consider an early account from just after LPS went into effect: public guardians could "apprehend the person at his home by force; commit him to a mental hospital for up to one year . . . authorize or withhold electric shock treatment . . . and, finally, authorize or withhold release from the institution."[91] The guardian was not directly exercising this sovereign power. Instead, guardians had the state-sanctioned authority to mobilize others to do so.

This book will paint a starkly different portrait of authority in the conservatorship system today. The ensuing chapters are filled with extreme examples of how narrowly grave disability is being circumscribed, in ways that disqualify from conservatorship people who appear to need it.[92] The explanation for this is not that LPS law has become stricter, since the law has largely stayed the same. Instead, the conservatorship system is facing a crisis of authority. At multiple levels, government fails to provide exclusionary reasons that would compel professionals to apply grave disability in a coherent and consistent way. Police officers cannot convince ER doctors to admit people in crisis into the hospital. Public guardians cannot make inpatient psychiatrists apply for conservatorship for individuals who might benefit from it. Judges struggle to get basic information out of doctors necessary to rule on whether someone is gravely disabled. And county mental health departments are overruled by private providers of long-term care.

In short, while many people can (and do) exert sovereign power over clients of the mental health system, government does not exercise authority to make law and medicine use that power in a concerted way. It is failing to coordinate interventions that would keep people from becoming gravely disabled and neglecting people when they do.

ABDICATION THROUGH DELEGATION AND DISCRETION

How did this happen? Government in California not only lacks authority over the conservatorship system. It has *abdicated authority*; that is, through active policy choices and passive neglect, government has given up authority that it could potentially wield. As you will see throughout this book, abdication has been a convenient way of escaping two dilemmas facing the state's system of involuntary care. First, laws like LPS sought to end the one-size-fits-all approach of interning everyone in state hospitals, creating a new challenge of organizing and funding the range of services that conservatees need. Second, legal standards like grave disability are vague, leaving open the question of who, exactly, should be subject to forced hospitalization or conservatorship.

Government has never comprehensively addressed either of these conundrums. The California legislature has hosted ferocious battles over reforming LPS, including two large, unsuccessful initiatives to expand grave disability in 1987 and 2000 (as well as in recent years). Yet you would be hard-pressed to find anything resembling a strategy for how judges, clinicians, or bureaucrats should be using the law as written. Two major task forces on California's public mental health system in 2000 and 2003, for example, included hundreds of pages of recommendations without a single one on conservatorship.[93] For all the more recent attention to conservatorship, a 2021 "Vision for All Californians' Behavioral Health," put together by just about every imaginable stakeholder, mentions conservatees only once as a "special population that should be considered by policymakers."[94] Instead of acting as an authority engaged in assuring the implementation of LPS, the state has *delegated* the organization of services to counties and private entities and granted them *discretion* to apply grave disability in inconsistent, and at times seemingly inexplicable, ways.

First, delegation: The United States is distinctive among developed countries in the degree to which essential state functions, ranging from health and welfare to incarceration, are farmed out to nonstate actors. It relies on charities to care for domestic violence victims, commercial insurance companies to disburse publicly funded prescription drug benefits to seniors, and privately run charter schools to replace failing public ones.[95] Mental health was once the great exception. States built enormous asylums long before they started paying for higher education or unemployment benefits. By the mid-twentieth century, psychiatry was an almost entirely public affair: nearly 90 percent of psychiatric treatment happened in state hospitals, which at their peak housed more than a half-million people. States spent an average of 8 percent of their budgets on these institutions.[96]

Deinstitutionalization—the closure of 90 percent of state psychiatric hospital beds in just a few decades[97]—was not just an exodus of patients (and before them of psychiatrists, who in the 1950s quit state hospitals en masse for private practice). It also meant that the state almost entirely ceased being a direct provider of services. Frank and Glied argue that the shift was "as dramatic as those in Eastern European nations after the Soviet Union's disintegration. In a matter of twenty years . . . mental health care moved largely from a centrally planned, state-owned and operated enterprise to a system dominated by market forces."[98]

LPS delegated responsibility for organizing local mental health services to counties. Then counties, following the pattern of other antipoverty programs of the Great Society in the 1960s, contracted out service provision to nonprofit organizations.[99] While counties paid for medical treatment for at least some people leaving state hospitals, they did almost nothing to meet these individuals' basic needs for income, food, or shelter. A shadowy world of for-profit residential board and care facilities and nursing homes emerged to fill the gap, harvesting the disability checks of deinstitutionalized ex-patients eking out survival on the margins of society.[100] The state's relinquishment of responsibility left families to try to stitch together these fragmented programs into a threadbare safety net for their loved ones.[101]

Delegation has a clear economic logic. It has allowed the state to shift costs onto others (as in the case of board and care homes, operating on federal social security checks). Yet the abdication of authority provides a way to avoid the challenge of organizing an effective conservatorship system even in moments of government largesse. Today, California state government pumps ten billion dollars per year into the mental health system. Yet while this money gives the state leverage to make the jumble of county and private providers it feeds fully serve people on or needing conservatorship, it largely has not used that authority. In fact, the state's data are so poor in quality, inconsistent, and incomplete that it does not even know how many LPS conservatees there are, where they are, or what happens to them. This is the consequence of delegation: a "complex hybrid of public and private actors" with such "convoluted lines of authority and accountability" that it seems as though no one has any authority or accountability at all.[102]

Delegation crisscrosses with another way the state has abdicated authority for conservatorship: granting extensive, underregulated, and privatized discretion. Psychiatrists, lawyers, public guardians, and police officers bring with them radically different philosophies about the merits of involuntary treatment and tools for intervention. But they all face the classic dilemma of street-level bureaucrats. As theorized by political scientist Michael Lipsky, these are "public service workers who interact directly with citizens . . . and who have substantial discretion in the execution of their work."[103] That discretion comes from scarcity: bureaucrats invariably face more demand from people legally entitled to their services than they have resources to provide those services. This bind obligates them to informally triage based on their own preferences, professional identities, and organizational constraints. Lipsky's classic insight is that "when taken together, the decisions of these workers . . . add up to agency policy."[104]

Discretion is an endemic feature of public services. But there are two distinctive aspects of discretion in the conservatorship system. In some government agencies, street-level bureaucrats can grant access to services on their own: a social security administrator qualifying someone for disability benefits, for example, or a prosecutor choosing whether to charge someone with a crime. In contrast, putting into place a conservatorship requires that a complex chain of bureaucrats exercise their individual discretion in a consistent way. All must agree that a person remains gravely disabled over the course of weeks or months, even as that person moves among institutions and receives treatment intended to change their state. As a result, the conservatorship system has myriad "veto points"[105] where police, ER physicians, or public guardians can stop someone from advancing toward conservatorship (instead shuffling them onto other agencies or abandoning them entirely).[106]

Veto points are a crucial protection against the overuse of sovereign power (indeed, multiple veto points are a key feature of the separation of powers among the legislature, the executive, and the judiciary in the federal government). Still, it is striking that while the legislature created criteria for when someone *can* be placed on conservatorship, it never identified the situations in which professionals *should* do so. The LPS Act expressly granted the California Department of

Mental Health, later merged into the Department of Health Care Services, the power to adopt "rules, regulations, and standards as necessary" for its implementation (such as offering guidance about best practices for applying grave disability).[107] But that authority is going unused. The first critical feature of discretion in the conservatorship system is that each actor exercises only *negative discretion*. Many people can say "no" to conservatorship, but no one exerts authority to make these actors, collectively, get to "yes."

The second key aspect of discretion in the conservatorship system is how many veto points sit inside for-profit entities. Critics of the mental health system deride a "non-profit industrial complex" of inefficient community organizations and hapless homeless service providers.[108] But the most restrictive end of the system is dominated by unabashedly for-profit enterprises. An analogy to for-profit prisons is uncomfortable but warranted: in both cases, state funds are used to pay for beds in private facilities, and state power is used to keep those beds full. But the comparison is also imperfect. Because of the risk that for-profit entities might try to maximize profits by serving the least needy (and therefore least costly) cases, government often tightly curtail their discretion, obligating them to "surrender" the prerogatives of "private judgment."[109] For-profit prisons can cut costs in all sorts of problematic ways, but one thing they cannot usually do is screen every person sentenced by the courts to weed out the most difficult inmates.

Yet the unwillingness of government in California to provide care directly has led it to show marked deference to the profit-driven preferences of the private hospitals, subacute facilities, or board and care homes that are willing to provide that care. As you will see, grave disability expands or contracts to fill the beds those entities make available. Those beds, in turn, depend on market forces, which are shrinking and shuttering these institutions across the state. Street-level bureaucrats in the conservatorship system have adapted their use of discretion to this new reality. They veto conservatorship for the people with the most complex and expensive problems, who could clog up those scarce beds for months or years. These factors, not an imagined cadre of die-hard civil libertarian lawyers and nihilistic disability rights activists, are driving grave disability to be defined in ever narrower ways.

In short, as you will see in this book, the California mental health system fits with scholars' image of a "many-handed" state.[110] People facing conservatorship could easily have a half-dozen agencies—from fire and police departments to parole officers to substance abuse and mental health clinicians—providing care and imposing coercion in their lives. But that state is hollow: many hands, but no brain telling them what to do.[111] As these public and private entities exercise negative discretion in incompatible and disconnected ways, the aggregation of discretion that is supposed to "add up to agency policy" adds up to no coherent policy at all. For better or worse, attempts to rewrite LPS law to make it easier to conserve people will fail, because they will not rewrite the informal definition of grave disability that has been created by delegation and discretion and government's abdication of authority over them.

COVERING THE CONTINUUM

I conducted the research for *Conservatorship* between 2018 and 2022. This book is based primarily on 268 interviews with professionals, policy makers, advocates, family members, and people subject to forced treatment. These interviewees come from thirty-four of California's fifty-eight counties, spanning hamlets in the High Sierras to Southern California beach towns. While jumping between counties might be jarring for the reader, showing disparities between them reveals a common lack of authority across the state. I also illustrate my findings by drawing on dozens of site visits to hospitals, ERs, board and care homes, and conservatorship courts, as well as days spent shadowing professional outreach workers, outpatient clinical teams, and law enforcement.

I supplemented my field research with an analysis of more than 1,500 newspaper articles on conservatorship, LPS, and the public mental health system published in California newspapers from the 1950s to the present, plus virtually every piece of academic literature, hearing transcript, or government report on LPS I could find. My conclusions have been shaped by my participation in work groups and policy discussions on conservatorship, as well as numerous preliminary presentations of this work where I received sharp and critical feedback from stakeholders (see the methodological appendix for more details).

Part 1 of this book traces each step in the "conservatorship continuum": the chain of street-level bureaucracies a person encounters on their way to a conservatorship. Chapter 1 starts with the voluntary outpatient services that too often fail to keep people out of crisis. Chapter 2 moves to how police and clinicians respond to those crises with 5150 "holds," a legal mechanism created by LPS that allows them to transport a person involuntarily to an ER for evaluation. Chapter 3 looks at the strict screening those ERs exercise before, in chapter 4, going onto an inpatient unit to see how financial pressures shape decisions to apply for conservatorship. Once an application is made, it is "investigated" by a public guardian (covered in chapter 5) and ultimately ruled on by a court (the subject of chapter 6). Across part 1, negative discretion, exercised in inconsistent ways, is king. It keeps the vast majority of people whom at least some professionals see as gravely disabled out of conservatorship—often leaving them deserted, not diverted into a less coercive alternative.

Part 2 focuses on the trajectories of those people who are in fact placed in conservatorship. Chapter 7 examines locked facilities, both state hospitals and largely private, subacute "institutions for mental disease" (more on that later). Chapter 8 brings us inside unlocked board and care homes. In both cases, the delegation of services for chronically ill conservatees to private entities allows those entities to decide who gets a bed and, indirectly, who gets conserved in the first place. Chapter 9 considers abuses, both active harm and passive indifference, that happen throughout the system. Chapter 10 analyzes, in contrast, the mechanisms through which conservatorship can achieve positive outcomes like stabilization, independence, and recovery. Abdicated authority means a lack of clear accountability for protecting conservatees from the worst possible outcomes or for the coordinated pursuit of the best possible ones.

Part 3 analyzes proposals for reform. In chapter 11, we delve into a pilot program in San Francisco to conserve homeless substance users who were generating high costs and citizen complaints. Chapter 12 looks at proposals to expand grave disability to capture people dying on the streets in Los Angeles. The impacts of both reforms, I will show, are limited by an absence of government authority to get hospitals to implement the new conservatorship pathway (in San Francisco) or to make the private sector build sufficient beds to house people who would be newly conserved (in Los Angeles, and statewide). Chapter 13 profiles a diverse range of alternatives to forced treatment, helping us envision what giving authority to people with mental illnesses themselves would look like. Such a system would not force potential conservatees to accept services they do not want but would instead compel providers to offer services their clients do want.

In the conclusion, I revisit my core argument: an absence of government leadership, coordination, and regulation creates the readily apparent failings of California's mental health system. Delegating care to private providers has been a convenient way to elide the challenge of designing a public system capable of meeting conservatees' complex needs. Granting discretion to myriad street-level bureaucrats has been easier than writing guidelines for when to use conservatorship that weigh the delicate balance between care and coercion, compassion and constraint. It is the abdication of authority over the conservatorship system, rather than an absence of power and coercion over the people it serves, that explains why people like Wally are dying on California's streets—despite all the frantic efforts to help them.

PART I

THE CONSERVATORSHIP CONTINUUM

CHAPTER 1

OUTPATIENT

U rban Mental Health (UMH), a public outpatient clinic in Northern California where I attended weekly team meetings in 2018 and
2019, is laser-focused on people with serious mental illnesses. Most
of their clients have schizophrenia or bipolar disorder, frequently coupled with
substance use, trauma, homelessness, and a history of criminal-legal contact.

UMH confronts these challenging cases with the best tools at the disposal of
California's public mental health system. One team, called a Full-Service Partnership (FSP), sends clinicians in pairs multiple times a week to engage clients
under freeway underpasses, in homeless encampments, or in the supported housing units their $24,000-a-year-per-client budget helps pay for. The evidence for
the effectiveness of FSPs is robust: according to UMH data, participants show an
86 percent reduction in hospitalization, 90 percent reduction in incarceration,
and 68 percent reduction in homelessness in their first year in the program.[1]
But this chapter shows why the state's promise to provide high-quality, voluntary services through programs like FSPs nonetheless sometimes falls short—thus
hurling some of the neediest individuals toward conservatorship.

At one meeting, the staff discusses a twenty-six-year-old Asian man diagnosed with bipolar disorder. Stu, a thirty-year-veteran social worker who has
watched UMH transform from a clinic offering psychotherapy to the "worried
well" (people with psychologic troubles but not serious illnesses) to one focused
on keeping people with psychosis and meth use out of ERs, handled his intake.
He explains that the man had his first mental health contacts a few years ago
through Kaiser Permanente, an enormous and wealthy nonprofit health system.
They prescribed him medication but failed to give him the whole range of social
supports crucial for someone experiencing a psychotic break. In the past year, he

has been seen by UMH's mobile crisis team on nine occasions when community members have called 911 to express concern about his fighting with invisible antagonists on the street.

In one recent hospitalization, he was referred to UMH for ongoing care. 'We tried to swoop in,' says Avril, a psychologist with mobile crisis, 'because it was clear if they discharged him too quickly, he'd wind up being readmitted.' But he refused treatment and left the hospital without follow-up care. Now, as they predicted, he's back in the hospital, where Stu carried out the assessment and found him paranoid, refusing food, and borderline catatonic (that is, nonresponsive). Stu thinks he'd be a good fit for FSP, which can give him the persistent outreach he thinks is necessary to engage him. But Blair, who oversees adult programs at the clinic, thinks it's too late: 'he needs to be a "captive audience" [i.e., in a locked unit] to get him on meds longer term. We should focus on getting him into an IMD.' To get into an IMD (Institution for Mental Diseases, a subacute facility where some will stay for months or years), he has to be conserved first. Neither UMH nor Kaiser was able to get him into high-intensity voluntary services, like an FSP, fast enough to keep him from declining to the point where he was considered gravely disabled and a conservatorship seemed the only option.

At other times, UMH struggled to catch people coming out of conservatorship. One morning, the new intake is a fifty-four-year-old African American who was brought to his appointment by his wife. He was, Stu said, 'cooperative for two minutes' before coming across as 'suicidal,' 'having no insight' into his illness, and 'aggressive.' He had spent nineteen years in a state hospital after being found not guilty by reason of insanity for setting a homeless person on fire (who, thankfully, survived). The hospital released him to a board and care home, where he stayed for ten years before leaving to get his own apartment. Now, he and his wife are on the verge of eviction. 'He has a long history of nonadherence to treatment and refusing follow-up,' Stu adds. Stu is recommending that he go onto Intensive Case Management (ICM). It is a level of care one step below FSP but still involves meeting with a clinician once per week.

'I don't think so,' replies Mary, the social worker at the head of ICM. 'This is a lot of scary stuff, he's not stable and it sounds like he doesn't want to come in on his own.' She thinks he should go onto FSP.

Charlie, the head of the FSP team, counters, 'Our responsibility is to people who have a high use of services and are highly visible in the community. He doesn't meet a single one of our criteria.' The man might have a severe mental illness, but FSP requires a certain number of recent hospitalizations, ER visits, or incarcerations, plus risk factors like current homelessness or violence. Nonetheless, Charlie agrees to go visit him at his apartment.

Charlie reports back to the group the next week: 'We started introducing ourselves and he just said, "Stop." He was very clear about refusing services. He said, "Never come back." He made that motion where you zip up your mouth.'

Kevin, the clinic director, summarizes, 'So now we have someone with a lengthy state hospitalization, a long period in residential care, now he's home and there's a history of some scary stuff . . .'

Blair adds, 'And he is not taking any meds whatsoever.'

Charlie insists there's nothing more FSP can do: 'The fact is he doesn't want services.'

Maybe not quite. Stu comes into the room and reports, 'I just heard from Angela'—a woman who used to be a client of UMH, and now works there—'that he came to our peer-led wellness group and was, quote, "delightful."'

Kevin tells me these kinds of cases (minus the nineteen-year hospitalization) are typical: 'All those people you see out on the street, they're not people that are looking for [UMH]. You have to be motivated to be treated here. And, as a result, we wind up cutting loose clients who can be very ill, but whose mother brought them in [rather than choosing to come themselves].' Therein lies the paradox. With some exceptions, California reserves its best services (like FSPs) for people who have already been repeatedly hospitalized and incarcerated or are homeless. But even then, they still have to actively consent to services. By that time, they might be too sick to do so. Or they've been burned too many times by the mental health system to want to try again.

This chapter is not about the people who stabilize and recover thanks to the tireless efforts of clinicians at places like UMH. It's about the clients for whom those efforts fail. There's no single explanation for why, but this chapter focuses on four possibilities. First, private insurance rarely provides sufficiently intensive services, pawning people off onto the public sector only once their condition has deteriorated significantly. The burden of navigating both falls on family members. Second, the public system has seesawed between expansion and austerity, creating extraordinary fragmentation and an unclear demarcation of responsibilities that leaves people to bounce endlessly between disconnected levels of care. Third, voluntary outpatient services allow people with anosognosia—a lack of awareness of their need for care—to decline services (a source of desperation for parents in particular). Finally, people refuse to engage with the mental health system because they perceive its offerings as superficial, incompetent, unwelcoming, and unable to meet their primary needs (often community and help with housing and income, not just medication and therapy).

This chapter points to a common thread of abdicated authority. There are many doors into the system, but nothing requiring mostly private providers to keep those doors open. No single entity is clearly accountable for serving the citizens of the state with the most serious mental health challenges, come what may.

PRIVATE AND PUBLIC FAILURES, FAMILY RESPONSIBILITIES

California's mental health system, which sharply divides between services financed with public dollars and those paid for by private individuals or commercial insurance, is a microcosm of the American welfare state. Public services are reserved for those too poor and too sick to go anywhere else. Parents can try to help navigate the chasm between the two systems, but as Kiley, the mother of a daughter diagnosed with bipolar and borderline personality disorder, put it, it's hard when the pathways into care are "clear as mud."

"Reflecting back," she told me, "we could see the signs of mental illness at a very young age." When her daughter Clarissa was twelve, she cut herself after seeing the movie *Thirteen* (which depicts self-harm among teenage girls). Kiley thought, "She's copying this stupid movie, it's frustrating." Her husband was more worried, fretting that "a normal brain doesn't copy a movie." By fifteen, Clarissa "wasn't able to control her emotions anymore," and Kiley called the police on her daughter, the first of many times.

Kiley, like 55 percent of Californians, had commercial health insurance,[2] but she quickly found that took her only so far. Psychiatrists are the least likely of any specialists to take insurance.[3] The providers she could find seemed ill-equipped to handle her daughter's problems. Her family doctor, she said, was reluctant to diagnose her, telling Kiley, "I don't want to diagnose someone, because they're just labels. The reality is that she is very sensitive." She got her daughter in to see a rotating series of psychologists and psychiatrists. Clarissa would "manipulate what they want to hear" for the first few sessions and "as soon as they started pushing back, she'd be on to the next one." Private providers are under no obligation to treat a patient if they don't want to.[4] Most private therapists are in the business of treating anxiety and depression, not psychosis and personality disorders.

Still, Kiley was lucky to be in a part of the state where she could find a mental health provider at all. There are three to four times as many psychologists and psychiatrists per capita in the Bay Area as in the Sierras, the Inland Empire, or the San Joaquin Valley.[5] Seven rural counties have no psychiatrist whatsoever. A lawyer who worked with families struggling to connect to mental health care in rural Northern California lamented, "The rural situation is the worst when it comes to access. . . . Anything more than primary care is not available. A lot of poor folks can't afford the transport" to the coastal cities where specialists choose to congregate.

Having been failed by more conventional outpatient services, Kiley—who works as an interior designer—paid out of pocket for her daughter to go to a private clinic in Southern California. The clinic promised that, with "a brain scan and a physical," they could "tell what's wrong with the brain." She recounted, "All these places supposedly know mental illness and you slap down your $5,000 and they're going to put her where she needs to go." The clinic gave Clarissa a regimen of medication and vitamins and recommended she go to a wilderness-based rehab center in Colorado.[6] She lasted a week before she fled and came back home. Kiley showed me a timeline cataloging Clarissa's stints in more than a dozen private residential programs that quickly discharged her—some within less than a day—saying she needed a higher level of care. They don't give refunds.

Over time, Kiley realized that the providers that take private insurance often don't offer the suite of services, like case management or a multidisciplinary team, that people with serious mental illness often require in addition to medication or talk therapy. Kaiser Permanente has 40 percent of the insurance market share in California,[7] and a particularly abysmal record. In 2013, the state Department of Health Care Services fined Kaiser for violating "parity" laws by providing slower and less comprehensive access to mental health services than to physical ones.[8] Kaiser mental health workers went on strike in 2022. They alleged that the company had let waitlists for a first appointment grow to eight weeks and underfunded psychiatric care so grossly that some Kaiser ERs had no mental health staff at night.[9]

Among Kaiser's many shocking practices—especially given that it made $8 billion in profits in 2021—is abdicating responsibility for its own clients.[10] A 2014 lawsuit alleged that Kaiser sought to disenroll people from coverage so that the public sector would pay for them to go into a locked residential facility.[11] Dr. Fazio, a doctor in one of those facilities, insisted, "If you're a young person with psychosis you're better off not having private insurance. . . . The data on first break episodes [that is, the early stages of schizophrenia, when hallucinations or delusions begin] for privately insured patients is horrible," he told me, citing a study that found young people with psychosis had twenty-five times the mortality rate in the year after diagnosis as those without psychosis.[12]

Family members like Kiley sometimes do the dirty work for insurance companies themselves. She had been writing letters to her county supervisors—she called them, "Oh shit" letters, of the genre "Oh shit, Clarissa is back in jail!"—and realized that "the county wasn't going to help her unless she was completely reliant on them." She promised herself she would stop taking her daughter home when the hospital called, instead letting them dump her onto the street. She disenrolled Clarissa from her family insurance plan, which was "unfortunate" because her daughter had a serious physical condition for which she lost access to her existing specialist.

There's no estimate of the number of people who drop private insurance to get public mental health services, but it's enough to be a vexing problem for county governments.[13] Michelle Cabrera from the County Behavioral Health Directors Association fumed, "The failure of commercial [insurance] plans . . . to really take seriously the behavioral health needs of their beneficiaries results in people who are allowed to become disabled. . . . And this puts additional pressure on our public system." By the time they reach the county mental health department, a crucial window of opportunity has closed: "it's unconscionable because if you do catch people at 'first break' . . . you can really help people live a completely different life that isn't filled with homelessness, justice-involvement, and forced treatment."

By the time Clarissa went off private insurance, she was in free fall. She totaled her car by leaving it on a train track. When she got on social security disability benefits, she bought another one (recipients often receive a substantial back payment for the period between when they apply for disability and are approved). Clarissa was convinced she needed to help "save a pregnant dog" in Tijuana, and drove to Mexico. Kiley recounted, "She called me [from Tijuana] and said, 'Mom, I'm in a police car, something happened to me.'"

The county put Clarissa in its Assisted Outpatient Treatment (AOT) program, a form of court-ordered outpatient care in which a judge mandates that a person accept treatment. But the AOT team couldn't convince the county's own hospital to keep her the ten times in the previous year police dropped her off for an emergency psychiatric evaluation. When Clarissa stabbed someone and ended up in jail, Kiley was hoping the AOT team would "swoop in" and ensure she got treatment while incarcerated. But after one of her infamous email blasts to county supervisors, the district attorney called her to let her know they wouldn't press charges. Clarissa would go back to the streets. "I call people in county government and they say, 'Oh, have you tried this, have you heard of AOT?' and I say, 'Yeah, she's already part of it.' . . . The right hand doesn't know what the left hand is doing. . . . Communication between the police, hospitals, AOT—it's a shitshow," she raged.

Kiley thought that after the private sector had thoroughly failed her daughter, the county would take charge of halting her decline. But becoming a client of the county was no panacea either, partly because "the county" is actually a host of disparate agencies touching on the lives of people with serious mental illness and following their own discretion in doing so. Parents like Kiley are the glue that holds this nonsystem together. They cart their children's medical records between providers who don't share them. Their frantic emails connect agencies that usually don't talk. They're the burned-out care coordinators who can never quit or take a vacation.[14]

As a result, Kiley sighed, "It's just trial and error while my daughter is drowning."

FISCAL FEAST AND FAMINE IN A FRAGMENTED SYSTEM

For Kiley, California's public mental health system was a last resort. For Ashley, it was a new hope. I spoke to her and her sister Meredith over Zoom in 2022, both of them sitting on a couch in a bare apartment in Stanislaus County. Ashley is not sure when her hallucinations started: "When I was young, 14 or 15, I saw these men out the window, following a little girl dressed in green. It could have been psychosis, it could have been real, but I freaked out." She told her parents, who called the police to check on her. Like so many I talked to, law enforcement—not clinicians—were her first contact in a crisis.[15] She didn't get treatment until she was arrested for drug possession and diverted to a residential substance use program at eighteen. While there, she was diagnosed with bipolar disorder and put on lithium. She stopped it when she became pregnant.

The next decade was a blur of aimless short-term psychiatric coercion. Ashley grew up in Florida, where the 1971 Baker Act mirrored LPS: it gave legal authority to law enforcement to place people on involuntary "holds" and transport them to an ER for evaluation. It is used even more frequently.[16] She recalls being "Baker Act'ed" when she was "completely erratic" and fought with a friend over a burrito. Another time, police found her outside her house, naked, fearful her whole family was dead inside. Ashley's sister chimed in to remind her of when she was held for throwing herself in front of a car.

Sometimes the ER would say her psychosis was from drug use and let her go immediately; other times, they'd attribute it to schizophrenia and keep her a few days. Ashley's care was constricted by Florida's decision to leave adults living in poverty, like Ashley, uninsured (Florida chose not to expand public health insurance through Medicaid under the 2010 Affordable Care Act, better known as Obamacare). The hospital would not be reimbursed for Ashley's stay and thus discharged her in a flash. Worse, her sister Meredith recalled, "They [the hospital] would send her home with scripts for Seroquel [a "second-generation" anti-psychotic with fewer side effects] that were $2,000 or 3,000 [a month]." So they switched her to Haldol, an older drug. Ashley hated it, but it was "one of the cheapest drugs. We could pay cash for it."[17]

Ashley encouraged me to go online to read her arrest record, which I did: it's a litany of drug possession and disorderly conduct charges. But in 2019, Ashley, now in her thirties, off medication and on methamphetamine, told her mother that she was a demon and tried to strangle her. An officer hauled her out of the bathroom and declared she would be Baker Act'ed. When she spit on him, he arrested her for battery instead. Things, improbably, turned around from there. Ashley went to the jail medical unit, which was "basically like solitary [confinement]." It was so bad that Ashley agreed to take meds just to go back to her cell block. There, Meredith tells me, "the girls in the pod were aware she was sick, and they'd all tell her to take her medicine every day."

Meredith had learned about AOT and was convinced Ashley needed it. Florida has an AOT statute on the books, but the program was unfunded and inactive.[18] Meredith lived in California, which has AOT (the program that Clarissa was on). Meredith asked the judge to let her take Ashley home, telling the court, "It's a liberal paradise over here, there are systems to help her, they have better healthcare." Ashley pledged to take her Haldol. The judge let her go on the condition she would "find a doctor and send a letter." As Ashley recalled it, "The judge was like, 'get out of here,' so I walked out of jail, my sister was standing there by a car, I had nothing"—not even a day's supply of meds. This all might sound implausible, but it's what her court records show.

Meredith had reason to be optimistic. In 2015, California spent the fourteenth most per capita on mental health care among states; Florida was dead last.[19] But that headline number misses the way California's public system has been alternately stuffed by new initiatives and starved by budget cuts, creating layers of delegated services—all of which have the discretion to say "no."

Alongside granting new civil liberties and creating the legal framework for conservatorship, the LPS Act took an existing program (Short-Doyle, enacted in 1955) that provided matching funds for local mental health programs and upped the state's contribution from 50 to 90 percent (leaving counties to pay the other 10 percent). Some counties ignored the opportunity; others ran their own programs; still others took the money and contracted with private organizations to provide services.[20] Who actually got served varied. Many community clinics appeared more interested in providing psychotherapy to people with less severe conditions ("pretty co-eds with interesting sex lives"[21]) than people whose only stories were of spending the last ten years in a state institution.

There's a well-worn tale about what happened next. As Nicolas Petris recalled in an oral history in 1988, "When we started keeping people out of state hospitals, it was under the intention that the state dollar for mental health was going to follow the patient. . . . That never happened. . . . [Reagan] took the guts right out of this state money for local treatment."[22] This is accurate, but incomplete: in the ensuing decades, every governor—not just Reagan—subjected county mental health programs to brutal cuts.[23] As the *Los Angeles Times* observed, once care for the severely mentally ill went from "wholly a state responsibility" to one delegated to the local level, "Sacramento's interest seemed to fade."[24] The original bargain of LPS was that those concerned about civil rights would get new legal protections and those concerned about providing care would get new treatment programs. The deal was almost immediately broken.

The late 1980s were particularly pitiless. Governor Deukmejian cut one-third of the mental health budget from 1985 to 1990.[25] The austerity was so bad that San Diego developed a triage plan that would withdraw care from half of its existing clients.[26] In 1991, legislators responded by further delegating mental health care through a process called "realignment." Counties would assume full responsibility not just for operating outpatient clinics but also for paying for expensive long-term residential treatment. Each county's mental health program would get a dedicated if inconsistent funding stream from a 1.25 percent sales tax increase and a hike in vehicle registration fees. The bill also established a clear set of objectives: "To the extent resources are available, public mental health services in this state should be provided to . . . persons experiencing severe and disabling mental illnesses."[27]

Realignment successfully refocused public mental health services on people who were poorer, less educated, and more impaired.[28] It expanded county bureaucracies to act much like insurance companies: managing contracts with providers, evaluating people for services, and authorizing (and withholding) continued treatment. Realignment also entrenched huge disparities in the services available across counties: some spent much of their realignment money on locked facilities while others went all in for outpatient care.[29] The Legislative Analyst Office concluded in 2001 that while realignment had successfully "stabilize[d] mental health funding," it did little to expand care to an estimated six hundred thousand "seriously mentally ill persons" in the state going without treatment.[30]

An attempt to reach that unserved population came with California's Mental Health Services Act (MHSA), which is second only to LPS in the amount of initial hope it sparked and later derision it received. The MHSA, approved by voters in 2004, imposes a 1 percent surcharge on incomes above one million dollars. Half its funds go to FSPs—outpatient teams assigned to do "whatever it takes" to keep people who have been cycling through jails and hospitals stable in the community (by tracking down clients in homeless encampments to give them antipsychotic injections, for example, or intervening with landlords to keep clients from getting evicted from supported housing). The rest of the funds go to prevention, early intervention, and innovation. In its first full year in effect, MHSA brought $1.3 billion new dollars into the system; within a decade, it was providing 24 percent of public mental health financing in the state.[31]

You might think that Ashley, with her history of hospitalizations and incarceration, would qualify for one of the 65,000 FSP spots MHSA made available.[32] She even posted on social media that there was one nearby that she thought would "bring me meds every three days" and that her sister could contact instead of the police in a crisis. But when Meredith called the county access line, which evaluates new cases and orients them to services, Ashley didn't qualify because, the county bureaucrat explained, she was "too stable." Meredith went to a public outreach event for the county clinic where they told her, "if it's not a crisis, we don't have anything."[33]

Meredith and Ashley were running up against the limits of what MHSA could do to plug the gaps in California's mental health system. Even as MHSA dollars were flowing in, realignment funds tanked in the Great Recession. The public mental health caseload dropped from 658,314 in 2007 to 442,691 in 2009.[34] A decade later, the basic infrastructure of care—clinics with case managers and psychiatrists—that counties are supposed to provide for people who don't meet strict FSP criteria were, at least in Stanislaus (where Ashley lived), just not there.[35]

The county mental health bureaucracy's determination that Ashley was "too stable" threw her into an entirely different, parallel public system. (If all of these layers of services and funding streams are confusing, imagine what it's like to try to navigate them in a crisis.) The 2010 Affordable Care Act ushered in a new expansion of care in California.[36] It also added another set of actors to an already convoluted system. In this regime, private care insurance companies would take public Medicaid dollars (in California, called Medi-Cal) to pay private mental health providers to care for people with "mild-to-moderate" conditions. Counties would refocus only on individuals with "significant" impairment (see figure 1.1).[37] This deepening privatization is visible nationwide: for example, since 2016, private

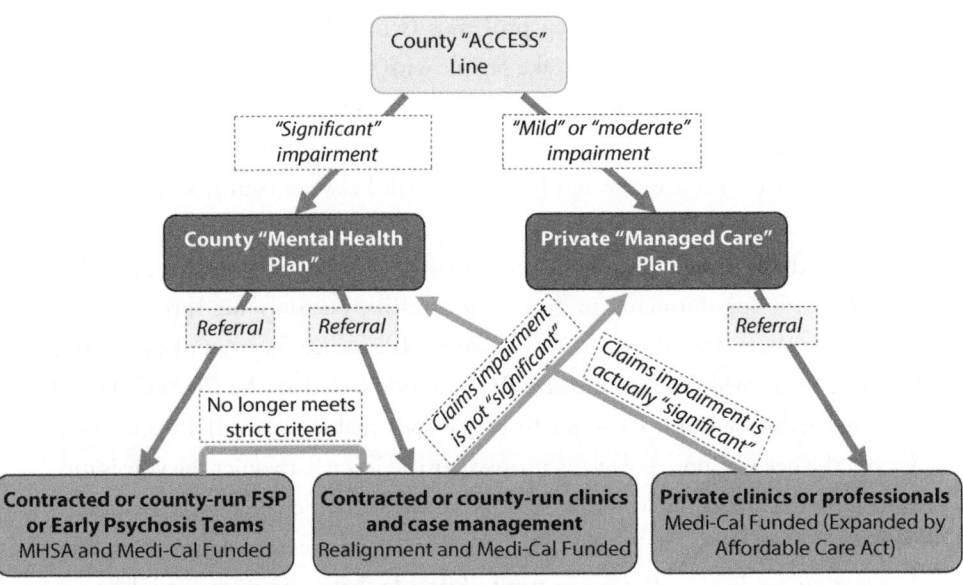

1.1 Access to services for Californians on Medi-Cal

equity firms have been snapping up community mental health clinics once run by nonprofits.[38]

According to Kevin, the director of the UMH clinic, the expansion of Medi-Cal was like a "firehouse" of newly insured people demanding care. About three-quarters of those individuals do not qualify for county services like UMH and are thrown back out to this privatized Medi-Cal managed care system. Dr. Stevens, the clinic's psychiatrist, was not optimistic about what happens next: 'They [the insurance company] will refer you to a therapist network, but they [the therapists] don't return calls, they cap the number of people on Medi-Cal [they will serve] because it doesn't pay well, they're too busy, or they're dead. Those lists are really horrendous. If someone is high functioning, they can connect, but I don't know what percentage makes it.' The head of one county's mental health department did know the percentage: 50 percent of the people they referred to the Medi-Cal managed care network never made it to a first appointment.

Meredith called the clinics on the Medi-Cal managed care company's list, desperate to get care for her sister. "I get violent," Ashley cuts in, explaining the urgency. But if the county thought Ashely was too stable, the publicly paid private providers that took Medi-Cal thought she was too severe. Given her criminal justice history, some programs wanted a "special letter [from a psychiatrist] saying I'm safe for community care," but since Ashley couldn't find a psychiatrist, that was a dead end. Drug programs (which have a separate Medi-Cal funding stream) said they didn't take people with serious mental illness and that she should return to the county system. This is exactly the situation some government watchdogs feared when California further subdivided its system: gaps in services as clients are referred back and forth between counties and private managed care plans.[39]

Meredith eventually found a psychiatrist who took Medi-Cal. She agreed to do telehealth appointments to give Ashley refills, but only for three months. Three years later, that doctor is still writing refills, since they can't find anyone else who will. Ashley wrote me after her interview to describe the "tactile and auditory hallucinations, messages from the gods making me suffer." She's convinced she needs a more powerful antipsychotic, Clozaril, to quiet the voices nipping at her. The doctor won't do a complex medication change over the phone. A few days after we spoke, she posted a despairing message online: "Literally begging for my life. . . . Put me in front of people that will understand. Remove my barriers to care."

In an odd way, for Ashley, that barrier was not an absence of providers, but a surfeit of them. On the ground, the multiplication of funding streams and programs in California makes it so every point in the nominally public system can say "no" to someone like Ashley, who seems too impaired for privately run services and not impaired enough for county-run ones. After all, there's always a different level of care more appropriate for her—except, in her case, there isn't.

DELUSIONAL REFUSAL?

Ashley couldn't get care when she wanted it. Some people can get it, but don't. Multiple parents insisted that, to understand why, I needed to read either D. J. Jaffe's *Insane Consequences* or Xavier Amador's *I'm Not Sick, I Don't Need Help.*[40] What these books share is their unswerving emphasis on anosognosia. According to Jaffe, *anosognosia* is the "clinical term for lack of awareness of being ill" (sometimes also called a lack of insight). He asserts it has "major policy implications": namely, that the law should not allow people with anosognosia—supposedly 50 percent of people with schizophrenia—to refuse treatment, since that refusal is itself a psychotic symptom.[41] From this perspective, because the community-based programs that LPS envisioned as an alternative to institutionalization were voluntary, they were guaranteed to fail people living with the most serious conditions.[42]

I can see why Michael and Julie would turn to anosognosia as an explanation for the seemingly inexplicable unwillingness of their son, Adam, to accept help. He was an Eagle Scout with a 4.0 GPA when, early in college, he started failing his courses. Over time, Julie recounts, "It turned into paranoia, blockading himself in his room, refusing to eat the food we served, stories about freemasons, etcetera. He took these spontaneous trips across the country in his car, we'd have to fly out to find him, impound the car." They tried to get him to a private psychiatrist, but Adam refused to go. Instead, he installed locks on his bedroom door, blocked it with furniture, and began accusing Julie of putting benzodiazepines in the tuna sandwiches she would drop off for him.

Michael and Julie mentioned this accelerating catastrophe to a friend at church who recommended they go to meetings of the National Alliance for Mental Illness (NAMI), an advocacy organization that provides support for parents. NAMI counseled reading Amador's book (where they learned about anosognosia) and reaching out to ALTER, a program for people experiencing a first psychotic break. Both federal and state lawmakers have been funneling money into such early intervention programs.[43] There is compelling evidence that quickly putting a young person on a low dose of an antipsychotic and providing a host of psychosocial supports to keep them in school, working, and connected with family can prevent a life of chronic illness.[44]

They only managed to get Adam to take a single phone call from the ALTER team. As Julie recounted, "He said, 'I'm not sick, do not call here, I will not go to your program,' and hung up." The ALTER social worker told Julie, "He's over 18, our hands are tied": he needed to consent to care. Without his agreement, ALTER also couldn't share information with his parents. Michael read me a letter he wrote to the program expressing his frustration: "First of all, your program is great, we wanted our son to be involved, but the whole approach that you take . . . is a violation of what you and all professionals know is 'anosognosia.'" I get their exasperation. Michael and Julie had been going to NAMI webinars where they heard the claim that "with every episode there's more brain damage," an image that psychiatrists have been popularizing to argue that first breaks should be treated with the urgency of a heart attack.[45] For them, letting Adam refuse care was as much medical malpractice as deciding not to revive someone unconscious from cardiac arrest because they did not consent to defibrillation. "It's just tragic," Julie added.

At home, Adam was becoming more hostile. Michael and Julie called the sheriff, but every time they'd come to evaluate him for an involuntary psychiatric hold, "he'd rally" and officers would declare that he didn't meet criteria (i.e., he was neither dangerous nor gravely disabled). Eventually, the officers recommended that Michael and Julie evict him; a social worker at ALTER gave the same advice, suggesting, "Throw him out, and he'll be back in a week, he'll be hungry, and maybe you can get him into care then." They weren't ready to make such a wrenching decision, but Adam ran away on his own. Michael and Julie tracked him to a motel and convinced a county mental health team to outreach him. "They went to the motel and he wouldn't open the door, he was just screaming at them, and [the team] told us, 'He really isn't cooperative, so when he's back home and more stable, we'd be happy to come out,' and we're like, 'Are you effing idiots? If he were home and stable, we wouldn't need you,'" she seethed.

It's not easy to watch a beloved child's life fall apart and to be continuously told the mental health system can't do anything about it. But there are both financial and pragmatic reasons why outpatient teams were not berating Adam into care: financial, because Medicaid won't reimburse clinical teams for going to motels to be yelled at by people whom they can't diagnose and can't treat; pragmatic, because the whole effectiveness of models like ALTER is to engage young people by enticing them with things they want—help with school and work, for example—and minimizing the imposition of things they don't, like heavy doses of antipsychotics.[46] Then again, even top-shelf early-intervention programs have "disengagement" rates ranging from 12 to more than 50 percent.[47]

Many critiques of laws like LPS argue that a mental health system that won't coerce people into care funnels them into institutions that will coerce them: prisons and jails.[48] The sheriff's deputies wouldn't bring Adam to an ER when Julie and Michael asked them to, but they did pick him up when he hit a woman with a rock. Julie and Michael begged the jail to give him a psychiatric evaluation. While waiting, he punched a guard and they put him in solitary confinement. Eventually, though, Adam made it to the jail psychiatric unit and received court-ordered involuntary medication. Julie and Michael hounded the county mental health director until he agreed to pressure the jail to release their son to a hospital and have him conserved.

He stayed four months, stabilized to the point where that the public guardian released him from conservatorship, and he went to live in a board and care home. The home was run by Jehovah's Witnesses and was pretty strict, but to his parents, the monthly injection and structured environment worked wonders. Julie told me, "It was like a miracle, honest-to-goodness. He went back to school, he had a car again, he was doing really well." But, to their horror, he convinced his county psychiatrist to titrate his medication downward. The psychiatrist, in their eyes, allowed Adam's disease—namely, his anosognosia—to drive his treatment. The resulting spiral ended when Adam committed a serious violent crime.

When I interviewed his parents, Adam was in jail awaiting trial but, Julie noted, "He's back on medication . . . and he's pretty normal. The crazy part of this is because he has anosognosia, he still doesn't think he's ill, he's only taking the medication because he thinks it's better for his case [to show the judge he's complying with treatment]." Michael and Julie were tireless advocates for getting their son the best voluntary services their insurance company and the county had to offer. Adam refused it all, even though when he was required to take medication, he did really well by all accounts (except maybe his own).

Anosognosia is such a powerful framework not only because it helps make sense of these cases but also because it seems to definitively resolve the intractable tension between medical care and civil rights they present. The psychiatrists who have popularized anosognosia argue that heavy-handed medical intervention can restore not just someone like Adam's sanity, but his very capacity for rational choice.[49] Indeed, you'll hear in this book from people who turned down treatment, were forced to receive it, and ultimately came to see their past refusals as a disordered symptom of anosognosia, leaving them grateful for the involuntary help in overcoming it. Medicine, it seems, can do great things when Law gets out of its way.

ACCESS TO SERVICES, QUALITY OF SERVICES

Cases like Adam's are like a Rorschach test, in which a psychoanalyst asks what images a patient sees in blobs of ink. If you look at treatment refusal and see anosognosia, you're likely to conclude that forced treatment is the solution. Critics, however, argue that there has been a "striking function creep" as anosognosia (a condition that neuroscientists use primarily for people who have had strokes or Alzheimer's, not schizophrenia) has come to "account for just about everything that goes wrong in community mental health care."[50] When you ask erstwhile clients themselves, you hear about a different set of barriers to care: social conditions that make compliance difficult, superficial and low-quality services, a lack of professional competence, and a failure of the mental health system to provide what they actually want. If you squint at people disconnected from services and see these alternative explanations, then expanding conservatorship—versus fixing the failings of California's outpatient treatment system while keeping it voluntary—starts to make a lot less sense.

Thatcher had nine involuntary hospitalizations throughout the Bay Area starting in 2016 during a series of manic episodes (which I will describe further in a later chapter). What's important here, though, is what happened when Thatcher's legally imposed inpatient treatment ended and they (Thatcher uses they/them pronouns) were discharged to voluntary outpatient care. As they recounted, "They would give me a couple days of [medication], and be like, 'You have to refill it at San Francisco General Hospital.' And I just wouldn't have my shit together to do it, you know?" Thatcher "remember[s] trying to take meds," but without stable housing or income, getting to the hospital in the right timeframe was a challenge.

Even if Thatcher did get the refill, navigating the system to receive follow-up care was frustrating: "I was on a waiting list for over a year to try to see a psychiatrist. They'll give you medication once you get arrested and 5150ed, but access to medication is actually really hard to figure out if you are not rich." As a report from the LA Department of Mental Health in 2020 observed, medication nonadherence from someone who might be unhoused or lack regular access to a phone is "multi-factorial": "choice or [lack of] insight" might be part of it, but so too are a "lack of transportation to clinics or pharmacies, lack of safe places to store medications, [and] concerns that medication side effects may place them at risk for violent victimization [on the streets]."[51]

Depending on who you ask, the single-minded focus on medications may itself be the problem. Gail, the mother of a thirty-year-old son with schizophrenia in Los Angeles, told me she is a fervent believer in "recovery," which she understands to be the ability of people with serious mental illness to "get a job, get married, [and] fulfill their dreams, just as they did before they got ill." And she believes that the key to achieving recovery is medication. To her, because schizophrenia is a "lifetime illness for which relapse is real," people should be required to take medication "for life."

Her son Alexander sees things differently. He claims his mom dragged him to see a clinician at age seventeen when he got caught at school with a bottle of tequila in a gym bag (she says he was showing signs of paranoia and delusions). His prior image of mental health treatment was similar to what many educated and middle-class people probably imagine: "I thought I could be open and talk to them and I would get a non-judgmental ear to listen." What he got instead was a series of pointed questions, like "Do you think there's an organized group targeting you?" He was being evaluated for schizophrenia, not getting therapy. This unwelcoming entrée isn't helped by the fact that mental health services act as if their clients are potential criminals: to get into a public clinic in LA, you might have to pass through a metal detector or receive a pat down.

Alexander described the treatment he received as superficial in exactly the way you would expect if your psychiatrist had an active caseload of three hundred clients.[52] "They like to hear that you can identify your symptoms," he expounded. But when his doctor told him, "You have disorganized thinking," Alexander figured they'd "clear it out, write down those thoughts, and organize them."

He expected an ongoing, multifaceted partnership. Instead, he received a never-ending medical monologue about complying with his antipsychotic medication.[53]

His doctors were the ones who ultimately applied to place him on conservatorship. This didn't exactly deepen the connection: "They'll always tell you that they want to help you, but I felt like any contact I had with them was risky." So he decided to go into his appointments "and think about the image they want to see, and try to get them to believe that everything is going well. I tell them that their solution"—that is, medication—"is working." Then, he laughed, "Every few months I'd get the spirit back and run away, totally avoid everything [treatment]." For him, "recovery" meant escaping the mental health system, not being permanently enmeshed with it.

Other interviewees tightly linked the quality of treatment with who was providing it. Advocates have increasingly called for "culturally competent" services that account for the unique experiences and beliefs of different social groups.[54] Lola, who is Latina, lamented the dearth of professionals who understood the distinctive forms of stigma she faced. She wished more could understand Spanish: she's bilingual, but some feelings just didn't translate. (Four percent of psychiatrists in the state are Hispanic/Latinx, even though 39 percent of state residents are.[55]) But Lola's care didn't just lack cultural competence; sometimes, it lacked competence, full stop.[56]

After one involuntary hospitalization, she was discharged to the care of a county psychiatrist who was "very validating" and open to talking about Lola's depression and self-injury as well as her challenges with her weight. One day, the psychiatrist told Lola she had to see her urgently. Lola drove eighty miles to learn that her psychiatrist was leaving for private practice. We often chastise mental health clients who don't stick with care, but underworked and underpaid public-sector professionals also don't stick with providing that care. Every one of a rotating cast of clinicians wanted Lola to recount the same checklist of traumas and failed treatments; every one piled on more medications for symptoms and those medications' side effects. Then a new psychiatrist, straight out of med school, proposed taking her off all ten at once. She crashed and ended up in an ER.

Lola was happy to see that psychiatrist go. The next one was skeptical of big pharma's pills and encouraged her to deal with her anxiety by "just taking a breath, breathe your problems away." Lola found this clueless: "I was like, 'What are you talking about? I have asthma! How do you want me to take a deep breath if I can't even breathe without an inhaler?'" Psychiatrists quickly dismissed her back to her primary care provider for any physical complaint; those primary care providers usually told Lola her problems were psychosomatic. Inattention to physical problems by mental health professionals is a frequent remonstrance. Meredith told me her sister Ashley once reported excruciating abdominal pain while in a psychiatric ward. Her doctor assumed it was a hallucination. It was appendicitis, and she needed emergency surgery.

Sometimes, people who supposedly lack the insight to accept mental health services suddenly gain it when the services offered change. Thatcher readily admitted that they had a mental illness and that the long-acting injectable Abilify they were getting helped them enormously (including making them well enough to participate in advocacy groups looking to abolish forced treatment). But they only got on that medication after finding a clinic that provided not just medication management but also peer supports, psychotherapy, information about gender confirmation treatment, and help applying for disability benefits.[57] In the new intakes I observed at Urban Mental Health, one-third of people said that their primary desire was getting help with housing or benefits. Only 13 percent said they wanted medication. Clinicians frequently attribute client disengagement to stigma or a lack of insight. But in a survey of clients, "the reason most commonly reported . . . was that services were not relevant to their needs."[58] Almost all agreed they could use help, just not the help the mental health system was offering.

Kate has a history of forced hospitalization that made her oppose involuntary treatment in all but the most extreme circumstances. ("Like, if I saw a child running into traffic, would I forcibly grab them? Yes.") But she also questioned the idea that the solution to involuntary, medicalized inpatient treatment is voluntary, medicalized outpatient treatment. As an advocate, she explained, "I go to a lot of meetings where they talk about 'access to services.' . . . And thinking back, all through my life, these were not services that I wanted to access." Instead, she wishes for "education, employment training . . . wilderness, camping experience, working with animals, creative arts." It may seem obvious, but any conversation about whether people are accepting "services" needs to consider what those services are, whether they are high quality, and if they match what people want.

CONCLUSION: THE RIGHTS ROAD NOT TAKEN

California's public mental health system provides care "to the extent resources are available." Even in its more generous moments, the state legislature never created an entitlement program, whereby funding would expand to match the needs of all people with serious mental illnesses in the state. As Michelle Cabrera, from the association representing county behavioral health directors, put it, the legislature defined a comprehensive public mental health system as something that would be "'nice to have,' not a 'must have.'"[59]

A "must have" system would not just establish an abstract right to care. Engaged government authority would ensure that there were specific clinics, professionals, or teams with an obligation to provide that care, even to individuals they perceive as difficult or resistant. This intuitive definition of "public service" as "for anyone in the public who qualifies" is the basis of public mental health services in countries like France, but jarringly absent in California.[60]

The limits of even the most intensive outpatient services were visible at the end of UMH meetings, when clinicians discussed clients whose files they'd be closing. Sometimes clients moved to another county or state. Mostly, though, they disappeared or made it clear they no longer wanted care. I almost never saw anyone progress out of the public system into the less intensive treatment organized by private Medi-Cal managed care plans, as consultants' flowcharts had envisioned.

At one meeting in 2018, Charlie (the head of the FSP team) mentions a forty-six-year-old white man with schizoaffective disorder (a combination of psychosis and mood disorder symptoms): 'Basically he's been disengaged since he left his housing [an independent apartment UMH helped find for him] in 2016. He was talking about 'wanting to teach the Star Trek opera.' My only contact is that I saw him at [local park] at 6 A.M. taking a walk in his bathrobe.'

Avril, a clinician from the mobile crisis team, declares in response, 'Well, we've got to close him. I always say "an open chart is not treatment."' He didn't want care, so UMH's responsibility to him had concluded.

Stu, the social worker who would handle his intake if he came back, adds, 'We can always catch him the next time he's hospitalized.'

That "next time"—the very much not-voluntary, not-outpatient part of the system—is where we now turn (figure 1.2).

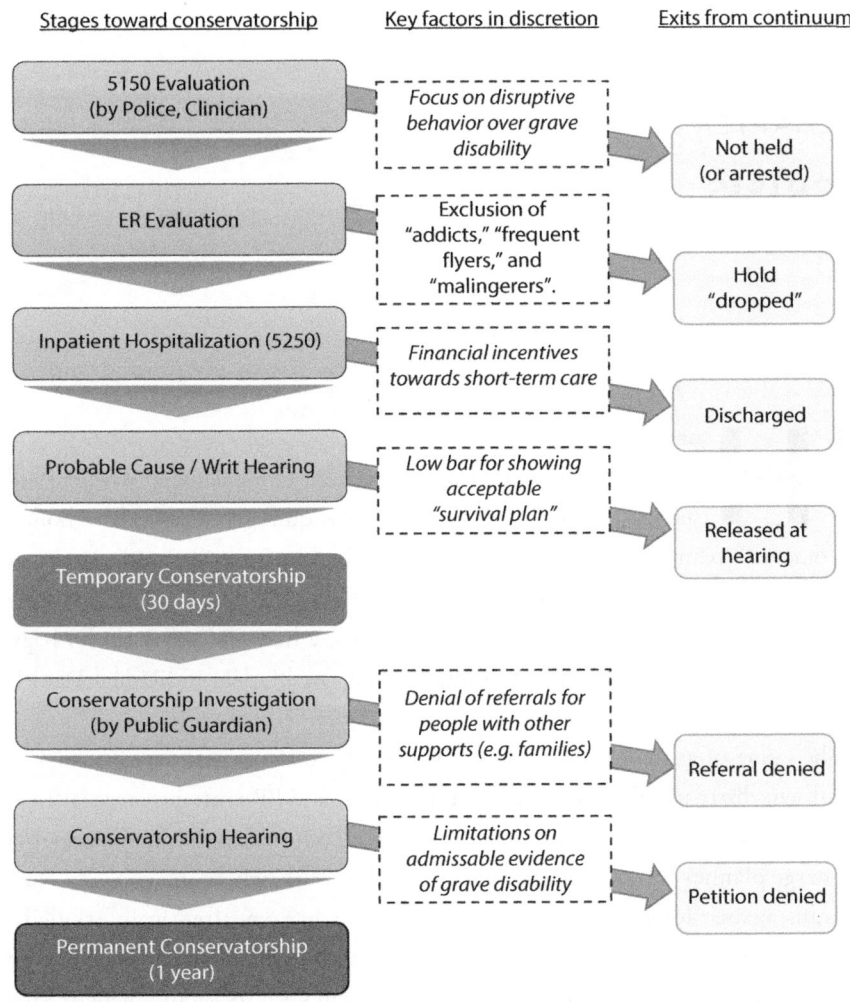

Stages toward conservatorship

5150 Evaluation
(by Police, Clinician)

ER Evaluation

Inpatient Hospitalization (5250)

Probable Cause / Writ Hearing

Temporary Conservatorship
(30 days)

Conservatorship Investigation
(by Public Guardian)

Conservatorship Hearing

Permanent Conservatorship
(1 year)

Key factors in discretion

Focus on disruptive behavior over grave disability

Exclusion of "addicts," "frequent flyers," and "malingerers".

Financial incentives towards short-term care

Low bar for showing acceptable "survival plan"

Denial of referrals for people with other supports (e.g. families)

Limitations on admissable evidence of grave disability

Exits from continuum

Not held
(or arrested)

Hold
"dropped"

Discharged

Released at hearing

Referral denied

Petition denied

1.2 The conservatorship continuum

CHAPTER 2

CRISIS

'Homeless or hipster?'

I'm driving with Dani, a licensed clinical social worker, and she's introducing me to a timeless quiz game played by homeless outreach teams in her Southern California beach town. She's referring to a white man who looks to be in his late twenties and is walking shirtless down the street with a pair of board shorts, cowboy boots, a hat, and a few duffel bags. But whether he's homeless or a hipster, he's not the kind of individual Dani is looking for.

She's part of a small team financed by the city to figure out creative ways to transform thirty ultrahigh users of hospitals, jails, and ERs into just regular high users. Dani came here two years ago after burning out making $35,000 a year as a discharge planner in a psychiatric hospital in the South, where she grew up. Now she rails against for-profit health care and spends her days frantically trying to meet her clients wherever they're at and keep them there. That means convincing them to switch from vodka to beer, providing them with socks and hygiene kits, keeping them from getting evicted from their supported housing, and sometimes even getting them some mental health treatment.

The team also occasionally subjects people to 5150s. A 5150 refers to the section of the LPS Act that allows "peace officers" and certain clinicians designated by the county to place people on a "hold" and transport them to an ER for evaluation. These holds are the first step on the conservatorship continuum. As you'll see in this chapter, 5150s are haphazard, emotionally fraught, sometimes violent, and often disconnected from any coherent project to get someone better. Who gets 5150ed depends less on whether someone meets the formal criteria of danger to self, danger to others, or gravely disabled and more on how a person fits into four archetypes of individuals who might receive a 5150 evaluation: people dying on the streets, in the wrong state of mind at the wrong place and time, in crisis in public, and decompensating at home.

Jerry is in that first category. He's the main topic of the morning staff meeting, before people hit the road (or, in some cases, the boardwalk). Although he's sixty-one, according to Dani, he 'looks like he's eighty.' A combination of alcoholism and depression has shriveled him to ninety-five pounds and confined him to a wheelchair. In his most recent stint in detox, he left (the program, like nearly all substance abuse programs, was unlocked and voluntary) and went back to his shelter after two days. Now the shelter is kicking him out because he keeps falling out of bed and fighting with staff while drunk. Courtney, a social worker who is going on her third year with the team, adds, 'It's very sad and emotional for us. We know the standard [for a 5150 hold] is that it has to be a mental disorder. But he has a traumatic brain disorder from a motorcycle accident. . . . It's related to the brain, but it doesn't count. So we're just watching him die.'

Dylan is the team's supervisor and the only one authorized by the county to place 5150 holds. 'This is not something I use lightly,' he reminds the team. In Jerry's case, it's not just a matter of legal criteria. Because Jerry has medical, psychiatric, and substance issues, 'If we put him on a hold, he'll be shuffled between psych and med [in the hospital]. Some psychiatrist will scream at me if I bring him to a psych ER,' saying he belongs in a medical unit better able to handle the physical effects of alcohol withdrawal. Still, Dylan says, 'based on what I'm hearing today, I might just try it. I can't use chronic alcoholism or TBI [traumatic brain injury], I'll have to lean on the depression,' even though everyone agrees it's not depression that is killing him. 'If he said all of this was happening because the demons told him to,' Dani offers, 'this would be easier [to do a 5150],' because he would be more obviously mentally ill.

I had imagined a 5150 evaluation to be a high-drama affair, but Dylan's once-over of Jerry is low key. We walk to the back garden of the homeless shelter. Jerry is sitting in a folding chair, rail thin with a checkered shirt and jeans hanging loosely from his frame.

'I'm in bad shape,' Jerry declares, lamenting 'someone stole my wheelchair. But I'm going to go to rehab on Friday. I'm not drinking anymore. I'm not going to go out until then, it's just too dangerous.' (It's Tuesday.)

'It's nice to see your resolve,' Dani offers.

'Have you been eating?' Dylan asks, sipping from a coffee cup.

'I hadn't eaten in three days, but this morning, I had two bites, and I have this,' Jerry states, holding up an empty bottle of Ensure. 'I also shaved and took a shower,' he adds, proudly.

Dylan rolls his eyes, and closes, 'I don't want to be harsh, Jerry, but this is a life-or-death situation for you, so I want you to go on Friday.' Jerry has cleaned up. He won't be 5150ed. This is the pattern: Jerry has been seen by fire department paramedics ten times in the past two months while passed out on the street, but has never been taken in against his will. When Dani runs into Courtney later that day, she reports, 'He looked better, but still so terrible. He shaved and there was no dirt on his neck. It made a difference. But that's the problem. He gets it together, and there's nothing we can do.'

We next head to the beach to see a fifty-year-old client nicknamed Professor Jolie. Dani says she once was 'housed and on meds' but was evicted for screaming racial epithets at her Black neighbors. (She also is Black.) She's now been on the streets for ten years, and neither this team nor the county's AOT clinicians have been able to dislodge her, despite four 5150s in the past few months. 'She does well on meds, which means she gets out [of the hospital]' and, of course, stops taking them. She is, according to Dani, '100 percent schizophrenic.' She is also Dani's 'favorite.'

I quickly get why. Professor Jolie's encampment is a five-by-five-yard plot of boardwalk adorned with artwork, ornate metal lawn furniture (including a table with a few finished bottles of liquor atop it), and a sleeping area covered by colorful, flowing fabric. 'It's a great set up, I'd like to live there,' Courtney told me. There's also a sign stating 'COVID-19: Sweeps Kill,' which is a reminder of the urgency of our visit: the city has put her on notice that she'll be evicted next week. Jolie emerges from her bedroom, wearing a sun hat, a colorful dress, and an array of bracelets, her curly, slightly greying hair perfectly coiffed.

Professor Jolie seems happy enough to see us: the team has been giving her medical supplies for a leg wound she suffered in a bike accident. She rolls up her bandage to show us that it's healing nicely. When Dani introduces me as a researcher, Jolie replies, 'I am a professor too, you know.' She holds up a small canvas with a painting that looks like Starry Night. 'It [space] really looks like this,' she tells me. The narrative that followed was well put together and emphatically stated—and hard not to see as delusional. As she explains it, when she was five, she wrote a book for Harvard Law School, which repaid her by sending her to the moon with Neil Armstrong, who then adopted her, which made her a member of the Swedish royal family and bequeathed her two-thirds of the world's wealth.

At this moment, Dani interjects, 'You know, they're clearing people out here—would you be interested in housing?'

Given what she's just told us, Professor Jolie's next response is not surprising: 'No. I actually own houses up and down here. I'm just waiting for someone to drop off the keys.'

Our conversation goes downhill fast. 'Would you be interested in talking to our doctor about taking medication?' Dani offers.

Professor Jolie stiffens, 'No, I'm fine, I don't need that. I'm actually a professor of physio-psychiatry. I do not teach calisthenics.' She seems more agitated, and Dani moves to leave.

Professor Jolie takes a few steps with us, and then spins and shouts, 'Bitch, leave me alone.'

There's no one there, but Dani asks sympathetically, 'Do those people bother you?' Professor Jolie nods. Dani closes, 'Okay, well, we'll see you soon.'

She tells me that, in Professor Jolie's recent 5150s, 'the police have had to go "hands on" because she's aggressive and volatile.' The risk of violence from police—and the lack of success on previous holds—means that there's no plan to send Dylan down to evaluate her. Professor Jolie represents a different type of situation where a 5150 becomes a potential intervention: a visible crisis in public.

Our third visit is to Guadalupe, decompensating at home. 'She really needs to be conserved,' Dani tells me, a process that will have to start with a 5150. She has schizophrenia, is frequently mute, and has destroyed her apartment based on paranoia that extraterrestrials have installed cameras inside. The team has had to use its finite funds to pay the nonprofit running her building for repairs. She's risking eviction, which is surprisingly common even in "permanent" supported housing.[1] In any case, she frequently doesn't sleep there, because she believes she is being sexually assaulted by the aliens. Whatever you think about the credibility of that fear, Dani speculates that these delusions likely come from a life of pretty unrelenting trauma.

We rap on her door. She's wearing a dirty T-shirt and looks like she hasn't been sleeping. Dani's pretext for checking up on her is an upcoming optometry appointment. When she asks Guadalupe if she remembers the appointment, Guadalupe holds up a finger, retreats back into her apartment, and comes back with a notebook, where she writes that she didn't. 'Is there anything we can do for you?' She writes 'no' and abruptly closes the door.

Outside, we run into Courtney and Jordan, the team's substance use counselor, who are here to visit another client. 'Dylan says we should be thinking all the time about whether she meets the criteria for us to put her on a 5150,' Courtney explains, 'but she's been hospitalized so many times that she's "institutionalized."' In the 1960s, "institutionalized" meant that someone had spent so long in the hospital they didn't know how to live outside it; for Guadalupe, it means she's been hospitalized so many times she knows what to say to the judge (who will review her case within a week if her 5150 leads to a hospital admission) to get out.

When I come back the following week, everyone is doing worse. We go to the shelter to give a client his antipsychotic injection and run into Jerry. He's quivering, 'It's real bad . . . You know . . . I had a four-day hangover and yesterday . . . I just couldn't do it, I drank.' The team is convinced it's so clear his problem is alcoholism, and not mental illness, that no psych hospital will admit him. His last, best hope is a detox program, which he'll have to go to voluntarily. We're in a rush and move on quickly to the boardwalk. Professor Jolie is much harder to follow. She is shifting between a Caribbean and an American accent, explaining, 'I am not node three, I am node five.' We try to tell her that her eviction is imminent, and she declares, 'Bye' and starts talking to someone who is sitting at her encampment's table, although we cannot see them.

But it's Guadalupe who is the real concern. The team received a call from her building manager that she was screaming in the hallway. Courtney went to see her: 'She was pointing to stains on her pants and said, "Do you see all this semen? They are raping me." But there was nothing there.' Worse, 'She had a golf-ball sized swollen cheek, and a gash in her head. She's probably doing this to herself.'

On Wednesdays, the team is joined at its morning meeting by a psychiatrist, who helps refill clients' meds: 'Why isn't she considered holdable [on a 5150]?' he asks.

Courtney replies, 'Because after I talked to her, she got in the van and we went to her appointment. She was functional, she was oriented.'

I join Courtney on a visit to Guadalupe's apartment. It takes a long time for her to open her door, and I can see a series of boards stacked chaotically against it. The walls of her apartment are lined with plastic bags. 'Can you tell me how you got that?' Courtney asks, pointing to a gash on her temple. Guadalupe shakes her head. 'Can you write it?' She shakes her head again. 'Is there anything else you need from us?' She starts closing the door. 'The doctor is going to drop by to see you.' Guadalupe makes a small 'bye-bye' wave with her hand and shuts the door.

Outside, I can tell the case is weighing on Courtney. We confab with Dani, who declares, 'I'm going to get LPS designated, so I can deprive people of their basic human rights!'

Courtney offers, in response, 'It's for a good cause.'

Dani replies, 'Sure, but I don't have a lot of optimism a hold will stick.'

For Dani and her colleagues, conservatorship is an almost mystical intervention that everyone needs but no one gets. The team has some incredible success stories. But many clients either die (one person was hit by a car while inebriated and passed away a week before I joined them), bounce endlessly in and out of jail, or alternate between living on the streets and staying temporarily in "permanent" housing until they get evicted. "Not being conserved" is thus far from "having one's civil rights respected."

As you'll see in this chapter, involuntary holds can feel like a potent and terrifying state power to the people subject to them. Yet they are not really coordinated by any public authority. We'll start this chapter by examining how police use their discretion in ways that concentrate coercion on people who are visibly disruptive, while also sweeping up some people who seem to have just been in the wrong state of mind at the wrong place at the wrong time. Then we'll see how the system overlooks people decompensating at home and gives up on those dying on the streets.

CRISIS IN PUBLIC

Alameda County, across the Bay from San Francisco and home to Oakland and Berkeley, is the 5150 capital of California. With 17,600 holds placed in 2017, its rate is nearly four times the state average.[2] To understand what drives high rates of 5150s, we need to examine how police respond to individual crises in public, which are themselves exacerbated by the collective crises of homelessness and substance use.

I've interviewed a dozen law enforcement officers since 2021. They all concurred that some 5150 holds are straightforward and unavoidable. Lieutenant Reid, head of the Los Angeles Police Department's Mobile Evaluation Unit

(MEU), which specializes in responding to mental illness–related calls, gives me two classic cases: the "person on the bridge wanting to jump off onto the 101 freeway" and the "naked man with a machete running down the street." MEU sends Systemwide Mental Assessment Response Teams (SMART), which pair an officer with a clinician, to some calls. But she says incidents like these are urgent enough to get a "patrol response"—that is to say, a regular beat officer. They'll usually write a 5150 on their own.

Most 5150s aren't so clear-cut. One ethnography of homelessness in San Francisco documented how policing of homelessness is increasingly "complaint-oriented."[3] Officers spend their time responding to citizens who are calling in (or reporting on a city smartphone app) people blocking doorways, accosting passers-by, acting bizarrely, or bothering callers by their very presence. Lieutenant Reid explained that for MEU, "it's all citizen generated. Even the SMART teams don't go out and proactively look for people to say, 'Hey, we're observing you right now, and you're unable to care for yourself.'"[4] Officer Herman, who handles community outreach with MEU, said she monitors community pages on Facebook and NextDoor.com to identify individuals irritating neighbors, business owners, or pedestrians.

There are more people than ever having crises in public to complain about. Starting in 2014, a decade-long decline in homelessness in California reversed. Homelessness increased 42 percent by 2020.[5] The unsheltered are increasingly in suburban and rural areas accustomed to viewing homelessness as an urban, coastal problem. In Alameda County, homelessness nearly doubled from 2017 to 2021. The vast majority of the unhoused were longtime county residents.[6] Calls to police for mental health holds grew in tandem.[7]

Perhaps a more significant factor is not the quantity of homeless people but a degradation in the behavior of a visible minority of them. Politicians and the general public view mental illness as ubiquitous among unhoused people, although both social scientists and federal data dispute this claim.[8] But clinicians and first responders on the ground saw something else behind the chaos generating complaints: methamphetamine.[9] In the shadow of the more mediatized opioid epidemic, meth overdose deaths in the United States went up 180 percent from 2015 to 2019.[10] In San Francisco, ER visits related to meth increased 600 percent between 2011 and 2016.[11]

Meth-induced psychosis looks a lot like schizophrenia-induced psychosis. Dr. Zeldes, who has been practicing street medicine in San Francisco for decades, reflected on the growing calls for his team to "do something" about disruptive homeless people: "The narrative is, 'We have all these people with mental illness [on the streets].' The reality is, what people [complainers] are responding to is people who are methamphetamine users, and who are acting bizarrely and behaviorally highly dysregulated." While psychotic symptoms due to schizophrenia are challenging to treat, those from meth seemed insurmountable: "It's really hard. . . . What could be more compelling than a blast of methamphetamine?" he mused. Antipsychotics can blunt the acute symptoms of meth psychosis, but chronic meth use can create permanent cognitive impairments.

Police officers' options for responding to drug-related complaints have dwindled. Proposition 47, approved by Californian voters in 2014 to limit mass incarceration, means an arrest for possession is unlikely to lead to jail time.[12] This seems to reflect a broader cultural shift. As Officer Herman recounted, "When I came on in 2000, I wouldn't get many mental health calls. Instead, people would call 911 and say, 'I have a person on drugs acting erratic, causing a disturbance, they're a criminal, I want them arrested.'" Today, though, "they [the public] changed their mindset of what they wanted to call 'crime' compared to 'mental health,' and they've bought the idea . . . that drug use is mental health." The public now expects officers to try to get drug users into services.

But substance use services are sorely lacking and inaccessible.[13] In early 2022, I went on a ride-along in Alameda County with Officer Harden, a real estate agent turned cop who is also a black belt in jujitsu and gives me compelling arguments for switching to a Keto diet. We start our day watching a webinar from the Health Department on the "precipitous rise in stimulant overdoses" in the past few years. Harden is genuinely excited about the new county CARES (Community Assessment, Referral, and Engagement Services) Center, which is a kind of one-stop shop for signing up for housing and treatment. Officers can drop people off as an alternative to arresting them for a misdemeanor.

I accompany a CARES sales team of four armed officers to a small encampment by the side of a freeway in Alameda. It's a well-maintained space, with a haphazard plywood wall surrounding three tents, propane stove, and a bathing area in an adjacent cistern. Officer Harden's partner, Sergeant Briggs, raps on a tent, declaring, 'Sofia, we know you're in there, could you come talk to us for a few minutes?' A Latina who appears to be in her thirties emerges, looking groggy. She has a black eye.

'What happened to your eye?' Harden asks.

Her speech is slurred. (Harden believes she has serious cognitive damage from meth use.) I hear 'fell,' and then 'fight.'

'Looks like you had a rough night. Would you be interested in checking out that CARES program I told you about'—he makes this pitch a few times a month—'get you some resources, shelter, maybe a job?' The woman nods.

'You want to be transported up there today?' he asks, clearly surprised. She nods again.

'Okay, let me make a phone call [to CARES],' Harden declares, exuberantly.

The woman starts throwing a few items in a backpack. Briggs steps in to explain, 'It's not to take you directly to housing, just helping you make connections. You can leave your stuff.'

While Officer Harden is on the phone, another officer is patting down a rail-thin, shirtless man, who had emerged from another tent. The officer comes over to Briggs, reporting, 'If she [Sofia] is going to CARES, he'll go too.'

But at this point, Officer Harden has some bad news: 'CARES said their clinician is on vacation, and the replacement didn't come in. But they say, 100 percent, we can bring them tomorrow.'

Sergeant Briggs exclaims, 'There's a 100 percent chance that meth will make it to this encampment tonight and they won't go tomorrow!' They were each 50 percent right: the next day, Sofia still wanted to go, the other man didn't. As both cops and clinicians will tell you, people's openness to substance use treatment might last just a few hours after a bad trip or a reversed overdose. But most substance use services are nine-to-five operations.[14]

Even in counties that have 24/7 detox or drop-in centers, people have to go voluntarily. So when officers are faced with complaint-generating behavior they can't ignore but for which an arrest seems futile, they feel they have only one option: writing a 5150. Alameda is a stand-out among large counties for how little it has invested in non-police crisis response teams: it has only five mobile crisis teams; equivalently-sized Santa Clara has twice as many.[15] So it is no surprise that at Alameda's main safety-net psychiatric hospital, John George, virtually everyone is originally detained by law enforcement.[16] But as you'll see in the next chapter, the kind of behavior we're discussing—at the border between illegal-and-dangerous and legal-but-disruptive, and maybe caused by meth use rather than a "real" mental illness—is likely to lead to a quick discharge.

One nurse working at John George explained the absurd back-and-forth created by police pushing people unwanted by the community onto hospitals that also don't want them: "We've had some tug-of-wars with law enforcement. . . . We get people that we discharge and they don't want to leave, so we have to call law enforcement to remove them. They approach the guy, who tells them he wants to hurt himself. Then the officer will say, 'I have to put him back on a hold.' We say, 'We will just drop the hold.' And we could do this all day." This seemed implausible to me, until several law enforcement officers described precisely this process playing out in the hospital parking lot.

One clinic director in Alameda County summarized the situation: 'The police see folks who are high. A 5150 is the easiest way to get them off the street. The ER is not admitting them, and the system is sort of functionally dysfunctioning the way it is supposed to.' This functioning dysfunctioning means some people wrack up extraordinary numbers of 5150s. One study from Alameda found that a small number of people with five or more 5150s accounted for 9 percent of all ambulance encounters and 39 percent of all holds in the county.[17]

These individuals, a confidential informant with access to county data told me, are not the sickest of the sick but, instead, people on the edge between multiple systems of care and control.[18] Police have the power to put them on a hold, but not the authority to make the criminal justice or mental health systems intervene in any enduring way—whether by providing voluntary drug treatment or pushing them toward a conservatorship.

CONFUSION AND MISUNDERSTANDINGS IN THE "STATE OF EXCEPTION"

Being 5150ed might be in someone's best interest and better than being arrested, but it's not a benign way to move a person off the street for a few hours. People who are 5150ed are handcuffed before being put in a squad car or tied down for transport in an ambulance. Captain Brian Bixler, head of the mental health unit at LAPD, told me proudly that according to department data, only 1.2 percent of 5150s in 2020 involved a "use of force," which would include "anything from a firm grip . . . to control devices, i.e.; TASER, baton, pepper spray, etc." He encouraged me to publicize this statistic to show the compassionate and competent way officers handle most calls. I heard about plenty of incidents where this seemed to be true. Still, when you start talking about many, many 5150s for a single person—in Los Angeles, five hundred people have had at least fifty (!)

5150s—those risks add up.[19] And since Black people are hugely overrepresented among those with many 5150 holds, the potential for harm is particularly stark.[20]

5150s have enough reach to crop up in song lyrics: by rap duo Luniz, punk band Tsunami Bomb, or rapper turned pop punk Machine Gun Kelly. This isn't proof that they're ubiquitous, affecting everyone regardless of fame, privilege, or musical genre; rather, it's a sign that they're a little bit random. Lola struggled with both her mental and physical health from a young age, but both deteriorated significantly when she slipped, injured her back, and was bedbound much of the time. She went repeatedly to the ER for pain medications, but was frequently turned away for "drug-seeking." Once, though, she confided to a resident that "my complaints [about pain] are true, but there's another side to why I'm here. I don't feel safe, I need support, I need help." The resident told Lola that she didn't think it was a good idea to go home. She'd be better upstairs, where the staff were caring and would listen to her. It wasn't until they wheeled her into the unit and she heard the click of the door behind her that she realized a 72-hour hold meant going to a locked ward: "I was freaking out, 'Shit, this is real.'"

The second time she was 5150ed, she had called a suicide hotline and told them she took eleven Tylenol PMs (a combination sedative and painkiller)—to sleep. The next morning, she woke up to a call from her mother, who reported that two police officers were banging on her door asking where Lola was. Lola let her mom give the police her address.[21] Within a few minutes, they showed up. "There were two officers, one male, one female. And they were nice, not threatening in any way." But they did tell her they would be taking her away in a squad car. "I was like, 'Are you kidding me? What am I, a criminal?'" She claimed they responded, "Well, we just don't know if you're going to harm yourself. So it's safest if we take you." She begged them to call an ambulance instead. They insisted it wasn't an option because she was at risk of harm. The whole "evaluation" lasted just a few minutes and gave her almost no opportunity to explain her situation. Lola insisted, "I was very compliant and I followed their orders. But it was so degrading" to be carted off in front of her neighbors—and, in her eyes, completely unnecessary, given that she had been the one who reached out for help.[22]

Even without physical force, there's an inherent violence to 5150s. Holds tear people out of their everyday lives and throw them into a fast-moving machine where restraints, forced medication, and confinement are constant possibilities. John Black is a fixture of the Stanislaus County public mental health scene, where he runs a drop-in space and gallery that showcases art created by people with mental illnesses. He's also a member of the California Behavioral Health Planning Council. When I presented my work there, he inveighed against the idea of expanding conservatorships and insisted on peer-run programs as the alternative. He wrote a few months later to update me that he was "personally . . . force treated" through an "unbelievable . . . mix of illegal methods." He was hoping his story would "increase your insight into the uncertainty of CA 5150 in reality style format."

Someone like John, who readily states that he lives with schizoaffective disorder, starts at a disadvantage, because a condition that can entail hallucinations, delusions, or paranoia makes his account unfairly suspect.[23] Yet John's story captures the enduring distress that can be caused by a 5150. He recounted how his life started spiraling: he and his girlfriend were separating, two good friends died, and he was scammed by his partner in his side business selling fireworks. He was staying with his brother and, at some point, "didn't know what was real and what wasn't" and took off running, wearing only a pair of flip-flops. Eventually, he lost even those and decided to walk back. It was 3 A.M.

I'll offer the next part of John's story nearly verbatim: "When I get home, there's a fire in the barn, there's police, there's ambulances, and I walk up, and I know they're going to shoot me, because police shoot mental health clients. I dropped to the ground. . . . And my brother had all my medicines, and I said, 'Just open the door and give them to me.' They wouldn't do it. I had one of my cars there, and I opened my trunk, and there were an old pair of jumper cables. The sheriffs, the firemen, the police were trying to get around me to tackle me, I just grabbed the jumper cables . . . [and] put the jumper cables around my head. . . . They said on my 5150 paperwork that I was trying to hang myself with jumper cables."

The political theorist Giorgio Agamben argues that the pinnacle of state power is the ability to declare a *state of exception*, suspending the very legal order the state is supposed to protect.[24] For many, the experience of being 5150ed is precisely that: being ripped from a world in which they are ordinary citizens to one where the normal rights in a democratic society are held in abeyance. For example, most people assume that police can detain them only if they're accused of breaking the law. Many interviewees expressed their shock upon learning through their first 5150 that they could be held against their will based only on a prediction that they will cause harm.

In this state of exception, police do not read *Miranda* rights (which tell a criminal suspect that they have the right to remain silent). People undergoing a 5150 evaluation don't have that right, since silence could be a sign that they are "internally preoccupied" (distracted by internal voices) and require hospitalization. In Oakland, police give people subject to a 5150 a Mental Health Resource Card (figure 2.1). It explains that "you will be told your rights by the mental health staff" later on. Those rights would not include access to an attorney or a

Detainment Advisement:

The Oakland police officer below is sending you to a mental health facility for an examination by mental health professionals.

You will be told your rights by the mental health staff.

The officer will tell you, if he/she is able, whether or not you are under criminal arrest. If the officer is not able to tell you, ask the mental health staff to look at the officer's paperwork which will indicate whether or not you are under criminal arrest.

The following is allowable if you have been detained at your own residence and you are able to communicate with the officer:

You may bring a few personal items with you which the officer will have to approve.

You may make a phone call and/or leave a note to tell someone where you have been taken.

Please let the officer know if you need assistance turning off any appliance or water.

OAKLAND POLICE DEPARTMENT
455 7th Street
Oakland, CA 94607

Mental Health Resource Card

This resource card is being given to you by the Oakland Police Department in an effort to connect you, your family, and/or caregivers to the resources available for mental health care in Alameda County.

TF-33S4 (3/14)

Officer Name & Serial #

2.1 5150 information card
Source: Oakland Police Department

right to contest the hold, because the LPS system actually suspends those rights during the seventy-two-hour 5150 and restores them only once a fourteen-day 5250 begins.[25] That card also notifies people that they may "make a phone call and/or leave a note to tell your friends or family where you have been taken." This phrasing, Esmé Weijun Wang points out in her book on living with schizoaffective disorder, "echoes the wording of kidnapping narratives."[26] This card is also misleading. A person can bounce from an ER to any number of hospitals based on bed availability. Any note is liable to be completely inaccurate.

In John's case, the start of his 5150 really did feel like entering a state of exception, one that shared features of an arrest and seemed to go beyond it. He elaborated: "They arrested me. They cut my wrists so deep with the cuffs. I have gashes. They dragged me to [the squad car], but I wouldn't fit. . . . So they put me on a gurney and tormented me all the way to the hospital." He continued, "Even if I was 5150ed, they had no right to force treat me, strap me down to a gurney, leaving me in my own puke for twelve hours [at the ER], put me in a hallway with bright lights shining in my face. That they didn't have the right to do." The point of a state of exception is that whether or not the government has the "right," it can do it anyway.

I was particularly appreciative of John's willingness to share his story, though, because it suggests how ambivalent some experiences of 5150s can be. To my surprise, later in our conversation, John told me, "So the 5150 was alright, because I had been going nuts, trying to figure out how all this happened to me. I have schizoaffective disorder, and I broke." People like John are typically deemed as needing a 5150 because they lack the insight necessary to seek treatment on their own. But John claims he was already taking medication and knew that he could use help. Given that John is avidly dedicated to self-advocacy and peer supports, I wonder how he would have responded if a clinician and a person with lived experience had showed up at his brother's house, not a gaggle of police officers.

DECOMPENSATING AT HOME

The first two parts of this chapter focus on the situations—from visible crises to serious misunderstandings—that lead people to get 5150ed. This third part looks at the contexts in which people who might seem to meet criteria for an involuntary hold do not get placed on one.

We'll start at almost the polar opposite from the people in visible crisis in public: individuals like Guadalupe (who was injuring herself and isolating in her apartment) whose decompensation at home is invisible to everyone but those closest to them. In the pre-LPS era, families collaborated with psychiatrists and judges to construct what Erving Goffman called a "betrayal tunnel" to strip relatives of their rights and funnel them to state hospitals.[27] The authors of LPS crafted a law that virtually eliminated families' ability to directly petition courts to order a commitment.[28] Now what families—or housing providers or outpatient teams—can do is call 911, over and over again, to plead for a 5150. The betrayal tunnel has turned into a betrayal merry-go-round.

Dorothy, seventy-one and living in Northern California, was being understated when she said her family has had its "fair share, or maybe more" of mental illness. She ticks off her family members who have been touched by it: an uncle with schizophrenia who ultimately died by suicide, a sister with bipolar disorder who lives and works independently but is often "on the edge" of a breakdown, and a daughter with depression who has been out of contact for a few months. Dorothy sends the occasional note encouraging her to reach out, but much of her worried energy stays closer to home.

Eight or nine years ago, her son Arnold—now forty—started sleeping less and less. She recalled, "He was having a schism from his own memories, increasingly consumed by guilt about things that happened in his life." He wanted to confess his shame to the police, which Dorothy discouraged. He walked to the police station a few miles away anyway, but "they weren't open or wouldn't let him in." Soon, the pattern changed. He stopped talking to his friends and, then, his mother: "He thought he was being poisoned and that I may have looked like his mother, but I was actually a prison guard spying on him." His weight started plummeting, and he became increasingly immobile on her couch.

Dorothy reached out for help. Arnold didn't want to see a therapist, and she couldn't convince him to go to the ER. So she called 911. Most of the family members I talked to specified they wanted medical professionals rather than law enforcement to come out. For a variety of reasons, it's often the police anyway. Mobile crisis teams don't exist in some counties, operate only in a narrow geographic area, or aren't available at night.[29] Even in Los Angeles, which has fifty mobile teams that patrol around the clock, some dispatchers recommend the police anyway.[30] ER staff can refuse to evaluate a person who is brought to them by a clinician. They can't if they arrive with law enforcement.[31]

Clinician-led teams might also declare a case too risky for them to handle. In Dorothy's case, "they told me they wouldn't come without the police coming first. So I called the police for welfare checks a number of times, with not very much success." I pressed her on what that meant, and she explained that—much as the LPS Act intended—police looked for visible behaviors and not inner suffering as the basis for a 5150.[32] "The evaluations were just a flash. I have a detached garage, and he [Arnold] would just lock himself in there. So the officers would say, 'We can tell he's not right, but there's nothing we can do.'"

Dorothy was running up against an odd contradiction: people can choose not to be evaluated for involuntary treatment if they have a door to hide behind. One week, the team at Urban Mental Health discussed an elderly white woman with schizoaffective disorder. She had more than a dozen hospitalizations and two conservatorships behind her but had been stably housed for years. According to her caseworker, though, 'she stopped her meds and is decompensating. She reported that Gavin Newsom was dead in her apartment and that Donald Trump wanted to have sex with her. She is no longer paying rent because she claims she owns the building.' The director of adult programs, Blair, is convinced there's only one route forward: 'A 5150 is key here. She needs a hospitalization to get her back on meds.'

The only problem is that the clinic's mobile crisis team visited her a week ago, spoke with her through the screen door, and determined she didn't meet 5150 criteria. 'Now I'm convinced she does,' the case manager reports, 'but she won't open the door.' The social workers on mobile crisis have no legal authority to break it down. The police could, but as Avril (from mobile crisis) comments, 'they're really unlikely to do that unless we can show there's an imminent health and safety risk.' Brian asks hopefully, 'Is she maybe diabetic?,' knowing this could lead to a life-threatening crisis. 'No,' Avril replies. For the moment, they figure, their best hope is that she will run out of food and have to come out. Absent that, they'll see her when she gets evicted.

I raised this kind of scenario with Lieutenant Reid from LAPD and asked, "When will officers force an evaluation for a 5150 hold on someone who is refusing it? When will you break down the door?" Lieutenant Reid paused, then laughed: "We won't. We just won't. We'll walk away from it. The last thing we want to do is rip down someone's door to do a 5150 hold." She elaborated: "Even if there's a weapon, we'll take the family out, and walk away. We call it 'tactical disen-gagement.' Otherwise, we wind up shooting people, injuring them, or damaging the house."[33] She clarified that there are incidents, such as a suicide in progress, where police will engage. (And, full disclosure, I once observed the police break down a door with the fire department's help to do a 5150 at a supported housing complex.) Lieutenant Reid's fears of both bad outcomes and bad publicity from imposing a 5150 evaluation are justified. Half of people with mental illness killed by police die in their own home.[34]

Dorothy kept trying. On the fifth or sixth call, she had a breakthrough. Arnold was lying on the couch. In came an experienced and sympathetic officer. She "showed him a picture from his [Arnold's] driver's license, and the officer looked at him, skin and bones, and said, 'I'm going to call him gravely disabled.'" But, she sighed, "it took that much—we're talking about eighty pounds, one hundred pounds weight loss for it to be addressed." The officer offered her son the option of going to the ER in the back of a cruiser in handcuffs or in an ambulance on a gurney. To everyone's relief, he chose the latter.

He stayed in the hospital for two weeks, came out on an antipsychotic, and, in Dorothy's view, was doing "much better." He then stopped taking his medication. "Now, we share a house, but he doesn't want me to speak to him, he tends to avoid me and spends most of his time around the house at night, when I've gone to bed. . . . He's clearly not a danger to himself or others, so I'm just kind of coexisting with him. I'm enabling him by letting him live here, [but] I can't not do this. That's my personal feeling." "That's tough," I offer. We both know that the police sometimes advise parents to throw their children out to render them gravely disabled. She can't bring herself to do it: "There are just too many people on the streets screaming and too many people with mental illness getting shot by the police."

An outpatient team calls occasionally to offer her son services, but she can't even get Arnold to listen to their voice messages. The county now has a joint police-clinician response team. She contacted them when her son smashed their refrigerator in a moment of heightened paranoia. They arrived three days later. He was calmer by then. So while she's waiting for her son to deteriorate enough to be placed on another hold, Dorothy is helping staff the local chapter of the National Alliance for Mental Illness support line. She encourages parents and siblings to take care of themselves. After all, there is often not a lot they can do for their family members.

Dorothy and Arnold's case is an ethical morass. "Welfare checks" are a warrantless police entry into a private space. Even if parents are inviting the police into their homes, these are their children's homes, too. Although Dorothy's son could be gravely disabled despite being housed, insofar as he had stopped eating, it's not clear-cut at what moment this becomes such a crisis that it merits breaking down a door. On the other hand, as Dorothy closed our conversation, "I'm concerned about people's civil rights, but what about my rights? I'm an almost seventy-two-year-old woman who is no longer traveling, can't have guests over. My rights have been invaded because I'm the only salvation that he has in having a safe home."

DYING ON THE STREETS

Many families would prefer that it not be police who respond to their pleas for help. Most officers would prefer not to be responding to them. For cops, a 5150 might mean waiting hours in an ER for a clinician to formally accept a handoff of a patient (after which they are frequently told the patient cannot be admitted). While they're busy processing the mound of belongings left behind in a homeless person's encampment, they could be watching calls for crimes in progress go unanswered. There's a reason that Dani, the outreach clinician at the start of this chapter, described caring for high utilizers of emergency services who are "dying on the streets" as a "game of hot potato where we're the only ones still playing."

Some officers, though, are still in the game. Detective Camacho responded to my first question, about how she wound up working for LAPD's Case Assessment Management Program (CAMP), with a standard disclaimer: "When I started as a police officer twenty-six years ago, I never thought that I would be working on a mental health unit." As she recalled, back in 1995, LAPD's MEU consisted of three officers stationed "in a basement at headquarters downtown, kind of a little dungeon." But she eventually worked her way into Threat Management, which handles high-profile individuals who might "have a delusion about being in a relationship with Brad Pitt" and wind up breaking into his home. Because some of those individuals "needed to be linked to services . . . to get them stabilized," she came into closer contact with a then expanding MEU. Eventually, Detective Camacho—who went into the force with an image of "I want to hook and book, put bad guys in jail"—applied for a job at MEU, which puts sick guys in hospitals.

LAPD's SMART officer-clinician crisis teams are recognized nationally as an intelligent response to mental illness.[35] But Detective Camacho saw their limits:

"I learned that we were putting people in the hospital to get the help they needed at that moment of crisis, but sometimes they were released not long after, and we continued to see the same individuals coming through." That's where CAMP comes in. It's the "detective component" of the city's response to "high-risk, high-utilizing subjects." Since she joined, she's been helping sleuth out elusive solutions for some of the hardest-to-crack cases. One solution is conservatorship. The first step to getting there is a 5150 that lasts more than just a few hours.

I spoke to Detective Camacho at length about an individual who was perplexing enough that, when I interviewed others in the Department of Mental Health, the public guardian's office, and MEU during 2021, they all immediately mentioned him. The subject, Mr. R, was in a wheelchair with severe abscesses and a colostomy bag. Mr. R would call 911 "maybe every other day, and that's no joke" to have his wounds dressed and his bag changed. He had 170 transports to an ER the year prior. He had one leg amputated after a court order saying it was necessary to save his life, and he was on his way to losing the other. In 2006, Malcolm Gladwell published an oft-cited story about Million Dollar Murray, a homeless alcoholic who cost the city of Reno, Nevada, a million dollars in hospitalizations and jail visits over ten years.[36] Chump change. According to Captain Bixler, the city spent two million dollars on Mr. R in 2021.

Regular visits to the ER afford plenty of opportunities for ER doctors to admit him involuntarily, but according to Detective Camacho, "the problem is that he presents very well. . . . He says, 'I can take care of it, it's my wound, it's my body.' You can talk to him, he's not delusional." I asked her if Mr. R had a mental health diagnosis. She chuckled, "I don't know, they said it was 'social something.' It's like being a grouch with people." It sounds like antisocial personality disorder. ER clinicians told her, "He is able to make decisions, even though they're bad ones and going to kill him." Critics of the protections against forced treatment in laws like LPS argue that they leave people to "rot with their rights on."[37] For Mr. R, this seemed quite literally true.

Mr. R was obviously showing up on just about every city agency's radar screen. Camacho noted, "We got the case because the fire department is seeing him every day. 'He's costing us resources that could be going to other cases.' But all they could do was say, 'Yeah, you can't call 911 every time you need your colostomy bag changed and you need to be cleaned up.'" CAMP's role was to bring together the public guardian, DMH, Homeless Services, Adult Protective Services, and the fire department on a regular basis to discuss the case. But whose responsibility was he? It's not DMH's job to deal with people with no clear diagnosis that are overusing the fire department, but the fire department doesn't really have "clients" and certainly doesn't organize locked placements for them. Police, on the other hand, are (in the words of one sociologist) "the terminal, all-purpose remedial agent" that can't walk away.[38]

Detective Camacho told me they worked up a consensus that Mr. R should be conserved and even had the courts "on board" to do so: "At this point, we've got the money situated, now it's just finding him a location." That was, ultimately, the sticking point. Lieutenant Reid, one of Camacho's supervisors, said this profile was catastrophically hard to place: "People who have severe medical health issues, mental health issues, and drug issues, nobody wants them. The medical side says, 'They're too agitated to treat medically,' and the mental health side is like, 'Yeah, I don't want the guy with abscesses and a colostomy bag that's in a wheelchair missing a leg.' So where are we? We pick him up and leave him at the train station." DMH, she noted, wouldn't push for a conservatorship until they knew there was a bed, and those beds weren't under their control. They were in private facilities that had the discretion to refuse unwanted and expensive individuals, like Mr. R.

Both Camacho and some clinicians I spoke to evoked a similar set of challenges in relation to an increase in people seeking to commit "suicide by cop." One individual CAMP was following had been going from station to station demanding to be shot, before ultimately climbing over a wall to get in. Camacho explained, "He was fixated on dying by the hands of an officer, he wasn't getting it out of his head . . . he was refusing treatment, just saying, 'I don't need services, I just want to die.'"

Unable to make their 5150s stick long enough to even contemplate conservatorship, the police did what they do best: they arrested him. They did so after consulting with the district attorney to make sure he would be offered a "diversion" program, whereby he could accept treatment and get the charges dropped. Detective Camacho knows how this sounds: "it's the last resort, we know this person isn't a criminal, we don't want to stigmatize what he's going through. At the same time, because he wasn't compliant and he didn't want to get help, we were able to use that criminal case to have the court mandate mental health treatment for him." When the mental health system won't coercively address behaviors that society deems (rightly or wrongly) unacceptable, the criminal justice system can step in. It uses the powers of law to overcome the recalcitrance of medicine.

You should note one feature of both of these "dying on the streets" cases: in each, the person was calling enormous attention to (or even soliciting) their own death. Most people aren't. A DMH clinician pointed out, "When we talked about that [Mr. R], we all agreed that there's a thousand more like him that aren't going [to the ER], aren't attracting the attention of medical services. There are human beings, clumped in blankets, everywhere in the city, with pretty heinous medical conditions, not being treated." But they weren't annoying the neighbors, soliciting the police, facing eviction from their housing, or causing fear in their families. And so, by and large, they weren't getting 5150ed.

CONCLUSION: DISORDER-DRIVEN DISCRETION

The LPS Act deputized clinicians and police to write applications for 5150 holds and transport individuals to an ER for evaluation. You'd be hard pressed to find any clear guidelines for when they should actually do so. A state official admitted that they had "failed consumers and family members in this space [involuntary treatment]." But to them, the state's levers of action were unclear: "[Our leverage] is pretty limited. It's this dance between the legal system and then local jurisdictions. . . . State law dictates who can place someone on a hold, but there's a lot of nuances in terms of people's interpretation of what meets the threshold." She mused, "Do we go in and do a lot of auditing to see the quality of that? No. Technically, do we have the ability to do some of that? Probably. But I'm not sure that it's been resourced in that fashion."

This abdicated authority leaves significant discretion in the hands of the police. A 5150 hold is one tool in law enforcement's sovereign power toolkit, and they use it, predictably, primarily on the audibly addicted rather than the silently suffering, the visibly disruptive and not the invisibly dying.[39] Even officers committed to helping people get treatment feel a sense of futility about what will happen to people like Mr. R or Jerry further along the continuum. They are thus more likely to lean on the criteria of danger to self and danger to others than grave disability.[40] As a result, people dying on the streets are ruled out of a conservatorship at step one.

Given all that, who in our Southern California beach town got 5150ed in the end: Guadalupe, Jerry, or Professor Jolie? If you've got the gist, you might have guessed Professor Jolie. The week after I went out with the outreach team, Jordan sent me a video of what happened when police showed up at Jolie's campsite for the sweep. She is in a dress and sunhat, folding her clothes, while six officers cluster nearby. You can see an officer approach her.

She tells him, "I'm not a homeless person, I'm allowed to be a vendor, and I have not fucked up anything." The officer nods, but suddenly two officers grab her from behind.

"What's going on?" she asks. The officer in front of her still seems to be listening when she announces, "I have a restraining order against the Department [of Behavioral Health]."

The officers start leading her off, and her voice raises, "I don't need to go to the hospital!"

Nearby, a bystander protests, "There's twenty people for one woman!"

Jolie is now shouting, "What is wrong with you, I'm a U.S. federal marshal, my credentials are real, what is wrong with you people, I have not broken the law, I am the title owner. You can't detain me for no reason."

No one replies.

Now she is screaming, "You are Nazis, you are fucking Nazis. What are the charges?" They lift her into the ambulance and close the door.

I get a text from Jordan a few days later, "Our girl got out on Monday." She didn't even make it to the end of the seventy-two hours, because "we think the police did a shitty job on the hold." That is to say, they couldn't (or didn't try to) convince the ER clinician to keep her. The next chapter asks why convincing them is so hard, and why it's sometimes not worth it to try.

CHAPTER 3

EMERGENCY ROOM

Thankfully, the videos of Serge Obolensky are now gone, but you used to be able to search for "No Hands," "Crazy," and "Hollywood" on YouTube and find him. In one that seems too Hollywood to be true, the cameraperson is focused on an LAPD officer who is laying out a spike trap in the road, presumably to put an end to a car chase in progress. The video pans over to a man with no hands, a grizzled beard, and caked and dirty hair. He is shouting at the sky and clapping his two wrists together as his pants fall to his knees. In another, Serge is pretending to shoot pedestrians across the street using his arm as a machine gun. He then spins and smacks the camera.

These videos capture Serge's external psychotic behavior, not his internal suffering. He doesn't give me a lot of details about his background but says that he suffered an accident with a firecracker in his late teens. He lost both his hands and one eye. His parents were Scientologists and staunchly opposed to psychiatric treatment, even though he showed signs of developing psychosis. They did pay for an apartment, from which he was evicted in 2001. He spent more than a decade homeless in Hollywood. "It was very hard. Very painful," he told me, "I didn't have shoes, my hair was all dirty, I was hungry all the time. I was freezing cold all night, I didn't have a blanket or anything. It was really bad."

Occasionally, an outreach worker from a church would give him a pair of socks, but Serge can't recall any concerted effort to get him housing or treatment.[1] What he does remember are many, many 5150s. The voices in his head would tell him to run into traffic, police would pick him up and take him to a hospital, and he'd be released within forty-eight hours. Sometimes, if he had been transported to a hospital in another neighborhood, they would even provide him a taxi back to Hollywood. He also took himself to the ER a few times. Back in

2013, "I kept thinking I had hypothermia from being out in the cold. I would call 911, and I would go to the emergency room. I was really cracking up." The ER would "give me really warm blankets to put on me to try to warm me up." One time they even "hooked me up with a social worker," who sent him to a homeless shelter, but "it didn't work out." Serge didn't elaborate why.

Serge was a source of constant consternation to Kerry Morrison, who was then head of Hollywood's Business Improvement District (BID). For her members, Serge was a bit like Hollywood's "feral cat," whom they were keeping alive with donations of food and water. BIDs have been roundly criticized for advocating the criminalization of unsightly homeless individuals.[2] But Morrison did much more than demand the police arrest or 5150 him. After all, Serge was already being regularly detained. What she realized was that "there was no accountability" for ensuring those detentions actually accomplished anything. She concluded that Serge and others like him were missing an "air traffic controller" to ensure that they actually progressed through the mental health system rather than just cycled in and out of it.

What's striking is that Kerry Morrison saw no one within any of the many agencies touching Serge's case—the police department, the Department of Mental Health, the Homeless Services Authority, hospital emergency rooms—taking on that role. So she decided to do it herself. She convened a group of volunteers from nonprofits and local churches, who set out to find out everything they could about the "Hollywood Top 14." These were the individuals in the neighborhood they identified as the most vulnerable, most difficult to house, and most likely to die on the streets.

They started by figuring out Serge's name and background. This took them only so far, because LAPD wouldn't share his records with them. A rogue DMH employee tipped them off that he had twenty-eight 5150s. A breakthrough came with the Santa Monica Police Department, whose jurisdiction Serge occasionally visited ("I just liked the ocean") and which had a robust homeless outreach program. They gave the team, in bullet form, a list of all his arrests for trespassing and various misdemeanors.

They assembled all of this information into a dossier and hatched a plan. Usually an ER doctor would make a decision based on a snapshot of Serge at the precise moment he was sitting in front of them, without considering the years of suffering that had preceded his arrival. The point of the dossier was to make the case that, despite this long history of failed interaction with the mental health system, Serge nonetheless desperately needed treatment. The group would wait for a day when a particularly sympathetic doctor was on call at a local hospital. During that physician's shift, the BID's foot patrol would watch for Serge to run into traffic and then call LAPD's Mobile Evaluation Unit. Meanwhile, someone from the Hollywood Top 14 team would "camp out in the ER so that, before he was released, they would show the doctor the dossier, to say, 'If you let him go, this has been the pattern, and he's vulnerable.'"

Everything worked "like clockwork," she told me. That didn't make for any less of a tragic scene: "the police had to handcuff him, but he doesn't have hands, so they used those zip ties, and he was kneeling on the ground, there's all sorts of law enforcement all around him." When Morrison talks about her work, "I say, 'Sadly, this is how we help people in America.'"

Serge expected that he would just wait a few hours before the doctor released him to the sidewalk. But the dossier followed Serge through a fourteen-day 5250 after his seventy-two-hour 5150 was finished. It eventually reached a judge, who put him under a one-year conservatorship. We'll revisit in a later chapter what life in a locked setting looked like for Serge (it was grim), but in retrospect, both Kerry and Serge think the results were worth it. When she visited him after four months in the hospital, she recalled, "My jaw was just in my lap." He had been "completely transformed as a human being, from being on the Boulevard, in his feces, hadn't washed in months, very intimidating, to being someone that you would want to hug." When we spoke, Serge was living in a board and care. Kerry had been teaching him how to use his new iPhone, donated by a philanthropic organization, right before we talked. "I'm trying to get my GED [the equivalent of a high school diploma]," he told me enthusiastically. I asked him what he wished worked differently in California's mental health system. His answer: "I wish they had conserved me sooner."

Regardless of whether you believe conservatorship was the only option for Serge, there's no doubt that he is an incredible survivor and success story. But his saga was shaped in stark ways by government's abdication of authority. Serge was far from abandoned in Hollywood: instead, he faced an ongoing barrage of involuntary holds and arrests. Law and Medicine were neither in collaboration nor in conflict; they were just working at cross purposes. There was no plan to align the police's decision to place a hold with the ER's decision to admit him. It took a passionate and compassionate private individual like Kerry Morrison to step up and coordinate how the state would exercise its own power.

ERs are one of the strictest veto points in the conservatorship process. Clinicians concentrate resources on those acting dangerously or disruptively over those who are gravely disabled. They filter out many people coming in on 5150s whose problems they attribute to criminality, addiction, or homelessness. Outsiders may see these decisions as callous, but they are not arbitrary. They reflect the legal constraints, resource limitations, and professional obligations that ER clinicians, acting as quintessential street-level bureaucrats, must juggle on every shift.

PEOPLE PROCESSING IN THE EMERGENCY DEPARTMENT

Serge couldn't get through an ER to become an inpatient until there was "nothing left between death and conservatorship," as Kerry Morrison put it. To understand why, you need to consider the onslaught of social and medical problems landing on ER clinicians like Dr. Rand. He's the director of the emergency department of a public safety-net hospital in a large, urban Northern California county, where he started practicing twenty-eight years ago. He's a "single-payer, access to care, bleeding heart liberal." We bond over our mutual affinity for the French medical and social system (he worked in *les urgences* of a Parisian hospital for a year and a half): "I think there [in France], there's a floor in terms of social services. . . . You can be an unemployed chronic alcoholic, and almost invariably have a place to live." That, he thinks, is what's missing for many of the psychiatric patients he sees: "For our people, what are the origins of mental illness? They're lack of housing, lack of food, lack of access to medication and affordable health care . . . and that social part is arguably more determinant than the actual illness."

He and "essentially an army" of nurses, residents, techs, and social workers are the rickety floor of social services for his patients, by design and by default. In 1986, Congress passed the Emergency Medical Treatment and Labor Act (EMTALA), which requires ERs to provide screening and treatment for anyone with an "emergency medical condition" walking through their doors (or being deposited by police, as in the case of many 5150s), regardless of ability to pay.[3] The Act helped turn ERs into a "modern day almshouse" for the poor, filling in for the safety net that President Reagan was eviscerating at the same time.[4] Transformations in the mental health system inadvertently increased the pressure. During the 2008 Great Recession and subsequent budget cuts, a range of nonhospital crisis resources—like drop-in clinics that could provide medication refills or respite beds for homeless people needing a night inside—closed.[5] People in distress had to go somewhere. The spike was dramatic: from 2006 to 2011, the number of visits to California ERs by people with a behavioral health diagnosis went up 47 percent.[6]

For flagrantly psychotic people brought in on a 5150, the marching orders for Dr. Rand's medical army are clear: "Our cog in the machine is that we provide stabilization and medical clearance for patients going on to a psychiatric hospital." His own hospital does not have its own psychiatric unit, but it does have three on-site sheriff's deputies, so it tends to get the "very violent, physically imposing patients." He elaborates: "If they're particularly aggressive or agitated, then they're put into a high-viz, acute care room for immediate stabilization. There are three or four different medications we'll use, usually as a shot or IV, to bring them down." Arjun, another ER physician, rounded out the picture: "The waiting time for severely psychotic patients is zero. They're kicking, screaming, and so we medicate and deal with them right away." Once sedated, they go to an observation room, where they could wait—sometimes for days—for an inpatient bed.

Having enough staff and beds to handle these crises requires dealing expeditiously with other, less legitimate pulls on the ER's resources. One such drain stems from police *burden shuffling* unwanted and unruly persons onto the health care system (which, as you saw in the previous chapter, is partly driven by societal demands that they limit arrests).[7] The ER staff I spoke to were not on board with this strategy of disorder management. Nurse Dwyer, who works with Dr. Rand, recounted, 'One time, the cop's [5150 paperwork] was literally just a description of a homeless person: "This person is living behind CVS [a pharmacy], their clothes are dirty." ' The ER provided a valuable service: dropping the hold and protecting a vulnerable person from continued, unjustified detention.

Another set of patients on 5150s suffer from "incarceritis"—a sudden health complaint (think "chest pain" or, more importantly for our purposes, "suicidal ideation") that forces an officer to take a person under arrest to a hospital for a screening.[8] Responses to these cases are swift. Dr. Rand grumbled, "It's very common to have patients who are arrested, and they'll complain they're suicidal, knowing this will create a detour. . . . It's just suspect on its face, and we know they're going to jail, so what's the worst case scenario? . . . They're not going to have access to a gun, they're not going to have a knife, this is purely manipulative behavior. . . . I'll consult with the psychiatrist and say, 'suicidal ideation in the back of a police cruiser' and they'll just say, 'clear the person [of a 5150 hold] and send them to jail.'"[9] (For the record, fourteen people died by suicide in Alameda County's jail from 2015 to 2019, while San Diego County saw thirty between 2010 and 2018.[10])

Then there are the patients who can plausibly be served elsewhere. A psychiatrist who told me he had evaluated more than 90,000 patients across his career explained that his goal was to "relieve suffering"—maybe with the quick delivery of an antianxiety medication—and "get them to the least restrictive level of care." The goal of an ER is "always not to hospitalize, but to turn an emergency patient into an outpatient." Dr. Rand, aware of many of his patients' social circumstances, was less sanguine about sending people out with a list of referrals: "Many of our patients are coming out of these tent city environments and they're just pestilent, horrible, awful places. . . . You look in the medical record, and it says, many times, 'Referred to County ACCESS line'"—the gateway to public mental health services—"and they get assigned a clinic, and maybe they go once, but they have no ability to get to the next appointment, no cell phone to even be contacted."[11]

These typologies help clarify the role ERs actually play in the conservatorship continuum. Scholars of street-level bureaucracy have differentiated between *people-changing* agencies and *people-processing* ones.[12] The social security administration is an iconic people-processing bureaucracy: its goal is to check someone's eligibility and then send them on their way with a check. Most of us would like to think of the conservatorship continuum as made up of people-changing bureaucracies. No one wants a person who is gravely disabled to stay that way. But people changing takes information, resources, and time, all of which are in short supply in an ER bombarded with all the misery left unaddressed by the rest of America's miserly welfare state. And people changing through hospitalization requires beds, of which there are fewer and fewer (figure 3.1).[13] Even when they are cleared for admission, psychiatric patients wait as much as three times longer than nonpsychiatric patients to be transferred out of the cramped, chaotic space of an ED into a proper inpatient unit.[14] Sometimes the humane thing is to process and release, rather than attempt to keep and change (and see that person released by the hospital a few days later anyway).

Unsurprisingly, then, the proportion of people in psychiatric crisis that Dr. Rand sees who are actually admitted into the hospital is low. Although there's

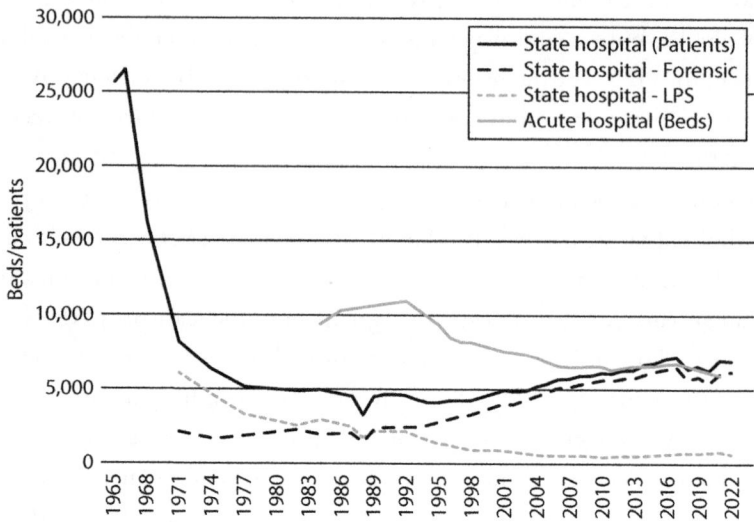

3.1 Psychiatric hospital beds in California, 1965–2022

Source: California Hospital Association; RAND (2022); Department of State Hospitals

no official statewide figure, the California Hospital Association estimates that only about 25 percent of people who had been deemed so dangerous or disabled they had to be forcibly transported to an ER on a 5150 are dangerous or disabled enough to keep past twenty-four hours.[15] Whether by connecting people to outpatient care, protecting their civil liberties, calling out malingering, or saving scarce inpatient beds for the most disruptive patients, ERs people process most patients off the conservatorship continuum.

THE FRUSTRATION OF "FREQUENT FLYERS"

But what happens if the people being processed keep coming back? Every ER clinician has tales of people visiting daily to have wounds dressed, weekly to help manage diabetes, monthly to get medication refills, or seasonally to have a hot meal and a cot when the weather turns. Research from San Francisco found that, among "super-frequent" utilizers of emergency departments (people with at least eighteen visits a year), 87 percent had some kind of mental illness or substance use disorder.[16] Psychiatric symptoms might be the direct reason for a consultation, but more often they are one part of a complex of social, medical, and psychological factors that make people unable to maintain their housing, attend outpatient appointments, or monitor their blood sugar.

Emily's son Jerad is, by her own admission, "definitely a frequent flyer." Almost two decades ago, he managed to get on medication that stabilized his psychosis. He went off it in 2004 ("the side effects were horrible") and since then he's been the quintessential revolving-door patient. Things got worse during the COVID pandemic. He has an FSP team, but they wouldn't come to him: he either gets videoconference appointments, which he frequently misses, or has to go to the clinic, which is an hour-and-a-half walk from the apartment Emily rents for him. He is afraid of going because people don't wear masks. As Emily described it, he is "isolated and alone" and goes to the one place where he feels safe and can get some attention: an ER.

The typical scenario, she said, is that he calls a suicide crisis line every few hours and then, at night, hits up ERs around the Bay Area. The doors revolve quickly. Here's what happened the week before I spoke to her in the fall of 2020. Jerad drank—"for some reason he thinks he has to drink to go there [to an ER]"— and went to a university hospital, where he stayed a few hours. They discharged him at 1:00 A.M., "when he had no way of getting home." He then went to a nearby nonprofit hospital, part of his predictable circuit. When Emily called, they said he stayed from 4 A.M. to 7 A.M. Next stop was a different private hospital, which found him a bed in a neighboring county, where they kept him from Wednesday to Monday and then discharged him. That night, he went to three different ERs. The public hospital kept him overnight and called Emily to pick him up that Tuesday. He returned that night. He had visited ERs at least 120 times since the start of the pandemic, with eight very short-term admissions during which he refused all medication.

It says something horrible about the world outside that people would want to go to a psychiatric ER repeatedly. Nurse Jones worked in psychiatric emergency services (PES) at SF General, the county's main public hospital, for the better part of a decade. I asked her what PES looked like, and she responded, "The word 'looks' is incomplete, because it's a full-on sensory experience. There's a lot of noise, a lot of smells, a lot of chaos, even on a good day." During a morning shift, she and a half-dozen other nurses were faced with up to twenty patients who had come in during the night: "Sometimes you walk in, and there'd be nobody in the staff area because everyone was in the middle of putting someone into locked seclusion or injecting them with emergency meds. So you jump in and help out." I finally visited PES in 2022. The staff I spoke to were warm, but the environment was cold. They were overflowing, so a half-dozen patients were crammed in gurneys inside a narrow common area. The rest were behind heavy metal doors that would fit right in at the county jail.

As Nurse Jones described it, her team's overarching goal was to drive the census down by midday to make way for a new round of homeless people walking in off the street or 5150ed. PES is legendary for its frequent flyers. One woman came 150 times, mostly searching for pregnancy tests. When one came up positive, she refused an offer of a hotel room or shelter bed and left.[17] PES is also mythical for the ruthlessness of its discharges. It seemed everyone working in mental health in the city had heard about the time it released a blood-covered man found eating a dead racoon in the street. He was, psychiatrists determined, meeting his basic need for food.[18]

The management of PES has tried a series of disturbing and sometimes illegal strategies to empty its beds (or, often, gurneys). Emily reported that back in the early 2010s, they'd interview people in the waiting room to turn them away before they were formally admitted (otherwise, PES would be required by federal law to give them a thorough workup). In 2018, Emily's son encountered San Francisco General's pioneering new approach to deter frequent flyers: "vertical therapy," or making it impossible for waiting-room chairs to recline. "It was just horrible," she told me. "He'd go to PES and wouldn't sleep for eighteen hours. . . . Do they do vertical therapy for people with a broken leg?" They relaxed the policy when patients kept coming anyway and slept on the floor.[19] (An 1845 article in the *American Journal of Insanity* recognized "Sleep['s] . . . Importance in Preventing Insanity," but the knowledge seems to have been lost.[20])

For many years, PES didn't have social workers on staff to help link frequent flyers to the things they were frequently asking for, like housing or income supports. Now they do, but social workers can refer people only to things that exist. Nurse Dwyer admitted to me, 'The main role of our social workers is to explain to people why we can't help them: "I understand you have no housing, no food, but that's not something an ER can help you with." ' It's not even clear what the ER should be offering to someone like Jerad. Emily would like to see him hospitalized and medicated, but when he's hospitalized and medicated his symptoms clear quickly, he wins his hearing asking for release, leaves, and the cycle begins again. She's convinced that he has been, in effect, blackballed from nearly every inpatient unit in the Bay.

Some counties' administrators have tried to skirt the dismissive connation of "frequent flyers" by relabeling them "friendly faces." This is a euphemism. These patients are frustrating. Nurse Dwyer shared Dr. Rand's pride at providing public services to the poor, but as a steward for the nurses' union, he was also witness to the burnout frequent flyers provoked: 'There are definitely people where everyone is rolling their eyes. . . . Patients who know what to say [to stay], "I'm planning to hurt myself?" "How?" "With a gun." Everyone is going through the motions. We resent them because we want to be treating people.' The nurses would lobby the physician to remove the 5150 hold. 'Sometimes they'll throw a tantrum, and we'll agree we're going to ignore it.' His sense of his medical vocation being thwarted aligns with the more callous financial concerns of hospital administrators, who have no way to bill for people whose diagnosis is "homeless and hungry."[21]

The response to frequent flyers presents an odd twist on that classical definition of insanity as "doing the same thing over and over again and expecting a different result." In Jared's case, ERs seem to be doing the same thing over and over again, recognizing that the result will be the same—another visit a few hours, days, or (if he's in jail) maybe weeks later. You can't understand this just in terms of resource limitations. It's also a product of the lack of external authority to snap an ER out of people-processing mode and make it participate in a coherent people-changing strategy.

I talked to Emily a few months later, and Jared was up to 181 visits in a year and a half. She had been lobbying the county to get him conserved, to no avail. Instead, he had recently been arrested for knocking over sidewalk tables in the street and damaging a car. He liked it in jail, she said, because he got to talk to the guards.

SPITTING OUT SUBSTANCE USERS

If there's one way to be spit out of an ER quickly, it's to be labeled as an "addict" rather than mentally ill.[22] This is a bit odd because literally everyone I talked to recognized that the two are not either/or. Psychiatry's very own bible, the Diagnostic and Statistics Manual (DSM), lists "methamphetamine use disorder" as an illness just like schizophrenia. And although California once sharply delineated substance use and mental health services, the current watchword is "integration" of the two under the single roof of "behavioral health."[23] On the streets, the symptoms of meth use look an awful lot like the symptoms of schizophrenia, justifying a 5150 hold as the logical response to either. As Lieutenant Reid put it, "You hear doctors saying, 'The police are just bringing us people who are under the influence.' And we're like, 'okay, 85–90 percent of the people we see have a combination of mental illness and drug use. So how do you expect us to parse that out?'"

ER clinicians are quick to do the parsing themselves. I could hear Dr. Rand struggling to balance his commitment to providing care and the sense that there might be people more deserving than substance users: "The number one [laboratory] test we do for patients who are young and otherwise healthy is for stimulant drug use [meth]. . . . I mean, there's obviously the coexistence of mental health and substance abuse but . . ." He hesitated before continuing, "We have patients who have chest pain, lacerations, broken bones. Sometimes they're with children. . . . And why are they waiting? Because you've got this patient who did a bunch of meth and is acting out." There's a difficult-to-shake sense that, despite methamphetamine's incredible addictive potency, users can white-knuckle their way into abstaining from them. People with schizophrenia can't kick their hallucinations so easily. An inpatient psychiatric nurse admitted, "Look, I do want people who are addicted to drugs to have access to treatment . . . but I think we all feel a little bit like, 'That's not what we're here for.'"

ERs have a highly effective treatment for the immediate symptoms of drug use, which is preventing people from using drugs. After a few hours, they'll no longer meet dangerousness or disability criteria for an ongoing hold. One community provider seethed, "I work with some of the highest utilizers of behavioral health services in my county. I have one woman who will take meth and then threatens others in the community. She'll go to the ER [on a 5150]. But if she takes her meds cooperatively while there, and she's not high because she doesn't have a pipe in front of her, they'll say, 'She's no longer gravely disabled.'" She went on, "Boom—they street her. Back on the street." Forty percent of patients at SF General are discharged without so much as a referral—likely because they're deemed meth users, frequent flyers, or both.[24]

As much as meth has come to dominate these discussions, the highest utilizers of emergency services in California are people struggling with alcoholism.[25] Over a five-year period, five individuals were transported by San Francisco's ambulances 1,781 times, at a cost of four million dollars.[26] When I visited in 2022, multiple city agencies were wringing their hands over one of them. He would be found belligerently drunk and screaming racial epithets in the street; other times, he would claim he was suicidal or planned to shoot someone. In two of his 501 encounters with emergency services in the past year, paramedics revived him because his heart had stopped. He would seem to fit pretty solidly under the danger to self and danger to others criteria for a 5150. But in the dozens of times he had been brought to PES on a 5150, he cleared up by morning, clearly articulated his desire to leave, and was drinking again as soon as he reached the first liquor store off hospital property.

The problem isn't the law. A separate section of LPS specifically provided for the involuntary treatment of "chronic inebriates," who were a sizable chunk of state hospital residents, in a "specialized facility." A later law permitted the same for "users of controlled substances."[27] But these provisions are basically never applied.[28] San Francisco actually tried to conserve one of its five super-utilizers with chronic alcoholism, but gave up when it couldn't find a "specialized facility" willing to take them.[29] Most drug treatment programs are voluntary. They aren't designed to serve people who also have a serious mental illness.[30] A spokesperson for one of San Francisco's largest drug treatment providers told me, "People who are actively psychotic, can't go to the bathroom . . . we can't manage that in a 100-bed [substance use] facility, it's not safe for them, or for other people. So, our [intake] assessor says 'This person needs a higher level of care' and I'll tell them, 'Guys, there is no higher level of care.'"

Nurse Jones was clear about the result. "It's a sad, sad situation. People get tossed out into the street wearing a hospital band or thin blue scrub pants, into the elements with a bus token if they're lucky and maybe a meal in their belly, and a list of resources on a piece of paper. And that's it." And then, the tragic irony: "So if you're trying to survive, it's dangerous at night, sleeping outside can put you at risk. You need to stay awake. Coffee won't cut it." So what do you take after the ER sends you to the street because you're using substances?

"Meth."

FUTILITY AND GRAVE DISABILITY

We've covered most of the archetypes of psych ER patients: people who are acutely dangerous, malingerers, frequent flyers, or substance users. There's one left: people gravely disabled by chronic psychosis.

When I spoke to Matt, a third-year psychiatry resident in Los Angeles, he told me he had initially planned to do emergency medicine. When he had his psychiatry rotation at the county hospital, he realized that "people with severe mental illness, especially psychosis—I just really enjoyed those patients" and switched tracks. But he was quickly socialized into a sense of futility around what to do with patients who, on their face, might seem like good candidates for conservatorship.

One of his clients on the FSP team where he was currently training was an elderly woman who lives on the street in a wheelchair, wearing seven layers of clothing through the summer heat. She has a "complex delusional system" that includes believing she won the lottery and needs to stay in place until someone brings her the winnings. This prevents her from accepting the housing her FSP has lined up for her. But she's still not gravely disabled, in the barest sense: "She has the wherewithal to use cash given to her to go to a 7-11, or eat yogurt from a homeless shelter." She does not, he noted, have the wherewithal to take medication. After decades on the streets, he wasn't optimistic about her prospects: "The longer the delusions persist, the less likely they are to be responsive to treatment. . . . Even if I had her conserved in the state hospital for years, on the best medications we have, she might make only a tiny improvement, like 10 percent, because she's been off medication for so long."

Among those responsible for the woman's current situation is Matt himself. He saw her a year before during his ER rotation. "Someone like her, you offer everything: board and care, residential treatment, intensive outpatient. They just refuse it, and so you discharge them with an Uber," he explained. He recounted what he wrote in her file: "Given her longstanding history of psychotic symptoms, we suspect that her limited improvement is consistent with her psychotic baseline, and she has likely reached the maximum benefit of inpatient hospitalization." Most importantly, though, "she was alert and oriented and able to consistently express her desire to return to the street. She has demonstrated that she is able to provide food, clothing, and shelter, despite her delusional system, and does not meet criteria."[31]

"Does not meet criteria," when properly documented, is the magic phrase that releases an ER clinician from liability for a discharge. It's also code. Now, when Matt's own FSP patients are released from a 5150 and discharged by an ER, he can easily read between the lines: "They say, 'They don't meet hold criteria,' but it's really that no hospital is going to take them."

At the start of this book I reviewed evidence that, shortly after LPS went into effect, grave disability became the catchall category that provided an easy route into an inpatient bed. A 1987 investigation in San Francisco claimed that three-fifths of holds were on that basis.[32] Today, clinicians see it as a losing bet for winning an admission. "I don't even know what it means anymore, patients losing weight, lying on the street. . . . I've never gotten someone in [for grave disability]," one outpatient psychologist told me. A psychiatrist at the same clinic concurred: "If you're filling out a 5150, you have to check a box, and I'll always do danger to self or danger to others. Grave disability, they [ER clinicians] are just not impressed by that."[33] As you'll see in the next chapter, hospitals see these kinds of patients as difficult to discharge once admitted, and thus as financial liabilities.

For psychiatrists like Matt, this endless cycle of holds and quick releases is just part of the package of working in public mental health care in California. For those who signed up for classic emergency medicine, the disillusionment is starker. Arjun, a resident rotating through public hospital ERs in Northern California, described the grim choices facing him: "As an ER physician, you have to fight your battles. You can't make sure every discharge is safe." Sometimes he would argue with doctors upstairs to admit someone, "but you can't do that with every single patient, or you lose your job." He saw plenty of patients who "you know they need to be conserved," but even if he admitted them for some "bullshit reason," in five days "they'll be discharged one way or another." Feuding with hospital administrators was not what he trained for: "after I've fought [for those patients], I am beaten to the ground emotionally and mentally." By comparison, "a trauma [like a gunshot wound] is so easy, quick, we know all the steps, [the ER] works like a well-oiled machine. Those cases are where my time, effort and energy go."

As with police doing 5150s, then, ERs can easily overlook people who are just really, really sick. Dr. Rand admitted, "If you're just hearing voices, but you're not peeing on the floor, basically behaving yourself . . . you're going to wait hours and hours to be seen." Nurse Dwyer concurred: 'That person who is sick in the corner, quiet, with a distorted reality of what is happening to them, and they're keeping to themselves, not drawing any attention,' he confessed, 'well, they don't get any attention. And when you finally get to them, you ask, "Are you ready to go?" and they say, "yes," and they just go.' This orientation may help explain why there are ultimately more men on conservatorship than women, given gendered disparities in whether serious mental illness comes out as loud disturbance or quiet withdrawal.[34]

"That's just the nature of emergency medicine," Dr. Rand concluded. "You're always making these decisions knowing that every decision to intensify care is a decision to ignore someone else's care. It's a zero-sum game."

CONCLUSION: NEGATIVE DISCRETION

It is often said that getting admitted to an inpatient psychiatric ward is harder than getting into Harvard.[35] I don't think that this claim makes any sense (and, in any case, the admit rate for 5150s is about 25 percent, and the Harvard admissions rate is 5 percent). But it is certain that many families, outpatient clinicians, and housing providers anxiously await the admissions decisions of ER psychiatrists and are frequently disappointed when they arrive. (For people held involuntarily, being "rejected" from an inpatient stay probably does not bring the same sense of disappointment.)

ER clinicians, for their part, can cultivate an image of personal potency that fuels the seeming arbitrariness of their decisions. As one ER psychiatrist wrote in her memoir, "I picture myself standing on the corner of Sane and Insane directing traffic. You're in, you're out. Step over the invisible line and see what happens."[36] Yet this apparent authority comes not from gatekeeping access to abundant resources, but from triaging allocation of scarce ones.

Resources play a role in *how many* people make it through an ER into a bed, but professional identities and preferences weigh heavily on *who* does. Sociologist Josh Seim spent two years with ambulance crews in a California county, shuttling between rich, white neighborhoods and poorer, brown ones. Paramedics weren't looking for the easy cases of seemingly deserving people—maybe a senior citizen needing a transport to the hospital for the flu—but instead sought out the hard, unpleasant ones—like gunshot wound victims from drug deals gone bad. That's not because they were "trauma junkies," he argued. Instead, they were professionals who wanted to exercise the "craft" of their "chosen vocation," emergency paramedicine.[37]

You could say the same for the ER clinicians who receive the patients those paramedics are dropping off. If you're a hammer, you look for nails. If you're an ER physician, you look for acute crises. Those cases fill up your available beds. You don't look for homelessness, substance use, and chronic psychosis. Put another way, in most cases, you don't admit potential conservatees. You discharge them.

CHAPTER 4

INPATIENT

Kate's forty years of contact with California's mental health system have given her the kind of window into the transforming role of psychiatric hospitals that you can only get from being locked, repeatedly, inside them.[1] Her saga started early: when she was eleven, her mother—battling her own mental health challenges without "any support, or treatment, or even acknowledgment" of her illness—decided "she didn't want to be a mom anymore." She sent Kate to a residential school in the Northeast, where she was left alone to cope with the accumulating effects of her traumatic childhood, struggles with her sexual orientation, and sense of alienation from the privileged children of Ivy League families surrounding her. She made a "kind of pitiful attempt to cut my wrists," went to the infirmary, and was sent back to classes the next day.

At fifteen, her mother returned and brought her to the Bay Area. Kate recounted that she was "suffering a lot from depression," then paused to say, "I don't really like the word 'suffering' because there are some interesting benefits to emotional pain: increased empathy and creativity." She put some of that suffering, and the creativity it brought, into poetry. Her mom read some (presumably without Kate's consent) and then committed her (definitely without Kate's consent). "I was horrified at the idea of being put in a mental hospital. All I had to go on was the kind of antique images of . . . *One Flew Over the Cuckoo's Nest*." She was sixteen.

To Kate's surprise, the hospital was not all "horrible and brutal and straightjackets." In 1981, the private hospital where she stayed had a "rehabilitative attitude." They wanted her to continue her education and get "job skills, social skills, life skills, cooking skills." Patients would leave a few times a week to go bowling or for a picnic. Most stayed one or two months. This was before a new generation of antidepressants like Prozac hit the market, and the available medications had such strong side effects that her doctor—who met with her in now unthinkable one-hour chunks to conduct psychotherapy—didn't even raise the possibility of pills. "It was odd [to be hospitalized] and I was scared," she reflected, "but it was not a horrible experience. It was actually a bit of relief, because I no longer had to pretend to be normal."

She didn't want to romanticize it, though. Once when she was upset and banging her wrist on a bedstand, they put her in a seclusion room "and told me if I acted up while I was there, they would tie me down." Even if she wasn't forcibly injected with medication or put in physical restraints, she saw those things imposed on others, "and living with that constant threat, in itself, is frightening." The situation was bad enough that Kate took advantage of the then less intense security measures to "AWOL" (run away) several times.

It was on one escape, after four or five months, that it became clear to her that the hospital's rehabilitative program wasn't helping her prepare for life in the community: "I remember walking down the street, being free . . . and thinking, 'I no longer know how to live in the outside world . . . what am I going to do with myself?' I had no money, I had nowhere to go, I didn't have any friends." She turned around and checked back in. Staff responded by taking away her shoes. As she neared eighteen, the hospital started taking her to visit residential treatment programs. She said "no" to five or six, and the hospital respected her wishes: "They kept me a month or two to find me a good placement. They weren't going to place me anywhere I didn't want to go."

Kate lived through the last days of a now defunct model of extended inpatient care. Some psychiatrists remembered this epoch wistfully. Dr. Salay, who works as a public psychiatrist in Northern California, recalled the difference when she was in training: "We had a patient that had bipolar disorder and she had children at home, and we kept her in the hospital until her mania went away, until she was safe . . . We must have kept her like a month or two months. I think there was more comfort with the paternalism involved with that." Now, she tells me, "you know there's a clock ticking. It [hospitalization] is so short, you have three days to figure it out. But meds don't work that fast. . . . Any kind of deep healing needs to happen in an outpatient setting."

There is little evidence that prolonged hospitalizations actually produced any outcome beyond dependence on the hospital.[2] Still, Kate describes a humanism to a previous era of inpatient care that had disappeared when she went back.

From twenty to thirty-five, Kate worked a range of jobs with children, domestic violence survivors, and people with disabilities; she saw a therapist occasionally, but was off medication. Then she enrolled in a PhD program, which was "excellent academically and horrible interpersonally." Within a month, she was seriously depressed and dealing with intrusive thoughts of hurting herself. She confided in a campus therapist. The therapist said, "Will you excuse me for a minute?" Kate waited, "and the next thing I know, there's a policeman at the door with handcuffs to take me to the hospital." The therapist may have felt obligated to report Kate because of a risk of self-harm, but for Kate, it was shocking: "The amount of force, threat of force, lies, and betrayal that's involved in trying to get people help is just outrageous."

Thus began fifteen years dominated by "hospitalizations, all kinds of treatment programs, lots of ambulance rides, lots of police visits, lots of suicide attempts." Out of both desperation and coercion, she tried thirty different medications, which gave her little but side effects. Hospitals saw her as "not only an object, but a bad and broken object." The Magna Carta that was supposed to give her the right to refuse unwanted treatment was a meaningless scrap of paper. She described going before a judge to contest her fourteen-day 5250 following a seventy-two-hour 5150: "It's the crazy person's word against the staff . . . and you always lose." The patients' rights advocate supposed to represent her "just sat there." With no real oversight, "they [hospitals] can do anything. I've seen other patients beaten; I've seen them spit at by staff; I've seen them tied up for no reason; I've been insulted, degraded, told horrible things by staff, threatened with all kinds of stuff. . . . And all these supposed rights that a mental health patient is supposed to have, ever since the [LPS Act], more and more rights—those don't mean anything."

These hospitalizations were nasty, brutish, but—at least compared to the months she spent interned as a teen—short. When she was forty-five, though, she had an intentional overdose serious enough that it put her in a coma. Her parents reappeared, armed with her father's discovery that "he could become my guardian and choose a locked placement for me for the foreseeable future." Yet Kate had a realization that is surprisingly common after near-fatal suicide attempts: she wanted to live. "The problem is that no one believed me," she recounted. "They just thought I wanted to get out of the hospital to finish the job." Her inpatient psychiatrist told her that he didn't want to conserve her. "If it were up to me, I'd discharge you now," he admitted, "but your family has threatened to sue me. . . . So I'm going to sign the petition for the judge to declare you gravely disabled." She was terrified: "I'd been in and out of the mental health system for so long that I knew about conservatorship. . . . And it seemed horrible to me. I would lose my rights and freedoms as an adult."

Kate had an unlikely savior. A week before her court date, her insurance company sent the hospital a letter announcing that, because she was not benefiting from treatment, they would no longer pay. "Bless the insurance industry," she confessed, reluctantly. Her subsequent "discharge plan" was far from the five or six visits to local step-down programs she was granted as a teen: "They opened the door and kicked me out. Put me on the curb with a plastic bag of clothing. Not a single referral, not a single medication, not a single person to pick me up. Nothing."

Fearful that her father would still pursue a conservatorship, and dedicated to "surviving rather than dying," she began to construct a new community support system. She found a therapist, an acupuncturist, and a bodyworker doing trauma release, Reiki, and breath therapy. She started visiting a peer-run Wellness and Advocacy Center (funded by the 2004 Mental Health Services Act): "I realized if I do not take responsibility for the care and feeding of my mental health, other people are going to in a way that's very painful to me." She hasn't been back to the hospital since 2016. Or, rather, she hasn't been back as a patient. At the time of her interview in 2021, she was starting to volunteer as a peer support worker at the psychiatric crisis unit in Sonoma County: "It's my old stomping ground, where I was held against my will multiple times." But now, she'll be talking to people to help them realize that hospitalization "is not all there is, and they have every right to be pissed off, and no, I'm not going to help them burn the unit down, but provide whatever sort of support and connection I can."

Debates in California often refer to "barriers to hospitalization" and a "lack of beds" but too often ignore what it means to be hospitalized and to be stuck in one of those beds. Kate speaks to how the harms of long-term institutionalization that disconnected people from the community have been partly replaced by the harms of short-term institutionalization geared toward medicating someone just enough that they can be abandoned anew.

Her story and this chapter are a window into a part of the conservatorship continuum where the state's delegation to private entities is particularly consequential. To put in place a conservatorship, an inpatient clinician must file an application with the county stating that, despite several weeks of hospital care, a person is still gravely disabled. As this chapter shows, financial incentives, market forces, and administrative pressures drive how psychiatrists make these decisions, frequently trumping legal criteria and medical judgment in determining who gets conserved.

MANAGING CARE, DENYING CARE

Inpatient psychiatrists can override a patient's desire to leave after a seventy-two-hour 5150 by placing them on a fourteen-day 5250 hold. But they have less leverage over the financiers of those stays. As Kate found, involuntary hospitalizations can be a rare instance where patients' interests align with those of insurance companies (or county behavioral health departments, which act like insurance companies): both want to shorten a forced stay in an inpatient ward.[3] They ensure that the vast majority of people on a 5250 don't stay all fourteen days.[4]

When LPS arrived in 1967, lengths of stay in state hospitals were already dropping dramatically. An article published that year quoted a social worker who observed, "The public has difficulty keeping up with rapid changes taking place in mental illness treatment. Whereas they are used to thinking in terms of three to four months' hospitalization, doctors now routinely turn them out in several weeks. The family is often bewildered and asks, 'He isn't cured, is he?' Then we tell them that the hospital goal is not cure but getting over a crisis."[5] Shortening stays reflected both the rapid closure of beds and a new optimism about medications that really did seem to calm symptoms quickly.[6] LPS accelerated the plummeting decline in length of commitments; in just two years after it went into effect, the average for state hospitals went from 180 to 15 days.[7]

Lengths of stay in hospitals kept collapsing, but the reason was no longer innovative new treatments or expanding legal rights. In the post-LPS years, private hospitals boomed, taking advantage of more patients with insurance covering mental health treatment.[8] (Frank Lanterman specifically hoped the law would encourage a "pooling of public and private resources" in new community hospitals.[9]) By the 1980s, psychiatric patients were such a lucrative proposition that private hospitals would send mobile teams to recruit patients in county ERs or advertise their services to people who, upon arrival, would be placed on a hold.[10]

In the 1990s, though, insurance companies cracked down with a vengeance. Psychiatry was, according to one analyst, "more severely walloped by managed care policies than any other branch of medicine."[11] The shifting winds of the market spurred waves upon waves of closures. Relative to the population, California had only 58 percent of the acute-care psychiatric beds in 2019 that it had in 1995 (see figure 3.1).[12] Private insurance introduced techniques like preauthorizations and doctor-to-doctor utilization reviews to keep patients moving.[13] After realignment, county behavioral health departments, which pay for all hospitalizations for people on Medi-Cal, piled on. 'Honestly, it [insurance oversight] can't get any stricter. Our length of stay can't go down further,' Dr. Swati, the clinical director of one psychiatric hospital told me. 'Yes, our average stay is seven days, but that's pulled up by a small number of people. Eighty percent of our patients are here for four days.'[14]

Inpatient clinicians vary in their willingness to wage quixotic battles with insurance and hospital administration.[15] Jenny, a nurse who worked in the same hospital as Dr. Swati, recounted, "We had some very old-school psychiatrists. When the utilization review people [from administration] were like, 'You've got to get them out [of the hospital],' they were like, 'Screw you, I'm not listening to you.'" She sighed, "But we've had a lot of turnover. Now, we have staff meetings where [the unit with the] shortest length of stay gets a pizza." Most professionals I interviewed were neither actively resisting nor enthusiastically collaborating with financial micromanagement; they were simply resigned to it.

I speak to an exhausted-looking Dr. Wagner, a twenty-year veteran of public psychiatry, in the cafeteria of the hospital where he has just finished a shift. He tells me that he prefers working with uninsured or Medi-Cal patients, because for the ones with private insurance, the pressure to discharge is overwhelming.

"The insurance companies want us to get the patients out as fast as possible. They have their own doctors who want to know in a detailed way why they [patients] aren't appropriate for an outpatient program. Honestly, I don't fight it too hard," he tells me.

"Because you know you're going to lose?" I ask.

"I know I'm going to lose, and their mind is made up before they even call."

"How does that even get set up?" I press.

"They'll schedule a review in a very specific timeframe, and if you're not reachable in ten minutes, you forfeit your opportunity to argue for a longer length of stay. They hold all the cards." Dr. Wagner knows that the ability to sign 5250 paperwork gives him apparent control over patients. But he feels bereft of authority over the faceless administrators who are the real deciders of who stays in his care.

One consequence of ever-tightening criteria for reimbursing inpatient stays is the virtual disappearance of voluntary hospitalization for the poorest and most severely ill.[16] Matt, the psychiatry resident in Southern California, recalled from his time training at a county hospital, "When I was there, I probably had a total of eighty patients. And one of them was voluntary. It was a big deal," he laughed.[17] LPS actually specifically envisioned that patients would be offered voluntary inpatient services and would be placed on a 5250 only if they were not "willing or able to accept [hospitalization]."[18] Today, though, if a person with Medi-Cal on a 5150 decides they want to stay, it's usually a sign that they need to leave.

Another consequence relates to who stays. Remember the previous two chapters, where people deemed a danger to self or others were more likely to be held on a 5150 and admitted by an ER, compared to those alleged to be gravely disabled? When it comes to who remains beyond the first few days, my interviewees suggested that the probabilities flip. Dr. Wagner reported, "If someone had a near lethal [suicide] attempt . . . I don't think one day of not being suicidal is enough. But some insurance companies will say, 'If they're not suicidal today, they need to go.'" Someone's acute risk to self might be quickly calmed on an inpatient unit. Someone's chronic inability to care for themselves, maybe less so.

DISCHARGING THE GRAVELY DISABLED

'That . . . can't be possible.'

Dr. Cai, my host on a tour of the psychiatry unit in a county hospital, is looking at a whiteboard listing upcoming discharges from her twenty-five-bed unit. There's only one name written. Her cry of dismay suggests that the implications are dire. There's an ER full of patients downstairs waiting to be brought upstairs, but the hospital's "bed flow"—consultant-speak for the smooth balancing of admissions and discharges—has slowed to a trickle.[19] How is this possible in a system of relentless pressure to get patients out as quickly as possible?

The paradox, Dr. Cai explains, is that while her unit and the one next door have fifty beds between them, only ten to twelve are "in play" at any time. The rest are occupied by patients who are, in effect, living there. There's a woman with developmental disabilities whose family won't take her back and whose application has been refused by every step-down program around. A younger man with a degenerative neurological condition 'doesn't really have a severe mental illness' but has been here for three years 'because he can't be managed by a nursing home.' Ditto for a woman with dementia: 'I don't really know why she's on psychiatry,' except that she keeps falling and needing to go to the medical hospital, so it's easier to keep her nearby. These patients are gravely disabled because no one outside the hospital is willing to feed, clothe, and shelter them.

Dr. Cai is facing a problem as old as psychiatric hospitals themselves. In the nineteenth century, state asylum superintendents complained that, even though they "cured" most patients rapidly, their facilities were nonetheless gradually "silting up" with intractable cases.[20] They argued for greater funding from state legislatures to expand their buildings or, absent that, simply crammed two or three times as many patients into wards as they were designed for. Neither option is available to Dr. Cai. Even as insurance companies have driven private hospitals to close, county governments have subjected public hospitals to harsh austerity. Her facility lost half its psychiatric beds in the Great Recession.[21] Many rooms already have three patients sleeping in them. So the solution is to find a way to declare patients no longer gravely disabled and to discharge them.

Discharge planning starts at day one of an admission. According to Jess, an inpatient social worker, the hospital begins at the same time to "push back" on anyone who would like to see a person conserved. The easiest option is to return someone to wherever they came from—even if that homeless shelter, board and care home, or family was the one begging for the person to be admitted. Devon, a social worker in a supported housing complex, occasionally writes 5150 holds on residents whose homes are overflowing with garbage and feces. She'll call her inpatient equivalent to try to pressure them to keep a resident longer, but it often backfires: "I'm shooting myself in the foot saying, 'I'm a licensed mental health provider and I'm on their care team [in housing],' because they'll say, 'Well, they have someone looking out for them, they have a key, that's a safe discharge plan, send them home.'"[22]

Board and care homes or families can refuse to take people back. This creates—like so many places in the conservatorship continuum—a back-and-forth between agencies and providers all claiming they're not the right setting for a complex case. Dr. Cai sees it this way: 'We're really the only people who don't say no. Shelters say no, IMDs [locked step-down units] say no, SRO [single-room occupancy] hotels say no. When we try to discharge, we get a big N-O.' As for those same entities' complaints that hospitals also say "no" to admitting their clients all the time? She points out, 'It's like Grand Central Station. If you don't have any trains going out, how can you have more trains coming in?'

A few years ago, these kinds of disputes might have been resolved by simply dumping patients on the street. California lawmakers have tried to crack down on the practice. A 2018 law requires that hospitals connect homeless patients to "community resources, treatment, shelter, and other supportive services" that have "agreed to accept the homeless patient."[23] Another discharge social worker I spoke to told me she likes the law: "it gives us guidelines, as a universal, 'these are the bare minimum things that people concretely need in their lives when they leave the hospital.'" But the bare minimum can be, well, really minimal: in some cases, it might be "just an overnight chair" in a shelter "and they have to leave in the morning."

Of course, patients have to actually agree to accept the resources proposed by that plan, which many don't. Jess told me she had recently discharged someone from a 5150 "with no follow-up appointments or linkages." The client's plan for self-care was "to take BART [Bay Area Rapid Transit] to live in People's Park in Berkeley, steal clothes from Target, and go to a free breakfast location down the street." Compared to many discharge plans she hears, it sounded "pretty fair and reasonable," which to her shows how low the bar for a "safe" discharge has fallen. Even with the law in effect, one recent study found that more than half of psychiatric inpatients in one Los Angeles hospital who were homeless when admitted were homeless upon discharge.[24]

There's one other way to get patients out, even when their previous shelter is refusing to take them back or the patient is holding out for a new housing option. The original LPS Act gave patients the right to file a writ of habeas corpus to ask a judge to be released from the hospital during a fourteen-day 5250. It didn't require a hearing if patients didn't ask for one. But in 1979, a Los Angeles District Court, later backed up by the Ninth Circuit, ruled that confinement without judicial review was unconstitutional. *Doe v. Gallinot* requires that all patients on a fourteen-day 5250 have a hearing within four days to determine if there is "probable cause" for their continued detention.[25]

This new intrusion of law into the realm of medicine may not have been as significant as it sounds. For hospitals, showing "probable cause" is a low bar.[26] The patients I spoke to did not find these hearings particularly rigorous. Individuals are represented by a patients' rights advocate, not an attorney, and heard by a hearing officer, not a judge, who is largely unbound by standard legal rules of evidence.

But *Doe v. Gallinot* did create a new discharge option. Jess explained that hospitals can "throw" hearings by choosing not to present evidence that a person meets grave disability criteria. Hospitals can also opt not to discredit a patient's plan for providing food, clothing, and shelter that is more grounded in delusions than reality.[27] Jess elaborated: "The doctor doesn't think there's any point in keeping them, and it's much easier to have [the patient] win their probable cause hearing because the psychiatrist can't be held accountable for what happens next, it's not on their license, it's not on the hospital." A hearing officer I interviewed concurred that this "definitely" happened, pointing out: "pretty much all the patients I see would benefit from [more] treatment . . . but most of the time, it's not in the facility's best interest financially to keep the patient."

Losing probable cause hearings solves multiple problems for hospitals. Dr. Cai tells me that when COVID shut down many of the housing and social service providers hospitals typically rely on,[28] discharges by the courts became one of the biggest ways to get patient "flow." Those winning a hearing technically leave "against medical advice," which means the hospital is no longer required to set up outpatient care or shelter on their behalf. That, Jess claimed, helps account for why you still see people dumped on the hospital sidewalk with a plastic bag of belongings, in an era when patient dumping is supposed to be illegal.

There's no evidence of how common thrown hearings are (although they're common enough that in San Francisco they have a moniker, "Cindy Lei hearings," after a doctor who supposedly perfected the practice). But they are revealing. Sometimes law and medicine are neither conspiring to control patients nor in conflict over the priority of medical care versus civil rights. Rather, in some cases, medicine leverages the legal procedures that are supposed to protect patients in order to release them. The sovereign power LPS grants hospitals over people with grave disabilities is power that hospitals actively abdicate.

OUTSOURCING REFERRALS

All hospitals face intense financial disincentives to keeping patients for a long period of time. But as Phil, the father of a thirty-year-old son with schizoaffective disorder living in Los Angeles, learned, who owns the hospital shapes how much sway those disincentives have over psychiatrists' decisions to apply for a conservatorship.

After a first 5150, Phil's son Jacob stayed for a month in a nonprofit hospital. He recalled, "That was the best psychiatrist he's had, a Russian guy, and he told me, 'Your son may never be back to what you think is normal, but we're going to do the best we can.'" His son was released on oral medication, quit taking it, and launched into a chaotic period during which he was hospitalized four more times, each in a different private facility. Phil (like Michael and Julie, in chapter 1) started taking classes with the local NAMI affiliate and convinced himself that his son needed a conservatorship: "What I learned is that every psychotic episode almost fries the brain. It's like shooting up a lot of heroin. That's why the sooner a patient is taken care of, the better, and that's not done in the current system unless you have a conservatorship."

Phil's pleas to the inpatient psychiatrists, though, were in vain: "On the third hospitalization, I called every day to talk to my son's psychiatrist, and I never could get him to talk to me." On the fourth, he cornered a psychiatrist in the hallway, but received a flat "no" when he asked him to apply for a conservatorship. Phil seemed to have better luck on the fifth hospitalization, in a small for-profit facility. A month in, "he [the psychiatrist] calls me in, and says 'What do you think is going to happen when he's discharged?' And I said, 'Oh, he'll probably be okay for a few months, and then he'll be hospitalized again.' And he said, 'It's worse than that. Your son has a good probability he'll die.'" Phil reiterated his plea for a conservatorship, adding "He's not welcome back at my home." Phil had learned from NAMI that refusing to take a family member back is one strategy to force the doctor's hand. The doctor replied, "I'll work on it."

It didn't pan out. A few days later, he received a call that Jacob was being discharged. Phil had no doubts about what was behind the decision: "Basically, it's cost. When a patient first checks in, they get reimbursed a substantial amount. . . . But after a few weeks, that goes down. They [hospitals] would rather have new people coming in because they make more money. I have argued the point, 'Isn't one good long hospitalization better than seven or twenty short hospitalizations?' And they said, 'Yes, but that's not the way it works.'" He's right. To be fully reimbursed by Medi-Cal, a hospital needs to convince the county mental health department that a patient meets strict "medical necessity" criteria.[29] Once someone no longer meets this standard, the hospital may be paid only an "administrative" rate that is hundreds of dollars a day lower.[30] Or the county might refuse to pay entirely. A patient stuck four months waiting for a conservatorship and a step-down placement could represent a loss of more than $20,000.

It's unsurprising that Jacob's hospitalizations were all in private facilities. Eighty percent of acute-care beds in the state are in private hospitals, and half are in for-profit ones.[31] In theory, explained Dr. Rod Shaner, the former medical director of Los Angeles County's Department of Mental Health, this improves the quality of care, as hospitals compete for contracts to take county patients. In practice, he said, a dearth of beds makes it hard for the county to actually impose quality controls.

It's particularly hard, he opined, to get private facilities to make conservatorship applications, even when it's clinically indicated. In Los Angeles, 54 percent of psychiatric beds are in for-profit facilities, but they make only 22 percent of conservatorship applications. Only 12 percent of LA's beds are in county hospitals, but they produce 39 percent of applications (see figure 4.1).[32] The pattern holds across three other counties that provided me with data. One county public guardian looking at these numbers told me, "There are [private] facilities that can do involuntary holds, and they don't do a single referral [to conservatorship] in the entire year. . . . They are admitting people on 5150s, they are holding them as long as they are getting paid on the [acute] Medi-Cal rate . . . but as soon as someone no longer meets 'medical necessity,' they are discharging them. . . . You're seeing those people cycling back into the hospital on a frequent basis."[33] Just like Phil's son.

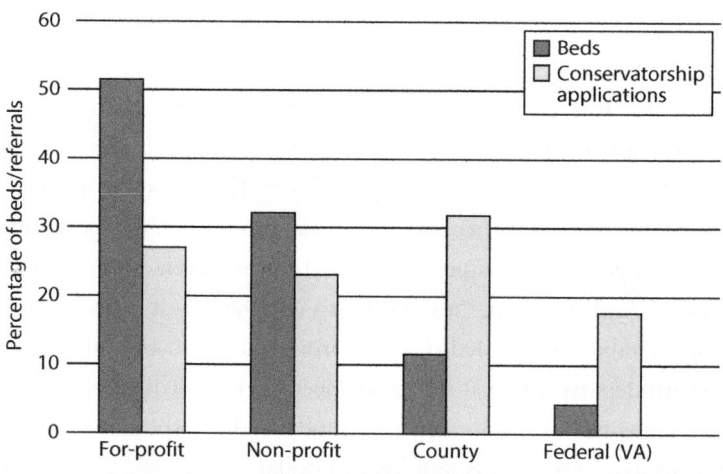

4.1 Conservatorship applications in Los Angeles, by hospital ownership, 2021
Source: LA Office of the Public Guardian; California Department of Health Care Services

Public hospitals also lose money on conservatorships. From 2016 to 2018, psychiatric beds at San Francisco General, the county hospital, were filled 79 percent of the time by people whose care was not fully reimbursed as "acute." It cost $21.4 million a year to pay for individuals who were occupying scarce beds not because they needed hospital care, but because they were waiting for a conservatorship or subsequent placement.[34] But county hospitals, under pressure from county supervisors, who themselves might be under pressure from parents with the resources and wherewithal to harangue them, are more willing to eat the financial loss that comes from applying to conservatorship.[35]

In private hospitals, the pressure goes the other way.[36] Matt, the resident introduced in the previous chapter, recounted, "In [hospital], if you want to conserve someone, you have to present the case to the 'conservatorship committee,' and they make the decision . . . with the knowledge that they'll sit in a bed for however many months, and not allow the hospital to make money on that bed. So the committee just denies everything. . . . [Clinicians] know that it's not part of the solution, you have to discharge." While there's ample debate about whether private or public facilities deliver better care, what's clear is that the "social control function" of a hospital—that is, whether it will continue to coerce and constrain a person past the point where doing so is lucrative—depends on who owns it.[37]

Public authorities do have some leverage. After learning his son would be imminently discharged—only a week after being informed that, absent a conservatorship, he would die—Phil made a phone call to Dr. Shaner, whom he had met through NAMI. Dr. Shaner, in Phil's retelling, warned the hospital that he could yank their authorization to take involuntary patients if they didn't make an application. When I talked to Dr. Shaner, we didn't discuss this specific case, but he confirmed it's a real if rarely used government prerogative. He explained, "The regulations give county mental health directors a tremendous amount of discretion about who is designated [to take LPS patients]." He went on, "So, at times, we would get complaints"—for example, from parents like Phil or county supervisors—"and we would go to those hospitals and remind them of their responsibilities as a designated hospital to be referring anyone that meets criteria [for a conservatorship.]"[38] What Dr. Shaner did was a risky gambit. Some private hospitals have deliberately dropped their LPS designation so that they can focus on voluntary patients with private insurance.[39] Dr. Shaner knew LA County couldn't afford to lose any more beds for involuntary patients on Medi-Cal. "Our bark was always worse than our bite," he admitted.

In this case, though, it worked. The hospital applied, Phil's son was conserved, and he was sent to a state hospital for half a year before being discharged back home. It's not a happy ending. For Phil, schizoaffective disorder had not so much afflicted Jacob as it replaced him with a new person: "As a kid he was the smartest in the class, but now, he's just sitting in a chair in his room. Doesn't have the TV on, doesn't read, just sits. I ask him what's going on, and he just looks at me." At least now Phil can make sure he gets his monthly antipsychotic injection. Phil is convinced conservatorship has kept Jacob out of the hospital for four years. But getting it exposed how, in California's delegated hospital system, the market trumps medicine—except when the state exercises the authority it has but rarely uses.

THE LAST RESORT?

The headwinds to applying for conservatorship are strong. Some inpatient psychiatrists apply anyway. When? No psychiatrist has ever answered this question by quoting the California Welfare and Institutions Code's definition of grave disability back to me. "The Code" is not an "external authority," an abstract force—like the Bible—that gives "exclusionary reasons" that clinicians feel compelled to follow.[40] The Code sets when a psychiatrist is allowed to file an application but creates no obligation to do so. So psychiatrists, like other street-level bureaucrats, make decisions that balance their professional ethos with an awareness that there are invariably more people who meet the grave disability criterion than there are resources to conserve them.

Given that a conservatorship is the most restrictive way to keep treating someone (outside of a prison, perhaps), we should be relieved that it's not the first tool for which psychiatrists reach. Dr. Wagner explained for whom he'd apply by ticking off what he would try first: "Usually, it's [for people who have] failed all lower levels of care. They've been working with an intensive outpatient team, they've tried an ADU [Acute Diversion Unit], residential placement, living independently, and repeatedly come to the emergency room. They just have a lot of trouble with medication compliance, end up in and out of different cycles of care, and don't seem to maintain outside of a structured environment." In certain counties, public guardians informally require that a person have a certain number of hospitalizations, with an unsuccessful discharge to the community, before they'll approve an application.[41]

This idea that someone is gravely disabled—in the sense of needing a conservatorship— only when they've "failed" (or been failed by) everything else is an illustration of a *social model of disability*.[42] The central idea is this: rather than being an inherent feature of certain kinds of bodies and minds (as posited by the *medical model*), disability is created by a society that is ill adapted to those variations. Being in a wheelchair is a disabling impairment insofar as businesses are unwilling to install access ramps; the limitations of being blind vary with whether a building put its signs in braille. Similarly, a "grave" disability is not something that kicks in automatically when someone's symptoms reach a certain level of severity. It emerges once someone has exhausted the available alternatives to conservatorship, which vary enormously from county to county.

In 2019, Los Angeles County conducted a thorough survey of its options for providing intensive care. "Peer respite centers"—where a person can stay for up to two weeks with nonmedical support from other people with lived experience of mental illness—are a "highly effective alternative to hospitalization during crises."[43] But the county has only two, with twenty beds between them. Other clients might be able to stay out of locked facilities if their board and care homes offered "enhanced residential treatment"—but board and cares are "closing rapidly because their business model is broken"[44] (more on that in chapter 8). Partial Hospitalization Programs (also known as day treatment) are a "great option." But Medi-Cal reforms have starved them for funds.[45] The report concluded that if all these crisis services were in place, the county would actually need only about half its current number of acute-care beds.[46]

Now, as Dr. Wagner told me, there are people who can't take advantage of alternatives to conservatorship, even if they exist: "If you have somebody who is really depressed or really psychotic and isn't organized enough, doesn't have the motivation or the will to take care of basic things," there's no choice but to apply. He went on: "Often people are gravely disabled who may have a place to live, an SRO or apartment, but they're too psychotic to sleep there, or worried that their place is bugged, or their food is being poisoned, so they won't eat, even though they have money and can go buy food. Those are examples of how illness can interact with one's normal circumstances and make them abnormal to the point of being gravely disabled." The point here, though, is that "normal circumstances" vary. People's grave disabilities are a function of both their capacity to use the supports in their environment and what supports aren't available at all.

This social model of grave disability is confirmed by the fact that whether someone counts as gravely disabled is, in practice, county dependent. The psychiatrist at a Northern Californian university hospital was initially insistent that nonclinical factors didn't play into decision making, telling me, "you're not going to send a person to the street if they're completely psychotic, covered in their own feces." Eventually, though, he conceded that, on the margins, conservatorship petitions depended on whether a given county had the facilities that would allow him to transfer a newly conserved person and liberate a bed: "If it's a wobbler and I think, 'this person is from San Francisco'"—which has longer delays in organizing placements than this psychiatrist's home county—"maybe it's not even worth applying."

Counties' political choices about how to fund and organize mental health systems can render some people, miraculously, not gravely disabled despite their clinical state—at least in the sense that the hospital will find some way to discharge them without a conservatorship.

CONCLUSION: DELEGATED DISCRETION

The simplest reason there aren't more people on LPS conservatorships in California is that there aren't enough beds in hospitals willing to conserve them. Far from being a legal category with a fixed and clear meaning, grave disability is a slippery standard that expands to fill inpatient beds when they're available and shrinks to justify emptying them when they're not. Evan, a Public Defender whom you'll meet in a later chapter, put it nicely: "We have seventy-two beds at [County Hospital]. If all seventy-two are filled up, then grave disability means one thing. . . . If we built a second acute hospital tomorrow, we doubled our capacity. . . . I think we would find that there's actually now 144 people who meet the criteria for grave disability. And if we shrunk it down to thirty-six, we'd find that a lot of people, it turns out, are not gravely disabled."

Financial factors weigh not just on the number of beds but on how they get used. For people like Kate, whose narrative began this chapter, insurance companies' tight oversight has the positive side effect of ensuring that most hospital stays are short, protecting patients from conservatorship when law fails to. For families and outpatient clinicians, on the other hand, reimbursement rules and utilization reviews create a cycle of short, ineffectual admissions. They represent an unjustifiable intrusion on decisions that should be purely in the realm of medicine.

Either way, inpatient psychiatrists serve as a veto point on the conservatorship continuum, but not an independent authority capable of pushing a conservatorship through. Instead, delegation means that insurance companies deciding who meets criteria for payment, county supervisors subjecting hospitals to budget cuts, and investors calculating whether it's worth staying in the inpatient psych business have the real discretion to decide who moves to the next step in the conservatorship continuum.

CHAPTER 5

PUBLIC GUARDIAN

Early in this project, a group of research assistants and I reached out to the public guardians in most of California's fifty-eight counties. We never heard back from the majority. A few declined our requests with a note of suspicion about why anyone was interested in their obscure agency. (This was before the Britney Spears story broke.) When my Bay Area–based team did hear back from California's hinterlands, it was a view into what mental health services look like in areas that live under the same laws but within almost alien economic and social conditions. California has delegated responsibility for conservatorships to counties for which conservatorships can be almost untenably difficult to fund and implement.

Frontier County (that's a pseudonym) is about half as dense as Mongolia. The county's Department of Human Services is tiny, so Patrick—a military veteran who worked his way up through the department over twenty years—has the entire caseload of the LPS public guardian's office (which has six people). He also covers programs for in-home supports, probate conservatorships, and adult protective services. There's something that feels more humane about the pathway onto conservatorship in smaller counties: "One day, the Sheriff called, and said, 'Where's that guy we always see on the corner on the way to work?' I check with a county staff member who usually gives him a couple dollars, and they say, 'We haven't seen him.' We send someone out to do a welfare check, and when we find him, he's decompensated." The public guardian convened a meeting—which is easy when everyone works in the same building—during which the mental health department recommended a 5150, the police went to execute it, and the public guardian was waiting in the wings to file a petition for conservatorship.

After that 5150, though, it gets complicated. When I talk on the phone to Victor, Patrick's now retired counterpart in the Behavioral Health Department, he's up at his apple farm "in the midst of planting some conifers." Like twenty-five of California's fifty-eight counties, Frontier has no psychiatric hospital.[1] Instead, they take people on 5150s to the local emergency department, which calls around to find a bed. If they can't find one, they drop the hold. Even if they do find a bed, getting patients there is hard. At night, there's only one sheriff on duty for the whole county. There's only ever a single ambulance. Neither can safely make the five-hour round trip to the hospital that contracts with the county. There's another, closer, hospital, but they don't take Frontier's clients. (I explore the chaos of contracting in chapter 7.) Sometimes the Behavioral Health Department sends folks in a county car with a screen between the driver and the back seat. It's not a great solution. A person in an adjacent county died by suicide while being transported in a vehicle like this one.

Once someone from Frontier County on Medi-Cal is in a hospital, they're a ticking financial time bomb. Victor tells me that the county has a budget of about $250,000 per year to pay for locked placements for all its clients (which wouldn't cover a year in a state hospital for a single person). The public guardian's office, with a yearly budget of around $120,000, doesn't have much to kick in. They thus assess quickly to determine if the person's problems are mostly substance use, in which case they can count on the hospital to release the person quickly. If they're going to require a conservatorship, the public guardian hustles to process their application and get them to a cheaper step-down. According to Patrick, locked subacute settings (IMDs) are "prohibitively expensive." Almost everyone goes to an unlocked board and care home, which can be paid for by the client's own social security check. The county has one privately run home. It is currently filled with easier-to-house unconserved clients, so all conservatees are stuck out of county.

Given these challenges, I'm not surprised that the number of people conserved by Frontier County has declined. The explanation is not stricter oversight from the courts, which, as far as Victor and Patrick can recall, have never turned down a petition for an LPS conservatorship. Victor has no doubt about the real reason: "It's crass but true: there's a lack of beds, there aren't the resources, the beds that exist are incredibly expensive." The public guardian's office (i.e., Patrick) is nominally independent. But the guardian's power to place someone in a locked facility doesn't give them any authority to make the county pay for that placement—meaning they don't actually have much authority.

Given the limited resources available, conservatorship is reserved for the squeakiest wheels. Victor tells me, "99 percent of the time [someone is conserved], there are community members and other agencies putting pressure on Behavioral Health. . . . It may be family members who are just exasperated. It may be the local sheriff who is intervening regularly and really getting tired of it. It may be merchants where the individual is hanging out and being disruptive." Like public guardians everywhere, Patrick feels these demands getting louder. Frontier doesn't have much in the way of a homeless population, but it is facing the pathologies of rural America: "We're seeing an increase in issues around drug use, substance abuse, opioid use. . . . And they're in the criminal-justice system versus getting treatment, and that's becoming an issue."

I had read enough of social theorists like Michel Foucault and Nikolas Rose to suspect that public guardians might seize on this opportunity to "govern risky populations" through an expanding web of surveillance and constraint.[2] But many public guardians talk like civil libertarians. "Philosophically, I am a fan of the Constitution," Patrick states. He adds, "You should have a high bar" for conservatorship because "it's a big deal to take away people's rights." He acknowledges that "we have a crisis with people on the streets and mental illness in jail, but I don't really see how this [expanding conservatorship] is a solution to that." Most proposals to increase conservatorships don't include more funds for public guardians. "You can conserve people all you want," he notes, "but what do you do when they're conserved? We have a paucity of placement options to help these people."

Public guardians' offices are the government agency to which the state has delegated responsibility for conservatorships. As with every other step in the continuum, guardians are a veto point that can disqualify people from conservatorship. They do so by delegating the burden of ensuring the survival of people with chronic mental illness even further—sometimes onto other agencies but more frequently onto families and those chronically mentally ill persons themselves. Guardians have a principled and strict interpretation of conservatorship criteria but also a practical recognition that neither the state nor counties have ever committed the resources necessary to conserve everyone whom others in the continuum might label as gravely disabled.

BACK-WARD BUREAUCRATS

Conservatorship was the unremarked third rail of LPS. The 1966 "Dilemma of Mental Commitments" report that became the basis for LPS declared that policy makers should carefully bifurcate a "voluntary system for providing prompt assistance . . . without any stigma or loss of liberty" and an "involuntary system for identifying and separating dangerous persons" through short-term hospitalizations.[3] The two-hundred-page report devoted only four, near the end, to its plan "to provide individualized treatment, supervision, and placement services by a conservatorship program for persons who are gravely disabled." The legislators predicted that most of the people conserved by the mental health system would be "aged senile persons or physically debilitated alcoholics" who belonged in "special facilities" (not state hospitals).[4] Shortly afterward, a major evaluation of LPS used a handful of pages to conclude that this conservatorship program "appeared to be operating smoothly."[5] It was the last real statewide analysis of LPS conservatorships, and it was published in 1971.

As marginal as conservatorship was to the vision for the LPS system (compared to voluntary outpatient services or short-term holds), the number of people on conservatorship rose dramatically: from 2,613 in 1971 to more than 15,000 by 2000.[6] Surveys conducted in the 1980s showed that most had schizophrenia or other psychotic disorders.[7] Conservatorship "help[ed] . . . eliminate their chaotic life styles, their cycle of admissions and discharge from hospitals and jails, and/or their living on the streets."[8] Early on, conservatorship provided this stability by placing many conservatees in the remaining beds in state hospitals.[9] County public guardians were back-ward bureaucrats acting, as a 1972 profile put it, as "father-protector, jailer, aide-de-camp and paymaster" for people assumed to be helpless.[10]

At a sparsely attended 2022 press conference, Scarlet Hughes, the executive director of the California State Association of Public Administrators, Public Guardians and Public Conservators, declared that this backstop system of institutionalization was "on the verge of collapse." The fissures start at the top. Public guardians are the only mandatory county social service program that receives no direct state financing.[11] Hughes bewailed that the association has pleaded with the legislators who have introduced bills to expand conservatorship in the last four years to include funding to pay for the offices that would be doing the conserving, to no avail.

Longtime public guardians sensed growing indifference toward conservatorship in state government over the course of their careers. As one who started in the 1980s recounted, back then the state Department of Mental Health (DMH) had an LPS point person who would attend the annual conference of county public guardians and would liaise with them about pending legislation. DMH, which apparently was deeply dysfunctional,[12] disappeared in 2012 and was merged into the Department of Health Care Services (DHCS). The LPS office closed with the transfer, and dysfunctional oversight was replaced with none.

Indeed, when I asked an official about DHCS's responsibility with respect to the conservatorship system, they responded, "it's more delegated [to counties] and it hasn't been a top priority given everything else going on"—namely, a huge reform to the $100 billion-plus Medi-Cal public insurance program, of which only a small portion went to mental health and substance use treatment. One consequence of the absence of centralized leadership is wildly different interpretation of LPS law by county around questions as basic as when conservatees can refuse medication or whether families can serve as conservators. This makes conservatorship's sovereign power seem arbitrary and capricious since fundamental civil rights vary by zip code.[13]

Public guardians have not fared much better at a county level. The Office of the Public Guardian can be a standalone agency or a subdivision of mental health, social services, or aging and disability departments. Whatever the location, guardians are marginalized, much like the people they serve.[14] Counties treat conservatorship not as an obligation toward people who need it but as an option available only as funds allow. One public guardian told me that her county essentially told her, "Okay, this is how much money we're going to give you for LPS [conservatorships], don't come back to the table for any more; if your cases go up, that's your problem." Economic crises might lead counties to impose belt-tightening on public guardians, forcing them to declare that some individuals have spontaneously recovered and can be expunged from the conservatorship case rolls.[15] A tenfold difference in the number of people conserved (relative to the population) between counties almost certainly reflects differences in funding, not need (Figure 5.1).[16]

State and county neglect filters into how public guardians perform their basic functions: investigating conservatorship referrals and serving conservatees. There is no standard profile for deputy public guardians (the actual public guardian is usually a higher-ranking county official who does not play any day-to-day role in the

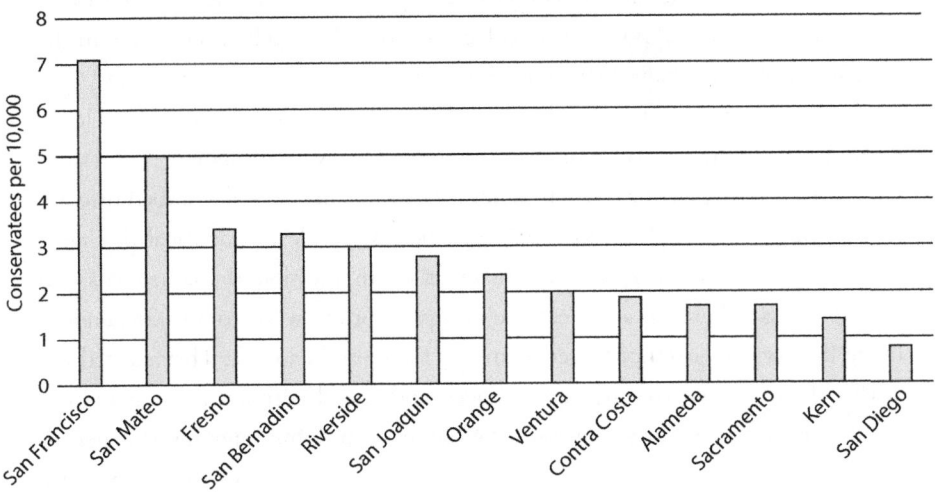

5.1 Permanent LPS conservatorships relative to population, 2020
Source: SF Budget and Legislative Analyst

office). In most counties, they need to have at least a bachelor's degree. The head of the department tends to be a social worker who has worked their way up through the mental health or social service system. But whatever their backgrounds, they face a similar dilemma: no new funding is automatically unlocked when someone gets conserved. More conservatees mean larger caseloads—frequently around sixty per guardian, but ranging up to one hundred in particularly strapped counties.

Once established, many conservatorships will be renewed year after year, so it makes sense not to keep the front door of the public guardian's office too far open.[17] The key moment to exercise discretion is during a conservatorship investigation. The process looks like this: five days before the expiration of a 5250, if the doctor wants to keep a person as an inpatient, they have to file for a thirty-day temporary conservatorship.[18] Judges usually sign that order without a hearing. Then the public guardian launches an investigation into whether to apply for a one-year permanent conservatorship. That means reviewing the medical record, speaking to family and outpatient providers, and, ultimately, interviewing the potential conservatee. The public guardian from a county even smaller than Frontier was frank about the purpose of these investigations: "[filing for] conservatorship is the last thing you want to do as a conservator."

A thorough investigation by a deputy public guardian is an important check on inpatient psychiatrists' power. Joseph Devico worked virtually everywhere in the system—outpatient team, IMD, inpatient unit—before coming to the San Diego Public Conservator's Office. He described one referral.[19] The individual had eleven hospital admissions in twelve months. "I thought, 'wow, he's a shoe in . . . for conservatorship," Joseph concluded. But, doing due diligence, he still combed through the hospital's records. He was shocked: "There were eleven identical discharge plans. Every time they stayed about the same length, they had the same meds—no attempt to get them on an injectable [antipsychotic]—went to an independent living facility—no attempt to get them in a board and care. . . . They started the year without an [outpatient] case manager, and ended without a case manager." He was, in his own words, "furious": "What are you doing referring this person for conservatorship after you've done absolutely nothing to get them more care in the community?" Refusing that referral, in his view, enacted the responsibility of guardians to ensure the system offers "every chance to keep that person free."

There are legal mandates and good ethical reasons for guardians to insist on trying every less restrictive alternative first. But it's also revealing. Community-based solutions tend to be provided by the private (for-profit or nonprofit) sector, and paid for partly by federal Medicaid dollars. A conservatorship makes someone a truly public responsibility, drawing on more limited county funds. And that's a responsibility that the public sector, through its inattention to public guardians' offices, is reluctant to take.

PLACEMENTS, PLACEMENTS, PLACEMENTS

Even taking these funding constraints into account, it's hard to look at the case of Mark Rippee, and not think some county public guardians are drawing sharp lines around grave disability that are inexplicable and inhumane.[20] Mark had schizoaffective disorder as well as a traumatic brain injury from a motorcycle accident that cost him both eyes and one-third of his frontal lobe. At fifty-nine years old, he had been almost constantly homeless since 2007, and during that time racked up one hundred arrests for illegal camping and vagrancy. He was a community fixture, frequently pushing his shopping cart into traffic, where he was hit, with near fatal consequences, twice. He was regularly beaten and robbed by other unhoused people.

Mark was long kept alive by his sisters Linda Privatte and Catherine Rippee and a town Facebook group that reported on him and brought him basic necessities. Linda spent enough time on the streets to sound credible when she stated, "He is the worst of the worst homeless person" in Vacaville, a town of 120,000 in Solano County, just north of Oakland and the East Bay. You could turn the failure of attempts to get him conserved into a parable of civil rights protections trumping common sense. But it is also a story about the inevitable imperatives of street-level bureaucrats who must adapt to a situation where the placements available to conservatees don't match the people who need conservatorship.

A few years after his accident in 1987, Mark began to develop delusions and became increasingly menacing. His family started calling the police, who usually arrested him but sometimes took him to the hospital. His longest stay was two weeks, which is to say the psychiatrist never asked for a conservatorship. That made his family his guardian by default. They put him in a subsidized apartment, from which he was evicted in 2007. His sisters and mother were ailing and were in no state to take him in, and the last time Mark's mother visited him, he threatened to kill her—or, in his mind, the person who was impersonating his mother—with an axe. Despite being constantly in the throes of unmedicated psychosis, in the ten subsequent years he was 5150ed only once. Linda speculates, probably accurately, that police in Solano just don't use grave disability as the basis for a hold.

A few times, they got closer to a conservatorship. Linda, her sister Catherine, and supporters they mustered from the family-advocacy community sent an avalanche of messages to everyone ranging from the county human services department to the White House. In 2017, the county took notice. Mark had been missing for a few weeks, but eventually Linda got a knock on her door from a Vacaville police officer and a social worker from a nonprofit who had found him. They promised there was going to be a meeting with the county behavioral health department and the public guardian to discuss a conservatorship. She got a message a few weeks later that "it [the conservatorship] didn't go through." They did find an alternative: a boarding home, where he lasted "about three days" before the supervisor called the police. "The manager was begging the police not to arrest him but to please take him to a mental health crisis place," Linda told me. "They did neither. They put him back on the streets."

The county did not give Linda an explanation for their decision, but my research offers a few hypotheses. Although public guardians describe substance use as ubiquitous among the people they conserve, they can refuse a petition by claiming that a person has only substance issues and not a mental disorder as required by the law. As with ER doctors, there might be a bit of moral judgment behind such a veto, but also a purely practical calculation. Locked psychiatric hospitals can force someone to be sober but rarely have comprehensive addiction treatment and won't hold someone they see as only a substance user for an extended period. As Joseph DeVico, the former deputy from San Diego put it, "There's literally no place, exactly zero places, where you can force a person to receive substance use treatment. . . . So it wouldn't make any sense to conserve somebody, officially crumple up their liberties, and then not be able to do anything with that authorization. That power would allow you to do nothing." That said, Linda tells me, although Mark might have run into other homeless people doing meth and join in, she didn't think his substance use was consistent enough to be used to disqualify him from conservatorship.

Public guardians can evoke other reasons to shuffle responsibility for unwanted (potential) clients onto other agencies, onto families, or onto those clients themselves. In September 2019, Mark was hit by a car. Officers visited him when he was crying in pain on the sidewalk, but he refused help and so didn't get any. It took Linda two weeks to get him to go to a hospital for a worsening abscess in his brain. When she heard that the hospital was planning to put him in a taxi upon release, Linda and Catherine mobilized their supporters into a "collective fit" until the county agreed to place him in a board and care home for thirty days. After twenty days, he jumped the fence in the backyard and took off. Then, in February 2020, he was struck by another car. After several surgeries, he ended up in a rehab hospital in neighboring Napa County. There, the physician and social worker (who apparently had heard about Mark's case even before he arrived) thought that he should be conserved and contacted the Napa public guardian, who concurred.

But they contacted the wrong public guardian. In a delegated system, counties are only responsible for their own residents. This creates plenty of opportunities for buck-passing, given how many of the people facing conservatorship are homeless and lack a fixed address.[21] In any case, Mark's application went back to Solano County. By that time, he had been fed, bathed, and on medication for six months—still delusional, but more lucid than Linda had seen him in decades. A social worker from Solano came out, met with him for thirty minutes, and declared that he did not meet their county's criteria. The disparity in definitions results from the fact that some counties put far more money into their public guardians than others, creating space for a more expansive application of criteria. Linda says that the hospital social worker cried with her when they heard the news.

Every once in a while, Linda managed to get someone from the county to talk with her about her brother's case. In one letter, the county's attorney pinned Mark's plight on LPS law, stating, "This is not a situation that we have ignored, nor that we condone. The law requires stringent standards [for] conservatorship, standards that so far we cannot meet." In reality, the law is vague, which is why some counties actually would declare Mark gravely disabled.

Linda got a more honest answer in a conversation with a public guardian: Mark was in a Catch-22. In the guardian's view, people with head injuries do not qualify for LPS conservatorships, whereas probate conservatorships, which are primarily for people with head injuries, dementia, or developmental disabilities (and give a different set of powers, more focused on financial management and medical care), were not for people with mental illness.[22]

While Mark's combination is rare, it is not unique.[23] The counties I spoke with diverged on whether they would conserve people with mental illness on top of dementia, traumatic brain injuries, or developmental disabilities under LPS. But they all agreed that the more of those boxes you check at once, the harder it is to find a placement. Mark, Linda once put it, "falls into a lot of different categories, that's why he keeps falling through the cracks." Josephine, the public guardian for a midsize coastal county, did agree to conserve someone with joint mental illness and a traumatic brain injury. She told me her office contacted a hundred facilities across the state on their behalf, to no avail.[24] Even when public guardians find a facility willing to take a complex case, the county behavioral health department—which, again, controls the budget for residential care—might not pay for it. That was probably the easiest explanation for Mark's plight: no available placement, no conservatorship.[25]

MANAGING THE "HOMELESS LIFESTYLE"

As a fourteen-day 5250 dragged into a thirty-day temporary conservatorship, most of the conservatees I talked to increasingly felt that doctors, social workers, judges, public guardians, and public defenders were all scheming in the same medical-legal plot to take away their rights. They're half right. There's a broad conspiracy among government actors in the conservatorship continuum, but sometimes it is actually directed toward restoring people's rights—and, in so doing, holding down conservatorship caseloads. Finding a (somewhat) willing third party, such as a family member, is one way to do this. The other is to declare some potential conservatees responsible for their own survival by showing that the miserable living conditions they inhabited before the hospital were a conscious choice.

Tamara has worn many hats in her twenty years in the mental health system, but the main thrust of her work has been revealingly similar across her career: getting people out of locked facilities and off conservatorship. At the very beginning of college, she had an internship in a state hospital. The unit was "dark, not well lit" and felt like a prison. She was "terrified, terrified, terrified" of the clients: "There was always a lot of noise. Initially, they were spitting at me, they were always trying to grope me, grab at me, all of those things. It freaked me out." Yet, when she managed to connect with an otherwise mute man who had been interned since he dismembered his family at age twelve, something clicked. She discovered that many of those individuals had been stuck in state hospitals for years, so "I really pushed for them to go to the socialization center, play games during the day, see people out in the community [on a day pass]."

Her desire to watch clients move to less restrictive environments continued when she became a deputy public guardian in a county in the Central Valley. As in the state hospital, there were "people who had been on conservatorship for twelve, fifteen, nineteen years . . . and I was like, 'So what's being done to . . . break this cycle?' I don't want conservatorship to be a permanent sentence." She would hustle to convince contracted outpatient teams to take a look at her clients or bring them from the state hospital to visit local, unlocked board and cares.

The biggest successes in passing the public baton were achieved when she could link conservatees back to their families. California's statutes are quite clear that "a person is not gravely disabled . . . if the person is capable of safely surviving in freedom with the help of willing and responsible family members, friends, or third parties."[26] For public guardians, convincing a family member to step forward provides an easy reason to turn down an application, while for public defenders, it is a cut-and-dried way to beat an application in court. Tamara admitted that "nine times out of ten times the family wasn't involved" (as you've seen, if someone has "willing" family, the hospital quickly discharges the person).

If she could, though, Tamara would ring up the family and say, "'Let's try a phone call [with the conservatee], see how that goes,' or 'You could come with me when I go visit, see for yourself, and be part of the treatment team meeting and give your input.' . . . Because I really saw that when family was supportive, there was a higher likelihood that the conservatee would be successful [in leaving conservatorship]."

A few years before our conversation, Tamara switched titles again and became a county patients' rights advocate. Advocates represent mental health clients in probable cause hearings (four days into a 5250), investigate complaints, and accompany them to meetings with doctors or public guardians. She kept pursuing the same goal: getting people out of locked settings. In her new position, she discovered that often she needed to show a hearing officer or the public guardian only that someone was, to borrow a phrase I heard many times, "successfully managing the homeless lifestyle" by acquiring some simulacrum of food, clothing, and shelter. As Tamara reminded me, "just because someone is homeless doesn't mean they're gravely disabled." Instead, a good conservatorship investigator or advocate is "out there looking at what their homelessness looks like."

She gave me an example. One individual told her, "'Yes, I'm homeless, but I'm not gravely disabled, I can get food at seven P.M. at this McDonald's on this street. I can go to this 7–11 on these days, and I can get something to drink. And I can go pick up cans and turn them in to get this amount of money.'" Tamara told me she would never defend someone's "survival plan" to a hearing officer unless she checked it out herself. In this case, "I went to the McDonald's, I asked those questions: 'Do you know this person? Do you feed this person?' The staff said, 'yes.' I went to the 7–11, and the staff were like, 'Oh my gosh, is he okay?' 'Oh yes, we'll give him this that and the other.' And then I went to the recycling company . . . and I verified it." She got that individual released. On other occasions, she'd dig through someone's tent at an encampment to make sure they had a stove or check in at the local Salvation Army to see if they came to get clothing.

Not everyone's plan for survival puts them above the "successfully managing" bar. Tamara's old boss at the public guardian's office, Darrell, explained that they would file petitions for people "coming in sunburned from exposure, lacking appropriate clothing, their lab work shows really poor food intake. . . . We look for those biological indicators that someone is not doing well." Being homeless was a skill that some, but not all, severely mentally ill people mastered.

He contrasted the case of "someone who has five or ten years of experience living on the street and not a lot of admissions or run-ins with law enforcement" with "someone who is nineteen, they've never been homeless, but now they're in the hospital saying, 'I can live on the street.'" Investigators would explore, "Do they really know what that means? You ask them, 'How would you get this and that?' and they can't piece it together. So that's an easier one to say, 'They don't know what they're getting themselves into' [and file for conservatorship]."

Around the state, I posed this question of when homelessness—which seems, by definition, to entail a lack of shelter—posed a grave disability. Nearly every public guardian spoke in terms of choice and agency. Josephine, the guardian from an ultraliberal coastal county, emphasized that her office was focused only on a small number of "mentally ill people who are unfortunately also homeless" and "constantly getting 5150ed or arrested for bathing naked in the fountain downtown or trespassing in a restaurant." Those individuals are "not making it as a homeless person. You're not managing the homeless lifestyle in an appropriate way, at least not enough to not bring attention to yourself." For her, the decision whether to conserve someone depended on which was the more effective strategy to minimize government involvement: not intervening at all or using conservatorship to reduce someone's expensive contact with law enforcement and ERs.

Tamara articulated to me her opposition to expanding conservatorships: "I don't like it. . . . People have a right to live where they want to live. If they want to live in a tent, that's fine." She'd like to see the system come up with "other solutions to work with the individuals one-to-one, to help them"—as she has her whole career. Tamara is Black and well aware that when you coerce people because they are poor and sick, you wind up coercing minorities for whom racism and exclusion contribute both to an inability to provide food, clothing, and shelter and to illness. Her emphasis on civil liberties is sincere.

It's also a necessity. "The act of defining a disability," the political scientist Deborah Stone posits, "determines what is expected of the non-disabled—what injuries, disease, incapacities, and problems they will be expected to tolerate in their normal working lives."[27] Drawing a perimeter around grave disability that excludes many homeless people's condition as normal and freely chosen is necessary to prevent public guardians from being overwhelmed by the tidal wave of misery washing over California's vacant lots, underpasses, and roadside encampments.

"DUMPED ON" BY DIVERSION

If there's one trend happening "industry wide" for public guardians, it's an "enormous shift of criminal-legal cases onto conservatorship," according to Scarlet Hughes of the state association of Public Guardians. Darrell, the Central Valley conservator, deadpanned, "Misery loves company. . . . The majority of us have noticed that the [criminal-legal] referrals have increased rapidly . . . [and they] tend to be a lot more of a challenge." This ongoing process of burden shifting from the criminal-legal system onto the mental health/conservatorship complex has created a shoving match that state policy has created but done little to resolve.

California statutes allow for conservatorship applications from the "professional person in charge of providing mental health treatment at a county jail," just like from a hospital.[28] But veteran public guardians I spoke to said such applications used to be rare. Rick Weiss, a forensic psychologist who worked for a decade in Los Angeles's infamous Twin Towers jail, had the same impression. Before he started his job in 2016, the jail was applying only for "squeaky wheel" cases when they were receiving pressure from law enforcement, families, or county supervisors. After all, since the jail provides food, clothing, and shelter, "the criteria [for grave disability] at face value is never met," making proving that an inmate qualifies for conservatorship complicated.[29] Then again, Rick assured me, the jail was crammed full of people who "cannot take care of their living conditions, they're living in squalor, gnat-filled cells, fecal matter, horrific scent, [and] that is someone not tending to their shelter. They're issued clothing, but they're not wearing it, they can't exchange out soiled clothing." He unapologetically upped the rhythm of applications: "If these patients were presented to a mental health professional in the community, [they] would be admitted to a psychiatric hospital 99 out of 100 times. . . . [They] are horrifically ill."

Some of the people on the receiving end of these referrals, though, are reluctant to take them on. Tod, who has been running the public guardian's office in a wealthy coastal county for fifteen years, is proud of having a comparatively large conservatorship program that defines grave disability broadly. But, he said, "We're seeing a lot more forensic clients coming our way. . . . Sometimes, it feels like we're being dumped on. 'This person is in jail, they're mentally ill, they're ready to go but not safe to go out on their own.' Thanks, but that's not really what we're here for." I heard that exact phrase—"dumped on"—from guardians in several other counties.

My research suggests that there are two poles to the population of people subjected to forced treatment: the "disruptive" and the "disabled." The former, as you've seen, are easier to 5150 and more likely to get through an ER, while the latter, when admitted, stay longer in hospitals. They're the group public guardians see as more deserving of and appropriate for their services. After all, a public guardian's ability to keep a person and the community safe is only as good as their ability to get someone into a secure facility. And public guardians don't hold the keys to those facilities, most of which are private. Mental health facilities have every incentive not to take clients who have a lengthy history of violence, which could put both other residents and their license at risk. As of October 2022, a person who had been conserved while incarcerated in San Francisco's jail had been waiting 1,200 days to transfer to a mental health facility.[30]

When we spoke, Tod was pulling his hair out over a conservatee who "has been banned from my own [county] hospital, he's been banned from Crestwood [a major private provider of locked beds], and he's been banned from everywhere." Tod suggested that this individual did not have a "real" mental illness like schizophrenia, but a "very serious personality disorder," which, like substance use, dementia, or a traumatic brain injury, can create some wiggle room for a public guardian to deny an application. On a previous hospitalization, this individual "talked absolutely crazy" to a psychiatrist, who managed to get him conserved and sent him to a state hospital, where he quickly ceased displaying any psychotic symptoms. He was a "hot potato" no one wanted: "We were stuck because the [state] hospital says, 'He doesn't need to be here,' and the community placement says, 'Well, we don't want him.'"

While he lingered in the state hospital without a discharge plan, he assaulted someone, went to jail, and was currently waiting to return to the state hospital's forensic unit. "I don't know if the state hospital gets to pick and choose, but they will [try not to take him back]," Tod speculated. In this case, he planned to push back on the jail, law enforcement, and district attorney by saying, "There's nothing we can do for this person, no place will accept him.'" Tod's goal was to convince a judge to just drop the conservatorship. He concluded, "He's a young guy, only like thirty years old, but he will probably be taken care of by the judicial system, not the mental health system."

But Rick, the psychologist back at Twin Towers jail, isn't willing to take no for an answer. When Rick manages to get clients conserved, they leave jail for the county hospital to wait for a locked subacute (IMD) bed willing to take forensic cases. He claims that as the months wear on, the hospital will sometimes persuade the public guardian that the person is stable enough to go off conservatorship and can survive in an unlocked board and care home with outpatient care from an FSP team. In Rick's experience, they make it "forty-eight hours and get rearrested." His approach, though, was to "continue [applying], despite knowing that there was a good chance that it wasn't going to work out. . . . I wanted to flood the system with as many appropriate conservatees as possible." He hoped the county would invest in more locked mental health facilities for justice-involved clients.

A rural public defender recounted a different strategy for using law to force medicine's hand. He told me the county mental health department had declared it wouldn't take conservatorship referrals from jail because "if you're in custody all of your food, clothing, and shelter needs are being met, no matter how crazy you are." His tactic—which, he told me, he had successfully exercised the afternoon before we met—was to beat his psychotic clients' charges in court, so they would be released from custody. He'd then call a mobile crisis team for a 5150 evaluation on the steps of the courthouse. That could get them into the county hospital as a regular, nonforensic patient.

The pathways for these criminal-legal referrals to conservatorship are multiplying over time, as part of well-intentioned attempts to downsize California's carceral system. State legislation passed in 2018 allows courts to refer people for conservatorship if they are unsuccessful in less restrictive diversion programs (in which a person agrees to treatment in order to get charges dropped).[31] Another route onto conservatorship begins when courts determine that someone is incompetent to stand trial and send them to a state hospital or an in-jail treatment program. Los Angeles County reported a 350 percent increase in such referrals from 2010 to 2015.[32] If at the end of two years the person is deemed incapable of being restored to competency, they too can be sent for conservatorship.[33] A 2021 bill, intended to clear a backlog of competency cases, made it so that people who are found incompetent to stand trial for misdemeanor charges can be referred directly to conservatorship, without passing through the restoration process.[34] For all these legislative reforms, the state has not limited public guardians' discretion to refuse these new potential clients. And as long as their budgets are stagnant and placements limited, public guardians like Tod will continue to do so.

Sociologist Armando Lara-Millán describes how government agencies engage in "people exchange[s]" as they "struggle either to abdicate or obtain responsibility for people, caseloads, and . . . the public revenue [or costs] attached to them." Lara-Millán puts it mildly when he says the result is "[not] coherent population management, in which the movement of people between state agencies is rationally coordinated." Instead, it shows how law and medicine are engaged in an ongoing process of "redistributing the poor" between settings that don't want them.[35]

CONCLUSION: RESIDUAL DISCRETION

Public guardians are obligated, by both the LPS statute and the Supreme Court's ruling in *Olmstead v. L.C. by Zimring*, to ensure that disabled individuals go into the "least restrictive" setting possible.[36] Many fervently believe that conservatorship should be a last resort. To understand how public guardians operate, though, you need to look not just at legal mandates and ethical precepts but also at the underlying logic of America's feeble welfare state. Public guardians are not charged with putting everyone onto conservatorship who might benefit from it. They instead operate on the principle of "subsidiarity," or the idea that the collectivity should step in only when the capacity of the individual and the family to provide is fully exhausted.[37]

Nonetheless, how public guardians act on these principles is remarkably inconsistent, thanks to the state's abdication of any role in standardizing practices. Paul, a conservator in a medium-size Northern California county, told me, "The definition of grave disability sounds simple . . . but operationally, how does that look? . . . You can look around fifty-eight counties, and we're all going to tell you something different." However it is exercised, discretion mostly goes in a negative direction. It's easy to turn down referrals, but conserving more people is hard: offices can only evaluate, not solicit, referrals. Budgets are fixed even if caseloads go up. More petitions do not magically create more beds in locked step-down facilities. It's unsurprising that so many potential conservatees wind up in criminal-legal institutions—often the only public agencies that cannot refuse the people "qualified" for their "services."

In the end, though, public guardians' negative discretion plays a residual role in the conservatorship continuum. Although public guardians in some smaller counties told me that they rejected as much as a third of applications, in larger counties like Alameda, Los Angeles, or San Francisco, the offices—under increasing pressure from county supervisors, law enforcement, and families—file on virtually every referral.[38] Most of the real discretion has been delegated earlier on the continuum to entities that are often private rather than public.

Resource constraints, regulatory requirements, and a lack of placements might explain why some individuals who seem flagrantly unable to meet their basic needs don't advance further along the continuum. That doesn't make the outcomes seem any less cruel. Public guardians' decisions left Linda Rippee feeling as forsaken as her brother, blind and psychotic on the streets of Vacaville. The day we spoke, it was raining, and Linda was leaving to bring Mark some dry clothes. At least she knew where to look. After his last hospitalization, he asked to be dropped off on the very street where he had twice been hit by a car. His favorite spot was right in front of a county office building. It houses the public guardian.

CHAPTER 6

COURT

'How many patients have you treated and evaluated as a psychiatrist?' Andy, the county counsel who represents the public guardian's office, asks. I'm one of the few people physically present in the courtroom for one afternoon's mostly virtual hearing for a Latina woman in her mid-thirties. She's sitting in a gray hoodie inside a hospital room, the camera a bit too close to her face.

The doctor, just three years out of med school but on the front lines of California's system of rapid, revolving-door involuntary hospitalizations, looks bemused: 'I don't know, thousands?'

County counsel is laying the standard foundation to establish that the county's star—and only—witness is an expert qualified to answer the question animating today's hearing. Judge Davis, who has been doing LPS cases almost exclusively for a year and a half in a Southern California county, explained what that question was a few minutes prior: 'Ms. Gonzalez, we're here today to determine if a conservator will be appointed for you. The issue today is to determine if you are gravely disabled as a result of a mental illness.'

That determination will depend on Dr. Park's *cultural authority*: his capacity, as Paul Starr explains it, to "define . . . [the] reality" of a patient's conditions and have that definition "prevail as valid and true."[1] But in this case, I'm struck by the weak underpinnings of this authority. The doctor has been treating her for four weeks, sees her 'once a week to check in,' and this usually takes 'about ten to fifteen minutes.'

Dr. Park gives his diagnosis, schizoaffective disorder. He adds, 'She has a history of multiple hospitalizations—'

'Objection,' the public defender cuts in.

Judge Davis looks up and rapidly declares: 'Sustained. Strike that from the record.'

This objection reveals a key dynamic of conservatorship trials—and why doctors' cultural authority within them seems so limited. In a 2016 ruling in *People v. Sanchez*, the California Supreme Court decreed that expert witnesses cannot testify to facts they have learned through inadmissible hearsay.[2] That case had nothing to do with mental health (the 'expert' was a police detective specialized in gangs), but the result was to tightly restrict the information coming into conservatorship hearings. An expert psychiatric judgment requires talking to someone's family members or outpatient providers, as well as reviewing records from previous hospitalizations. At a minimum, psychiatrists rely on ward staff—the nurses or techs who spend eight-hour shifts with patients, rather than fifteen-minute rounds—to fill them in. None of that is admissible in court if there's a public defender savvy enough to object and a judge who is caught up on the case law.

Sanchez explains county counsel's stilted introduction to his next question: 'In answering, I would like you to limit yourself to your direct observations and interactions with the patient. What are the symptoms of schizophrenia that you see in Ms. Gonzalez?'

The doctor replies, 'She is quite paranoid. She talks nonsensically and makes illogical statements about where she will go if released. Sometimes she says she will go home, other times she says that she will go to the Fourth Street Bridge [a notorious, and pseudonymous, homeless encampment]. We've talked to her about going home with her family, but she refuses.'

'And how is her judgment?'

'It's fair, but she has no insight into her condition.'

Prior to LPS, a commitment hearing might have stopped there. Ms. Gonzalez has a mental illness and doesn't recognize her need for treatment.[3] But that's not what this hearing is about. County counsel then asks, 'Is the patient gravely disabled?'

'Yes, she does meet grave disability criteria.'

'And what is the nexus between her mental illness and her grave disability?'

'Nexus' is an odd term, but it's another thing Judge Davis is looking for: a clear cause-and-effect relationship between Ms. Gonzalez's pathology and her inability to provide for her basic needs.

The doctor reiterates, 'Well, she has very poor insight. She could not care for herself on her own. I suspect that she was noncompliant with treatment, which led to her relapse and readmission to the hospital.'

County counsel asks if he thinks Ms. Gonzalez would continue taking the two antipsychotics she's prescribed outside the hospital. 'I haven't asked her, but I have a high suspicion that she would not,' Dr. Park concludes.

The public defender's cross examination is short. 'Have you looked into where she wants to go at the Fourth Street Encampment?'

Dr. Park offers a curt, 'No.'

'Are you aware that there are resources for people who choose to go to the encampment and want to avail themselves of them?'

The doctor's response is impassive: 'I'm sure there are. But she would basically be discharged with no follow-up. It's not a good plan.'

The public defender turns to Ms. Gonzalez (or rather, her image on the screen) and asks if she'd like to speak to the judge. The woman says 'yes' and, without prompting, starts explaining why she doesn't want a conservatorship, except that she's too quiet to hear. The court reporter throws up her hands in exasperation. Her lawyer cuts her off and asks her pointedly where she would go; she says Salvation Shelter, right by the encampment.

'When were you last at Salvation?'

'A month ago.'

'How long have you relied on them?'

'Four years . . . two years,' she fumbles.

'Is staying with your family what you want?'

'No,' Ms. Gonzalez replies, emphatically.

The public defender summarizes: 'Okay. So, if you were released, you would go to Salvation for shelter. What would you do for food and clothing?'

'I'd just use what they have there.' There's a certain tension in this discharge plan. When I spoke to the head of Salvation, he moaned that the residents they sent to the hospital were coming back barely stabilized and unwilling to participate in the shelter's programming.

You can tell that a case is straightforward if county counsel doesn't bother subjecting a patient to cross-examination. Here, though, Andy isn't taking chances: 'The doctor testified that you have a mental illness. Do you believe that you have a mental illness?'

Ms. Gonzalez gives him, I'm sure, the answer he's looking for: 'No, I don't have a mental illness.'

Counsel goes on. 'The doctor says that you take medication for a mental illness. Why would you do that if you don't believe you have one?' There's a pause. 'You'd keep taking it even though you don't believe you have a mental illness?' he continues, skeptically.

'Yes.'

'And how would you avoid coming to the hospital again?' he asks.

'I would stay in the shelter.'

The testimony is done, and there is no time for deliberation. Judge Davis starts haltingly. She notes, 'Ms. Gonzalez's affect seems very unusual . . . I'm not sure what adjective to use. . . . She is monotone, her expression is not changing. Could this be an effect of the medication?'

The psychiatrist replies, 'It could be. Sometimes the negative symptoms [of schizophrenia]'—like a dulled affect or slow cognition—'become more pronounced with medication, especially with what she is prescribed.'

'Okay,' Judge Davis goes on. 'This complicates my job a little bit. I don't have a good take on her personality, or where she's coming from. Is there any argument?'

The public defender gives a brief statement, remarking, 'She has a plan for food, clothing, and shelter. She discussed being with her family, but it's her choice not to. Fourth Street is where she wants to return. It's her community. She is med compliant, and she can get services at Salvation.'

County counsel replies, 'Salvation is a really unstructured environment. She's likely to regress and decompensate.'

Judge Davis knows that however she rules, people will be angry at her. When she decides against granting a conservatorship, she's lacking in compassion for people dying on the street. ("I worked as an attorney at a public interest law firm doing homelessness prevention," she counters to me.) If she does grant a conservatorship, others will claim she's failing in her role as the last line of defense of people's civil liberties. (She's aware: "The Britney [Spears] case has made me think hard about what we're doing here. Are these conservatorships abusive? It's my worst nightmare that this is *One Flew Over the Cuckoo's Nest*, and I'm playing a role in it.")

When I commented on the lack of oversight of conservatorships, state officials I interviewed reminded me that was supposed to come from the courts.

It's consistent with a long-running pattern in American government to use adversarial court proceedings to substitute for what might come from specialized civil servants enforcing detailed regulations in much of Europe.[4] The result is a guardianship system that "relies heavily on the discretion of individual judges, thereby creating a system in which decisions are unpredictable and potentially inconsistent."[5]

This is true, to a point. Judges have substantial discretion in deciding who goes onto conservatorship. But as I show in this chapter, many are frustrated by their lack of authority to get lawyers to represent conservatees effectively, make conservatees show up in court to assert their rights, or extract useful information from psychiatrists. While courtrooms are supposed to be the place where law and medicine come into visible and open conflict, conservatorship hearings reveal the weaknesses of both.[6]

ENSURING THE "RIGHT TO HAVE RIGHTS"

In a 1966 hearing held in the lead-up to the passage of LPS, Dr. Stubblebine, the director of Community Mental Health Services in San Francisco, tried to defend the state's involuntary commitment standard (which allowed for internment of people who needed treatment but who were not dangerous) to skeptical legislators: "Commitment . . . if you look at the etymology of the word, means . . . 'to connect' in the sense of 'putting in touch with, or entrust.' . . . It is an agreement or pledge to do something for the patient's welfare." He was articulating the justification for commitment based on *parens patriae*, the state's obligation to serve as a guardian for vulnerable citizens. Chairman Jerome Waldie had none of it: "That may be ideally what it should be, but in fact, what it is, is simply extreme punishment to the person committed."[7]

Waldie's argument won out. The equation of civil commitments with criminal detention is a powerful strand in legal approaches to conservatorship.[8] In a 1979 ruling, the federal Ninth Circuit Court of Appeals concluded that "from the perspective of the person who resists this confinement [involuntary commitment], there is little to distinguish it from incarceration in a penal institution. Because the mental facility is authorized to administer drugs to him against his will, detention there might be considered more severe than confinement in a penal institution."[9]

The courts have installed legal protections to match. Evan, a twenty-seven-year veteran public defender in a large Northern California county, observed, "When I started doing this work [LPS cases], it was astounding to me the due process protections for people on conservatorship, which are pretty robust and pretty generous." He sounded enthusiastic in the way only a public defender might be as he ticked off those protections: a right to a jury trial, a requirement that a unanimous jury find someone is gravely disabled "beyond a reasonable doubt" (the same standard as in a criminal case), and the ability to recontest a conservatorship every six months.

The philosopher Hannah Arendt once observed that, in a modern era when politicians and advocates declare that "human rights" are universal and inalienable, not everyone has a "right to have rights."[10] That meta-right can only come from a legal or political system willing to empower someone as a legal subject.[11] The point could apply to conservatees. In New York State, a 1964 reform to commitment statutes was coupled with the creation of Mental Hygiene Legal Services, a state-financed group of specialized lawyers, stationed within psychiatric hospitals, that represent everyone whose rights are restricted in the name of their mental health.[12] California's reformed commitment laws gave patients more rights to refuse treatment than those in New York, but the state never created a comparable infrastructure for making those rights real.[13] That role, instead, was left to counties, which have in turn charged already overwhelmed public defenders' offices with the task of representing potential conservatees.[14]

The barriers to effective advocacy start with how public defenders wind up in that role in the first place. Evan had already been a public defender for more than a decade when "my boss called up one day and said, 'Hey, we're going to move you into the mental health unit.'" Evan couldn't remember if he had ever actually expressed interest in it. But he thought, "I'm always up for learning new things, broadening my knowledge. [And] it's a nice break from the really heavy-duty felony caseload, which is very stressful." Since the process of being assigned seemed a bit haphazard, I asked him what preparation he had upon starting: "No training at all, zero. I walked in there the first day and my colleague who had been there six months trained me. It was all on the job." As he described it, "I got out the Diagnostic and Statistics Manual and I started reading."

Honestly, being assigned to take LPS cases for no apparent reason is better than some of the motivations I heard. One public defender recounted, "Our county says, 'If you've done a death penalty case, you can take a break and do conservatorships.'" Another huffed, "I was banished to our LPS unit because of office politics" and, with no preparation, "I was pretty ignorant and ineffective for two years." Depictions of how judges get the assignment can be equally bleak. A 1992 profile of Los Angeles's Department 95, which handles LPS cases, described it as the "equivalent of being shipped off to judicial Siberia" (both metaphorically and spatially, as cases were heard in an infamously run-down converted pickle factory).[15] Judge Rojas, who handled LPS cases in a larger southern county, told me that, after spending most of a decade as a criminal judge, 'They asked me to go to mental health court. . . . I was crestfallen. . . . It was the least prestigious assignment there is.' His preparation was 'zero, on the job.'

When Evan started, he had a startling realization: "Holy shit, our office is really, really poorly educated on this aspect of our work." Getting up to speed was an eye-opening experience: "Our county is a big place, and I had no idea that there were board and cares or a subacute facility for elderly people in [City]. It opened my eyes to a whole part of society that I had no way of knowing about otherwise. I felt sort of honored, gifted to learn all of that." Outside of large, urban counties, the logistics are more complicated. Josh handles 'all the weird civil stuff that public defenders' offices do,' as well as juvenile justice, for a small, rural county. His county has no psychiatric hospital, so his LPS clients are sprinkled around the state. As a result of the distance, 'I'll go a half-hour or maybe forty-five minutes before a hearing to go over the papers. . . . That's my first time meeting someone.' Other public defenders shared similar challenges tracking down their clients as they bounced among placements in a privatized, fragmented, and decentralized system.

Other barriers to rendering individuals subject to involuntary treatment into people with the right to have rights are more ethical than practical. The guidelines governing lawyers' conduct in cases involving people alleged to be mentally ill are clear. attorneys "shall, as far as reasonably possible, maintain a normal client-lawyer relationship."[16] This means following someone's "stated interest"— i.e., fighting for them to get out of the hospital, if that's what they say they want. This approach was comfortable ground for a seasoned public defender like Evan, who told me, "I've been a public defender for almost thirty years, so I don't have a hard time just promoting what [a client's] stated interest is, even if in my heart of hearts, I knew this person would be better getting treated in a facility rather than the hairbrained discharge plan they have."

Others, though, are more ambivalent. One researcher who observed hundreds of LPS hearings in the late 1980s reported that public defenders were frequently "just as anxious to see some of their clients hospitalized as were the [county counsel] and psychiatrists who opposed them in court."[17] None of the twenty or so public defenders I spoke to described going so far as to ignore their clients' wishes. Still, some admitted that not all cases merited quite the same vigor. Josh, the rural public defender, told me, 'With LPS conservatorships . . . if my client says, 'I want to contest,' I do that, I don't try to strong-arm them out of that . . . but sometimes you kind of want them to stay on conservatorship, because they still obviously need it. Sometimes you don't want to win.'

Ultimately, even Evan—who vaunted the fact that conservatees benefited from similar protections to those accused of serious crimes—admitted that LPS cases were not the same kind of work: "Liberty is at stake, obviously, but these are civil commitments, not criminal holds." No matter how much he learned, he felt, pitting legal versus psychiatric expertise in LPS cases was a losing battle: "I enjoyed cross-examining the doctors, but obviously I was only going to get so far. I wasn't going to have a Perry Mason [a fictional lawyer in a 1960s TV show] moment where the doctor on the stand changed his opinion."

Evan finished his assignment but stayed involved in a county task force focused on diverting people from incarceration into treatment—sometimes even involuntarily. From many public defenders' perspectives, conflict between law and medicine seemed to serve the interests of people with mental illness less well than collaboration, and rights sometimes lost out to (coerced) care.

CONSENTING TO COERCION

'Welcome to the machine,' Andy, the county lawyer representing the public guardian, greets me as I show up in Judge Davis's courtroom one afternoon. I quickly understand what he means. Mornings are for contested hearings to determine if someone meets the standard for conservatorship: grave disability beyond a reasonable doubt. Afternoons are for everything else.

There's a report that one conservatee had his tooth extracted (this seems to be happy news) and another for whom the court needs to authorize blood draws to check medication levels. Judge Davis has demanded updates on several conservatees who have been waiting months to transfer from an acute-care hospital into an IMD or state hospital. No news. The public defender asks that the court order the public guardian to provide her client a new set of pants, shoes, and underwear. Many, many hearings are rescheduled because the client isn't there, the lawyer isn't there, the translator isn't there, the doctor isn't there, or the paperwork isn't there.

But mostly, there is a parade of instances where Judge Davis calls a case and the public defender stands up and says, 'Submittal, non-appearance.' The psychiatrist has applied for a conservatorship, the public guardian has approved it, and the soon-to-be conservatee isn't contesting it and didn't come to court.[18] Arguably, the biggest reason the formal legal rights to due process against conservatorship aren't effective is that many potential conservatees don't exercise them.

This really surprised me. Shouldn't involuntary treatment be something that, by definition, people want to challenge in court? But my observations that afternoon are backed by a 2008 study from San Diego that found that 75 percent of conservatorship hearings went uncontested.[19] I was flabbergasted when one judge told me that, in his first year as the LPS judge in a large county in Northern California, he had "never actually had a full-blown conservatorship trial." I asked how he thought that was possible. He wasn't sure: "I don't really know what the public defender is advising the patient, in terms of, 'Look, do you understand you have a right to a trial?' I'm really reliant on them to, kind of, ferret out [what the patient wants] and protect their rights."

It's not clear that public defenders are consistently playing this role. Indeed, some arm-twist their patients into agreeing to conservatorship.[20] Phil (whose son Jacob was conserved only when the Los Angeles County DMH threatened to yank a hospital's LPS designation) recounted that, for one renewal, "My son didn't show up, but the public defender said, 'Call your son.'" Phil did, and the public defender told Jacob, "Listen, your father wants to continue to be your guardian. If you fight it, it's not going to be good for you. . . . Do you want to be out in the streets? [At home with your father] you get your own bedroom, you eat well, your father loves you, he's a terrific guy." As Phil remembered it, "My son says, 'Well I don't know . . .' and he says, 'It's yes or no. You agree to it or not, and if you don't, I think your life is going to be worse.' And my son says, 'Okay,' and he says, 'Great,' and he goes up to the judge and says, '[Jacob] agrees to it.'"

The under-resourcing of the LPS system creates additional pressures on clients to abjure other rights. Jury trials require an enormous mobilization of time and personnel and, according to some interviewees, are more likely to lead to a conservatorship being denied. In one case, Judge Davis asks a woman if she wants a jury trial or one with just the judge. The woman takes a long pause before saying, 'Jury.'

Her public defender tells her, 'That's okay, that's your right.'

But when the bailiff comes back with a trial date months in the future, the woman asks, 'Before then, can I leave [the hospital]?'

Her attorney replies, 'No, I think you'll go to a nursing facility.'

'I think it would be an IMD,' Judge Davis, looking at her paperwork, adds.

The woman's next response seems confused, because she states, 'So I can leave today?'

'You can have a trial with the judge today,' the defender replies.

'And if it's a jury, I stay in the hospital?'

'It's likely you will stay in the hospital [until the trial],' her public defender reiterates.

'Then judge,' the woman relents. Judge Davis then declares her waiver of her right to a jury trial 'knowing, intelligent, and voluntary,' which feels odd because the rest of the trial focused on how she is neither knowing nor intelligent about her condition and thus requires involuntary treatment.

Another explanation for the high rates of conservatees' consenting to constraint is simply that they have accurately assessed their low chances of winning. As Josh, the rural public defender, told me, 'If they say they want to contest their conservatorship, I tell them, "They'll ask you about your plan if you're not on conservatorship." If they can't come up with good answers, I say, "It sounds like conservatorship is helpful for you, your plan isn't very good, you haven't figured this out, so probably the court won't let you off." Frequently, they'll say, "Okay, I can live with conservatorship." ' Some conversations don't get that far. Clients who are acutely psychotic, catatonic, or mute might not be articulating any clear preference about their conservatorship. Lawyers have neither the time nor the training to help them develop one.

Then there are reasons that have little to do with legal advocacy by attorneys. When I raised this contradictory idea of consent to coercion with Judge Rojas, he responded, 'Many times the patient comes into court, they want the conservatorship, they like what they're getting, food clothing shelter, medication, activities, they don't want to be homeless. Anyone who has lived through hearing voices knows that's not a fun thing.' That's the happiest rendering: that services are high enough quality that people, eventually, realize they want them.

But why does someone need to be conserved to get shelter and services? Perhaps, in some cases, they need a period of forced medication to clear the haze of anosognosia, which could have blinded them to their own ailment. But as another public defender more cynically told me, the appeal of conservatorship for many conservatees hinges on the dire alternatives: 'You would expect that if anybody is told, "You're on a psych[iatric] hold . . ." [they would contest it] but if the alternative is, "I have nowhere to go, I need help finding housing, I don't have the support, I'm not doing well," a lot of people are willing to stay when they're getting three meals a day, there's shelter, and nursing for their medical needs.'

It's an endemic problem. Medicine often won't or can't treat someone until the law is involved (whether it's mental health care in prison or a civil commitment to a hospital that doesn't take voluntary patients). This means that, for some conservatees, the right to have "social rights" to housing and care—the kind guaranteed in other wealthy countries—requires renouncing civil rights to freedom and choice.

MISSING EVIDENCE

When cases do make it to trial, outcomes may depend less on the strictness of grave disability and more on the limitations of doctors' cultural authority to identify it.

For one thing, the *Sanchez* decision sharply curtails the evidence judges can consider. This comes to a head in the hearing for a young man diagnosed with a litany of psychotic, mood, and developmental disorders. Andy, the county counsel, asks how these symptoms affect his ability to provide food, clothing, and shelter. His psychiatrist replies, 'Well, he has been hospitalized twenty times . . .'

'Objection,' the public defender interjects.

'Sustained,' Judge Davis declares.

Later, the psychiatrist tries to explain that staff told him he was 'cheeking' his medicine (hiding it in his mouth to avoid taking it), testimony that meets the same fate. The psychiatrist then attempts to discuss the man's unrealistic discharge plan, observing, 'He says that his plan is to go home, but his mother won't accept him unless he's in a recovery program . . .' The public defender objects to hearsay, and the testimony is stricken.

On cross-examination, the lawyer presses on some of the behaviors to which the psychiatrist had previously testified: 'You said he was talking to himself in his room. How could you know that if you weren't there?'

'Staff observed it,' he replies.

'And you said that he attempted to go AWOL from the facility?'

'Yes,' again.

'Did he tell you that?'

'No, it's in the records,' the visibly irritated doctor responds.

'I'm going to object to this testimony, which is not based on the doctor's observations or what my client has told him,' the public defender declares. Judge Davis sustains again.

At the end of the hearing, Judge Davis concludes, accurately, that she 'didn't have much here, as I struck the testimony about hospitalizations, cheeking, and going home with family.' She releases the patient.

Here, we can see a genuine incompatibility between the organization of medicine and the requirements of law. The medical system assumes that highly paid specialists can spend a miniscule amount of time with their patients on the premise that staff will fill them in. They rely on social workers to determine if patients' discharge plans check out. But this division of professional responsibility means that psychiatrists frequently cannot meet the requirements under *Sanchez* for providing expert testimony.

Another core check on psychiatric testimony is the mandate that courts "may not consider the likelihood of future deterioration or relapse" in making a determination.[21] Judge Davis's reading of this case law is stringent: "Sometimes there will be evidence that the person has been gravely disabled in the past and even though he or she looks fine now, is stable, things are going well, there's a risk that if this person is taken off conservatorship, the person is going to fall apart in a couple of weeks. . . . That's kind of a tough situation, because the case law, as I understand it, is that I have to look at how the person is today." But therein lies the bind for clinicians: the very success of treatment in making a patient temporarily capable of meeting their basic needs undercuts any attempt to convince the court to allow them to continue treating that patient.

Given this, many conservatorship hearings (like public guardians' investigations) focus on whether the patient can present some minimally plausible blueprint for self-care and whether a psychiatrist, circumscribed in what they can tell the court, can invalidate it. Doug, a veteran county counsel in

Northern California, bragged that "I win 95 percent of the time." In fact, "I've only lost twice, and it was for the same person." Doug's description—which undoubtedly could be read as pejorative—captures how the legal process often seems to set pathology to the side: "He was as crazy as crazy could be. He believed he was really from another planet. He believed there was a mechanical device in his chest that called him to do things he didn't want to do. He believed the president was Abraham Lincoln. But he could articulate very well . . . that he has SSI [disability income] and that he would budget and wouldn't buy filet mignon and run out of money. He was street smart. He was familiar with the shelter system and able to articulate to the satisfaction of the jury that he could provide for food, clothing, or shelter." Doug closed his narrative: "He's been in the system. Round and round. Doesn't take his meds. We'll see him again."

Even taking these limitations into account, there were still cases in which Judge Davis seemed locked into making decisions that, to an outsider, bordered on unfathomable. Ms. Castillo is a young-to-middle-aged Latina who came before Judge Davis for an initial appointment for a conservator. Her soft voice is made even harder to interpret throughout the trial by the choppy quality of her WebEx connection and the fact that her wheelchair seems to be parked too far away from the mic. Her psychiatrist at the county hospital, Dr. Morton, is a psychiatry resident one and a half years out of medical school. She greets the judge with a 'Hi!' so chipper it prompts a guffaw from Andy. Yet Ms. Castillo seems to be benefiting from the greater attentiveness of trainees versus attending physicians: 'When did you last evaluate the patient?' counsel asks. 'This morning.' In fact, she's been seeing Ms. Castillo every morning—and 'sometimes twice a day'—since she was admitted three weeks prior.

Dr. Morton testifies that Ms. Castillo has schizophrenia, has 'no insight,' and has explicitly told her she will not take medication if released. Moreover, she has 'delusions of persecution' from the county's Homeless Outreach Team (which, given their involvement in a hospitalization she didn't want, is not baseless). 'She believes that HOT is trying to poison her, that they are trying to eliminate the "Sisters of the Divine," and that they're taking the form of nurses or police officers to sneak into the hospital.'

The public defender's cross-examination strips basic needs down to a minimum: 'You testified she wouldn't accept food from the HOT team on the outside?'

'That's correct,' Dr. Morton responds.

'But would she accept food from people not from the HOT team?' the public defender presses.

'We're worried she would be paranoid and think they're the HOT team,' she replies.

'So, she would not accept all food, but she could accept some?'

'Yes,' Dr. Morton concedes.

When it is Ms. Castillo's turn to talk, she seems—any paranoia aside—to have been well coached on the crux of the procedure. Before she is sworn in, she states, 'I just want you to know that I can take care of myself.' Still, her plan is less than half-baked. She says she will 'go into long-term housing' and, while waiting, 'the minister from my church will put me in a hotel.' She can't name which church. Her plan for food and clothing is that 'the long-term housing will give me everything I need.' Her public defender, perhaps aware that getting into long-term housing is not so easy, switches to hypotheticals: 'So you would accept help from a case manager if offered?'

'Yes.'

Her lawyer then pivots to discussing Ms. Castillo's plan for addressing her mental health. She might quickly regret the switch: 'Where would you seek mental health treatment if you were released?'

Ms. Castillo replies confidently, 'I don't need mental health treatment, I don't have any history of mental illness, and so I wouldn't go.'

On cross-examination, county counsel brings the court back to its central issue. 'When you were on the streets, what were you doing for food?'

'I asked people to buy it for me,' Ms. Castillo states.

'And you weren't staying in a shelter, were you? You left.'

'No, I wasn't,' she admits.

The public defender jumps in to pose one more question, 'On the street, you were staying in a bus stop?'

'I was close,' she replies. And that is all the information Judge Davis has to weigh this woman's survival against her fundamental civil rights.

Judge Davis starts her explanation slowly and methodically: 'What I have here is a delusion of persecution by the HOT team, that they are going to sneak into the hospital and take away the Sisters of the Divine.' She goes on, 'the nexus testimony'—about the relationship between her illness and her ability to meet her basic needs—'is that she may refuse shelter. Conservatorship is not used to conserve people just because they're homeless. I am very concerned about the homeless. But I'm not convinced that her inability to be sheltered is based on a grave disability from a mental illness. That linkage might seem natural, but the testimony strikes me as a bit tentative.'

The public defender, smelling an opportunity, declares, 'Your honor, may I submit an argument?'

Andy waves her off, sounding incensed: 'The court has already made its decision.'

Judge Davis sighs, and announces softly but firmly, 'The petition is denied.'

Before Ms. Castillo signs off, her lawyer pleads with her, 'Ms. Castillo, if the hospital offers to transport you to a nursing home, you should go, okay? Okay?' No response.

The standard of grave disability is supposed to exclude people with "unusual or nonconformist lifestyles," the kind of eccentrics or deviants that critics argue involuntary treatment is deployed to repress.[22] What frustrates psychiatrists,

TABLE 6.1 Key LPS case law

Conservatorship of Chambers	1977	Determinations of "grave disability" must "exclude unusual or nonconformist lifestyles."
Doe v. Gallinot	1979	Requires a "probable cause" hearing to authorize continued detention within four days of a 5250.
Conservatorship of Early	1983	A person is not gravely disabled if they are "capable of safely surviving in freedom with the help of willing and responsible family members, friends, or third parties."
Conservatorship of Benevuto	1986	Grave disability must be identified based on a person's current state, not a "perceived likelihood of future relapse."
Riese v. St. Mary's Hospital	1989	Patients subject to civil commitments must have a separate hearing on their "capacity" to refuse medication before they can be involuntarily medicated.
Conservatorship of Guerrero	1999	A person can be found gravely disabled if they "lack insight . . . does not believe he or she needs medication and will not take medication without supervision and as a result will be unable to provide for his or her own basic needs."
People v. Sanchez	2016	Experts may testify only about direct observation or conversations with a patient; generally precludes testimony based on the medical record or third-party observations.

families, and sometimes judges and lawyers themselves is that Ms. Castillo's situation—sitting in a wheelchair by a bus stop, sometimes accepting food— doesn't seem like a lifestyle nor, given her psychotic symptoms, a choice. But in the end, Dr. Morton's cultural authority to diagnose the woman as medically gravely ill did not translate into being able to convincingly define her as legally gravely disabled.

TOO SICK TO LOSE

At the risk of whiplash for the reader, I want to emphasize that, for all these legal protections and their exacting application by some judges, the vast majority of people for whom a petition for conservatorship is filed by the public guardian are conserved. The public defenders and public guardians from more than two dozen counties I spoke to estimated that the proportion of cases that go to trial in which petitions are granted ranges from 70 to 100 percent (and remember, as many as three-quarters don't go to trial and are granted automatically based on a conservatee's "consent").[23]

One explanation is that, in some counties, the public defenders don't use *Sanchez* to limit testimony. Some judges seem unconcerned with the complexity of showing a "nexus"; being homeless and mentally ill is enough. Another is that public guardians do their jobs correctly. "In our county, they [judges] know when we bring a case, it meets criteria," one guardian told me. "We don't bring cases and go in front of the judge to say, 'Ehh, it could go either way, he's annoying the cops, so we filed just in case.'"

Even when conservatorship may be legally warranted, many hearings still unfurl as what sociologists call a "status degradation ceremony" that brings about the "ritual destruction" of the once autonomous subject and their replacement with a pacified object, someone whom sovereign power has consigned to a social death.[24] The hearing for Ms. Johnson, a Black woman confined in a county hospital, begins with its own twenty-first-century ritual: technical issues. Initially, the doctor appears to have called in from a cell phone, with no video; the public defender objects, declaring, 'My client has a right to confront the witness.'

When Andy proposes rescheduling, the public defender insists, 'No. I've received many calls from Ms. Johnson. She's been waiting for this hearing for a long time. I'd like to request the petition be denied.'

'That seems harsh,' Andy replies.

Ms. Johnson, at this point, starts talking loudly into the microphone, 'I've never been in no hospital in my life, I want to go. I'm ready to leave. I take my meds and everything . . .' The public defender, the county counsel, and the psychiatrist are haggling over a trial date, and the woman begins crying in the background, 'What about being discharged?'

When Judge Davis indicates that she's likely to summarily deny the petition, the psychiatrist suddenly discovers that she might actually have access to a video connection (I'd speculate she finished driving and got to the hospital). She comes on-screen and testifies to a litany of problems: Ms. Johnson experiences hallucinations, reacts to internal stimuli, and is 'abusive' toward staff. She refused medication until she was ordered to take it (through a separate court procedure called a *Riese* petition). As for her self-care, 'she hasn't taken a shower since she was admitted' and 'can't even transfer herself from a bed to the wheelchair using a lift.' Her plan to live independently is 'not realistic. She is bedbound, she has no plans for her meals or coming to her medical appointments.'

The public defender rises to defend her client, but I can see why it's unlikely to be convincing: 'What is her physical condition?'

'She is morbidly obese,' the doctor replies.

'So, she doesn't require a wheelchair for paralysis or anything like that?'

'No, but she can't walk.'

When it's Ms. Johnson's turn, the public defender guides her testimony, but only gently. 'Do you need conservatorship?'

'No,' the woman shoots back.

'And what would you do if you were released?' she asks.

'I would go to Miami.'

'Do you mean Miami, Florida?' her lawyer queries, hopefully.

'I have no idea,' Ms. Johnson responds. 'I've lived forty-eight years on my own, I can do things for myself.' The woman states that she has no mental illness but takes her meds every day—and doesn't need them.

'Can you tell us what meds you're taking?' her attorney asks, opening an opportunity for Ms. Johnson to show a bit of insight.

'I've got the brown pill, the purple pill, and the green pill.' County counsel doesn't bother with questions.

Judge Davis asks if there is a 'closing argument' and the public defender states, unenthusiastically, that 'I will just note for the court that she does not want to continue this conservatorship.' Judge Davis declares, rapidly, that the public guardian has shown grave disability 'beyond a reasonable doubt' and that the 'least restrictive placement' for Ms. Johnson is a skilled nursing facility.

'Oh wow, oh wow . . .' Ms. Johnson sobs.

'Take care,' Judge Davis closes.

CONCLUSION: BLINDED DISCRETION

What I see in Judge Davis's courtroom is a straightforward application of the law—as she reads it. That law is strict. But when she rules against conservatorship, it often seems less a product of the rigorous standard for grave disability than the mediocrity of psychiatric expertise. When I ask Judge Davis about Ms. Gonzalez, the woman whose case started this chapter, she expresses her exasperation: "I wish I could get better testimony from the doctors. All this doctor said is that she was paranoid and she talked to herself. That was really pretty much it." At least this doctor was present for the hearing. One of the most common reasons conservatorship petitions get denied, it turns out, is that physicians fail to show up to testify.[25]

Then again, you don't need great cultural authority to see that the people before the court are often really, really impaired. Like the public guardian, the other key public institution in the continuum, courts can only exercise discretion in the small fraction of cases brought before them. Police, ERs, and hospitals have expelled so many people from the continuum that, once a petition reaches the courts, hearings often seem like another step of rapid people processing rather than a delicate balancing of health care and civil rights. As one public defender told me, 'I've been doing this for seventeen years. Some people, I've seen them so much they're like family.' She sighed, 'I used to be able to win [and get them out]. Now, they're just too sick.'

Despite the lack of authoritative evidence, Judge Davis feels Ms. Gonzalez's woolly survival plan is determinative. She declares, 'Based on the testimony today, I find that the public guardian has met its burden [to show grave disability beyond a reasonable doubt]. I'm granting the conservatorship. Take care and thank you.'

Ms. Gonzalez is expressionless. The hospital turns the camera off, and she disappears into the world of mostly private chronic-care facilities that are the centerpiece of the next part of this book (figure 6.1).

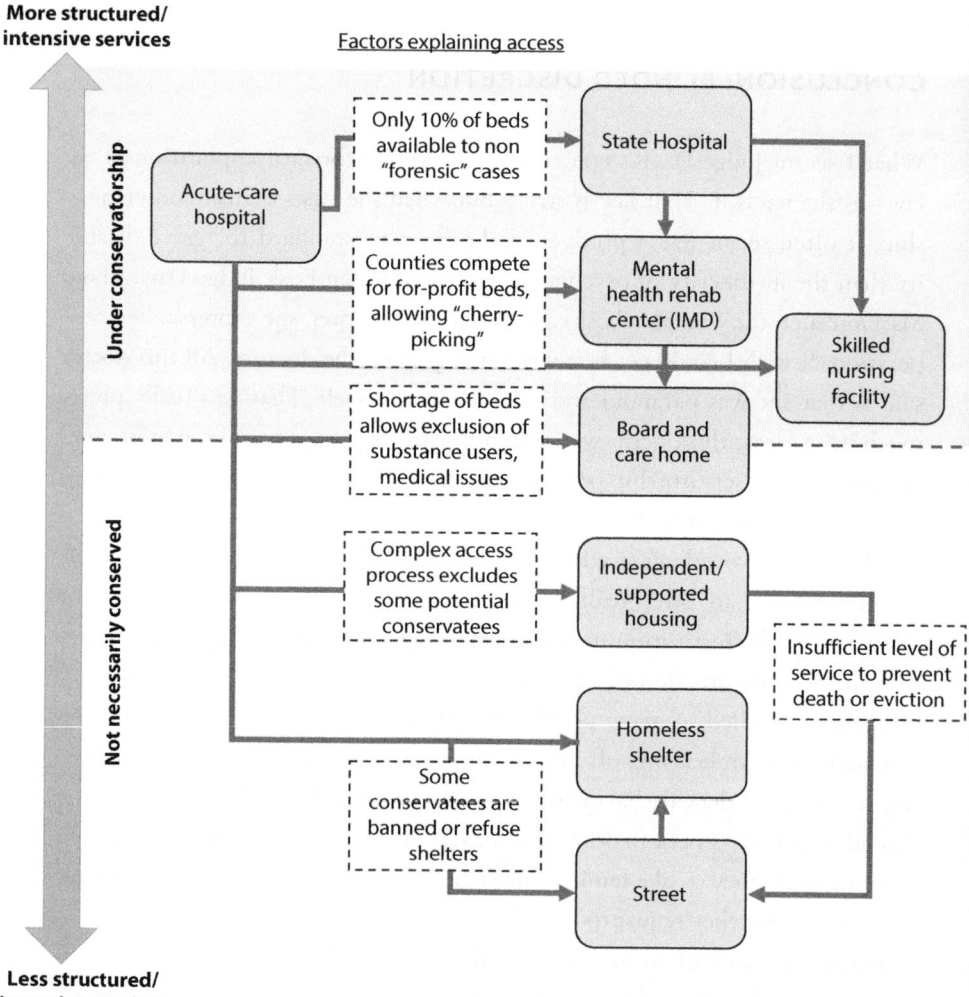

6.1 The placement continuum

PART II

CARE AND COERCION UNDER CONSERVATORSHIP

CHAPTER 7

LOCKED IN

The first time I visit a locked Mental Health Rehabilitation Center (MHRC)—colloquially known as an IMD (Institution for Mental Disease)—I'm almost in tears. So, too, is Kristen, a nurse from a county health department touring it with me, albeit for almost exactly the opposite reason.

IMDs are sometimes referred to as a community placement (in contrast to a state hospital) for conservatees. This one is at least an hour's drive from the community where most of its residents come from (two hours by public transport). It's an inauspicious place. You have to look carefully at the vine-covered fence around an exercise area out back to realize that it's topped with barbed wire. When I pass through the sliding glass doors, I'm greeted by a reception area that might welcome me into a dentist's office. The next door, though, is locked. It keeps more than one hundred people behind it, sometimes for years at a time.

My host is Simon, the facility's manager. "When I grew up, this was not on my list [of careers]," Simon tells me. He started in food service for institutions like nursing homes and eventually jumped over to administration. "One day I got a call from a woman who said, 'How'd you like to work in mental health?' and I said, 'probably not,'" he recounts. But he went for the interview and, somehow, "fell in love with it." He should have retired five years ago, "but I didn't want to." There's an incongruity to how he describes the people he works with, one that I encountered frequently at the most restrictive wing of the mental health system: "Our clients are people who . . . made bad decisions for whatever reason, had a tough life, been abused for lots of reasons, a lot of domestic violence"—and, he adds, "are very sweet to be with."

The ward itself has the wide hallways and linoleum floors of a nursing home, which makes sense, because it used to be one. What gives the IMD a vastly different feel from the nursing facilities and inpatient units I've visited, though, is how quiet it is. The IMD has no staff psychiatrist. Instead, it contracts for physicians to meet each resident once every two weeks. Federal regulations mean that people in IMDs cannot receive mental health services paid for through Medi-Cal, which means there are no licensed therapists coming in for one-on-one sessions. Most of the activities are groups on anger management or living skills put on by "program counselors," who, Simon explains, are "uncertified people who would otherwise be working at McDonald's."

The single study I could find on IMDs identifies the vast majority of people in them as having a history of violence.[1] I don't feel remotely unsafe. Residents are shuffling through the wide corridors, largely alone, largely silently. Some are sitting in spartan rooms with not much more than a locker and a divider between two beds. There's an activity room with some empty plastic deck chairs around a TV. I get the impression there aren't a lot of visitors, because people start clustering around us. One tall, middle-aged man with scars across his face comes to shake my hand; another man tells me he, too, is a professor, as he gazes intently over my shoulder.

'You've got to see this,' Kristen tells me; a young woman has shown her a notebook of poetry with titles like "My Incarceration" and "Locked Up." It's at this point that Kristen announces, "I'm not crying, really," explaining away welling tears. I don't say anything, but I figure we feel the same way. An IMD seems like a really sad place.

IMDs are usually the first stop for a conservatee after an acute hospitalization.[2] This is the point where a careening trajectory through the conservatorship continuum slows down dramatically. Treatment is measured in months and years, not hours or days. The difficulty of getting someone into an IMD weighs on the mind of almost every decision maker upstream. When I ask Simon about admissions, he pulls open a filing cabinet stuffed with folders: "We get ten or twelve of these referrals a week!" he announces.

"For how many openings?" I press.

"None. All the beds are always full."

Counties contract with IMDs to get access to a certain number of their beds, but the IMD can refuse any referral as too dangerous, too unstable, too noncompliant, or too medically compromised (sometimes, tragically, from conditions like diabetes that are side effects of medications). Almost all IMDs are run by for-profit companies, and in California it's a seller's market for locked, sub-acute care.

Simon's company mostly manages nursing homes. But it has realized that IMDs are a lucrative business. Sure, Medicare might pay a nursing home eight hundred dollars a day, while counties pay this IMD only three hundred dollars. "But you can't fill a nursing home, they're always 70–80 percent full," Simon explains, while "here we have a waiting list of seventy people." Plus, in a nursing home, "the feds are always coming to do an audit and are going to take the money back" for violating regulations or for "adverse outcomes." To drive home the point, he pulls out an enormous binder: "These are the regulations for nursing homes." He then prints off the regulations for MHRCs. There are seven pages.

Counties are clamoring for new IMDs, and his company is obliging with a new two-hundred-bed facility. And that's why I felt like crying. I had been hearing about the desperate need for more access to IMD beds for conservatees. I feel intense admiration for Simon and his team. I believe him when he says he loves the residents. But when I finally see an IMD, I realize we're clamoring for people to shuffle between injections for months.

It turns out, though, that Kristen is almost-crying for a different reason. "That's so great," she comments when Simon mentions the new facility. Everything is relative. Kristen helps run the county's programs for board and care homes and supported housing, which are supposed to provide the less restrictive alternative to locked facilities. Yesterday, she tells me, she consoled a caseworker who was having an emotional breakdown about a resident going in and out of the hospital every couple of days.

"The client refuses to be in a higher level of care. . . . Last time, we found him in the bathroom, defecating on himself, blood sugar over 700 [an extremely dangerous level], almost in a coma. He's thirty-one and going blind. So, what do we do?" she asks.

"How many of those folks should be living independently?" Simon muses.

"None of them," Kristen concludes.

"For some people, this [an IMD] is just better and safer," Simon comments, while Kristen nods. One of this IMD's residents has been safely here for twenty years.

Getting people into long-term care is, in theory, the point of conservatorship. As the courts have recognized, "one of the principal powers which the court may grant a conservator is the right to place a conservatee in an institution" like an IMD.[3] It turns out that this is an overstatement. Authority is actually fragmented among public guardians (who sign off on placements), county mental health departments (who pay for them), and private institutions (who exercise discretion in which conservatees they take). The almost wholesale delegation by the state of the locked part of the conservatorship continuum to private entities have given those entities the upper hand in determining where and how conservatees get served—and, as this chapter concludes, who gets conserved at all.

THE LAST ASYLUMS

Well, hold on. There's one place that conservatees can get long-term care in a locked setting that definitely does not make them a delegated, for-profit responsibility: the state hospital. Despite the narrative that Governor Reagan closed the state hospitals circa 1967, California's Department of State Hospitals is a two-billion-dollar-a-year, 13,000-staff behemoth.[4] In fiscal year 2021–22, its five hospitals' average daily census was 6,920 (up 50 percent since its nadir in 1989).[5] This makes it the largest state hospital program in the country (which is unsurprising for the largest state) and the fourth largest relative to population (which is less obvious for those convinced that California is uniquely underequipped for inpatient care).[6]

In most cases, the route into those beds is not an LPS conservatorship. As California turbocharged its criminal-legal system in the 1990s, mass incarceration spilled over into the state hospital system. Over time, people deemed incompetent to stand trial, found not guilty by reason of insanity, committed as sexually violent predators, and transferred from the state prison system came to constitute nearly 90 percent of the population (the national average is closer to half) (figure 3.1).[7] That leaves all of about seven hundred beds for gravely disabled conservatees.

The actual criteria for accessing those beds are opaque. None of the wary public employees working in state hospitals would go on the record to explain them to me. When I asked public guardians what the typical profile was, they often reached for the most extreme examples: a client convinced there were spider eggs in his neck, who spent all day in four-point restraints to keep him from clawing them out; a person so paranoid that he thought a state hospital guard was a ghost and who cut off his penis to be transferred to a medical facility and escape him. A less dramatic way to characterize the population that state hospitals serve is people who combine multiple challenges that, even on their own, would be difficult to address: treatment-resistant schizophrenia and serious comorbid medical needs; deep trauma and a developmental disorder; cognitive impairments from substance use and a history of violent behavior.

Even for people who seem to fall into many of these categories, the pathway into a bed is arduous. Counties used to be able to buy access to a certain number of beds and decide who got one. Now there's a common waitlist controlled by the state. One inpatient psychiatrist told me that "state hospitals are basically not an option" while another dismissed, "state hospitals? You might as well just forget it." Dr. Cai, a psychiatrist at a county hospital in Northern California, expressed the desperation of waiting for patients she had concluded could not be appropriately treated by her acute hospital unit to be transferred: "We have weekly meetings with the county [mental health department's] 'Transitions Team.' . . . It's ridiculous because they don't have any news for us: 'He's number forty-two on the Napa [State Hospital] waitlist.' Well, he was forty-two three months ago."[8]

The backlog is getting worse. California has seen an extraordinary rise in people found incompetent to stand trial (IST). These individuals, charged with a crime but deemed unable to participate in their defense, are referred to state hospitals to be "restored" to competency.[9] The spike in IST referrals (driven by well-intentioned efforts of public defenders to keep mentally ill people out of prison) is a startling window into the failures of California's county-run mental health system. According to state data, 84 percent of these individuals have a psychotic or mood disorder, 46 percent have sixteen or more prior arrests, 47 percent were unsheltered homeless at the time of their alleged crime, and nearly half received no mental health services through Medi-Cal six months prior.[10] Some commentators are convinced that this group is condemned to forced treatment in the criminal-legal system by the strictness of laws around civil commitment.[11] Throughout this book, I have also pointed to resistance among community providers to treating these sorts of individuals, who might have co-occurring substance disorders and are disproportionately poor and nonwhite.

In May 2021, Governor Newsom proposed addressing the growing IST waitlist by shutting state hospitals to LPS patients entirely within three years. A range of stakeholders, led by the County Behavioral Health Directors Association, had an understandable conniption. They observed that local facilities (most of which are private) "have the option to accept or deny mental health patients," meaning there are often "no suitable or willing" providers for the "high-risk populations" at the state hospital.[12] Most local facilities can't even get a license to take sex offenders. As one state hospital doctor quipped, "We're the end of the line."

Dr. Howie, who works in a state hospital's LPS unit, confirmed that his patients are not just clinically complex but also unwelcome elsewhere. This is not only why they go to the state hospital in the first place but also a barrier to their leaving (and thus a roadblock preventing other patients, lingering inappropriately at an acute hospital, from coming). He opined that at weekly team meetings, "The social worker will say, 'We've applied to this place, this place, this place' and I can put in my notes that the person is ready to go, but the limiting factor could be those other facilities." I'll discuss blacklisting and cherry-picking by private providers later in the chapter, but he saw both starkly: "They [private facilities] might look at a person's history and say, 'This person is not able to come here because they did such and such back in the day.'" It was, he said, tragic to tell patients who had battled for months to get better that they would stay at the state hospital, arguably the system's most constrictive level of care, for lack of an alternative.

The pushback to the governor's plan to shut state hospitals to LPS patients was successful, and he withdrew his proposal. But the saga goes on. In June 2021, an appellate court ruled that the state had "systematically violated the due process rights of all IST defendants" who remained stuck in jail while waiting for a spot in the state hospitals.[13] It ordered that all such cases be admitted to the hospital within twenty-eight days of being found incompetent. LPS conservatees would have to get to the back of a line that had swollen (according to interviewees involved in the process) to more than two thousand people. LPS conservatees wait more than a year on average for a level of care that their physician and a judge deem necessary but that neither acute-care hospitals nor county mental health departments nor public guardians have the authority to actually get for them.[14]

Even when beds are available, counties must pay the state to use them—at a cost of more than three hundred thousand dollars per year. Public guardians all reported that state hospitals remain an essential piece of the continuum, where around 3–5 percent of their most challenging conservatees are placed, sometimes for many years. But the rest don't move up into the most public part of the continuum. They step down into an almost entirely private world of locked IMDs, to which we now turn.

BUYING BEDS IN A SELLER'S MARKET

Advocates for deinstitutionalization from state hospitals envisioned replacing them with a robust system of voluntary, unlocked community-based care.[15] In practice, they got IMDs. The story behind that clunky moniker, Institution for Mental Disease, is a little dry. It is also essential for understanding who exercises power directly over conservatees (it's not public guardians) and who has authority over the conservatorship system.

When Congress passed the Social Security Act Amendments in 1965, creating Medicare and Medicaid, it included a provision barring Medicaid funds from going to IMDs. An IMD is a facility with sixteen or more beds, of which the majority are used to treat people with "mental diseases" who are between the ages of twenty-one and sixty-four.[16] The legislators' intent was clear: they didn't want the federal government picking up the tab for the hundreds of thousands of people shut away in state hospitals nationwide.[17] Medicaid's IMD exclusion may have contributed more to deinstitutionalization than civil rights lawyers, pharmaceutical discoveries, and community-care programs combined.[18]

In the 1970s, private entrepreneurs started offering California a (fiscally) great alternative to organizing and paying for custodial care in state-run facilities.[19] In 1973, the company now called Crestwood Behavioral Health created a skilled nursing facility with a "special treatment program" for chronically ill people on conservatorship. Nursing facilities could bill Medicaid so long as they claimed that most residents' principal diagnosis was something other than mental illness.[20] In 1987, the feds realized this was a scam and required California to pay back some of the money. This left the state on the hook for both state hospitals and these IMDs. In the 1991 realignment reform, which further divested the state from responsibility for constructing a coherent continuum for conservatees, it passed costs for both entirely onto counties.

Because state hospital beds at the time cost the counties nearly five times as much per year as an IMD,[21] the delegation of responsibility accelerated counties' efforts to get LPS conservatees out of state hospitals.[22] Enterprising companies like Crestwood were increasingly rebranding these facilities as Mental Health Rehabilitation Centers (MHRCs), not just warehouses. (Most people still informally call them IMDs.) Cynics disagree. Betty Dalquist, of the nonprofit California Association of Social Rehabilitation Agencies, insists that most people going into IMDs could be in unlocked placements if counties showed a bit more financial commitment and imagination.[23] To her, MHRCs are just "nursing homes with fewer nurses." Indeed, explained one IMD administrator, the logic of turning a nursing home into a "rehabilitation center" is that "instead of having two nurses, you could have one nurse, which lets you take that money and hire three recovery coaches." This hints at the wages and credentials of these coaches (if not their quality and dedication).

That brings us to today. California has about 2,000 beds in MHRCs and 2,100 in psychiatric nursing homes.[24] State government has thoroughly abdicated responsibility for financing and structuring this part of the continuum. Medi-Cal cannot be used for IMDs, and the 2004 "millionaire's tax," or MHSA, cannot go to involuntary programs. So counties pay for IMDs out of the limited pot of tax dollars they get through 1991 realignment. Virtually all IMD beds are run by private for-profits (figure 7.1). These businesses have managed to expand even as waves of austerity have closed nonprofit providers of unlocked residential treatment and tightening insurance regulations have shuttered acute-care hospitals. Counties have occasionally tried to set up their own IMDs, but the costs of unionized public staff make delegating them out much cheaper.[25]

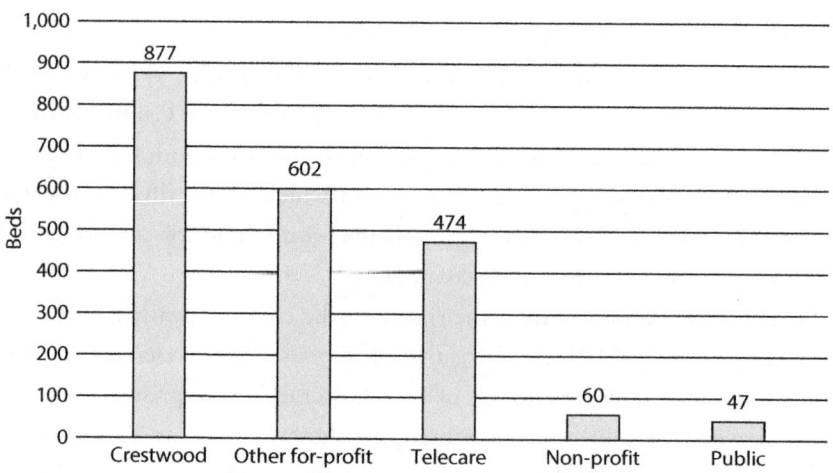

7.1 Owner/operator of Mental Health Rehabilitation Centers (MHRCs), 2022
Source: Department of Healthcare Services

And here's the kicker: counties compete with each other for these limited spots. An anonymous representative of one of the two main IMD providers, Crestwood and Telecare, insisted that they don't let counties bid against each other. But there's plenty of documentation of this long-running practice: as early as 1985, San Francisco was throwing in an extra fifty dollars a day to snap up nursing home beds for conservatees in neighboring Santa Clara.[26] Jon Sherin, the former mental health director from Los Angeles County, was not apologetic when I asked him about it. "We are the 800-pound gorilla, we can get people's attention," he told me. "We are going after facilities saying, 'If you've got eighty beds, we want them all, and we'll keep them full.'" I pressed him on whether this created a zero-sum battle between counties, whereby one's conservatees got into the appropriate facility at the cost of another's conservatees being stuck in inappropriate ones. He replied, "We're not bullies . . . We have 30 percent of the population, but 50 percent of the need. So don't tell me, 'It's not equitable.'"

This system of contracting with private providers makes public guardians feel, correctly, that they lack authority over where conservatees end up. County departments of mental health negotiate the contracts and hold the purse strings. A deputy public guardian in one large, rich, and stingy county recounted, "We tried to get a contract with [IMD], it has a recovery model [and] they care about their clients. I got my boss to agree to take a tour. But we didn't [get the contract], because [her county] doesn't pay as much as other counties." Her county "lost" six beds in the last year, "and they [the IMD] were clear it's because LA County paid more."

Clearly, this system has losers. For one thing, minnows like Frontier County often can't place their clients in IMDs at all, even if the public guardian, department of mental health, and inpatient psychiatrist all agree it's the right level of care. Meanwhile, private companies build where land and labor are cheaper and community resistance to facilities for a stigmatized clientele is weaker, which means away from the coast. Consistent with the state's general lack of oversight of the conservatorship system, there are no data on where conservatees end up. But many public guardians reported that a majority of their conservatees were placed out of their home county (including 54 percent of San Francisco's, for example).[27] Josephine, the guardian in one coastal county, reported she had "conservatees as far north as Sacramento and far south as Long Beach."

This dislocation of conservatees inland is probably inevitable; it's happening to disadvantaged people with and without schizophrenia throughout the state.

But contracting makes it worse. One public defender lamented, "We have a locked institution with 120 beds, and our county only contracts for four of them. So most people go out of county, away from family and friends, away from their support system, into an environment and climate that's totally different. It's not great. People don't want to get shipped out."

BLACKLISTING AND CHERRY-PICKING

The consequence of delegating IMD care to contracted providers is not just that conservatees get scattered across an immense state. It also gives IMD providers enormous leverage in deciding who to take. On paper, counties have the primary discretion to decide who goes into an IMD. I reviewed Santa Barbara's contract with Crestwood, for example, which states that Crestwood "shall admit clients to Contractor's programs unless compelling clinical circumstances exist that contraindicate admission." But everyone I talked to, on either side of the IMD admissions process, agreed where the real veto power rested. "We are at the mercy of the operators," one public guardian put it. It's one of the purest illustrations in the continuum of authority as the capacity to give exclusionary reasons: IMDs can say "no" to a given client and that's enough for the county to have to look elsewhere.

People generally go to IMDs when they've been repeatedly unable to stabilize at other levels of care. Dr. Fazio is the medical director of an IMD in Northern California. He's an institutional psychiatrist through and through. He worked in a county hospital, a jail psych unit, and a state hospital. He has been a vocal advocate for LPS reform since the very first time he saw "patients who were released where I was in shock, getting calls from loved ones, 'Why did you let them go?' and I'd say, 'I didn't let them go, the [judge] let them go,' 'Well now they're in jail, I'm going to sue you.'" He has never understood "this idea of allowing someone who is so mentally impaired to make their own decisions and then having them end up in the criminal-justice system." He'd like to see someone's first hospitalization for a psychotic break last at least a month, followed by the slow, structured rehabilitation program his IMD offers.

The morning we speak, he's dealing with a case that, he tells me, captures both the need for IMDs and patients' chaotic trajectories into these facilities. The patient is a twenty-six-year-old child of Nepalese immigrants with a degree in microbiology and philosophy. "Shortly after graduating, she had a bipolar break, believed she had a religious awakening, and needed to spread Buddhism throughout the world," he recounts. In the space of eight months, she traveled from India to Kenya, gave away all her money, had fifteen hospitalizations, and deliberately got herself arrested for burglary to help bring Buddhism to inmates of the Los Angeles County jail. "The bottom line is, here is a bright young woman who was having a psychotic break, this is an emergency, like a heart attack of the brain, and yet she had to go through fifteen really ineffective hospitalizations"—they usually lasted about a week—"and two jailings before the inpatient psychiatrist finally said, 'Enough is enough, they need to go to the [IMD].' But it's only after these repeated failings." Her parents had even hired a private attorney to pressure the county to push the conservatorship through.

Dr. Fazio made it sound as though it's just obvious that someone like this would be admitted if referred to an IMD. But when I spoke to an occupational therapist who worked for more than a decade in an IMD run by Crestwood, I realized there are a host of reasons even someone with a very serious mental illness might be refused entry. When she looked at a hospital referral, she would make sure that someone continued to have severe symptoms even though they were "taking their meds, compliant with all treatments." For example, "if they're diabetic, are they compliant with their finger sticks?" She would also like to see that "they're not punching walls, beating the shit out of anybody, cutting themselves, hanging themselves, for at least two weeks."

All these criteria make sense. IMDs don't use mechanical restraints, generally can't physically force medication, and expect residents to participate in as much as thirty hours a week of group therapy. But a situation in which IMDs obligate someone to show their stability for weeks before admission is "onerous . . . unrealistic . . . arbitrary and exclusionary" toward many people with chronic mental illness.[28] Such criteria almost guarantee that an insurance company or county will deem someone too stable to be in a hospital—thus cutting the hospital's reimbursement—during the three to six months, on average, they wait for an IMD bed.[29] Hospitals have a reason not to rush it, though, because IMDs also have the discretion to send someone back if a person commits a violent act or refuses medication.

From Teresa Pasquini's perspective, many IMDs are engaged in "cherry-picking" from a pool of applicants within which, admittedly, everyone is seriously ill, but some more so than others. Her son has been on an LPS conservatorship for twenty years, but it hasn't kept him stable enough to prevent forty 5150s and repeated sojourns in IMDs. After one long stay, he was discharged to an outpatient provider. They failed to give him his injection, and he was hospitalized again. At this point, she explains, "my son had 'bombed out' of several Crestwood Facilities and they said, 'Nope, he can't come back.'" Getting a bad rap with Crestwood is a bad deal, since the company controls 43 percent of IMD beds in the state (figure 7.1). It's particularly a problem for people who live in Northern California, like Teresa's son, where Crestwood's market share is even higher.

So the acute hospital sent him to the only place that would admit him: Napa State Hospital. Teresa said a state hospital was "everything I was trying to avoid" in years of advocacy, and he was stuck on the inpatient ward ninety days waiting for a bed. Still, the state hospital managed to stabilize him. They even convinced the one Crestwood facility he hadn't been to and with which her county contracted to come take a look. "His case manager thought he was ready to go, his conservator thought he was ready to go," but the representative of the company declared, "No, we think you need a little bit more time." For Teresa, it was the prime example of the risks of "hav[ing] private companies like Crestwood and Telecare monopolizing this whole thing": "The private organizations get to decide, 'Nope, we're not taking you, you don't look good on paper,'" she sighed. Her son was so frustrated, she says, that he "acted out" against staff, got arrested for felony battery, and spent the next four years bouncing between solitary confinement and the forensic wing of that same hospital.

Ultimately, Teresa convinced her county, Contra Costa, to send her son to an independent IMD, California Psychiatric Transitions (CPT), and after that, Psynergy, an unlocked residential treatment program. To get him into the latter, she had to convince her county to make an exception and send him to a facility with which they did not already have a contract (most parents probably don't have the access to decision makers and wherewithal to do this). When we talked, Teresa said her son was one of Psynergy's "stars" and about to start college. To be clear, both CPT and Psynergy are private and for-profit. Psynergy has a mission of taking clients that have been blacklisted everywhere else and finding ways to get seemingly undischargeable people out of locked settings. If you want to see the power of entrepreneurialism, think about these facilities' owners taking on mountains of debt to start programs for people the state hospitals want to get rid of, counties want to farm out, and nonprofits don't want to touch.

I am not the only one wondering why private IMDs get to exercise so much control over what happens to conservatees. Rick Weiss, the psychologist in the Los Angeles County jail who spent years trying to get formerly incarcerated conservatees into IMDs, observed, "What I've found shocking over the years is that there's not some kind of county-run IMD that doesn't have those kinds of issues [cherry-picking], compared to an IMD that's run privately and can make decisions without anybody taking all that much notice." The reason is partly that publicly run facilities cost more, and partly that companies like Crestwood have built up a genuine expertise in treating this population. Still, counties like San Francisco are increasingly considering having their own dedicated facilities because competition for contracts between counties "often leads to delays in client placement and a lack of transparency about those delays."[30]

Even without a revolutionary seizure of the IMD industry, you could imagine a more rational system. I asked a state official about the issue, and she replied, "This is a question that we're posing right now to counties, 'Why, if you're contracting with IMDs, doesn't the contract require that certain people be taken?'" She understood, of course, that the fear is that if a county becomes too demanding, IMD operators will "just run to the hills" and either go out of business or only serve less exigent counties. If only there was some government entity, hovering over the counties, that could bring order to this delegated system.

THE HUMAN LOGJAM

When a judge signs a conservatorship order, they also determine what level of placement is the least restrictive appropriate option. That order is no guarantee someone will get there. Instead, the conservatee gets to take a proverbial number and enter a "human logjam" of suffering bodies waiting for locked beds.[31]

Judge Rojas described how it looked from his vantage point: 'The first place that people tend to go on conservatorship is a locked IMD. Those beds are just completely filled up. When people are ready to leave that locked setting and go to a board and care, the beds are incredibly oversubscribed. . . . So that means you then have people in acute psychiatric hospitals who can't move. . . . And at the top of the food chain, you've got people that are in psych ERs that have been sitting there for weeks and months. . . . The whole system is just incredibly backed up and doesn't allow people to be in the setting they're supposed to be in.'[32]

I'm going to close this chapter by reflecting on how this drives discretion throughout the continuum.

This human logjam means that many conservatees are in restrictive levels of care in direct defiance of court orders. You might think this gives law some authority to get medicine (and bureaucracy) to take action. Some public defenders told me they would demand repeated "placement hearings" and ask courts to hold counties in contempt for not getting their clients out of acute hospitals fast enough.[33] But Doug, a lawyer who represents a county on the receiving end of these complaints, told me the courts knew there was nothing he could do: "It's not only 'most appropriate' and 'least restrictive placements,' it's also the 'available placement.' . . . [The court] can't expect us to place someone in a place that doesn't exist. What do you do? The legislature needs to be building more facilities. I'm not a legislator."

Public guardians are also taking the logjam into account. One told me bluntly, 'If there is no availability of an ongoing treatment facility, our office will refuse conservatorship until the [county] department of mental health gets that in place.' Although there is no reliable topline number for the state, many individual counties reported that, as the number of (largely private) acute-care hospitals that make conservatorship referrals and the (almost entirely private) subacute institutions that conservatees go to have closed, the number of LPS conservatorships has fallen to match. The public guardian in a large southern county reported a one-third decline in conservatorship referrals in the past decade and insisted "the reason . . . is strictly that there's no place for people to go." The number of conservatorships in San Francisco declined 21 percent from 2012 to 2017, just as the availability of long-term care in the city collapsed.[34]

Earlier in the continuum, inpatient psychiatrists applying for conservatorship are balancing the same considerations. Dr. Cai, working in a public Bay Area hospital, admitted, "We always weigh the realistic limitations of the system. Like where is the patient going to go once we put them on conservatorship? Are there any places for them to go? A lot of times, there aren't." As such, "I wish I could be idealistic, 'We put everyone who meets criteria on conservatorship.' . . . But you think down the line, 'All the facilities will have a waitlist of three to six months, and in the meantime, the patient is going to be in the hospital, waiting.'" That last line is important. She might decide the ideal option would be for someone to go to an IMD, but when the choice is between forcing someone to stay in an acute-care hospital—an environment that is absolutely not designed for deep healing or quality of life—and letting them go back to the streets, the less cruel option might be the latter.

And, to take us all the way back to those streets, the police are also learning from experience who is and who isn't likely to find a placement further down the line. Lieutenant Reid from LAPD reflected on why her officers were 5150ing people who were acutely dangerous and needing short-term stabilization while driving by those who were dying on the streets: "We could scoop up people with minimal effort that very much meet that criterion [grave disability]. My kids could probably say, 'Wow that person should have some help.' A lot of these are obvious. But where do they go? . . . How do we ensure they're not back here in three days? How do we get people help that's of any longevity? . . . We don't have an infrastructure to support and serve that community."

Let's revisit the social model of grave disability. In chapter 4, I quoted a report from Los Angeles cataloging the county's lack of alternatives to inpatient hospitalization. This meant that some people are being classified as gravely disabled not because of their internal pathology but because of a lack of services that they could access without being classified as gravely disabled. That same report also recommended that the county triple its stock of IMD beds (by adding three thousand).[35] In one sense, this analysis implied that there are three thousand gravely disabled persons in LA currently not conserved because there is nowhere to put them. If you look at it from a social model, though, you flip the relationship: currently, those three thousand people—whatever psychiatric state they are in—are not gravely disabled, because the institutions that would make that label meaningful don't exist.

CONCLUSION: DELEGATION AND THE DECLINE OF PUBLIC AUTHORITY

This chapter should drive home two recurring points. The first is that, whatever the statute says, grave disability is defined by economic and bureaucratic forces. The state abdicated its role in ensuring long-term care for conservatees by downsizing state hospitals and converting them to serving a forensic population. IMDs thus became the destination for most LPS conservatees. The number of IMD beds, in turn, reflects a mix of Lyndon Johnson–era federal Medicaid legislation, the funding formulas of realignment (created to deal with a 1991 state budget crisis), and a monopolized market for twenty-four-hour care dominated by an offshoot of the nursing home industry. There has been no government leadership to match the number of IMD beds to the number of people who are unable to provide their food, clothing, or shelter as a result of mental illness. There is no evaluation as to whether those individuals benefit from IMD care.[36]

The second point is about the distribution of power in the conservatorship continuum. Reforms to expand conservatorship are predicated on the assumption that public guardians have the capacity to transform an expanded definition of grave disability into more people being conserved. It also presumes that they can use their placement power to put those conservatees somewhere. But guardians' control over conservatees on paper does not extend to authority over the conservatorship system. The institutions that exercise sovereign power to intern conservatees for years at a time are paradoxically private entities over which sovereign governments have surprisingly little leverage.

Tod, the guardian in Northern California, described how his many years in the job had made him modest about what he could do. "We come across as the ones who have the, quote-unquote, 'legal authority' to put someone somewhere, but the Behavioral Health Department is the one who hold the purse strings," he observed. His years of experience gave him a strong sense of where would be best for his clients, but he could not overrule the people handling intakes at the IMD. He sighed, "This creates problems, it creates strife, but I will say that after fifteen years of battling those battles, I've sort of given up and decided we don't have the authority that we're given legally." When California decided that the keys to placements would be held by private providers and the budgets to pay for them controlled by another agency, they abdicated Tod's authority for him.

CHAPTER 8

STEPPED DOWN

I'm on a tour of a fifty-four-bed board and care, the Guest Home, in Southern California. Cindy, the facility's psychologist, is explaining the facility's "token economy." Residents get thirty-five points for going to a "group." With forty points, they can buy a Diet Coke at the facility's commissary; with fifty, they can skip the aspartame and get a regular.

George, a white man who looks to be in his fifties, shows me his notebook. He has 300,000 points. Any way you do the math, 300,000 points means that George has been at the Guest Home a very, very long time. With the fortune he's amassed, he could buy out the entire commissary—a small closet with a rack of clothes, cups of noodle soup, toiletries, and a fridge with baloney and yogurt—except that Cindy has been limiting him to two purchases at a time.

She's been working with George on his behavior in other ways, too. When I meet him in the activity room, George launches into an intense recounting of how he took his accumulated five-dollar gift cards (you get one if you go to five groups in a week), bought a hat at a nearby strip mall, and tried to return it: 'They sold me a hat that was from Vietnam, I only wanted one from Malaysia, I told them, "I have my rights . . ."'

'Yes, you do have rights,' Cindy interjects, 'but there's also appropriate behavior.'

She proudly tells me that, ultimately, he returned and used the interpersonal skills he had learned in one of the thousands of groups he has attended to get a refund.

There are several observations to make here. The first is that George is lucky to be in a board and care that has programs and a token economy. Alan, who has been the administrator at the Guest Home for thirteen years, proudly tells me, "We provide a higher level of care than most board and cares do." The Guest Home has a unique partnership with the local Department of Mental Health to provide case management and psychotherapy in-house.

"Our hospitalization rate is a lot lower than anywhere else," Alan tells me, explaining "in most board and cares, the activities are just bingo or arts and crafts—"

"Whereas we have process groups, codependency groups, anger management, interpersonal groups," Cindy elaborates.

Alan goes on, "Our ultimate goal here is for someone to move out on their own and become independent and a productive member of society. Does that happen?"

He answers his own question: "Not very often."

That's the second observation that I make on my visit: for someone like George, the Guest Home is home. "We're a fifty-four-bed family," Alan tells me, observing, "we have clients where their families live [in the same city] and they don't see them. Every year, we do a big Thanksgiving meal, because they're not going to go home." There's no doubt this is closer to what many of us would recognize as a home than an IMD. Residents' (shared) rooms are chock-full of their possessions; most have phones, and many have computers with internet. Cindy tells me they discourage sex between residents, but it happens, which is why the commissary has a big box of condoms. Most important, this is a home people can leave; the front door is unlocked, and people can spend the day outside walking around (in a suburb far from the city center).

It is, also, a particularly institutional kind of home. While the front door is unlocked, I realize during my tour that life within the Guest Home is pretty restricted. Clients have to ask for a key to go the showers, so staff can keep tabs on who is taking care of their "activities of daily living." Clients can do their own laundry, but the soap, too, is locked. We walk past a "med room" filled with filing-cabinet-like drawers and a woman sitting in front of a tray with a few dozen paper cups. The woman is calling out names over the loudspeaker, 'Natasha, *wake up*,' 'Dan, *it's time for meds*.'

My third observation is that George may never get to spend the nest egg he's earned through the token economy. After our tour, we are joined by Joel, who owns this board and care as well as a network of nursing homes for seniors. I had been hearing about how board and care homes in California were closing en masse. Clients' social security disability (Supplemental Security Income, or

SSI) checks, the home's main source of financing, have not kept up with a rising minimum wage, workers' comp costs, and the temptation to sell off buildings that, given the spike in property values, could be put to more lucrative uses than housing people with schizophrenia. So I throw the question out there: "I hear a lot that the industry of board and cares is collapsing. So how are you able to provide such a higher level of service?"

Alan quips, "By losing money."

Joel provides a slightly more thorough explanation, but it's basically that. The facility used to have seventy beds, but "we were forced to reuse a portion of the building for a higher and better use," which was expanding the nursing home next door. He catches himself: "That doesn't sound right, because we were helping the clients, but a different use. That helped to right-side financially the collective operation, but things have become more and more difficult." I can see that, in front of his staff, Joel is being careful: "I'm not patting myself on the back, but other operators would have abandoned this type of program a long time ago. . . . This brings so much meaning to me in my life. But there gets to a point where you can only be so charitable. Losing $20,000 a month . . . only the government gets to do that."

Indeed, it's a sense of rejection by local government that is so frustrating. In the past year, the mental health department pulled the plug on the clinical program the board and care was running, leaving Joel on the hook for covering the enhanced services the Guest Home had been providing. Alan, the manager, has been trying to take advantage of a county program to provide augmented funding for particularly serious clients, but there are delays in getting approvals. Joel has the impression that county government "is so focused on the homeless, they're redirecting their funds" to pay for shelters and supported housing. This is, we all agree, a ludicrous robbing of Peter to pay Paul: "The sexy thing is to talk about homelessness, without acknowledging that ARFs [adult residential facilities, the formal regulatory name for a board and care] closing will contribute to homelessness, because so many of our clients, if not for us, they would be living on the streets."[1]

There's a lot to criticize about board and cares. My hackles certainly rise when Joel reminds me, "These are businesses. It so happens that the product involves human beings, people taking care of people, but it's business."[2] But then I retell myself how much money he has been losing to keep this business going. Whatever the motives of their owners and operators, board and care homes provide a service no one else in California's mental health system seems particularly interested in: custodial care for people who, even after thousands of sessions of group therapy, may still not be able to live independently. Board and cares have been delegated an essential role by the failure to develop any alternative.

Board and cares like the Guest Home are frequently the point where the conservatorship continuum ends. Conservatees in IMDs typically step down into them. Most public guardians reported that at least half of their clients were placed in board and cares. This is the level of care at which some clients will be stable enough to come off conservatorship and others will, at the very least, require no more than a once-every-three-months check-in from their public guardian. When conservatorship gets someone into a board and care, it has succeeded in "enabling individuals who would otherwise be long-term residents of psychiatric hospitals to live in the community and achieve a considerable measure of autonomy in their lives," as two psychiatrists optimistically put it decades ago.[3]

But that continuum can loop back. Clients depart through the unlocked doors of board and cares and decompensate. When their fragile equilibrium breaks, clinicians like Cindy fight, often unsuccessfully, to get them back into the hospital. And if and when places like the Guest Home close, these individuals wind up back on the streets—the very insalubrious situation that put some of them on the conservatorship continuum in the first place. This chapter is about the risks of delegating care to private institutions that the market might decide should no longer exist.

BORED AND THE STATE DIDN'T CARE

There's a typical pattern when I bring up board and cares. The person I'm speaking to decries the sorry conditions within them. In the next breath, they mourn that these sorry structures are rapidly closing. This is no paradox. California's negligence toward board and care homes goes hand in hand with its dependence on them.

It has become a common trope that the deinstitutionalization of state hospitals happened as an unplanned, pell-mell dash for the exit.[4] This is not entirely fair. Starting in 1938, the California Department of Mental Hygiene created a Bureau of Social Work. It cultivated a network of small boarding homes to support discharged patients, who would also continue receiving care in state-run clinics.[5] The head of the bureau in El Monte, outside Los Angeles, explained, "What we're seeking primarily is not houses but people [to run boarding homes]. We need warm, loving women. . . . Perhaps older women whose children have grown up and flown the nest, or younger ones with small families who are interested in providing a community service."[6]

The situation changed in 1963, when people with mental illness became eligible for Aid to the Totally Disabled (which in 1972 morphed into SSI).[7] This, in the words of sociologist Andrew Scull, "transformed mental patients into a lucrative commodity" for a new, unabashedly for-profit industry.[8] Community resistance pushed board and cares into low-income, minority neighborhoods.[9] Economies of scale led them to grow from small homes into large institutions.[10] As the *Los Angeles Times* fretted in 1972, the attempt to "put an end to 'warehousing' at state hospitals ended up creating scores of miniature 'warehouses'" that operated as "poorly-staffed, poorly-equipped miniature mental hospitals."[11] By 1980, this system of "privatized malign neglect"[12] housed 35,000 people with mental illness statewide.[13]

Since then, the main public policy California has maintained toward board and care homes is no policy at all. The state eventually closed the Bureau of Social Work on the assumption that counties would pick up the slack in organizing ongoing residential care for a chronically ill population. They didn't.[14] While state government kept responsibility for licensing these facilities, the Departments of Public Health, Mental Hygiene, and Social Welfare all spent years arguing that doing so was not in their purview.[15] Board and cares are not just the cheapest place to put someone with a severe and chronic mental illness (figure 8.1). They're also almost entirely paid for by a federal entitlement program (SSI). As a result, they were often the last structures left standing when state and county governments slashed funding for other mental health programs.

Low funding, minimal oversight, invisible and dependent people, and the profit motive: a cocktail for cruelty. Until recently, the board and care industry has been visible only in moments of spectacular abuse. In 1985, investigators from the Department of Social Services visited an eighty-three-bed "home" where residents were "filthy, unwashed, and dressed in grimy clothing," living amid "rodent droppings and spoiled produce swarming with flies" and sleeping on mattresses "so filthy and roach infested that the state team ordered [them] destroyed on the spot."[16] In 1995, the state closed down a home where "one schizophrenic man beat another to death" while the seventy-three-bed facility's lone staff member

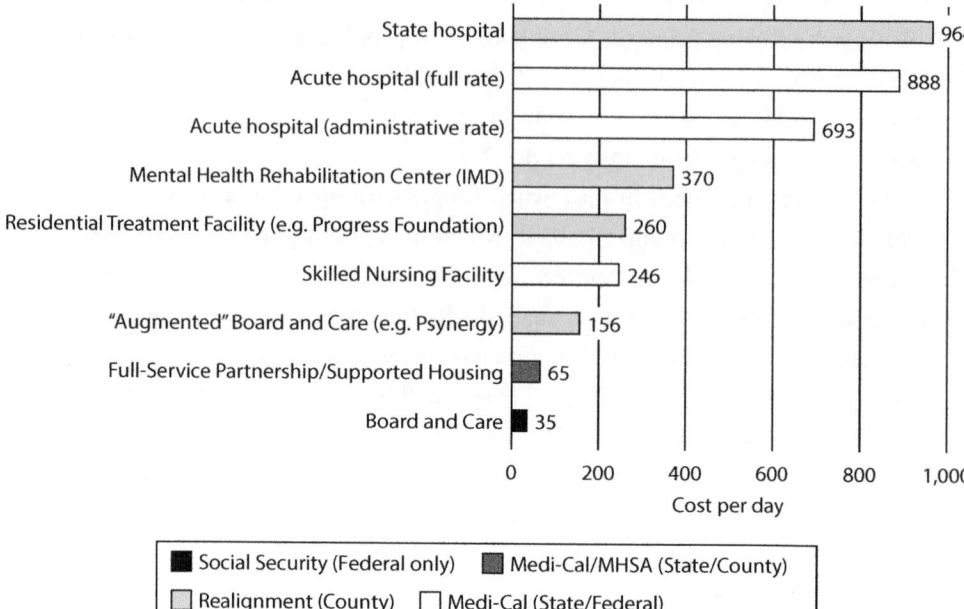

8.1 Estimated costs of 24/7 care, 2022

Source: Department of Healthcare Services; Department of State Hospitals; county contracts
Note: Costs of programs vary by facility and region.

was washing dishes.[17] One home in Long Beach accumulated years of citations for unsanitary food, thefts from residents by staff, and an overdose death. County mental health officials only stopped referring clients there when a staff member was killed.[18] Occasionally, policy makers floated proposals to better fund or more carefully regulate board and cares, but delegating responsibility for the most chronic individuals was too convenient to risk upsetting.[19]

This abdication of any active government role in organizing the "care" in the board and care system is apparent in individual facilities. My interview with Saul, the owner and operator of one ninety-bed facility in Southern California, eventually turned into (in his words) a "therapy session." He told me, "My facility is an older facility. It's a bare-bones facility. Your mother would not want to live here." Pre-COVID, they tried to have the occasional activity, but "my residents don't have an attention span of more than a minute. You can try something, but they're highly schizophrenic, they walk in circles and smoke all day. They don't want to do anything else. They don't socialize, they don't talk to anyone." He returned to self-flagellation: "An outside person can critique me all they want, and I would say, 'You're 100 percent right.' But what do you expect for thirty-five dollars a day?"

Thirty-five dollars a day is what you get when you take a resident's social security check, give them four dollars a day to cover personal expenses, and hand the rest over to an operator. Operators are charged with transmuting that into food, lodging, supervision, assistance in taking medication, housekeeping, transport to medical appointments, and, if residents are lucky, "activities." I ask Saul how he's surviving on this paltry rate. Much like Joel (the owner of the Guest Home), he replied, "I'm not. I owe the landlord over $350,000 in rent. I haven't paid myself in three years." While SSI benefits have barely kept up with inflation, the minimum wage he pays his staff, the workers' comp policy he has to purchase, and, more recently, extra hygiene precautions in response to COVID have pushed his expenses through the roof.

When Saul confesses that taking over the business from his mother-in-law in 2006 was the "worst decision of my life" and that "the day I walk away, which is very soon, I will never turn back," it's no idle threat. He had another hundred-bed facility that investors agreed to renovate and turn into a high-end drug treatment facility—on the condition that the current residents leave. "We vacated them, they all ended up homeless or in the hospital," he admitted. He's unapologetic: "I have gone to every public forum, I've gone to the city council, I've gone to the board of supervisors and I yelled and I yelled and I yelled" about the need for more funds, to no avail. Before COVID hit, he was negotiating to "basically shut it [his remaining board and care] down and lease it out to some homeless shelter that pays fifty-five dollars a day, and they don't provide any care, any food, any medications, or anything."

Saul is, comparatively, a holdout. A report from Los Angeles in early 2018 observed that board and cares were closing at an "alarming rate."[20] Four years later, 38 percent of board and cares beds serving adults with serious mental illness in the county had, indeed, disappeared.[21] Some owners have sold off their smaller six-bed homes to make luxury dwellings for millennial tech workers.[22] Others have emptied and refilled larger facilities with people living with developmental disabilities, addictions, or experiencing homelessness.[23] After all, the state and counties have taken a direct interest in housing these populations, often paying two to four times as much per day as SSI.[24]

CONTROLLING THE FRONT DOOR

As always, I was curious about how these financial forces shaped who winds up where in the continuum. Back in the 1990s, a series of exposés revealed that some board and care operators in Los Angeles were snatching people off of Skid Row or abducting them from their competitors to fill empty beds.[25] The ongoing catastrophic collapse of the industry has one clear upside for operators like Saul: they not only don't have to worry about open beds but can be choosy about who fills them. Private board and cares, like IMDs, can cherry-pick clients who are referred to them by county hospitals, community mental health teams, or court-ordered diversion programs. Saul feels completely powerless in the face of economic and policy forces beyond his control— but for individual admissions, he has enormous discretion.

He gets, he told me, "twenty referrals" faxed per day from "every hospital" and has one to two openings per month. He prefers not to take people with depression because they "sleep the whole day." He won't take anyone with a serious suicide risk because he had a resident die by suicide and it was "living hell" even though "there's no way to prevent suicide." He'll make an exception for someone who was hospitalized as a danger to self for "running in front of traffic" because "that's a really weak" attempt. The other operators I talked to had their own preferences. Lucas, who owns another large facility, said that he stopped taking referrals directly from hospitals because they were discharging people too quickly: "at thirty-five dollars a day, it's really not worth the risk of bringing someone [with repeated hospitalizations] in." Saul is a bit more forgiving. He won't take someone with five 5150s if every time it was because "he slapped the staff, spit at the staff, broke windows [in a placement]," but if those five are "because he was gravely disabled, which means he was just living on a park bench and not taking his meds," he'll take a chance. He reckons, "I know I can get him his meds four, five times a day to keep him stable." For another operator, whether or not someone showered regularly in their IMD was a key metric of whether they were ready for less structured congregate life. The point is, the owner of a board and care is sovereign over whom she or he serves.

Some of the informal admissions criteria are consistent. Saul, Alan, and Lucas all screen out people whose primary issue seems to be substances (which, according to Saul, is a lot because "the entire California homeless population is on meth. That's just a fact"). Lucas elaborated his reasoning: "I would say 60 to 70 percent of my residents have a dual diagnosis history . . . [but] I have a big population here that has been sober, so one seed can create havoc really quickly." He's a realist: "There are a few that still go out and have a beer behind the liquor store, and I 'don't know about it,' but I know about it." And he'll make exceptions to help the county outpatient teams with which he has a good relationship. But you can quickly see why ER clinicians, hospitals, and public guardians might be reluctant to advance people further along the continuum if they seem more substance user than psychotic: there's a void of step-down options for them, which means they could get stuck upstream in the human logjam of acute-care hospitals and IMDs.

Another population being squeezed out of board and cares by declining availability is people with comorbid medical conditions. At one forum on board and care closures held near Sacramento in early 2018, a social worker from a small, rural county stood up and griped, "We only have one place that takes SSI in our county. I know the guy who runs it very well. . . . He gets to be so picky and so specific because he's the only one. He can practically choose based on the color of someone's hair. And he can certainly say, 'No one with a walker because I just put in new floors.'" As always, there's a financial logic here that, like it or not, is pretty inescapable for facilities operating on a tight margin. "If we need to check someone's blood pressure or give them an insulin check, I can't take them unless they're on Medicare, because it covers for a nurse, and Medi-Cal does not!" Saul told me. He is the all-purpose bookkeeper, handyman, and activity coordinator for his facility, but he's not a nurse and, by regulation, is not allowed to pretend to be one.

Board and care owners get a bad rap. Some certainly deserve it. But while these facilities might look like the place in the continuum where naked capitalism has completely displaced public service, owners are still basically street-level bureaucrats. They have an essential mission for a needy population and not nearly enough resources to meet that need. So they triage. Unlike a county clinic's staff, owners are paid only whatever is left from the pot of resources they have to dole out for operating costs. Given that one report estimated that the average thirteen-bed board and care loses $255,688 a year, it's easy to understand why owners just quit.[26]

BOUNCING UP AND SLIDING DOWN

While the board and care industry is in free fall, individual board and cares are usually where conservatees stabilize—or, less generously, stagnate. One report from Los Angeles profiled an eighty-bed facility where 50 percent of people had been there five years or more. This is an impressive tenure for a population that previously might have been cycling among shelters, hospitals, and the street. Seventy percent of those individuals were receiving no therapy.[27] Once someone gets into a board and care, then, they often become what Neil Gong calls "lumps": people from whom little progress is expected and for whom little service is provided.

Some board and cares really do offer more "care," but this usually depends on the willingness of a county to use its own funds to pay a facility that could otherwise be left to survive (or starve) on federal SSI funds. Alan, the manager of the Guest Home, again vaunted his facility as a standout: "Most [board and cares] operate like a retirement community, people are on their own and all staff is helping with is medication management. We don't operate that way." Having therapists and groups on-site is a way for the facility to avoid crises, as Cindy explains: "We have qualified professionals who are able to spot things. . . . We can say, 'so and so seems a little off,' 'so and so isn't taking her meds.' And we work together to maintain stability." More robust treatment helps avoid two ways this supposed end point of conservatorship can circle back: being bounced up to higher levels of care or dropping down toward no care at all.

Let's start with those bounced up. Conservatees are frequently a small portion of board and care residents: the operators I spoke to estimated between 10 and 30 percent.[28] Lucas said that he preferred conserved clients because, for residents suspended just above social death, "it's nice when someone else is involved." It also helped him keep residents in line: "I have one resident who doesn't want to take any medication. So I say, 'Here's the options: I can call the conservator, they'll send you to the hospital, or you can take your meds, and we'll be okay.'" This is, in theory, one of the conservator's mightiest powers over conservatees. Welfare and Institutions Code section 5358.5 states that "when the conservator . . . deems it necessary to remove his conservatee to the county designated treatment facility"—that is, an acute hospital—"the conservator may take the conservatee into custody and return him to the facility."[29] Potent stuff.

Except that a public guardian's official power is sapped by their lack of authority over other actors, none of whom is playing by Welfare and Institutions Code section 5358.5. When I asked Saul whether he saw a conservatorship as a plus for his residents, he exclaimed, "It doesn't make a difference." He recounted the story of one conservatee who "broke six windows" before the cops came. He complained, "They did not want to do anything with him. The guy [resident] said, 'I'm not getting on the gurney.' I said, 'Put him in handcuffs,' and the police said, 'We're not going to do it.'" He, like a number of providers I talked to, was not on board with the police's growing reticence to use force to impose a 5150. He went on, "Do you know what happened? He broke four more windows, ran around, beat someone up in the parking lot, and then got arrested."

Eventually, the client went to the hospital for five days: "It was just like a time-out," Saul bewailed. "Going back to a board and care" is an easy discharge plan for hospitals: "I go down to the hospitals all the time. I bring [hospital staff] Starbucks, bring them cakes, bring them lunches, I know all the case managers. . . . But certain hospitals, they don't care what you say. They'll just [discharge them and] drop them off [at the board and care] with an Uber, and you're done."

More frequently, the pathway from a board and care back into a more structured institution happens not from an acute crisis but via a downward slide toward death. Lucas proudly told me that his facility had kept alive clients who, upon arrival, seemed as though they would have a tragically short stay. But the very forces that kept residents psychologically stable also led to physical decline: "I think the longevity of taking certain meds really has an impact in terms of onset of dementia, some side effects like tardive dyskinesia"—involuntary movements such as grimacing and eye blinking—"and just making them a lot more frail."[30] He reflected that "50 percent of my residents have been with me more than ten years. The reality is that the only reason why they're moving is that they need a higher level of care, in terms of oxygen, or their [activities of daily living] can't be dealt with—bathing every day, feeding, etcetera."

Unlike bouncing people back up to a psychiatric hospital, the trajectory into a nursing home is smooth. Lucas recounted, "Usually what happens is we'll send the patient to the [medical] hospital and, in coordination with the medical doctor at the facility, they'll run a series of tests and at that point we'll make a decision about whether to bring the resident back. I have one lady who really just didn't get out of bed and wasn't doing well, she didn't want to eat, she was losing weight." Once her blood pressure dropped low enough, they sent her to the hospital against her wishes. The hospital transferred her to a nursing home. Lucas told them, "'If she is able to come back, she can come back,'" but, he said, "the reality is she won't come back."

THE END OF THE LINE?

State-level discussions sparked by the collapse of board and cares usually pay lip service to the idea that they are temporary way stations toward greater independence. But such step-downs are vanishingly uncommon. Lucas told me, "I rarely have someone move out of the facility who has been with me a long time. I would say that is something that happens, maybe, once a year." He was happy to report that "I had one lady who gave me thirty-day notice, she's lived with me eighteen years, and she's just doing so well . . . that her family has said, 'We want our sister to come live with us.' . . . I'm sad to see her go."

I asked Alan about whether he thought the higher level of services they provided residents meant that more were able to move on. He admitted that aspiration often clashes with reality: "We hope to get the low functioning [people] into moderate functioning, but we all know that's not realistic. So, what we do is provide programming that will at least get their mind going. The number of people that end up moving out on their own is very, very low. In the twelve years I've been here [in a seventy-bed, then a fifty-four-bed facility], we've had seven or eight move out on their own." Cindy adds, "And they did not do well." Once you recognize that board and care homes are homes, a long length of stay moves from a sign of failure to a metric of success.

A more common way out is via eviction. Alan insisted to me this was really a last resort: "I'd rather not do evictions because that means I'm giving up. I don't want to give up. It's the hardest thing you could do." The last person he evicted was pregnant. Both he and the conservator agreed that the Guest Home was no place for a person with a baby. For clients with behavioral problems or drug use, he explained, they would try to devote extra staff time to them or make staying contingent on attending their Recovery Anonymous group. One of Alan's best tools, he said, was to expose clients to the execrable conditions at other board and cares: "I tell them, 'Look, if you don't want to comply with the rules, your choice, you're welcome to go elsewhere' and it's amazing how quickly they straighten up, because a lot of them have been to other board and cares." Sometimes he'll even propose, 'Let's drive you over, take a look around, see if it's a fit . . .'" They usually decide to stay.

Still, a board and care is not a locked facility, it can't force medication compliance, and for every recalcitrant resident, there are dozens of people waiting for a bed who might be more pliant. Saul again: "If we have someone that does drugs, or we can't meet their needs, I give them an eviction notice. We have a resident that doesn't want to pay rent, that's too destructive, it happens. The number one thing is—if you're not med compliant, you can't be here. I don't care how much rent you pay . . . I know it's their right [not] to take their meds, you can't force anyone to take meds, and our house rules state, if you don't want to take meds, that's okay, you can't live here. If the doctor writes the order, you have to take it." People in board and cares have rights and freedoms, but exercising them has consequences.

In the end, more residents seem to leave of their own volition than are pushed out. Charlie, who headed up the Full-Service Partnership team at the UMH clinic profiled in chapter 1, observed, 'We're fighting harder and harder to get our clients into substandard housing that doesn't want our clients.' He reported at one weekly meeting how he had spent months begging board and cares to take a client with multiple evictions and hospitalizations. The day after he got in, 'he high-fived the operator and walked out.' As always, this might have stemmed from a lack of insight and an unwillingness to comply with treatment. Or it might be because, for a grown adult, being housed but living on four dollars a day left over from an SSI check may seem less dignified than having the whole check and being homeless.[31]

I've seen a range of board and care homes. One that I visited, which served primarily veterans (who receive much higher disability payments), had a small movie theater and a fountain in the courtyard. Another was depressingly decrepit. The walls were bare because, the owner told me, residents would tear posters down or crush cigarettes on them. The cafeteria was sweltering, but the windows were too rusted to open. Flies buzzed around an open trash can in the pantry used to store rice, next to a few boxes of wilted produce donated by a church. There was a cement patio in back; it used to have trees providing shade, but the owner uprooted them to get rid of rats. A few residents sat around a metal barrel in complete silence, smoking.

Everyone seemed bored. Beyond the owner, a first-generation immigrant desperately struggling to stay open, and some community members trying to turn that empty lot into a small garden, I'm not sure anyone cared.[32] Leaving might not be good for the residents (or the public guardians that put them there), but I couldn't blame them if they decided just to walk out.

CONCLUSION: COLLAPSING CHRONIC CARE

Many lament that the United States has no comprehensive national policy guaranteeing universal health care. But it has no long-term care policy at all, much less a guarantee of it.[33] Usually when the state abdicates, families are next in the line of succession, left picking up the tab for nursing or in-home care for aging relatives.

California's state government has been lucky that the nonpolicy for organizing residential care it adopted after closing state hospitals has been partly compensated for by private entrepreneurship. Operators' ability to make do with small but steady SSI payments from the federal government rendered board and cares resilient, compared to other mental health programs that expand in moments of state largesse and shrink when austerity strikes. These facilities have been places where conservatees can be subject to abuse (the topic of the next chapter) or sites of stability or even a stepping stone to recovery (discussed in the chapter after that).

In any case, this suboptimal solution to chronic mental illness may be nearing its end point. At a 2019 forum held in the state capitol, I heard an unpublished estimate that one-fourth of adult residential facility beds [including board and cares] in California had closed in the previous five years.[34] The state has suddenly taken interest, promoting new legislation to improve tracking of closures, finance improvements to dilapidated buildings, hike the SSI rate to forty dollars a day, and give counties first dibs for buying up private facilities that are closing.[35] Jon Sherin, the former director of the Los Angeles Department of Mental Health, led LA's aggressive efforts to save board and cares. He told me it's time to recognize that they are "permanent housing for certain populations. 'Congregate living' is not a bad word for people with profound illness and fractured families, who aren't going to do okay in a permanent supported housing unit with some social worker who comes once a week."

These efforts may be too little, too late. Saul tells me that when he gets off the freeway each morning for a twelve-hour day, he's "sick to my stomach. It's not because I don't like my work . . . I love my residents. I can't look at them and say, 'Hey, you're going to be on the street one day.' I can't tell them that." But, he admits, "it comes to the point where there's helping other people, and there's helping yourself . . ." He said the other operators are "hoping, hoping, hoping" that the state will salvage their businesses model, but, "I'm telling you, there is no hope."

CHAPTER 9

NEGLECT AND ABUSE

Among the people interviewed for this study who have lived through conservatorship, Florence took one of the hardest lines against it: "I don't understand why people involuntarily commit other people. . . . It hurts on all ends. It hurts the relationship with the family, it hurts the relationship with superiors, with authority. It just puts [the conservatee] deeper inside of a sinkhole that gets harder to get out of every time." People with mental illness shouldn't be "punished" by years under conservatorship. They "need some place to reform, as opposed to some place to rot, locked away like criminals." Whether or not you agree with her, after hearing her story, I hope you empathize with why she says "abolish[ing] conservatorship" is the number one change she'd like to see in the mental health system.

Florence, now thirty-seven, says she grew up in a "very strict, authoritarian household." She laments, "[My mother] kept me isolated . . . I couldn't have that connection [with peers] I wanted in my early childhood and teens." At age fourteen, she started experimenting with marijuana and alcohol until, at age sixteen, she moved to party drugs and meth. Her mom never believed in mental health treatment. When Florence told her near the end of high school that she wanted to be a psychologist, her mother replied, "Psychology is a quack profession."

When Florence was in crisis, her mother instead turned to the police. One evening when Florence was seventeen, "My mom and I were fighting, and she was hitting me, and I had nowhere to go. So I grabbed a knife, I put it to my throat, and I said, 'If you come near me, I will kill myself.' I didn't mean it, I just wanted her to stop hitting me." Her mother backed off. Florence drove to her friend's house. The police found her there, discovered she had a knife, and took her to a "suicide ward" in a private psychiatric hospital.

Kate, profiled earlier, recounted her first hospitalization as an adolescent with ambivalence, remembering both humane treatment and an ever-lurking threat of violence. Florence recalls it with horror: "I was shocked to be there. The girls were taking the screws out of the doors and cutting themselves in the stomach. Then they were offering them to me." She stayed a couple of weeks, then they "gave me a whole bunch of suicide pamphlets and let me go." Her mom was not helpful with aftercare: "She was like, 'Don't take those meds, you don't need them, don't go to therapy and tell all our business, you don't talk to nobody.'" Nonetheless, Florence made it to community college and was studying prelaw until, in her last semester, she had "a mental meltdown" filled with racing thoughts and paranoia. She was twenty-three and having a psychotic break.

The next few years were a chaotic mass of hospitalizations and stints in drug rehab. 5150s were, for Florence, another weapon in her mother's arsenal of abuse: "One time, I had a glass of water and my mom's boyfriend grabbed me . . . and I was pushing past him, and the water got everywhere, and he called the police and said, 'She's elder-abusing me, she threw hot water on my face.'" The police took Florence to the hospital, "and they were like, 'Did you have a glass of water?' and I was like 'Yeah, I did,' and they said, 'Aha, so you admit it!'" Florence might as well have been describing a wrongful criminal incarceration: "I felt like they were trying to trap me" into agreeing with the "charges" against her.

Her experiences taught her that "mentally ill" is a form of stigma that, as sociologist Erving Goffman put it, is "deeply discrediting."[1] If her mom called the police and said Florence was sick, they assumed Florence was the problem: "I could say, 'This person hit me, here is my bruise,' and they say, 'She hit me!' and I'm the one with the bruise . . . but I'm always the one at fault." As someone who's mixed race and disabled, she feels doubly at risk when anyone calls the police on her while in crisis. Other patients in the hospital taught her to "memorize a passage in case you come into contact with law enforcement: 'Please don't shoot, I have a mental health disability, I'm seeing things.'"

Florence has been to enough hospitals to have seen okay ones and abominable ones. She wound up in a facility where the kids of celebrities could stay in wards that looked like a log cabin and had access to a coffee machine. In another for-profit facility, the cruelties were flagrant: "The staff was pitting patients against each other in fights. I was told to fight my roommate, I did it, I won, and they gave me a treat. . . . And it was just crazy, they were really mean to us there." She read in a patients' rights pamphlet that she was allowed to make phone calls, "but they monitored your calls . . . and they'd hang up the phone and say, 'She's not getting any calls for a week!'" Her conclusion was that "a lot of these places don't take mental health seriously; they just see it as a business."

As Florence lived it, conservatorship is a form of punishment. People are conserved when they've been "hospitalized so many times within a certain period of time, like nine times in six months or a year, there's a quota" and they get "red-lighted." Eventually, Florence found herself in an IMD with her mother as a conservator. It's hard to overstate, as author Esmé Weijun Wang puts it, the "absolute terror that coincides with not knowing when, or if, you will get out of such a place."[2] It's for that reason that some people compare the indeterminacy of conservatorship unfavorably with time-limited incarceration in the criminal justice system.

Florence claims staff told her she didn't seem like someone who "belonged on conservatorship" or in an IMD. She was locked with dozens of people with severe mental illness, but felt she "couldn't carry on a conversation with anyone . . . I felt so alone." Every time she talked to her mother about it, "she would threaten me, 'If you get off this conservatorship, I'm gonna make sure you live in the streets.'" Meanwhile, though, Florence was making progress. I've derided IMDs so far, but to her it was much better than a hospital: "[the hospital] had really basic like, idiot groups. They give you crayons, you know?" But the groups at the IMD, which kept her busy from 7 a.m. to 8 p.m., were "very informative, very insightful. . . . They give you first-rate information, life skills—I still have all my notes that I took. . . . I couldn't tell you how much I didn't understand about mental health, and what I learned in the IMD."

She finished the program and went to an unlocked facility. But it took her five years to get off conservatorship. When a forensic psychologist was interviewing Florence for one of her yearly renewals, Florence reported that her mom had been inappropriately sharing her medical information with family members and lying about whether her daughter was living with her. The court dropped her mother's petition for renewal. Thus ended what Florence saw as a state-sanctioned extension of the domination her mother had been exerting since childhood.

It's cold comfort to say this was all Florence's mother's fault, because bureaucrats and clinicians throughout the mental health system enabled the abuse. One could take a small bit of solace from the fact the Florence is doing well, which must take almost unfathomable inner strength and resilience. And, for once, she feels genuinely helped by mental health professionals. Florence says her therapist encouraged her to go back to school, but her mom was once again blocking her. "Have your mom come talk to me," the therapist said. When they met, "I was outside the room, and I don't know what [the therapist] said, but when my mom came out, she had her hand over her heart, and said, 'She [the therapist] is scary.' . . . Next thing I know, I'm enrolled in school . . . and I have a 4.0 average."

Today, Florence resides in a quiet group home with a "live-in mom." She also has an FSP team and "they're great." As busy as they are, frantically running from one client to another, "they always get back to me in twenty-four hours" if there's a problem. She adds, "I am physically active . . . it helps me subside a lot of side effects" from medication, which she takes consistently. "I'm an active student, I participate in clubs, I do volunteer work. I've written to women on death row for Christmastime with one of my clubs at school." After her bachelor's degree, she's planning to go to graduate school—in forensic psychology, of all things.

In the first part of this book, I focused on the way discretion allows agencies all along the continuum to decline conservatorship, and thus responsibility, for individuals in dire straits. So far, in this part, I've emphasized how delegation creates barriers to getting people who are conserved into the facilities that clinicians and judges deem appropriate for them. But this chapter flips the script to talk about what people face when they do get conserved and do get into "appropriate" facilities. There's a story here about active misuses of power, of the kind that cases like Britney Spears's have brought to light. But this chapter adds another consequence of abdicated authority: where a lack of regulation, funds, and faith in people with mental illness leads not just to exploitation and overbearing control but also to neglect and abandonment.

PATERNALISM AND EXPLOITATION

Almost as soon as LPS went into effect, some advocates sounded the alarm that declarations that someone was gravely disabled were serving as a back door to get around the law's new limits. Dr. Francis Rigney, chairman of San Francisco's Mental Health Advisory Board, blew the whistle in the pages of the *San Francisco Chronicle* in 1975, citing "evidence of widespread abuse" of conservatorship, which clinicians and judges were using as a "blanket device to sneak people into custody to enforce treatment."[3] Notably, the highest rates were in counties with large African American populations.[4]

There are, indeed, cases throughout the historical record of what looks like "wrongful conservatorship" (à la Britney Spears): people who wind up at risk of being shut away because of a concatenation of "contingencies" rather than an overriding illness.[5] In 1978, a reporter from the *San Diego Union* interviewed twenty-eight-year-old "Michael P" while he sat "behind five trophies marking him as an outstanding real estate salesman, studiously answering questions about his business success, alternately straightening his tie and pushing his black-framed glasses against his nose."[6] Michael, although it "seem[ed] inconceivable," had been deemed "gravely disabled" by the county public guardian, despite the fact that he was employed and lived with his parents—who themselves opposed the conservatorship.[7] He seemed to be a victim of San Diego county's "bounty system" for conservatorships, whereby the judge colluded with lax defense attorneys, who made seventy-five dollars per three-minute hearing, and board and care homes looking for new residents.[8]

Of course, the long line of victims of guardianship are not chosen at random: they're people the courts, doctors, or society at large find inconvenient, burdensome, or potentially lucrative. In medieval England, the king was "entitled to pocket" the estate of an "idiot" under guardianship, while "keeping him in poverty."[9] Early in the twentieth century, judges in Oklahoma put Native Americans under legal guardianship once oil was discovered on their lands. This "legalized plunder" left "Indian children . . . to die for lack of nourishment because of the heartlessness and indifference of their professional guardians."[10] There are more recent examples. Hillary Moss, an eighty-three-year-old woman in Simi Valley, California, dubbed "Dirty Sally," was a "pack rat with an unrelenting determination to keep a yardful of dilapidated furniture."[11] In 1976, the city jailed her for unpaid fines for code violations and then, in response to public outrage, conserved her. They shipped her off to a nursing home, even though a doctor determined that she "was and still is sane." (None other than Frank Lanterman spoke up that this case seemed to violate the law.)

If you'll recall from the introduction, there are actually two conservatorship tracks in California: LPS and probate. It's not surprising that the abuses that have received the most media attention are of probate conservatorships. The legal protections against these conservatorships are flimsier. Courts can establish probate conservatorships based on "clear and convincing" evidence of someone's incapacity for self-care or financial management, rather than "beyond a reasonable doubt," the higher standard for grave disability (which, itself, is a narrower criterion) required by LPS. A request for a probate conservatorship can be filed by any interested party, and the conservatee has to actively petition to be let out. For LPS conservatorships, the public guardian is required to investigate, file a petition, and renew it every year (table 9.1).

These two types of conservatorships are more or less open to certain kinds of misuse by the nature of the people subject to them. The statutes do not prohibit someone with mental illness from being placed on a probate conservatorship, and some public guardians told me they did so in certain circumstances (such as for a mentally ill person with a large estate). This seems to have happened to Britney Spears, whose probate proceedings started after she was hospitalized via a 5150 for mental illness.[12] But stifling paternalistic control and financial

TABLE 9.1 Comparison of LPS and probate guardianship

	LPS conservatorship	Probate conservatorship
Who can file	Only the public guardian (with petition from inpatient/jail clinician)	Family member; state or local agency (including public guardian); "any other interested party"
Criteria for conservatorship	Grave disability: current inability to provide for food, clothing, or shelter as a result of a mental disorder	Lack of capacity to provide properly for personal needs for physical health, food, clothing, or shelter
Evidentiary standard	Beyond a reasonable doubt (highest standard, used in criminal trials)	Clear and convincing evidence (lower standard)
Population	Mental illness (can also include dementia or chronic alcoholism, but not other substances)	Not specified: generally developmental disability or cognitive impairment (can also include mental illness)
Conservator	Primarily public guardian (can also be family or private professional, depending on county policy)	Primarily family and private professionals (but can be public guardian)
Key powers	Placement in a locked facility; involuntary psychiatric medication; control of disability income	Medical decisions; finances and estate; placement in a "secured facility" (dementia only)
Review and renewal	Must be renewed yearly; can be recontested every six months at request of conservatee	Reviewed every two years by court; conservatee must petition to terminate conservatorship

exploitation—which have become the iconic abuses of guardianship[13]—are usually visited on probate conservatees with intellectual/developmental disabilities and elderly people with dementia, respectively.

Consider financial exploitation. In 2005, a *Los Angeles Times* investigation found that there were five hundred professional guardians in the state, holding legal authority over 4,600 people and $1.5 billion in assets.[14] California stepped in to regulate the budding industry in 2006, but it remains the case that unscrupulous private guardians can file and be granted guardianship at "emergency" hearings with their potential wards not even present. The guardian might then show up at someone's home to announce they'll be moving to a nursing facility, with their assets sold to cover the guardian's "services."[15] These cases almost always involve elderly people alleged to have cognitive impairments.

Paid private guardians seldom serve as LPS conservators. People with serious mental illness rarely have time to accumulate assets that would make them of interest to exploitative professionals, since psychosis typically kicks in at the transition to adulthood.[16] If a person with mental illness did have real assets, they would likely be disqualified from an LPS conservatorship. One clinician involved in screening for a conservatorship program described a woman who is "incredibly dysregulated to the point where she injures herself, severely, in every hospitalization. Dislocating arms, she's flipped a hospital bed, will frequently need to be medically sedated to unconsciousness. Horrendous." Yet, the woman "has a house, she has food, and she has clothing, so we can't do LPS." To the clinician, making grave disability the criterion for conservatorship resulted in "missing a whole subset of people who really, really do need additional help, but have what they need."

There's also a stark difference in the trajectories onto conservatorship between people with developmental disabilities and those with mental illness. Disability rights groups have lamented the rise of a "school-to-guardianship pipeline." They allege that special educators encourage parents to seek guardianship to keep watch over their "forever children" when they turn eighteen.[17] This denies people with developmental disabilities the "dignity of risk": the opportunity to make choices and live with the consequences.[18]

There's virtually no way to have this kind of preemptive guardianship for people with mental illness through LPS. Rather than collaborating with concerned mothers and fathers to construct a pipeline onto conservatorship, many judges, psychiatrists, and public guardians I spoke to believed that part of their role was blocking overeager parents. And many people living with serious mental illness have been granted the dignity of risk (without the dignity of needed support) repeatedly: released from hospitals with little follow-up after winning a probable cause hearing or evicted from supported housing because their psychotic symptoms were too disruptive to their neighbors.[19]

Linda Kincaid is the head of the Coalition for Elder and Dependent Rights. She's been monitoring guardianship abuse in California since her mother was institutionalized, sexually assaulted, and bilked for $250,000 under a probate conservatorship. She told me, "Whatever you call it—probate conservatorship of an elderly person, or limited conservatorship [a variant of a probate conservatorship] of a young person with autism or a developmental disability, or LPS conservatorship for someone who may or may not have mental health challenges . . . [conservatorship] takes someone's civil rights away from them. Makes them less of a person . . . and Britney Spears illustrated that beautifully." She's right that major restrictions of fundamental rights, and the ethical questions they pose, occur across different types of conservatorships. But when we look at the LPS system specifically, a different set of harms come to the fore.

OVERBURDENED AND UNDERSERVING

I raised the question of abusive conservatorships with Scarlet Hughes of the County Public Guardians' and Conservators' Association (CAPAPGPC). Six months after the Spears story made headlines, Hughes had clearly been fielding such concerns unceasingly. She ticked off a series of "checks-and-balances with the public guardian that don't exist in the private sector," like public guardians' independent yearly investigations and oversight from patients' rights advocates (who are paid for by behavioral health departments to provide representation and respond to complaints).

These public agents' capacity to protect conservatees, though, is sapped by raw fiscal realities. There is no direct state support for public guardians and, as one report concluded, "across the board, public guardianship systems are underfunded."[20] This has predictable effects on public guardians' caseloads, their offices' ability to recruit and retain staff, and the rhythm of their contact with clients. Although some public guardians proudly describe themselves as helicopter parents, many conservatees wind up closer to latchkey kids.

You met Tod, the public guardian of a wealthy northern county, in a previous chapter. He is pleased with the intensity of supports he offers to LPS conservatees. In contrast to some counties, "we actually do everything for our clients, we manage finances, medical, psychiatric, all of that." He has many clients in board and cares, who require more regular check-ins than if they were in a structured locked facility. But when we spoke in late 2020, he was down one deputy, whom he struggled to replace. Another was on maternity leave. This pushed them up to one hundred clients per conservator. Thanks to the pandemic, "we're not doing any face-to-face contact with clients, it's all by phone, [so] one hundred clients are more or less manageable," but he was worried that "when we start going back to facilities, it's not going to be manageable."

Others are more resigned to the limited level of services they can offer. I asked Chelsea, head of a large public guardians' office in Southern California, how often deputies see their clients. She responded mournfully, "Unfortunately, it's not very often. Our minimum standard is we need to see them quarterly. We can see them more frequently if there's an emergency, end of life. Those sorts of things obviously become very urgent. . . . I would love to see our clients more frequently, but the caseloads do not allow us."[21] The situation is worse for agencies with many conservatees placed out of county. One guardian lamented that her county would only reimburse the six-hour drive to visit a conservatee in a locked facility once every six months.

Serge Obolensky, who spent more than a decade homeless in Hollywood until Kerry Morrison, head of Hollywood's Business Improvement District, helped mobilize a group of private citizens to get him conserved, takes a generous attitude toward the people involved in his conservatorship. He remembers being "really upset" when his psychiatrist testified that he needed conservatorship, but "now I look back, and it's all normal." He had never heard of a public guardian before he first spoke to one during the conservatorship investigation, but he appreciated that "they said they were going to get my ID card, my social security card, my Medi-Cal card. They helped me out a lot."

At that point in our interview, Kerry jumped in to fill in some less rosy details. As Serge's conservatorship referral marched forward, one of the outreach workers who had been seeing him on the streets visited him regularly in the hospital. The worker had Serge sign a release so she could be notified when he stepped down into an IMD. But after four months, Kerry and the worker "went up to the floor [of the hospital], [staff] said, 'Oh, he's gone,' and they would not tell us where [Serge] was." Although the public guardian could consent to the release of this information, he or she was nowhere to be found. "If we did not go looking for you," Kerry reflected, "nobody in the whole world would have known where you were. You would have been completely alone."

Kerry and her compatriot eventually found a contact in the Department of Mental Health willing to stretch privacy rules to tell them where Serge had wound up. Kerry drove out to the "far reaches" of Los Angeles County to meet him. There, she made a distressing discovery: although Serge had been conserved for months, he had not met his public guardian. Concretely, that meant the public guardian was not transferring to Serge any spending money from his social security check, which meant he couldn't get food from the IMD's small snack bar. Kerry raised "holy hell with the county," and within a day or two Serge's public guardian reached out. For Kerry, it was symbolic of a "lack of accountability" in a conservatorship system that "does not want to even acknowledge that there might be someone out there who cares, who could be the lifeline, the connector, could provide people with five bucks."

When Serge left the hospital for an IMD, he was placed in what anthropologist Joao Biehl, studying private institutions in Brazil where the elderly and disabled are left to die, calls a "zone of social abandonment." Residents became "unknowable . . . with no one accountable for their condition."[22] But while Brazil's zones were created by the failure of the state to organize any more dignified alternative, in California the state both financed the place where Serge was relegated and used its sovereign power to place him there. It was private initiative, not engaged public authority, that brought Serge back from the brink of social death.

Public guardians, like all overwhelmed street-level bureaucrats, have a range of what Lipsky describes as "coping behavior and adaptive attitudes."[23] Coping and adapting within budgetary and staffing limitations means, as one evaluation in Los Angeles observed, that public guardians focus on keeping up with "paperwork . . . which must be done to ensure the conservatee receives the minimum level of care." They thus leave to the side "'quality of life' tasks [such] as personal visits and observation of living conditions."[24] As the next section details, some of what guardians might see on visits to and observations of the places where conservatees live are quite disturbing.

LOCKED IN THE "CLOSEST THING TO HELL I'VE ENCOUNTERED"

Not all of the powers that LPS gives to conservators actually get exercised. In spite of anecdotal reports documented by journalists digging into guardianships post–Britney Spears,[25] public guardians and judges insisted to me that LPS conservatees almost never lose their right to vote or are sterilized by court order.[26] Pushing back against depictions of conservators as all-powerful, one public guardian admonished me that "many people think we have the power to do things we don't actually have the power to do." In that guardian's county, "really the only two powers that we are granted by the court . . . [are] to place someone in a locked setting and to consent to medication." But these are fearsome tools. Public guardians are not the one physically pinning people down to give them injections or shutting them behind locked doors. Instead, these powers are delegated to facilities that can subject people to degradation and death.

The last-ditch retort to critiques of involuntary hospitalization is that at least it keeps people safe.[27] The record suggests otherwise. In-depth investigative reporting from the *Los Angeles Times* in 2019 found one hundred preventable deaths in psychiatric facilities statewide over the course of a decade.[28] Government's failure to protect people from whom courts have stripped any power to protect themselves (for example, by not allowing them to leave a facility they find unsafe) is harrowing. At La Casa, an IMD in Long Beach run by Telecare, two patients died by suicide over two years.[29] The facility was already under scrutiny for hundreds of police calls tied to patient violence and dozens of escapes per year. Staff, some of whom made a little over nine dollars an hour, argued that residents (all of whom were conserved) were moving too quickly from jails and acute hospitals into this less restrictive, less controlled facility. Telecare faced no regulatory consequences for the deaths.

Counting deaths, however, only captures a fraction of the harm that some patients experience under involuntary psychiatric holds. Thatcher is a thirty-seven-year-old genderqueer, mixed-race person; after graduating from college, they moved to San Francisco to become a tattoo artist. Thatcher left a bad relationship and was being stalked by their ex. They "basically developed a lot of paranoia, like a trauma response," which "activated a manic episode." They pursued therapy and medication "for a really long time" via Medi-Cal but were stuck on waitlists.

Thatcher only got "help" when visiting a friend in Pomona who, out of concern for Thatcher, called the police. Officers extracted Thatcher from the bathroom and hurtled them into what I have previously described as a "state of exception" where violence and humiliation seemed routine. It started with the 5150. Thatcher was having "delusions that they were federal agents, not police." While being strapped to a gurney, Thatcher spit on a cop's shoes. The EMTs responded by putting Thatcher in a "pain restraint hold" (applying force to the joint of Thatcher's jaw) and gave them an injection of sedatives and antipsychotics.

Outside of emergency situations (like Thatcher's 5150), psychiatric facilities can only forcibly medicate a person not under a conservatorship after a *Riese* hearing, where a judge determines if a person lacks capacity to evaluate the risks and benefits of medication. But once someone is conserved, the public guardian can consent to medication on their behalf, without going back before a judge. One public guardian, Tod, told me that this consent-by-proxy rarely required physical force. He elaborated: "The most powerful authority we have is medication. . . . I can say, 'Off to the hospital you go' and shoot them up with medications. It's a powerful deterrent, which we don't frequently have to use. Most clients are in settings where they comply . . . either willingly or with a 'show of force.' . . . In other words, get a bunch of burly nurses around them and say, 'You're going to take that shot.' You're going to comply."

Beyond involuntary medication, Thatcher received little that they saw as "treatment" during nine involuntary hospitalizations between 2016 and 2018. Several were in John George Psychiatric Hospital, a notorious facility in Alameda County. Thatcher remembers only "very brief encounters with doctors who seemed to have already made up their minds about where my mental health was at." Thatcher saw their paperwork extending their 5250, for example, and were certain the doctors had switched their chart because it said they were "despondent and stayed in my room" even though "I was manic, staying up and talking a lot, in a high energy place and not staying in the room." There were a few art supplies and occasional "dog therapy that everyone wanted to go to," but that was it. One former nurse from John George concurred that it was a therapeutic desert: "There's a great myth that we're able to . . . work some kind of magic by virtue of it being labeled a psych [hospital]. . . . But we're in the business of crowd control. . . . We just have to make sure that nobody's fighting."

They weren't that successful. Violence was omnipresent. Thatcher said (sarcastically), "Another cool moment was when this super-young woman at John George—it's like, very skewed, mostly men—some dude tried to touch her while she was sleeping or something, and she clocked him in the face."[30] Women, unsurprisingly, tend to see psychiatric hospitalizations as more traumatic and coercive than men.[31] Lorraine, whom I'll profile in the next chapter, ultimately wound up in a state hospital, where assault seemed banal: "You get hit a lot. . . . I would just be sitting down playing cards with somebody, and then I would have my back towards [other patients], and they would come and just hit me in the back of the head." In 2019, the state hospital system logged 3,513 incidents of violence between patients. (In fairness, this number has gone down over the decade.)[32]

Although patient-on-patient violence is more common, in 2004 a doctor was strangled to death in John George.[33] Risks to staff further down the hierarchy, who spend far more time on wards, are greater. The Bureau of Labor Statistics reports that psychiatric technicians and aides have some of the highest rates of injuries of any occupation.[34] A psychiatrist at a public hospital explained to me, "I tell my staff, 'Just like we use universal precautions against infection, assume everyone is violent until proven otherwise . . . because you can't sort it out [who is at risk and who isn't]." You can imagine how these kinds of admonitions reverberate back on patients—either through retaliatory violence or a wariness that makes a supposedly healing environment feel like a battleground.

Perhaps the only thing Thatcher got out of their stay at John George was solidarity with others who perceived the place as equally traumatizing. "A lot of Black people in particular who had experienced incarceration at John George would be like, 'Oh, we're familiar with that situation,'" Thatcher reported. They went on, "When I left John George . . . some random person in San Leandro gave me a cigarette. And I was like, 'Why'd you give me a cigarette?' and she was like, 'I saw your sandals. [They mean] you're either coming from Santa Rita [Jail] or John George, and I know you need a cigarette.'"

Experiences like Thatcher's capture the disparity in perceptions that polarizes debates around involuntary care. The "Alameda model"—in which all involuntary patients are funneled to a single, specialized hospital like John George—has been hyped in academic journals by its founders and was even considered by legislators as a statewide model.[35] Meanwhile, a recent Department of Justice investigation lambasted John George, quoting an ex-patient who characterized it as the "closest thing to Hell I've encountered."[36]

As Esmé Weijun Wang writes, "My hope is that I'll stay out of those cages for the rest of my life. . . . I believe that being held in a psychiatric ward against my will remains among the most scarring of my traumas."[37] To look at the experiences of people like Florence or Thatcher and assume that their skepticism of inpatient treatment is only a product of anosognosia means discounting their experiences—which, the data are clear, are far from aberrations. One study of public psychiatric patients found that 59 percent had been placed in seclusion, 29 percent "taken down" by staff, 24 percent strip-searched, 14 percent bullied or abused, and 8 percent sexually assaulted in mental health settings.[38] Conversations about increasing the number of beds should not sidestep why some people are too afraid to fall asleep in those beds.

ENDLESS INSTITUTIONALIZATION DIDN'T END

Thatcher's repeated hospitalizations were awful. They were also short, usually lasting just few days. Such rapid discharges appear to confirm the widespread narrative that LPS has made long-term institutionalization "virtually impossible."[39] Yet on my visit to an IMD, I meet a woman who had been inside for twelve years. "Nobody will take her," Simon, the director, tells me, because in addition to treatment-resistant schizophrenia, she had a stroke (despite being in her forties). "She could go to a nursing home, but she'd have no life there. She'd be with people in bed all day."

I muse in response, "Sometimes I think our society doesn't want to believe people like her exist."

"They don't," Simon tells me. "She's invisible."

Extended and expensive institutionalization is cause for bureaucratic finger-pointing across the continuum. A hospital administrator I spoke to, for example, explained that some people "live in" acute hospitals because county behavioral health departments give up on finding a placement for them. IMD clinicians blame public guardians, who can decide that a person has "failed" in the community so many times that it is safer to leave them indefinitely interned. Public guardians, for their part, accuse contracted outpatient teams of refusing to consider conservatees for step-down programs. (They are likely to be difficult clients that hurt their performance metrics.) And courts, which LPS's boosters believed would "very effectively end the possibility of throwing people in a mental hospital and forgetting about them,"[40] might mechanically sign off on renewals of conservatorship year after year.

Lengthy internments can also be reinforced by dependency engendered by a loss of self those institutions themselves can cultivate. Sociologist Erving Goffman, in his 1961 exposé of state hospitals, documented the rituals that stripped away all the markers that a patient was an "adult . . . [with] self-determination, autonomy, and freedom of action" (think of giving up all one's personal possessions and replacing them with hospital pajamas, or losing control of with whom one's intimate personal details are shared).[41] Yet even in places where "existence is cut to the bone," Goffman argued, people find ways to "flesh out their lives."[42] That indomitable capacity to adapt to extreme circumstances, though, ultimately converts "inmates" into "programmed" or "built-in" creatures of these "total institutions," unable to return to the world outside them.[43] Subsequent research has confirmed the catastrophic consequences of prolonged institutionalization for people's capacity to live autonomous lives.[44]

The story of a beloved son, who received so much institutional care yet was left with so little on the other end of it, speaks to the continued relevance of this framework six decades later. Joyce, a sprightly eighty-nine-year-old, recalled that her son Joe, now sixty-five, actually did pretty well once he started medication after his first psychotic break (at age nineteen). That summer, he, his brother Jack, and some friends went swimming in the river near their home in the Central Valley. Jack got caught in the current, and Joe went in after him. Years later, Joe still comforts Joyce, telling her she doesn't have to feel bad about the incident. His brother Jack, Joe reports, is living happily in Los Angeles, working at a 7/11. Except that he isn't. Jack drowned. And, Joyce told me, the experience sent Joe "clear over the cliff."

Joyce is as sharp as a tack, but she'd have to dig up her old journals to count how many times Joe was institutionalized over the subsequent fifteen years. He went onto conservatorship in 1976, in order to participate in an "orthomolecular treatment" trial at Napa State Hospital, which entailed consuming huge doses of vitamins (the approach seems not to have been effective enough to make it into psychiatry's therapeutic arsenal).[45] She hoped the conservatorship would "guide him [Joe] towards rehabilitation," but his public guardian had the mentality of "'Well, he's on conservatorship, so we'll just send him here or send him there,' not because it's the best place, but because there's an opening." In the late 1980s, the place with an opening was an IMD where sixty patients were "drugged out and walking around like zombies." Joyce and her husband accompanied Joe to his austere room, where he sat on the bed and told her, "It's okay Mom, I'll stay." But once they got to the parking lot, Joyce's husband started sobbing, "I can't do this. I just can't do this." They took him home.

She did everything she could for her son. She went back to school to become a nurse. She joined the county mental health board. She found a private residential treatment program in Los Angeles whose psychiatrist called her and said "if you just have the money, I can heal your son." She was ready to put her house up for sale to pay for it, until her friends talked her out of it. She still had to think of herself and her other children. In 1991, she nagged Joe's conservator to put him on Clozaril, a potent new antipsychotic. When the public guardian wouldn't, she found a doctor on her own who made the medication switch. Within six months, she recounted, "you could have a conversation with him" for the first time in years. By some metrics, her efforts turned Joe into a shining success: for three decades, he has stayed out of psychiatric hospitals, has not had a single arrest, and has spent zero days homeless. But he has never come home and never lived on his own. By the time Joe got effective treatment, Joyce thinks, "too much damage had been done" to his brain. "I always wanted him to get well. And it took a long time before it dawned on me that he's probably not going to be able to function in society on his own," she confessed.

For twelve years, Joe lived at Psynergy, an unlocked residential treatment facility. Joyce said he did "really well." Partly, that meant he adapted to institutional life, "able to bathe himself and take care of himself—with prompting. Able to negotiate the facility, follow instructions." But mostly, Joyce meant that he was "doing well" because he was happy and had friends. Those friends would finish their therapeutic program at Psynergy and step down into independent housing. They were being given what disability rights organizations call a "right to fail," a chance to live independently even if success is uncertain.[46] Joe stayed. Joyce admitted, "I feel really guilty, because my son probably could have survived on the streets, but I just couldn't do that." He had failed too many times for her to want to see it again. A staff member at Psynergy had the same realization: "When I started here, one of my goals was, 'How do we get these clients off conservatorship and make them independent?' But I realized that 20 percent of our clients need that level of support [conservatorship] forever . . . so you realize the question should be, 'How do we make sure people's needs are being met?'"

But Joe got older, and his needs changed. Decades of heavy medication made him increasingly unsteady on his feet until, in 2021, he fell and broke his arm. He was confined to a wheelchair. His conservator moved Joe to a nursing home for "rehabilitation," without even telling Joyce beforehand. (Conveniently, the move shifted Joe from the county's ledgers to the federal government's, since Joe was now old enough for Medicare.) Regulations make it almost impossible to put people who have a mental illness and people who are elderly in the same board and care. The rule makers seemed to assume people like Joe would die young.[47] Psynergy would like to take him back, but the public guardian told Joyce, "You're getting old and Joe's getting weak, so this is where he will end up the rest of his life."

It's a sorry denouement to what Joyce insists has, all in all, been a "wonderful life." When Joyce goes to visit Joe, "the bed isn't clean, he's wearing somebody else's clothes, or he's dressed inappropriately." They don't even have a dedicated phone for patients anymore, claiming COVID makes it too hazardous. Joyce doesn't blame the staff; she, like Goffman, blames the place: "It's the facility. It's the way it's governed. It's old and crumbling. It's dirty. It's depressing. It's not conducive to a person getting well." Joyce often leaves her visits crying: "My heart is breaking. Because I don't have the strength or ability to bring him home." Joe would like to go home too. He tells her that if only he could go home, Joyce and his father would get back together—even though they were still married when he died a decade ago.

Joe had long been adapted to institutional life, but he wasn't resigned to it. He used to ask for a new hearing to contest his conservatorship every six months, so he could "get my life back." Perhaps he implicitly knew, as Goffman argued, that while "some roles can be re-established . . . if and when he returns to the world, it is plain that other losses" that people suffer from lengthening internment become "irrevocable and may be painfully experienced as such."[48] For the past year, though, Joyce recounted, he's stopped going to court. "There are a lot of things he would have fought before," she sighed, "but now he's tired."

For all of this, Joyce still believes Joe has a guardian angel. Decades ago, he tried walking sixty-five miles from his board and care to see his grandma; when night fell, he rang a stranger's doorbell, and they let him sleep on their porch. Another time, a cop picked him up off the streets of Los Angeles and called Joyce to say, "I don't want to take him to a hospital, they are so bad." He's certainly had a public guardian—or many—over the course of forty-six years, but recently they've been as distant as an angel and less magnanimous. Mostly, though, Joe has a mom, which is why Joyce is so afraid of what will happen when she's not there anymore. "I will do everything I can for him until my dying day," she confided, but "I'm afraid I'm going to die before him." Nothing in five decades of advocacy throughout the mental health system gives her, a deeply religious woman, faith that it can provide her son a life worth living when she's gone.

Joe received what many parents desperately want: a stabilizing conservatorship and consistent treatment. Thanks to that, he has avoided the worst abuses described in this chapter, be it handcuffs, mechanical restraints, or a forced injection. Yet decades spent inside highly structured settings, at the cost of quite literally millions of dollars, could not equip him with the skills and supports he needed to successfully leave. Sixty years of deinstitutionalization, which commentators like Goffman helped spark, has left most families afraid of seeing their loved ones abandoned outside of institutions. But it hasn't entirely eliminated the fear of seeing them abandoned inside, very much alone.

CONCLUSION: NO ONE CARES ENOUGH

What's missing in many of the stories in this chapter is any clarity about who is accountable for these multiple failures and who has the authority to correct them. Public guardians frequently stress how overstated their powers are: they can't make someone stop taking meth, for example, or force an IMD to accept an assaultive patient. But if they don't have the regulatory authority, capacity, or incentive to tightly surveil the facilities they depend on to intern and medicate conservatees, who does? As coercion gets delegated, responsibility gets dissipated.

The examples in this chapter suggest it is not just scarcity that explains why clinicians use their negative discretion to pull even very sick people off the conservatorship continuum. It's also a weighing of the relative risks of being abandoned into autonomy versus coerced into institutions that cannot be depended upon to heal. One county hospital psychiatrist admitted, "I know what our hospital is like. It's a really horrible place. It's really scary. I would not want my relative up there. It might be more traumatizing for the patient [than being released]. If there's any other way to help them, if they're on the border, then I really have to try that [alternative]."

This chapter contributes to a burgeoning body of investigations into the mistreatment of people on conservatorships. But the harms faced by people with mental illness with public guardians may be, in aggregate, different than those of other people subject to conservatorship. If the critiques of for-profit probate guardians are well summed up by the ironic title of the Netflix film *I Care a Lot*—i.e., overbearing control and exploitation—the problem for many LPS conservatees is that no one cares enough.[49] The abuses of sovereign power over conservatees are compounded by the absence of external authority overseeing its use.

To close, I'll return to the question with which I began this chapter. People like Florence think that we should abolish conservatorship. Can you blame them?

CHAPTER 10

STABILIZATION AND RECOVERY

I've never heard someone say they grew up wanting to be a conservator. Debby might have been born to be one without knowing it. She comes from three generations of college professors and got her degree in English literature. She spent a lot of the 1970s on spiritual pilgrimages in India. "I was kind of at loose ends, and one thing led to another, and just to pay the bills, I took a job at a private psychiatric hospital," she explains. She was "line staff": "When clients would be brought in on a 5150, hauled in by the police . . . you took care of them, you did the admissions paperwork. . . . We put people in a tub that we had in a nurse's station, because oftentimes they could be filthy or covered with lice." She learned "what it's like to deal with a schizophrenic coming in off his meds and putting him back on the street." It was the "very front-line work" of a street-level bureaucrat people-processing in a shriveling public mental health system.

She went back to school to be a marriage and family therapist but was "not really feeling it." She applied for a job as a public guardian in Marin County, with no idea what it entailed. She caught a "bug" for the job. She's convinced that what made her a good conservator is probably what would have made her a bad therapist: "You have to realize you're following a legal code. . . . It's not for everybody that is working on mental health, you need a more directive, assertive kind of personality." Her office occasionally brought in psychologists with doctorates, but they "are not good at it because it's dirty work. This is not sexy. You're with people who are not well. That's why there's a lot of turnover in public guardians, a lot of people come in and say, 'This is not what I spent five years in graduate school for.'" Except for a brief hiatus in the 1990s, Debby stayed in the profession until retiring a few months after I talked to her in 2021.

In states like New York, a person can be involuntarily committed to a psychiatric facility for a long period without a court ever appointing a legal guardian. In California, longer-term institutionalization requires a conservator, who is yet another player in the professional mélange of psychiatrists, case managers, police, probation officers, and judges intervening in a person's life. I wondered, what value do conservators actually add? In some cases, not much. Public guardians sign off on placement changes and ensure that papers are filed with the court. But Debby shows how the key contribution of a conservator comes from acting as an engaged authority within the mental health system, rather than from exerting power over conservatees themselves.

In her first position, she had a caseload of 160 conservatees, which was manageable only because 90 percent of them were in nearby Napa State Hospital. Back then, it was still the era when, as the *Los Angeles Times* put it, conservators appeared to have "total power" to decide "when they [conservatees] get to see the sunshine again."[1] Even though Debby had realized she was a "more practical person" than her academic parents, she was nonetheless keeping up with the science of serious mental illness. In 1989, she learned about Clozaril, a new "magic bullet" antipsychotic for people with treatment-resistant psychosis that was being marketed as "bring[ing] patients back to life."[2] She had a client at Napa State who was in restraint and seclusion 24/7 because "everything they devised to keep him from hurting himself, he'd one up them [by finding a new way to self-harm]." She went to her boss at the county mental health department and said, "We should try getting this guy on Clozaril." He said there was no protocol for procuring such an expensive drug in the public system.

So she drove to Sacramento to meet with the head of the then-existent State Department of Mental Health. "Long story short, I got a protocol [to purchase and use the drug]," she recounts, "and I got everyone in county management mad at me, they threatened me, and I had to go to the union to defend myself, because it, quote, 'Had never been done before.'" (Rod Shaner, from LA DMH, told me the barriers to using Clozaril at the time also included liability concerns, since it can lead to seizures and a potentially fatal decline in white blood cells.) In any case, her client went on Clozaril and was out of Napa in six months. "Of course he's not cured," she cautioned, but thirty-five years later, "he's doing okay . . . at the baseline that he was probably meant to be at." She believes her advocacy helped open the door for other conservatees to gain access to Clozaril in the state hospital system.

Debby saw an engaged public guardian as wearing another hat: "when judges ask me, 'How do you see your job?' I say, 'good parent,' a parent that will help the person find their highest level of functioning." In his ethnography of super high-end mental health services for the children of the rich and famous, Neil Gong describes how clinicians use "concerted constraint": an intentional and deliberate application of psychiatric coercion to develop people's capabilities.[3] Conservators like Debby might be offering the cheap, public equivalent.

Debby told me about Laura, who was one of those "famous street people" that everyone wants managed but for whom no one wants responsibility. She was "bipolar with a bad meth problem," a long sheet of 5150s, and many arrests. Debby would see her in the neighborhood where the public guardian's office was located. Eventually, she asked her boss, "Why hasn't anyone ever tried to get her on conservatorship?" They concluded that the local hospitals, with their "treat 'em and street 'em" approach, would never do it on their own. So the next time Laura was 5150ed, Debby called her outpatient case manager and said, "Let's see if we can get her kept in the hospital."

Debby—acting a bit like an official version of Kerry Morrison, the Business Improvement District head who served as a "mission controller" for the conservatorship process—shepherded Laura onto conservatorship. It wasn't a panacea: "For eight years, she was volatile, menacing, kicked out of one program or another. . . . She'd run away from programs. . . . I'd go over and chase her down, bring her back." Debby recalls that Laura showed up at one conservatorship renewal hearing having escaped from a facility, high on meth: "She was sitting at the table with her attorney, screaming obscenities at the doctor who was trying to testify." The judge declared, "Enough, I'm ruling this grave disability." Debby and another deputy guarded her on a bench until law enforcement showed up to take her to the hospital. "She was sitting there screaming at the top of her lungs, 'I hate you all, you are concentration camp rejects.'" Debby laughed: "I was thinking, 'Not only are you in a concentration camp, but you're so bad, they don't even want you there!'"

Most programs wouldn't try Laura on Clozaril, because she was too unstable and flighty to monitor for the medication's side effects. But Debby kept searching until she found a psychiatrist willing to take the risk. "It helped her immensely," she recalls. "It was the first notch in getting her a little more cooperative." After fifteen years of unstable placements, Debby fought hard to get her into a Crestwood-run board and care. She didn't want to give too much credit to private for-profit providers—"I'd maybe give Crestwood a C+"—but Debby liked the staff there, and so did Laura.

"She's in her sixties now," Debby reflects, "and a few years ago, she really started to settle down." Debby confesses that she "just got a call about her this morning, she's acting out." But she is no longer a person defined solely by her problems. Laura even reconnected with her one remaining family member and started writing poetry. A few years ago, a social worker at the board and care assembled the poems into a book, "and in the title, front page of the book, she wrote, 'This is for my conservator who really helped me find out that I could be me, in a good way.'"

The handful of studies on the outcomes of conservatorship mostly show where conservatees wind up: in placements like locked IMDs or unlocked board and cares.[4] But as you'll see in this chapter, conservatorship can achieve a range of other outcomes beyond simply keeping people out of jails or off the streets. Individual street-level bureaucrats, facing little state oversight, define a positive outcome in radically different ways. Some professionals aim for bare stabilization. Others pursue choice, independence, or recovery. The tactics they deploy to get there range from litigating over graph paper to haggling over medication compliance.

What these uplifting stories at the end of the conservatorship continuum share is that they do not emerge from the exercise of legally anointed authority and the deliberate design of public mental health care. Instead, they frequently depend on the scrappy resourcefulness of professionals like Debby and the resilience of conservatees, working against and around the system.

CYCLES OF STABILIZATION

Most people who go onto LPS conservatorships get off of them alive. This may surprise you. The widespread depiction is that "It's nearly impossible to escape a guardianship except in a coffin."[5] Guardianship really may be a life sentence for many elderly people with dementia and might have been the case for Britney Spears had she not had an international movement agitating for her freedom.[6] Yet both the limited quantitative data available and my interviews with public guardians paint a bifurcated picture. In San Francisco in 2018, 60 percent of LPS conservatees had been on conservatorship for at least five years. Among new referrals, though, two-thirds remained for less than a year.[7]

These latter cases capture that, for some public guardians, the point of a conservatorship is to pull professionals together and buy them some time to address a crisis.[8] Darrell, who manages a public guardian's office in the Central Valley, has a libertarian streak well-adapted to his county's more limited social service infrastructure. So I wasn't surprised that, when I asked for a "proud moment" in his long career, he reached for a case that suggested his ability not to promote lasting personal transformation but to alleviate immediate suffering: "I made a really strong case many years ago about a client who was 'successfully homeless,' she loved being on the street, she was thrilled to get pocket change from people, that was a rush for her," he recounted. The public guardian stepped in because "she broke her ankle trying to get into a dumpster [looking for edible discarded food], [and] it wound up healing badly, holding at like a 40-degree angle from her foot."

We'll talk in chapter 12 about how challenging it is to get medical and psychiatric services to work together. In this case, having a public guardian brokering between multiple systems was crucial. Darrell's office provided evidence to the judge that the woman was gravely disabled (you can't dumpster dive with a broken foot!), overrode her objection to invasive surgery (by showing her mental illness interfered with her capacity to understand her medical condition), and used its placement power to keep her in a medical facility long enough for her foot to fully heal. The outcome was that she was "back on her feet" (literally) and "able to live the lifestyle that she was used to" (being homeless and dumpster diving for food). He's convinced it's an outcome that neither law nor medicine could have achieved on its own.

This narrow aspiration can be frustrating to some people who fought hard to get someone onto conservatorship. I checked back in with Kiley (who, after years of trying to find good care for her daughter Clarissa, concluded that the system was "clear as mud"). Kiley was convinced that the constant "oh-shit, Clarissa is back in jail" letters she sent across county government finally got them to "all look around the room and say, 'Oh my God, who's in charge? This is embarrassing, this is ridiculous.'" A county supervisor leaned on the hospital to keep Clarissa longer and apply for conservatorship. Kiley would "put her life on it" that if they hadn't "gotten [Clarissa] conserved when we did, by the end of that year [2020] she would have been dead. There's no other way. She was so close."

Clarissa's public guardian did what he arguably was supposed to do and tried to place her in a less restrictive, unlocked residential program. But "she kept

AWOLing, and they would find her drunk, somewhere else, out of it." Eventually, the public guardian sent her to an IMD and ordered her to take medication. For Kiley, the results were a sudden ray of hope: "Probably within three weeks, you could start feeling that she was turning around. You could start conversations with her, she was lucid. [Clarissa] was coming back. It was amazing."

After a few months, the IMD discharged her to another unlocked residential treatment program that her public guardian lined up. The cycle seemed to be restarting. Kiley told me, "It was an unlocked facility. And supposedly they had control, but they didn't. There was no support. . . . The staff were all watching TV together, and the patients were walking the streets. There was no structure . . . [and] a liquor store [across the street]." Kiley pressured the public guardian to transfer her daughter to a different program, which was still unlocked but had tighter rules and no adjacent liquor store. Clarissa, again, seemed to stabilize.

Unfortunately for Kiley, Clarissa's public guardian joined the "Great Resignation" of 2021, which gutted social service bureaucracies around the state, and quit. The new conservator called Clarissa and, after a short conservation, concluded that she was no longer gravely disabled. He would let the conservatorship expire at the one-year mark. (Remember that LPS case law requires that someone be gravely disabled in the present, not just the past or the future.) Kiley pleaded with her daughter to stay in the program, telling her, "You're not ready, you're close, you're starting to get some insight." Clarissa was insistent, though, that when she got out, she'd go to a homeless shelter in the north of the state. Kiley hoped for a rainy winter so she would reconsider.

"We've gone through this marathon, and we're so close to the finish line, and it's being ripped out," Kiley lamented. As the end date for the conservatorship approached, she forwarded me a new "oh-shit" letter. She wrote, "Is it responsible or even legal to basically go from 'taking care of someone' to releasing them into a homeless situation? . . . Not sure how in good mind or conscience you can sentence her to a life on the street. She has come close on several occasions to killing herself and others. . . . She has civil rights, but she should also have human rights." Kiley's plea was unsuccessful. When Kiley and I spoke ten months after Clarissa left conservatorship, she had been to four hospitals and eight detox facilities and had been arrested four times.

A 2020 state audit found that conservatorship was a revolving door for many. Of the sixty cases auditors reviewed, eighteen had already been on a conservatorship before their current one.[9] Advocates for a robust, paternalistic response to serious mental illness might take this as a sign that the conservatorship system is failing. Indeed, for some family members, the fact that conditions like schizophrenia are chronic is precisely why conservatorship should be indefinite, as is the case with probate guardianships. (Kiley just wishes Clarissa's conservatorship had lasted two years instead of one.)

Some counties, on the other hand, treat conservatorship like the governmental responses to wars or natural disasters. Conservatorship suspends normal rules and rights in a state of exception that, ideally, should be as short as possible.[10] One public guardian told me, "The goal of conservatorship is to have someone come off conservatorship. . . . If they're stable, med compliant, and have housing, we should be thinking about terminating conservatorship." Some people would stop their medication, get hospitalized, and have a new conservatorship petition, and "we understand that. We in a way, expect it, because this is a chronic condition."

Focusing on a minimal degree of temporary stabilization as the metric for conservatorship's success is one coherent if controversial way to balance law and medicine, in a way that leans toward civil rights. Whether that's the right objective is ultimately a philosophical, not a clinical, question.

CHOICE AND DIGNITY AMID CONSTRAINT

Other conservatees, far from revolving in and out of conservatorship, remain stuck in institutions, sometimes for decades. But even people facing ongoing restrictions to their rights can benefit from being given dignity, choice, and an attentive ear.

The conservatees I interviewed often depicted conservatorship hearings as a nightmarish medical-legal conspiracy to strip them of their autonomy. Alexander, who had been conserved twice and hospitalized more times than he could count, felt that public defenders "repeat basically what the psychiatrists are saying. . . . They're claiming they're defending you but then they're on the other team." As for the judges, "it's like he's going through a rehearsal, like it's staged. . . . They just want to find the criteria that justifies the incarceration, the internment, whatever." He pointed out that "legally, you're innocent until proven guilty," but from talking to peers, he believed that "99 percent of conservatorships are awarded," which suggested to him that maybe he didn't have a right to have that right.

I wonder how he would have felt had he been represented by someone like Ali. Her trajectory into the role of LPS public defender for a suburban Northern California county wasn't a deliberate one. 'I decided to go part time because I had twins,' she explained, 'and I wound up on conservatorship because it tends to be something that's seen as easier. They call it the "mommy track."' Operating on her own, she nonetheless assumed the role of zealous advocate. When we first spoke in 2018, she had defeated a surprising number of conservatorship petitions by insisting on a client's right to a jury trial (which I can only assume caused all sorts of consternation for professionals looking to people-process conservatees quickly). 'We are a more conservative county, and on the jury, I want that white male who voted for Trump who says, "He's allowed to mumble to himself on the street. Why are we going to spend our tax dollars on someone who doesn't want to be housed? Why is government involved in this? Leave him alone,"' she elaborated.

Ali is not, in principle, opposed to involuntary treatment. If anything, she'd like to see LPS reformed "so they can file [for conservatorship] based on meth." She knows that "it sounds so harsh, but the reality is they [her clients] are going to end up in jail. It's not like conservatorship or nothing, it's conservatorship or jail." What I really found distinctive about Ali's advocacy was not how forcefully she wielded law against medicine, but the extent to which she wanted both of them to pay attention to the desires and preferences of the people they were supposed to serve.

I first spoke to Ali in 2018, and followed up with her in 2021 partly because I wanted the full story of the "graph paper guy." As she recounted, after a long conversation with her client, she went before the judge to make an unconventional request: "I told him, 'My client will accept [conservatorship] with the one condition that he be provided graph paper.' And the judge, who struck me like an engineer personality himself . . . leaned in and said, 'What size graph paper?' And I said, 'Oh, I hadn't thought to ask' and he said, 'It matters. Why don't you ask and come back?'" She queried her client, who had an immediate answer: one-eighth of an inch. She reported to the judge, who replied, "That's what I thought." The judge brought in the public guardian, and lectured, "'I can't technically order you to provide him with graph paper, but I'm going to strongly suggest as the judge in this case that he be provided with graph paper one-eighth of an inch square.' So they did."

I wanted to know why he wasn't getting graph paper before then. She replied, "I think maybe he was getting some, but he was going through it at a quick clip.

It just wasn't part of the flow of things . . . [at his] locked [IMD]." It is, the story suggests, easy for facilities to assume everyone needs the same things, namely medication and some coping skills. "Other than that, he wasn't contesting [his conservatorship]?" I asked, a bit incredulous. She insisted, "That was the reason he wanted out of there. They didn't have graph paper."

Ali has an incredible basket of stories like this: 'Seriously, we had a guy who just said he wanted Doritos. He was diabetic and the doctor put him on a restricted diet. But we got the judge to say, "Doctor, this person has no control over his life, he doesn't control his meds, he doesn't control where he lives . . . Just give him some Doritos!" ' One conservatee would agree to be conserved if he could leave his facility to go to a jazz concert; another wanted a green dress. Others would accept being in a locked institution—if only they could smoke: 'You've taken away their alcohol, you've taken away their meth, they're being put in a crappy place, they're taking meds that make them feel terrible, make them fat, spaced out, no sex drive, sometimes they're not allowed caffeine, and it's like, "Just let them have this cigarette." '

In a debate over conservatorship that pits fundamental civil liberties against a risk of death from grave disability, it's easy to lose sight of the constant indignities imposed on psychiatric patients. Thatcher recounted a host of abuses in psychiatric settings, a few of which were covered in the previous chapter. They also had stories like this one: "When I was in [hospital], we campaigned to be able to watch a DVD, 'cause there were sports on the TV all day, and not a lot of us were interested. So they were like, 'Fine, you can watch a DVD.'" Thatcher and a few other eager residents "cracked open the case, and there was no DVD inside. . . . They were all empty." I hope this was just a careless mistake by staff, not a malicious act, but the effect for patients like Thatcher was the same either way: feeling ignored and invisible.[11] (As an aside, Thatcher recalls that the empty case was for *A Beautiful Mind*, the story of a math professor who lived with schizophrenia, which, they pointed out, was "super ironic for a psych ward.") I'd like to imagine Ali would petition a judge to order a better movie selection.

Conservatees' views on conservatorship are usually on a continuum between outright opposition and passive acceptance. Ali speculated, 'I'd say for 10–15 percent of the clients, they simply think they have no mental illness. The doctors love testifying about it, "anosognosia." . . . Those [patients] are the people who say, "Why is this happening to me? This is a travesty. If I am conserved, why aren't you all being conserved?" ' For clients in the gray middle ground, though, there are windows of opportunity—if only someone takes the time to listen. Ali goes on: 'For the largest percentage, they simply don't like their placement. I think 70 percent of them would stay under conservatorship if they could go to an open board and care [rather than a locked facility]. Most people don't want to be homeless; they want a place to sleep and they want food.' And then, '5 percent of my clients go to trial [contesting a conservatorship petition] for completely random reasons.' Like graph paper.

These kinds of interventions may be less about getting people off conservatorship or out of institutions and more focused on their quality of life within them. Research has consistently found that someone's legal status matters less for how they experience involuntary hospitalization than whether they feel listened to and respected in the process.[12] With attentive judges or attorneys like Ali, conservatorship procedures can become sites of "therapeutic justice" that reinforce that conservatees are rights-bearing individuals with preferences that matter.[13] As we'll see in the next section, though, some programs assume that many people really can live outside of institutions so long as we override just one of those preferences: the choice to refuse medication.

FORCING MEDS FOR FREEDOM

The original "Dilemma of Mental Commitments" report in 1966 envisioned that the courts would grant the conservator powers "individual[ly] . . . tailored to the disabilities of the ward."[14] Conservatorship would be carefully calibrated to the areas in which a person's judgment was afflicted and otherwise leave their autonomy intact. In practice, most conservatorship courts nationwide default to granting "plenary" guardianships, which give conservators the whole range of powers allowed by the law.[15] Judge Davis, for example, did a bit of tweaking but generally ticked off the same list of powers granted to the public guardian, including the right to place someone in a locked facility, restrict driving and firearm ownership, and impose medication. (I never saw her grant power 11(a), withdrawing someone's right to vote.)

By contrast, some pilot initiatives are working to titrate the coercion public guardians exercise in order to maximize client independence. I saw one such example when I attended court hearings for a "community conservatorship" program (these programs exist in San Francisco and Alameda Counties). The conservatees—all of whom were coming in from unlocked placements in the community, rather than locked facilities—were here for a monthly check-in with the court. They told the judge about a recent family reunion, a dispute with other residents in their board and care home, and a new volunteering gig at an animal shelter. The judge responded to nearly every report with copious praise and a common refrain: 'Keep up the good work. And keep taking your meds.' A deputy public guardian was waiting in the wings with a goodie bag of snacks to give the conservatees on their way out.

There's a simple theory underlying community conservatorship: many conservatees could live safely outside locked institutions if only they were medication compliant (usually meaning they accept a monthly shot of a long-acting antipsychotic). As a public guardian involved in one community conservatorship program explained, her office looks for applications for individuals who are gravely disabled but have a low risk of violence. The individual's public defender then meets with the candidate and explains the public guardian's bargain: if they agree to conservatorship (that is, don't contest their hearing), they can live in the community on the condition they "consent to being involuntarily medicated if needed."

Admittedly, I think it's a misrepresentation to say, as the guardian told me, that community conservatorship programs are "100 percent voluntary" with "no coercion." These individuals are still subject to the sovereign power of a standard LPS conservatorship, which means that if they refuse, they're likely to go to an IMD. Still, there's some truth to the somewhat Orwellian framing that, under community conservatorship, 'if you take your meds, your rights won't be taken away.'

The program has benefits for both conservatees and conservators (and the counties that pay for them). It enables conservatees who otherwise would be lingering in a hospital waiting for a locked placement to leave faster, freeing up that bed for someone who might actually need inpatient care. While many counties won't place conservatees in any level of care less structured than a board and care, 11 percent of San Francisco's conservatees live at home or in their own apartment.[16] For individuals on community conservatorship, agreeing to an injectable antipsychotic one day a month might be a good trade to be largely left alone the other twenty-nine.

Luke, a social worker whose outpatient team works with clients on community conservatorship, described a client with autism and psychosis who had a compulsion to continually trespass in the same places. This earned him the sad distinction of being the "most arrested person" in his city. While he agreed to go on community conservatorship, the client resisted his monthly shot. Typically, in cases of noncompliance, the public guardian coordinates a "show of support," which means going to the client's house with a fire department paramedic and a police officer in tow. A police sergeant who frequently participated in these missions recounted, "I'll just say, 'You're going to need to do this, there's a court order, the judge says it needs to happen.' Nine times out of ten, I can coax them into rolling up their sleeve." Luke's client, though, continued to refuse.

Ultimately, the power of a community conservatorship is predicated on the public guardian's authority to get a conservatee back to a locked facility or ER. There, a client's "voluntary" agreement to involuntary medication can be translated into being physically forced to take it. The problem, Luke told me, was that this individual, who lived with his parents, "locked himself in his room" during the shows of support. The police declared, "We're not going to go out there and drag him out." Like most clinicians I talked to, Luke would like to see police less involved in handling mental health crises in principle but was well aware how their increasingly hands-off approach enfeebled the coercion on which the conservatorship system rests.

Eventually, the individual was rearrested and transferred to the psych ER, where he was given his shot. Luke explained that there is often this kind of "learning curve" whereby someone might have to have a few such interventions before they realize that "the shot isn't as bad as I expected, it is helping me reach my goals, and it is something I have to do." For others, the "black robe effect" (that is, being pressured and praised by the judge overseeing the program) provides an authoritative push toward medication compliance. Luke's client went back home, and "we don't tell him what to do during the day, we don't force him to wear certain clothes, or any of the other things people are afraid conserved clients will have to do. He can do his own thing." He hasn't been back to jail in three years on the program.

Insofar as we define "independence" as "staying out of institutions," community conservatorship programs have shown their potential. In Alameda County, an entire cohort of twenty-five conservatees kept out of hospitals and jails over two years.[17] For them, forced meds—and intensive community services coordinated by the public guardian's office—really were a ticket to greater freedom.

THE REALITY OF RECOVERY

There's a ubiquitous buzzword in the mental health system: "recovery." The Substance Abuse and Mental Health Services Agency, a federal entity that provides guidance and grants for state mental health systems (but exercises little regulatory authority over them), describes it as a "process of change through which individuals improve their health and wellness, live a self-directed life, and strive to reach their full potential."[18] Recovery was a key principle behind the 2004 Mental Health Services Act and has become the default stated goal of many county mental health departments. For some conservators, though, it's irrelevant to their work. One told me: "When we get a referral saying, 'gravely disabled,' we want the psychiatrist to confirm that the prognosis is not for any sort of recovery, no chance of participating in normal life activities."[19]

Then there are the people who prove that recovery is a real but painstakingly gradual process—one facilitated when conservators are patient enough to take small steps by a conservatee's side. Lorraine, now thirty-two, believes that she's "always been bipolar," but her story is as much about overcoming trauma and the substances she used to dull it. Lorraine "grew up fast." She had to serve as a parent to her five siblings because their adoptive mother "was a drug addict . . . had a lot of men over, and didn't really pay attention to her children." There was "abuse in the home, hitting us with belts and spoons, and sticks." When she was thirteen, she was "fed up" and pushed her mom in a dispute. By this point, she was touching all sorts of government agencies, but "I just felt I wasn't ready to tell them [child welfare workers, police, or her therapist] what was going on. 'Cause, I'm like, 'Why do I have to go to this stupid doctor? Am I that crazy?'" Instead of getting support, she got sent to juvenile hall.

She later found inner stability in a residence for transitional-age youth coming out of the foster system, but fell victim to the external instability of California's welfare system. The facility "closed down . . . [and] they didn't give us too much time to find a place." The next period of her life was "foggy." Lorraine was in and out of shelters. She started smoking crack and meth. She married a much older man, who "had me having sex with people for money. And I would cry and be like, 'I don't want to do this,' and he didn't care, he was like, 'We need the money, so you're gonna do it.' . . . I felt like straight-up shit."

Conservatorship was one more blow to her sense of self-worth. She was visiting her outpatient case manager and, after a dispute, hid in the bathroom and tried to self-injure. They 5150ed her, and "told me that because I continually kept going to the hospital, using drugs . . . they had given me all the chances I could get, and I did not listen, so they put me on conservatorship." It "sucked, because I like to be independent" but, she told herself, "I had been warned many times." The hospital set her up with an interview to go to a board and care, but "I kept hurting myself." She instead went to Metropolitan State Hospital. Lorraine was a long, long way from the "hope, healing, connection, and empowerment" that people in recovery are supposed to be reaching for.[20]

I spoke to Dr. Howie, a psychiatrist in the state hospital, about what people like Lorraine get there that they couldn't get in a regular acute hospital. There's a high staff-to-patient ratio to contain at risk patients, of course, and the ability to combine multiple, complex treatments, like Clozaril and electroconvulsive therapy. But what seemed really distinctive, in a system where hospitalizations are usually focused on achieving the bare minimum of stability necessary for discharge, is the focus on helping people progress along multiple dimensions: "We meet every single month to say, 'Here are your goals, here's what you need to do.'"

Lorraine reported that the state hospital's arrivals unit was terrifying and riven with violence. But she quickly moved to a ward that offered dialectical behavioral therapy, an approach designed to help people with severe trauma build skills to regulate emotions and manage interpersonal relations. Dr. Howie explained that when patients like Lorraine start following through with attending groups and taking care of hygiene, they move to level 2, where they gain access to a "patients' only lounge" and "small jobs based on their ability." He qualified, "Some patients might not have the capability of mopping a floor," so they might just end up "wiping door knobs or picking up trash." Menial though that might sound, Lorraine appreciated it. "I got the opportunity to work [for the hospital], they gave us money for cleaning, and you could buy stuff from a catalog." Level 3, Howie said, was for those "on their way out" who might be able to benefit from the hospital's GED program.

Lorraine worked her way through the levels. After six months, she stepped down to California Psychiatric Transitions (CPT), an IMD that numerous people described to me as the gold standard for locked subacute care. So far, I've painted a pretty disparaging portrait of IMDs. Alexander, who lives with schizophrenia and has been conserved twice, described being sent to an IMD one hundred miles from his hometown. It was "like a really bad prison" where he had no visits, no cigarettes, and no TV. "Maybe they cleaned the floors," he offered. "If I had to say something good about it, it's that you weren't slipping on human waste on the floors." At another IMD, though, his experience was different: "At the hospital, everything seems like it's behind closed doors. They're more transparent at the IMD. It's less ambiguous: they have criteria [for progression and discharge] and they watch your progress. All of the sudden there's a lot less fear. You're not sitting on the edge of your seat [wondering when you'll get out]."

For Lorraine, progress was measured in MP3 files. CPT kept its residents on a relentless schedule of group therapy, and "every week, if you did good, you would get to choose sixteen songs to download. . . . And that was one of the things that helped me get through the year. . . . That was an incentive for me." (If you're curious, her choices ranged from country singer Carrie Underwood to the death metal band Slipknot.) There was also a cooking group that motivated her to get up early and a walking group that allowed her to escape from behind locked doors. She appreciated the "token economy" that gave her tickets for showering or attendance, which allowed her to buy hygiene products or candies and chips from the IMD's commissary. She was seeing a doctor, but the most impactful people at CPT were the other residents: "Processing with other people is a benefit, because other people will jump in and say, 'Oh I've been through that, too.'"

She graduated to Psynergy, an unlocked residential treatment program in Morgan Hill, south of San Jose.[21] The facility is nestled in the back of a cul-de-sac, near an elementary school and surrounded by private residences. It has some of the features of a mental institution—the wide hallways are a holdover from the building's previous life as a nursing home—and some that make it pretty distinctive—like equine therapy with horses.

In deciding whom to admit, Psynergy is willing to overlook assaultive behaviors or a history of AWOLing, one staff member told me, if someone is "working their ass off in a locked setting [by] doing all their groups." As with CPT, Psynergy is built around different "statuses" that give clients concrete objectives and intermediate steps to get there. The staff member insisted that a patient's identification with their diagnosis is not the key factor in that progression: "I don't give a shit if you have insight. I want you to be nice, get along with others, participate in our therapy." On my tour, we walk through a room with yoga mats set up for an upcoming mindfulness class: 'Our goal is to have them spend as little time watching TV as possible,' my guide tells me.

Psynergy allows people to experiment, in a structured way, with the freedoms denied to them in other settings. The program prefers that people sign in and out, but it can't stop anyone from leaving. They care more about whether people shower first, because, my guide explains, "We want someone to go out and just look like a person, because we're trying to reduce stigma in everything we do." They'd also like clients to use their paltry funds left over from SSI to buy something other than a Frappuccino at the local Starbucks, but they aren't going to stop them. The program can't even prevent residents from using drugs on the outside.

After years of enforced sobriety and unrelenting self-work, though, Lorraine used her freedom in a new way: "You get freedom . . . to do what you want. And the thing was that once I had that freedom, I didn't go and do drugs a single time. . . . It really helped me to know that you could live life drug free, that you don't have to go and smoke dope to have a good time, be more social." Lorraine even started running the Alcoholics/Narcotics Anonymous meetings at Psynergy, for which she got paid in gift cards (not cash, because Psynergy, like CPT or the state hospital, doesn't want people to lose their disability benefits). Suddenly, "I felt like a lot of people really looked up to me and told me that they liked my group." Being at Psynergy, Lorraine says, was "the biggest blessing of all."

She moved into Psynergy's on-site step-down apartments, and then, a month before her interview, into cooperative housing back in her hometown. Staff come in occasionally to offer support, but most of her contacts are with her housemates, who also live with mental illness. She's thriving. After seven years, she's also looking to get off of conservatorship. It's a big change. Her conservator has been the behind-the-scenes coordinator for her trajectory between institutions. "I talk to my conservator all the time," she offers, "he sends me money, we just talk about different things." Conservatorship serves as an insurance policy for programs like Psynergy, which is more willing to accept someone with a checkered history knowing that a conservator can help move a client back up a level of care if things go wrong.

Lorraine's story is inspiring. It's a testament to the important work being done by facilities like CPT and Psynergy, which combine a for-profit status with a zeal for doing right by their residents. The story is also, from the perspective of some approaches to disability rights, all wrong. Lorraine's gradual transition

from acute hospital to state hospital to IMD to residential treatment to cooperative apartment is indicative of a "step-down philosophy," which the Department
of Justice has observed "does not comport with the [Americans with Disabilities
Act's] requirement that people receive community-based services."[22] The DOJ
has moved aggressively to shut down "sheltered employment" that pays below
minimum wage.[23] From the outside, it looks degrading to meter out MP3 files
based on good behavior or offer tokens in exchange for polishing doorknobs so a
person can buy a bag of chips.

But perhaps the right approach in general for people with disabilities might
not be the right approach for a small subset of people identified as having *grave*
disabilities. Critics argue that recovery-oriented mental health programs embrace
a very American conception that equates citizenship with independence.[24] This
emphasis embodies the requirements of a residual welfare state that often does
not want to provide enduring, and expensive, support. It thus "places heightened
and potentially stressful expectations on patients."[25]

What should we say to people like Lorraine, for whom independence so often
looked like vulnerability to mistreatment? Is it a mistake to have put her in "seg-
regated" contexts with other people facing similar challenges, in which she at
last found solidarity and understanding? I don't have an easy answer. Certainly,
Lorraine should not have needed conservatorship to get housing, care, and com-
panionship. But the reality is that she did get it through conservatorship. And, in
her words, it was "the best thing that has ever happened."

CONCLUSION: AMBIGUOUS OUTCOMES

The past two chapters present two diametrically opposed visions of what happens
to conservatees. Depending on where you stand, you might read stories of neglect
and abuse as reflecting the real functioning of the conservatorship system and
tales of recovery and stabilization as a jumble of unrepresentative anecdotes—or
vice versa. Florence might seem to be a whistleblower calling attention to widespread problems—or (as one reviewer suggested) just voicing her delusions about
her mother. Debby could be a paragon of public guardians' dedication to their
clients or a self-serving bureaucrat telling me what I wanted to hear.

I highlight both negative experiences (exploitation, neglect, maltreatment, and
institutionalization) and positive outcomes (stabilization, dignity, independence,

and recovery) of conservatorship that my research finds are happening through-out the state. What remains to be done is to weigh the prevalence of one versus the other. Disturbingly, the agencies that should be doing this kind of analysis aren't. There is no statewide reporting or, in most cases, countywide data. We don't know even the most basic outlines of what happens to conservatees: where they are, how long they stay there, what services they are receiving from their conservators, and, perhaps most important, whether those conservatees are sat-isfied with any of the above.

The conservatorship system is lacking not just in authority, then, but also in accountability. As you'll see in the chapters that follow, this hasn't stopped policy makers from pushing to widen conservatorship's net. These reforms seek to bring more people into a black box producing everything from abuse to recovery in uncertain measure.

PART III

REFORM

CHAPTER 11

PAVING A NEW PATHWAY

The June 2018 hearing was, staff of the California Assembly Judiciary Committee told me, the most emotional one they had ever seen. Four years later, the bill that provoked all that sentiment had led to the conservatorship of just three people.[1]

Senate Bill 1045 targeted individuals "incapable of caring for the[ir] . . . health and well-being due to a serious mental illness *and* substance use disorder, as evidenced by frequent detention for evaluation and treatment pursuant to section 5150."[2] "Frequent" was defined as eight 5150s in the past year. You could say its target was people like Professor Jolie, whose near-constant crises in public attract endless community attention but who are nonetheless cast out by ERs hours after police place a hold. In presenting the bill for a final vote at the June 2018 hearing, SB 1045's author, State Senator Scott Wiener from San Francisco, obliquely critiqued LPS: "When we see people who are dying on the streets, people who are sleeping in their feces . . . people walk by and they wonder and they get angry, 'Why is no one doing anything about this?' And the reason is our current conservatorship laws." He noted that the expansion was something we "need to handle with great care, because these are civil liberties we're talking about." But, he riposted, many of these individuals were "currently being conserved in a place called 'jail.'"

San Francisco's mayor-elect London Breed—on her first lobbying visit to Sacramento—repeated the mantra: the bill "offers us a way to help some of our most vulnerable residents, who are not just suffering on our streets . . . [but] also dying on our streets." She echoed Wiener's redefinition of coercive treatment as a progressive act of mercy: "I want to make sure we're not just allowing people who can't care for themselves to be left on their own . . . because they have 'rights.' . . .

What we're doing [currently] is not humane. It's not compassion." Raphael Mandel-man, newly elected to the County Board of Supervisors, declared that "no issue is more frustrating for my constituents, and no public policy failure is more obvious, painful, and embarrassing . . . [than] our inability to provide care for so many obviously sick people." Their chaotic trajectories were, he said, a "relentless and costly merry-go-round that carries them from the streets, to the hospital, to jail, and around and around and around. It is inhuman, it is expensive, and it has to stop."

The chair of the committee then called for statements from the opposition, and a familiar litany of groups offered a familiar litany of arguments against involuntary treatment (arguments that, to be fair, have had validity for decades). A spokeswoman for an advocacy group, the Western Center on Law and Poverty, blasted SB 1045 as a distraction from the "complete failure" to fund "upstream solutions" like "supported housing with wraparound services [or] early mental health or drug treatment." She hammered that a "failure to control the real estate market, a lack of affordable housing, [and] the criminalization of poverty" were the real culprits for the "extreme human rights violations" happening on the streets, not a "lack of conservatorships." Curtis Child, the lobbyist for Disability Rights California, declared that his group was adamantly opposed because "we've spent decades . . . working at de-institutionalizing individuals," which the bill (despite Wiener's promise that "our goal here is housing and services, not locked facilities") threatened to reverse.

This implacable opposition was met by committee members' torn, emotional, and ultimately unanimous support for the bill. David Chu, a Democrat from San Francisco, was the most unequivocal, stating, "We've often expressed the perspective that the definition of insanity is doing the same thing over and over again. I support this because, with folks who are dying on the streets . . . I do think we have to try different things." The vote from Jordan Cunningham, a Republican from San Luis Obispo, was clearly harder. "This is a tough vote," he stammered, haltingly. When he was an attorney, he defended a woman who was sued when her son with "severe schizophrenia," who had been 5150ed "numerous times," stole a firearm from her garage and "murdered his next-door neighbor because he thought she was a vampire." He fidgeted uncomfortably, "You know . . . When we talk about people falling through the cracks . . ." He was fighting back tears, "That's real. So let's do this."

It's rare for every member of a committee to explain their vote, but the official displays of angst continued. Ash Kalra, a Democrat from San Jose, noted that the eight-5150s-in-one-year criterion for the new conservatorships "really speaks to the degree that someone is struggling to stay alive." As a former public defender who worked years in a drug treatment court, he remarked, "I have a visceral reaction to any kind of involuntary detention." But he shook his head sadly: "There are many occasions, heartbreaking occasions, where I wanted to do more, and I couldn't. Many clients . . . we closed their cases because of their deaths."

Wiener gave his final statement, summarizing that this discussion was "personal, because ultimately this is about people. . . . There are people I see in my neighborhood, in the Castro, who over years I see them decline, decline, decline, and then one day they're not there anymore. . . . This is a human tragedy that plays out . . . everywhere in our state." Then the chair called the roll, and every member voted in favor of the bill.

This chapter follows the torturous, costly, and ineffectual implementation of SB 1045. It's a story about the public's and policy makers' growing intolerance for homeless substance users, balanced against their ongoing uneasiness with forced treatment. In the case of SB 1045, legislators salved their discomfort by adding protections that granted negative discretion to even more actors than the traditional LPS conservatorship pathway. What happened in the ensuing four years is a warning about the massive amount of passion, effort, and acrimony that can go into helping—or harming—a small number of people, so long as the system remains so fragmented and delegated that no one has clear authority for helping—or harming—them.

THE "METH CONSERVATORSHIP" BILL

San Francisco is experiencing, in microcosm, a particularly acute version of California's more general crisis of drug use and homelessness, collapse of a private system of residential care,[3] and gaps in the public voluntary outpatient system. It's easy to understand how politicians might conclude that desperate times call for desperate measures.

How that measure wound up being the expansion of conservatorship is less apparent. Governor Newsom mooted the idea in 2008 when he was San Francisco's mayor.[4] The effort didn't go anywhere. Then, in late 2017, Heather Knight, a *San Francisco Chronicle* columnist and advocate for taking a harder line on homelessness, reported on Alice, a "neighborhood fixture" who lived outside a Burger

King at Sixteenth and Mission, "her belongings piled high in shopping carts and stuffed into suitcases spread all around her."[5] Alice believed it was 2006 and had such bad back pain that sometimes "she can't walk and other homeless people have to carry her to nearby bushes to relieve herself." City workers offered her housing sixty times, but she refused. Knight critiqued LPS's civil liberties protections, explaining that "in the name of compassion . . . [they] cannot compel her to move inside, where she would be warm, and have a bed and bathroom." She asked Mayor Ed Lee about Alice, who replied, "I don't think we have strong enough conservatorship programs." Alice ultimately accepted an offer of housing but passed away shortly thereafter.[6]

Mayor Lee himself died abruptly a few weeks later, but others picked up the baton. In February 2018, Scott Wiener declared at a press conference that the city was in a "midst of a crisis . . . a life-or-death situation, and it is beyond inhumane to sit back and watch as these people die."[7] He announced that "current conservatorship law is inadequate to meet our counties' needs around chronic homeless people with severe mental illness or drug addiction" and promised to "craft a bold and comprehensive bill that will save lives."

Elected officials stumbled over themselves in support. London Breed, who appeared at Wiener's press conference, touted her efforts to ramp up conservatorship in the mayoral election—but so did her opponent.[8] The San Francisco Chronicle pronounced in an editorial that while "concerns" about civil rights "merit consideration, they're dwarfed by the human toll that every onlooker sees. . . . Conservatorships should play a role in ending a persistent and disturbing side of homelessness."[9] The discourse was emblematic of what the anthropologist Andrea López calls San Francisco's regime of "brutal compassion": in a context where housing and treatment resources are far from sufficient to address the scale of suffering, aggressive last-ditch interventions are prioritized based on individuals' "proximity to [their] own death[s]."[10]

While Wiener et al.'s mantra was that the bill was necessary to stop people from "dying on the streets," the bill's design suggested a target population distinctive from the people traditionally subjected to LPS conservatorships. The draft legislation would allow conservatorships for people who were chronically homeless and substance users—no mental illness required. The mayor's office wrote to the Assembly, "The LPS Act falls short in serving modern needs . . . [because] substance use disorder is not considered [for conservatorship]" even though 67 percent of users of the city's Psychiatric Emergency Services had such a diagnosis.[11] The bill initially proposed qualifying someone for conservatorship based on four 5150s in the past year, which would hypothetically nab those individuals being rapidly dumped from an ER once they came down from a high. Although advocates described it as a "housing conservatorship" bill to emphasize that it was geared toward getting homeless people into supported housing, one social worker put it bluntly: "SB 1045 is not the 'housing conservatorship' bill, it's the 'meth conservatorship' bill."[12]

Given the overwhelming public support for forced treatment of homeless drug users,[13] sources in the legislature told me that by the time Wiener's draft reached the Assembly, its passage was certain. I asked one legislative aide if the bill's authors came armed with any research about the effectiveness of conservatorship as a solution to drug use and homelessness. (It was a trick question, because at this point I knew the evidence was scant at best.[14]) The aide told me, "It's not clear cut that [involuntary treatment] is a highly effective solution . . . but for the folks in the legislature who are voting on this, their constituents with political capital to spend . . . are of the mindset that this is an effective way . . . of dealing with homelessness that they view as problematic to their communities."

The staff of the Assembly Judiciary Committee, where negotiations took place, were unwaveringly opposed to the bill. They wrote in their analysis that the "danger is evident" in moving away from a standard of grave disability toward one based on the number of times someone was 5150ed.[15] It was "unclear," they argued, "why seeking medical care in an emergency room would provide a basis to hold a person involuntarily for at least one year." Moreover, including only people who were "chronically homeless" would "create a different standard of treatment and involuntary confinement that is based solely on one's economic status." The optics were not great, given Breed and Wiener's support for sweeps of homeless encampments and opposition to Prop C, a 2018 ballot initiative that imposed a surcharge on wealthy corporations to fund homelessness services.[16]

With the tacit support of the committee chair and the help of opponents of the bill like Disability Rights California and the ACLU, staff "chewed [the bill] to bits" (as one lobbyist put it). The final version required that someone have eight, not four, 5150s in the past year. Potential conservatees needed to be diagnosed with both a substance use disorder and mental illness by the ER during each of those 5150s (chronic homelessness disappeared as a criterion entirely). Amendments transformed the bill into a five-year pilot program for San Francisco, Los Angeles, and San Diego only, with onerous reporting and evaluation requirements. Most importantly, the bill required that the county mental health departments try a less restrictive option, assisted outpatient treatment (AOT), before applying for conservatorship. The bill then passed the Assembly 61–0 and the Senate 39–0. At a press conference, Mayor Breed recounted, "I probably harassed Governor Brown every single day until he signed it," which he did on September 27, 2018.

Although civil rights advocates had been publicly defeated, in a practical sense their mobilization against SB 1045 had been successful. With the amendments, one disability rights lobbyist told me, "we knew that they'd have a really hard time actually putting the program together and getting anyone in it." Wiener had initially told the Assembly in June 2018 that "approximately 1 percent of the homeless population [which was about eight thousand in San Francisco] meets the criteria in the bill." But when it came time for the San Francisco Board of Supervisors to consider its implementation early the next year, the city was estimating that, while fifty-five individuals met the eight-5150s criterion, only five had already "failed" AOT. "I'm not willing to back down. . . . If it's four [people], it's still worth doing. If it's one, it's still worth doing," Supervisor Mandelman insisted.[17]

In a rare move for a bill that had not yet been implemented, Wiener returned in early 2019 with new legislation, SB 40. The revision would allow the county mental health department to apply directly for a conservatorship once a person hit eight 5150s if it was determined that trying AOT "would be insufficient to treat the person."[18] Civil rights advocates once again extracted their pound of flesh, shortening the duration of the new conservatorships from one year to six months.[19] That bill also passed unanimously. It testified to legislators' desire to be seen as "doing something" about the nexus of mental illness and substance use (and, implicitly, homelessness). But it was indicative of the hesitation about how far beyond the traditional boundaries of involuntary treatment set by LPS that "something" should be.

COMPLAINT-DRIVEN REFORM

SB 1045 and SB 40 required that the three counties authorized to implement the program meet a series of stringent criteria. The board of supervisors needed to find that a host of services, from supported housing to medication management to family support, were available in "sufficient quantity, resources, and funding levels to serve the identified population."[20] It further had to confirm that "no voluntary mental health services" would be "reduced as a result of . . . implementation." Legislators and county supervisors in Los Angeles and San Diego had initially indicated their enthusiasm for the bill.[21] But they quickly realized there was no plausible way to claim that both of these were true.[22] The City of San Francisco, which had always been the motor behind the bill, pressed on.

In December 2018, I attended an event in San Francisco City Hall to discuss the mayor's Draft Implementation Report. A reader of the report could be forgiven if they forgot that the housing conservatorship program was about involuntary treatment. The program would "provide the most appropriate care in the least restrictive setting" by "requir[ing] the provision of Permanent Supportive Housing," a focus which was "novel" relative to regular LPS conservatorships. Clients in the program would be "engaged to participate actively, and whenever possible, to direct their own service and recovery process." At the event, representatives from the mayor's office and the Department of Public Health opened by explaining that their focus was on 'trying to offer them [people targeted by the law] coordinated and better services.' The law would provide 'more time to hear what they are saying to work with them' to get onto a 'pathway to wellness.'

At the end of the presentation, the organizers called for public comment. A sharply dressed, middle-aged white woman stood up and declared that she was a representative of the neighborhood association in a wealthy area. 'I get what everyone is saying about voluntary services and people with trauma, but we've had it up to here!' she declared, waving her hand above her head, the pearls around her neck jangling. 'You walk down the street and you're worried someone is going to bop you on the head. My assistant was threatened, seriously, twice this week. Twice!' She closed: 'Three people were killed in the Castro this year. There are homeless people who just shouldn't be there. Period!' An activist from the Coalition on Homelessness, which was steadfastly opposed to the bill, called out 'How many homeless people died during that time?' I could see the person from the mayor's office grimacing.

Supervisor Mandelman, who remained the bill's most consistent champion, was direct when I asked him how much pressure his office was receiving: "Constant. Constant. Daily. A mixture of fury, sadness, angst, [and] concern" about specific homeless people in the district. As he explained in that December 2018 meeting, what he saw in his own district were 'people the city already coerces a lot, on the margins of law [LPS]. We get a bunch of complaints, and we finally pull some resources together to get them housed or maybe some care, because the person has generated enough community outrage to have a twitter account [reporting on their behaviors].' To Mandelman, housing conservatorships were a more coherent and consistent way to respond to community pressure. Ignoring it would, in one official's phrasing, otherwise lead to 'neighbors lighting [homeless peoples'] tents on fire.' SB 1045 was thus emblematic of what sociologist Chris Herring calls the city's shift to "complaint-oriented services."[23]

While the bill's main proponents seemed to have mutually decided to mention in every public statement that SB 1045 focused on people "dying on the streets," the concern was not about those who were dying quietly. Alice, the woman whose refusal of sixty offers of housing was profiled in the *Chronicle*, would not have qualified, since she wasn't being 5150ed. A more likely target was a woman who came to an "upscale salon near Union Square" on a daily basis and "plant[ed] herself outside the front door to strip her clothes off and scratch herself violently."[24] The salon owner got a TV station to cover the woman, which "prompted visits from police brass and the Mayor's staff." The woman was hospitalized briefly and then went back to scratching herself at Union Square. Some of the most enthusiastic proponents of the bill were the Chamber of Commerce, the Travel Association, and the Hotel Council.[25]

This target group was the source not just of vexing complaints but of enormous expenses.[26] Supervisor Mandelman, sounding exasperated at one of many hearings where SB 1045 was being discussed, focused on 'nine people who visited PES [Psychiatric Emergency Services at San Francisco General] 168 times over four months.' He went on: 'Aside from the human cost, there's a public cost—we're spending a lot of money on those emergency visits. . . . We need to get them off this merry-go-round' (another supervisor's chosen description was the "homeless hamster wheel"). Chief Simon Pang, from the fire department, told the supervisors that 2.5 percent of the people about whom 911 calls were placed ate up 19 percent of their total resources. 'We have a meth user who has an abscess in his spine and sits in his wheelchair in excrement all day,' he told the supervisors. 'We had 122 calls to 911 about him in the last year, and in 99 meetings, offered him shelter, assistance activating benefits, and an ID—he refused it all. I'm dumbfounded how he was allowed to leave a hospital [after a 5150].'

I am disturbed but not dumbfounded. A failure to provide for one's own medical care is not, for now, a criterion for grave disability. As soon as clinicians deemed his problem substances rather than mental illness, there was no legal basis for holding him even if he was a danger to himself. That's, in theory, what reformers sought to change.

COERCION WINS

The bill had widespread public support but was far from unopposed. In late 2018, a coalescing Voluntary Services Coalition brought together some of the typical skeptics of a coercive response to homelessness and mental illness—such as the Mental Health Association and the Coalition on Homelessness—with gray-haired veterans of the civil rights movement, a self-styled Mad Mob of people who had been subjected to forced treatment, the occasional representative of the Democratic Socialists of America, and outpatient drug treatment providers who feared that funds would be diverted into involuntary programs.

The group organized public protests in 2018 and 2019, including one in which activists held signs declaring "treat us, don't beat us" and "housekeys, not handcuffs." They distributed flyers depicting the city's public conservator as a sinister man in a trench coat brandishing a dogcatcher's net (figure 11.1). In public events, the Voluntary Services Coalition hammered that the law was a

11.1 Flyer opposing SB 1045 "housing conservatorships" in San Francisco

Source: Senior and Disability Action

"grave violation of civil rights" and that conservatorship was "the most extreme deprivation of civil liberties aside from the death penalty."[27] But what seemed the most compelling argument against the law was also the most obvious one: it was unfair to force people into services that thousands of people in San Francisco couldn't access voluntarily.[28] The head of Senior and Disability Action stated, "There is not enough housing, in shelters or permanent housing, and people are not being offered voluntary mental health services. The City must give people the services they need before rushing to scoop them up to get them out of the public eye."[29]

In aggregate, this critique was obviously on point. Even the mayor's draft plan estimated that they had only two hundred apartment units in "buildings with the highest level of supportive services," a number transparently way below overall need (given the size and acuity of the city's homeless population). Nonetheless, officials claimed that, for the small group targeted by SB 1045, misgivings about the availability of services were a red herring. The bill focused on an identified group of fifty-five people who were already receiving a huge amount of attention (as evidenced by their eight 5150s over a year). As a vote in the Board of Supervisors neared, Senator Wiener insisted, "Clearly, we need to invest a lot more in mental health and addiction services. There's no doubt about that. The safety net is not where it should be. But to suggest you can't get those voluntary services in SF, it's inaccurate in the extreme. The people most in crisis, we're investing huge resources in them, cycling through ERs [and] jails. The voluntary services are available for this small universe of people, but they're not capable of accessing [them] because of the condition they're in."[30]

Proponents of SB 1045 attributed people's "service resistance" to a mix of anosognosia and addiction. Opponents blamed services that were unable to provide them what they most wanted. A source from Health Right 360, the city's main provider of substance use treatment, told me that 94 percent of people entering their residential programs were homeless upon arrival—and 45 percent were discharged into homelessness months later. Dr. Zeldes from the city's street medicine team commented on how this statistic made it harder to get people to engage: "I can reach out to someone and say, 'Hey, you should go into a program.' They reply, 'Well, what do I get?' 'You don't use drugs for six months, and then you get to be homeless,' or 'You'll go to an SRO in the Tenderloin [a neighborhood with an extremely high concentration of homelessness] where everyone will be using drugs.' That's not compelling."

By May 2019, it seemed as though SB 1045 did not have enough support to pass the Board of Supervisors. But revealingly, the reasons given for skepticism toward SB 1045 suggested that the debate among policy makers had shifted from whether to coerce people to where and how. Supervisor Hillary Ronen, in a hearing before the Rules Committee, dismissed impassioned pleas, like that of one speaker from the Voluntary Services First Coalition, that 'involuntary treatment does not work.' Ronen riposted that 'abandoning mentally ill people to wander the street without care and medication is morally wrong and dangerous.' She added, 'some people need forced treatment. . . . It's a no-brainer to me that LPS should include drug addiction.' What she doubted was whether the city had enough dual-diagnosis mental health–substance use beds to actually send people to under housing conservatorships.

Two developments shifted the political dynamic. First, the city committed to expanding services—albeit not the ones the Voluntary Services Coalition wanted. In early 2018, the city announced that it would be opening a fifty-four-bed "Healing Center" at St. Mary's Medical Center, which was actually a locked IMD run by Crestwood.[31] In the run-up to the board vote, Ronen extracted a promise from the mayor to spend $50 million the next year on another hundred beds for people with co-occurring disorders.[32]

The second factor was a threat by Mandelman and Mayor Breed to take SB 1045 directly to the voters. They had reason to be confident: polls showed that 77 percent of San Franciscans supported expanding conservatorships.[33] The Voluntary Services Coalition, seeing the writing on the wall, released a statement that "a ballot measure on conservatorship would lead to a dehumanizing campaign against homeless people. . . . With the threat of a ballot measure, the supervisors who supported us were not left with any good options." A supervisor's vote against SB 1045 would anger many constituents while likely failing to prevent the legislation from going into effect.

When the legislation came up for a full vote on June 4, 2019, Mandelman announced that he had accepted a few amendments, which would require even more offers of voluntary services before someone could go onto a housing conservatorship. In the end, only one supervisor dissented. Supervisor Shamann Walton observed that "every time we take freedoms away from people, it's typically Black people and people of color." He lamented that "5150s usually involve law enforcement" in a moment when his goal was to protect people of color from them. An appalling 50 percent of people with eight or more 5150s in 2020 in San Francisco were Black (5 percent of residents are Black).[34] Nonetheless, it appeared that, for a small group of San Franciscans, the merry-go-round of short-term holds, arrests, and the street was going to stop.

NO CONSERVATORSHIP WITHOUT COOPERATION

Proponents claimed the adoption of SB 1045 had symbolic significance beyond the small cohort on whom it would have a direct impact. Senator Wiener, in that emotional June 2018 hearing, declared it was part of a broader effort to reverse "our state's retreat" from providing for people with severe mental illness. Afterward, Supervisor Mandelman made the same claim: "It's the job of the government to take care of people who cannot take care of themselves. That's what this legislation is about." Yet SB 1045's revamping of the role of government in the conservatorship system foundered against precisely the bureaucratic discretion and private delegation it was supposed to reverse.

By 2020, the city had put together a twelve-member implementation working group, added staff to the public conservator's office, and hired a consulting company to evaluate the pilot. The consultant's first evaluation report was chock-full of filler, taking until page seven to note that "at the time of this preliminary report's submission, the Housing Conservatorship pilot has yet to serve any individuals."[35] At a hearing in July 2020, Supervisor Mandelman grilled staff from the public conservator's office and announced, sarcastically, "I always said this would be worth doing if it helped just one person. But I did think that it would help *at least* one person."

One source involved in the implementation of SB 1045 characterized it as a "turd of a law" that was significantly more difficult to exercise than a regular LPS conservatorship. It mandated that, as a person marched toward eight 5150s, clinicians document that they had notified the person that they were at risk of a conservatorship and that they could receive voluntary services instead. Implementation required developing and approving seventeen different forms. Thus followed months of finger-pointing between the city attorney and the Superior Court about how to enact the many protections that had been tacked onto the bill.[36]

The real nightmare for city staff, though, was created by the hospitals. Although debates about SB 1045 centered on what was happening at the county hospital, SF General, it actually holds only about a third of the city's LPS-designated beds.[37] Initially, data suggested that private hospitals received about 56 percent of 5150s. By 2021, the consultants had dug deeper and found that 79 percent of 5150s were passing through hospitals other than SF General.[38] This is a point worth emphasizing: prior to the housing conservatorship pilot, no one in city government actually knew how many people were subject to coercive psychiatric interventions in San Francisco.[39]

If your target population is people with eight 5150s, you need someone to be counting. It turned out some hospitals just wouldn't. A clinician who was tracking people on the housing conservatorship pathway told me dejectedly, "Some hospitals are choosing to participate, and others are choosing not to." Even SF General's PES apparently told the public conservator that it would accept a list of only ten names of people for whom it would provide the housing conservatorship notices and file the necessary documents with the city. For other clients on the program's watch list, the hospitals "don't let us know that they're there."[40]

When this clinician did learn that someone on her radar screen was at a certain private hospital (because they had been 5150ed by a city mobile crisis team, for example), she'd call and ask, "Are you thinking conservatorship?" and ER staff would reply, "We don't do that here." Other ERs were writing "malingering" or "personality disorder" as their diagnosis, which rendered that 5150 unusable (since it did not show mental illness and a substance use disorder). "The Housing Conservatorship notice [offering services and telling someone how far along they were toward eight 5150s] is one page, it's check boxes and a signature," she told me, adding, "it's amazing the amount of pushback I'm getting about even that additional documentation." One petition the program had filed failed because the judge found the paperwork incomplete. "At this point it really does seem like a total joke," a social worker who had contact with some of the fabled fifty-five people initially targeted for housing conservatorship told me.

Even when the city did get someone into a housing conservatorship, the results were not stellar. One person was rehospitalized, and the judge determined that they met criteria for a regular LPS conservatorship. Another was placed on a housing conservatorship while in the hospital and was set to be transferred to an unlocked facility (the kind of less restrictive option the program envisioned). They jumped out of the car on the way there. Since then, they've been "continuously AWOL" (according to one source), pinging in and out of emergency services and hospitals, with the person's conservator finding out where they had been only after they were released. The public conservator successfully filed to terminate the conservatorship. It's a huge liability to have legal responsibility for a vulnerable individual, absent the authority to get other agencies to help meet that responsibility.

There are some positive stories around the margins of the housing conservatorship fracas. A clinician with San Francisco's AOT program described a woman who had refused to engage despite a court order and instead racked up two dozen 5150s in a year—at least seven of which actually counted toward the eight-5150 criterion (because the ER diagnosed her with both a mental illness and substance use disorder). Then COVID saved her. She had refused a room with a shared bathroom in an SRO in the Tenderloin. But when her partner was offered a converted hotel room as part of the city's shelter-in-place program, she joined him—and, as far as the housing conservatorship program was concerned, disappeared. "She is not society's definition of successful," the clinician told me, but "she's not hanging out at one of the police stations pooping on their cars anymore." She had made it a year without a 5150. "She's a shining example of what consistent shelter can do for somebody,"[41] the clinician summarized, before speculating that when the city wound down the hotel program, she'd likely return to the streets. You can't make this stuff up.

Senator Wiener finally broke his silence about the bill in 2022 to condemn the city's "uncoordinated and lackadaisical" implementation.[42] This might be true, but implementation required engagement from a range of other delegated service providers, and the bill gave no authority to the city to actually force them into participating.

CONCLUSION: THE UNMET MANDATE FOR FORCED CARE

I spoke to Supervisor Mandelman in April 2021 about his waning advocacy for the housing conservatorship program. "The trouble is that, maybe we go up from one conserved person to five—the bang for the buck is pretty minimal. So, I don't know how much further to push 1045," he admitted. It showed in his eyes, the lack of government infrastructure necessary to pave a new pathway to involuntary care on top of the creaking LPS conservatorship continuum: "These reforms are predicated on an assumption that the counties can step in and take on the public health, criminal-justice, [and] involuntary detention obligations

[and] responsibilities that the state is throwing off. San Francisco is very wealthy, but . . . our systems [in the city] don't act like they can meet the need, or are even trying." I share his doubts.

"Any attempt to amend LPS is bound to be an uphill slog," Mandelman mused. But to him, the broader fight was a worthy one: "The need [for reform] is so obvious. As the state goes out of the prison business and San Francisco goes out of the jail business, we're conveniently shutting down all of our options [for managing disorderly behavior]" outside of forced treatment. The barriers that both civil liberties groups and half-sympathetic legislators threw up to SB 1045, he insisted out, were out of sync with the general population, which was more stridently in favor: "I think there is such a disconnect between how San Franciscans feel about what is happening on the streets and the response of government. . . . I mean, we're a democracy, right? So you think the people are always right. But they don't get their way." Mandelman is certainly correct that ceding defeat on SB 1045 will not make community pressure go away. But as he himself was seeing, legislative reform matters little if no one has clear responsibility for acting on it.

The next chapter considers another reform attempt that, unlike SB 1045, was not an effort to create an entirely new pathway onto conservatorship. It took aim, instead, at the "grave disability" criterion itself. SB 1045 came with the pretense that this was a gentler, less restrictive conservatorship, focused on getting people into independent housing. The reforms considered in the next chapter, though, emphasize rebuilding and refilling longer-term institutions.

CHAPTER 12

ASYLUM FOR THE DYING

I t's not just rhetoric: people are dying on the streets in Los Angeles. A total of 1,988 homeless people perished in the first year of the COVID-19 pandemic (starting March 2020), four times the tally from 2014.[1] The mass mortality is similarly sobering statewide (figure 12.1).

But homeless people are dying when they get off the streets, too.

In the summer of 2021, when I met Wally with Dr. Partovi, she assured me that there were hundreds of cases like his throughout the city. And, she told me, nowhere had a greater concentration of people debilitated by mental illness than Skid Row, where she has worked at the Homeless Health Care clinic for more than a decade.

It's disturbing to describe a visit to this fifty-three-block gallery of human misery as a "tour," but the reality is that there's no better place to see the crystallized consequences of decades of neglect. So I reached out to Dr. Bollom, a street psychiatrist who collaborates with the Department of Mental Health on a pilot conservatorship program, to show me around.

The futility of existing attempts to govern Skid Row are visible as soon as we leave DMH's office on the outskirts. A group of workers is power-spraying the sidewalk on one side of the street. On the other, mounds of objects that seem to intermix valued possessions and refuse are heaped between partly collapsed tents. 'Later today, they'll sweep that side of the street,' she tells me, 'and people will just move everything to the other side.' Indiscriminate cleaning operations like this have partly replaced endless citations as a way to push people off the streets and go . . . somewhere.[2]

We step into the street but have to pause as a man with no legs wheels past us into the center of the intersection, screaming at the sky. Next to us, another

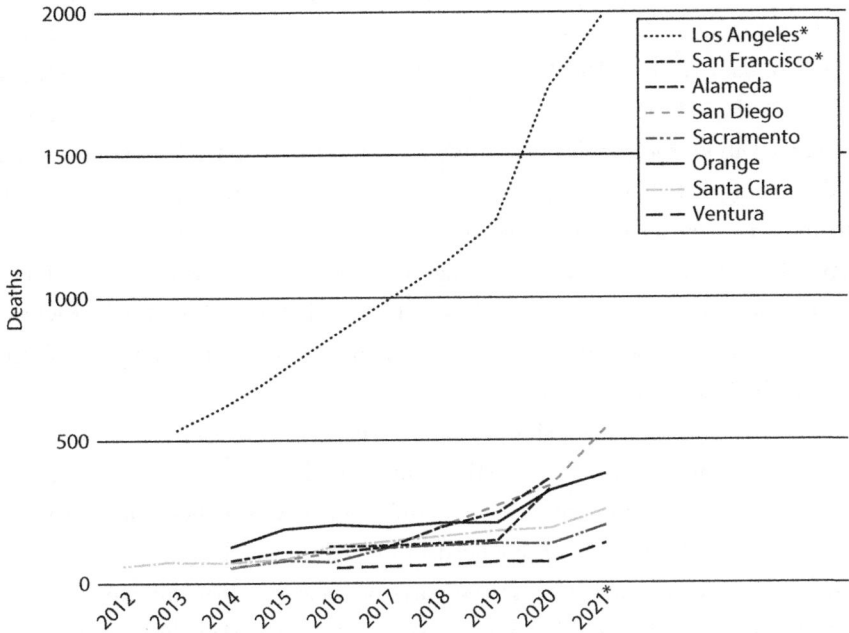

12.1 Deaths of people experiencing homelessness in select counties, 2012–2021

Source: County Coroners; Cawley et al. (2022)

* Data for 2021 are for the first year of COVID-19 pandemic (March 2020–March 2021)

man is rolling on the ground, with what looks like peanut butter coming from his mouth. I have no doubt that Dr. Bollom wishes she could help these individuals, but if you stop each time you see someone in visible crisis on Skid Row, you don't get very far. And the point of our visit is to give me a sense of psychosis not in its most jarring form but in its more subtle—and fatal—manifestations.

We're walking past a series of tents, and Dr. Bollom explains why the individuals here would not qualify for LA's Homeless Outreach and Mobile Engagement (HOME) team, which is working to facilitate conservatorships for the county's most chronically gravely disabled individuals. '[HOME's] clients would not have a tent,' she notes.

'Because it gets stolen, or because they can't manage to pitch one?' I wonder in response.

'Mostly the latter,' she replies. They're also often 'individuals who aren't showing up in any system' because their failure to attend to basic needs rarely leads to arrest or hospitalization, and they're easily overlooked by traditional outreach teams.

For privacy reasons, Dr. Bollom doesn't introduce me to any of HOME's clients.[3] But she's clearly on the lookout for potential referrals (and just genuinely concerned about the people we see). We walk over to a man lying on the sidewalk under a scraggly tree. He's alone, which she says is frequently the case for HOME clients, who often have severe paranoia and struggle to tap into the usual support networks between people experiencing homelessness. 'He has shoes,' she comments, and 'kind of a pillow,' which is just a wadded-up t-shirt, both of which seem to indicate some capacity for self-care. She thinks he's probably just sleeping off a high, and we move on.

We're walking along the side of the Union Rescue Mission, a mega-shelter that, Dr. Bollom assures me, HOME clients would never use and whose strict rules around congregate living they couldn't follow even if they wanted to. We see an individual lying with their head in one cardboard box and their feet in another. She's concerned because the parts of their legs that are exposed look very chafed, and she kneels down to investigate. It's a surprisingly common issue among HOME clients: abscesses or edema of the legs, putting them at risk of amputation. On the other hand, she observes, 'this is a pretty good box set up.' I know she sees the absurdity of this statement. But when your pilot program is serving fifty homeless people out of seventy thousand, triage is going to be brutally strict.

Toward the end of our tour, I admit to Dr. Bollom that I'm feeling pretty emotional. 'Do you think this exists anywhere else?' I ponder.

'This is pretty unique to LA,' she reflects, 'and the length of time these individuals have been going without services.'

In New York, at least, nearly all of the chronic homeless are on some agency's list. Until recently, 'HOME's clients were just invisible,' she reiterates. Another psychiatrist I spoke to who worked with the same population put it to me this way: "The people I care most about, they don't make a stink. . . . They don't fit any of the criteria, as they're currently defined, so [we] leave them there and they die there. . . . We have lots of people like that, and nobody has ever asked them a single question. They are just out there all by themselves, just forgotten people."

By this point, we're in front of a large supported housing building. For the past two decades, the momentum in homelessness policy has been toward Housing First, or the approach of placing people immediately in permanent, independent housing—no strings attached—and offering voluntary services afterward.[4] The evidence that this is an effective way to get people off the streets and keep them housed is robust.[5]

But what works for most homeless people may not work for HOME's clients. Many have refused housing offers because they have a delusion that keeps them fixed in place, sometimes unwilling to move even to go to the bathroom. If they did agree to be housed, 'most of our folks would not get a place, they would not make it through an interview, the facilities [mostly run by nonprofits] would cherry pick,' Dr. Bollom tells me. It might be for the best, because independent housing 'wouldn't be safe for them. They need 24-hour monitoring.'

A few days earlier, I visited one of those supported housing buildings where HOME clients who win the housing lottery and accept their winnings might go—and, tragically, die. Devon, my guide, is a social worker managing support services for several complexes that exclusively house once-homeless individuals. I've seen some pretty abysmal single-room occupancy hotels that qualify as "supported housing" over the course of my research, but this building is new and clean. There's a well-tended garden and barbeque area, neither of which seems to be getting much use.

While Devon is a Housing First believer, she also has a front-row seat to its failings. There was, for example, a woman who threatened repeatedly to blow up the building. She had a colostomy bag that she often did not attach. "There was blood and poop all over her unit," Devon recounts, "clearly not taking care of herself, so depressed and anxious, saying, 'I want to bomb the unit, just make this end.'" Devon called the county mobile crisis team, insisting, "This person needs emergency medical care." They came in a few hours, but by then she had "put on a clean T-shirt and walked back everything." The team left when she made a promise to see a primary-care doctor.

The experience was one reason Devon decided to pursue county authorization to write LPS holds herself. Still, 5150ing someone for grave disability "is so hard, because you're supposed to be writing a hold only when someone will imminently die because of their choices. It's so subjective. The line between self-determination and dignity of the person is so blurry."

That balancing act is trickiest for people refusing medical treatment for physical health issues. The week before, Devon did a wellness check on a resident and found him "actively dying . . . he smelled like death and decay." But he insisted, "I don't want to go to the hospital, don't call the ambulance." When the paramedics arrived, "They came and said, 'It's not okay for you to say "no," if you stay here you will die.' And he said, 'I don't want to die.' 'You have to come.' 'I don't want to go to the hospital.' Then they asked him, 'Do you want to die at home?' And he said, 'No, I don't want to die.' And the responders said, 'According to your vitals and your presentation, you will die.'" Eventually they took him in on grave disability. Devon says that LA County DMH has been sending signals to hospitals and clinicians that physical health needs should be considered in 5150 evaluations.

It hasn't been enough. In the past year, there have been thirty deaths across her nonprofit's supported housing projects. It's an endemic problem. In one audit from San Francisco, 7 percent of people placed in supported housing in 2010 were dead within five years.[6] The death rate in shelter-in-place hotels, where homeless people were sent to protect them from COVID, was distressingly high.[7] Fentanyl, a potent synthetic opioid increasingly finding its way into supplies of both meth and heroin, is a lethal accelerant (Figure 12.2).[8] Logan, a social worker in San

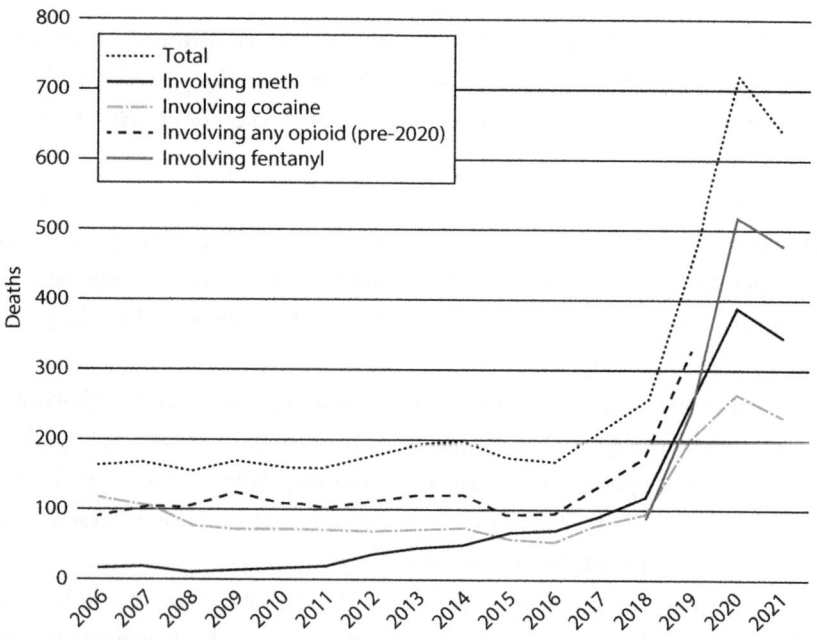

12.2 Overdose deaths in San Francisco by substance, 2006–2021

Source: San Francisco County Coroner

Francisco, told me that most of his clients' deaths were due to an overdose that was hidden behind apartment walls and so discovered too late to be reversed with Narcan, a nasal spray. He wondered, "Well if they had been on the street, would people have revived them? Did they lose their community when we housed them?"[9] He sighed, "It's very sad. But at least they died housed."

This chapter looks at proposals that target a different set of individuals from SB 1045—not the audibly addicted but the silently deteriorating. Concerns for this population congealed in a set of legislative proposals to revise grave disability to include a failure to attend to one's physical health. Those bills have so far failed. But efforts to get the dying into twenty-four-hour institutional care—not just independent housing—have continued to advance. Whether new approaches to imposing treatment will actually translate into more coercive care, I argue, will depend on budding efforts to rebuild long-term beds and partly roll back the de-institutionalization LPS is credited with helping spark.

REDEFINING GRAVE DISABILITY

How to define "grave disability" was a sticking point in the original negotiations over LPS. Prominent psychiatrists wanted it to include an inability to "manage [one's] personal affairs" or having "pronounced disturbance in judgment, thinking, or conduct."[10] The final bill kept only the narrow triptych of food, clothing, or shelter. An expansion of grave disability was a piece of the failed proposals to reform LPS in 1987 and 2000. Amending it to include cases in which a mental illness interferes with someone's ability to provide for their physical health became the centerpiece of a push for reform starting in 2017. In a later section, I will show that the failure to address the medical needs of people with mental illness is a key exhibit for the absence of any authority to make California's siloed systems of care work together. But first let's look at these proposals.

Among those pushing for a grave-disability rewrite is Dr. Partovi, the "renegade doctor of Skid Row." In 2007, she wrote an op-ed about "William," a patient she saw at the Venice Family Clinic after he was released from a hospital for congestive heart failure.[11] William consistently refused to take medications for his heart condition and a debilitating stroke; Partovi at various times asked Adult Protective Services and hospital psychiatrists to force him to, but one psychiatrist apparently told her, "It's his free will not to take his medications."

Without them, William died a few weeks later. Partovi used William to illustrate a stark reality: people with serious mental illness die on average twenty-five years younger than the general population, and "60 percent of premature deaths . . . are due to medical conditions such as cardiovascular, pulmonary, and infection diseases."[12]

In 2017, Partovi and Kerry Morrison (the Hollywood Business Improvement District director) convened a who's who of the mental health community in Los Angeles. At one event, Dr. Partovi delivered a PowerPoint presentation showing the bulging, untreated hernia of one patient to illustrate why grave disability should be amended to include an "inability to make informed medical decisions." By 2018, the working group had come up with a "checklist" to document factors suggesting a grave disability, such as "severe bodily infestation" (e.g., lice, scabies, maggots), "covered in bodily fluids" (e.g., blood, feces, vomit), and "untreated medical conditions" (e.g., unintentional substantial weight loss, serious open wounds). As Dr. Partovi explained it to me, "Everybody had their own definition of grave disability. . . . So I thought that if everyone was on the same page of what grave disability really was, we would all follow the law."

The problem, as the public guardian of LA repeatedly reminded Partovi when she pushed them to use the checklist, is that "the law" does not explicitly include unmet medical need as a criterion for grave disability. Partovi was part of a push to change that. In 2018, the Los Angeles County Board of Supervisors approved a resolution urging the state to "pass legislation that broadens that definition [of grave disability] to include people unable to seek medical care because of their mental illness." For one city councilmember, this effort was focused on "find[ing] a way to bring back institutionalization" for the permanently debilitated.[13]

Politicians were building on a local Department of Mental Health report that cited data from the coroner. It showed the rise in deaths among homeless people from "preventable and/or treatable medical conditions." The report admitted that "while this data does not indicate whether or not the deceased individual suffered from a mental illness," more forced mental health treatment was necessary because "individuals with cooccurring mental illness and homelessness . . . may account disproportionately for the increased death rates."[14]

The interpretive leaps here are worth calling out. Lots of mentally ill people are dying young. So, too, are many homeless people. But not all dying homeless people are mentally ill. And even for those that are, the main causes of death are overdoses, heart disease, transportation accidents, and homicides—to which mental illness may or may not have contributed. Suicides, where the linkage is clearest, accounted for only 4 percent of homeless deaths in LA in 2021.[15] The decision of people like William, from Partovi's op-ed, to refuse lifesaving treatment might seem irrational and inexplicable, but that doesn't mean it's pathological. Yet these caveats have been lost as policy makers and media draw increasingly direct lines between limits to forced treatment and people dying on the streets.[16]

The proliferation of bills to reform LPS is remarkable. A 2017 bill, AB 1539, would have added unmet medical care to the definition of grave disability. Two similar proposals followed in 2018, three in 2019. I counted nearly a dozen bills to expand forced treatment in 2020. A lobbyist who had been involved in attempts to reform LPS for decades told me that this was a grassroots effort: the "farm team" coming to the legislature from city councils and school boards was inundated with public concerns about homelessness. He explained, "We've seen an uptick in the number of elected [officials] at the state level that want to carry mental health legislation . . . it has become sexy. Everybody wants a bill." All this was driven by learning "how many people are dying on the street, from preventable health conditions that they're too gravely disabled to manage."

AB 1971, which a group of legislators from around LA introduced in 2018, made it the furthest. The bill passed a series of committees and a unanimous initial vote on the Assembly floor. As initially written, the legislation would have amended grave disability to include someone "unable to provide for his or her medical treatment, if the failure to receive medical treatment results in a deteriorating physical condition or death."[17] Senator Henry Stern, one of the sponsors, declared, "You can either walk past them, watch them die on our doorsteps, or we can do something about it."[18]

As with SB 1045, legislative staff panned these proposals. In one evaluation, staff quoted at length an argument from the association of county mental health directors that "the bill does not rule out abuses" because "it allows for virtually unfettered discretion to consider any medical condition without regard to its severity, likelihood of harm, or the person's capacity to treat it." Moreover, the legislation would allow someone to be forcibly held in a hospital as a result of their medical condition but "does not require that the person actually receives treatment during their detention." For good measure, they observed that "the capacity of med-psych beds"—the presumably appropriate setting for someone with comorbid issues—"are few."[19]

Legislators responded the way they typically have when civil rights concerns collide with a desire to take action: forging ahead while heaping on new protections. The psychiatrist Paul Appelbaum aptly calls this approach "ambivalence codified."[20] AB 1971 was shrunk to a pilot in LA, and it would require that a medical professional attest that a person's medical condition would "lead to death within six months." At this point, you could imagine AB 1971 leading to as many conservatorships as the SB 1045 housing conservatorship program did (recall: three). But the sponsors sensibly realized, as the lobbyist told me, that "the bill had been weakened beyond the point where it would be helpful" and pulled it.[21]

Reformers hit pause while waiting for a state auditor's report on the functioning of LPS in Los Angeles, San Francisco, and Shasta County, the first serious investigation in decades. Virtually everyone I talked to assumed it would provide compelling ammunition for a change to LPS criteria. Virtually everyone I talked to was surprised when the report, released in the summer of 2020, didn't. Instead, after reviewing documentation for sixty 5150s and sixty conservatorships, the auditor found "no evidence to justify . . . expanding or revising the LPS Act's criteria."[22] Opponents of rewriting grave disability, like the *Los Angeles Times* editorial board, crowed that the audit showed that "the real problem . . . is not the patients' right to self-determination, but the failure of the state and counties to provide sufficient ongoing care and housing."[23]

The audit, and the concomitant coronavirus pandemic, temporarily took the wind out of the sails of the movement to expand conservatorships. But in January 2022, Governor Newsom was again talking about "lean[ing] into conservatorships" in the legislative session later that year.[24] This means that it might be a good moment to analyze what reforming LPS—and, particularly, expanding grave disability to include someone's physical health—might actually do.

"OPERATION DIGNITY" FOR TRI-MORBIDITIES

Dr. Aaron Meyer is the kind of person you'd think would be on board for expanding who counts as gravely disabled. He deferred medical school for a year so he could work at a homeless shelter, where he encountered people with "untreated schizophrenia whose medical conditions were inadequately addressed." He wanted to be a family physician but switched to psychiatry when he realized that otherwise his training would not sufficiently cover mental health. He is currently working with UC San Diego's hospital system providing psychiatric care for people hospitalized for physical health problems. In 2021, he risked his career as part of "Operation Dignity," a project to conserve people dying of substance use, cognitive impairments, and physical disabilities. So I'm surprised when he tells me that rewriting grave disability, billed as helping to conserve people dying of substance use, cognitive impairments, and physical disabilities, is "garbage."

Like so many efforts across California, Operation Dignity emerged from what Dr. Meyer described as the "moral injury" that comes from working in an ER where "time and time again you have to click the discharge button because there's nowhere to send anybody." Sam, a hospital psychologist who works with Meyer, told me that, over time, they both realized that many frequent flyers had not only chronic alcoholism and mental illness but also serious cognitive impairments as a result of both being left unaddressed. He explained that "a lot of times when we saw someone coming in struggling with homelessness and a long history of substance use disorder, biases would come into play: 'They're not engaging in these things [medical care] because they're addicted. If they could kick their addiction, they could do self-care.'" Sam began doing some psychological testing and saw that cognitive impairments like dementia were kicking in at as early as forty years old for homeless people with heavy meth or alcohol use. This raised the question: "Well, are these people even *capable* of self-care?" The conclusion was that, no, they weren't. They needed conservatorship.

Many of these individuals were already being targeted by the Resource Action Program (RAP), a team led by the San Diego Fire Department to deal with super-high utilizers of emergency services. Since some were visiting the ER hundreds of times a year, Dr. Meyer had plenty of opportunities to cajole sympathetic colleagues into admitting them. Once they were inpatients, he badgered his colleagues on the medical floors of the hospital to keep them. He told me, "We've called it Operation Dignity, because what I want is for people not to be found daily in the street covered in their own feces and urine with skin breakdown. Until there is a better alternative . . . [conservatorship] is the only way to not have people found [by the fire department] covered in their own bodily fluids." He filed ten petitions in a few months, all for people with substance use and cognitive impairments. Seven were refused by the county public conservator.

There are two defensible reasons why the public conservator would be resistant to applications for individuals with "tri-morbidities" (psychiatric, medical, and substance use disorders). First, of course, there's nowhere to put them. "Integrated care" is a policy buzzword, but the system is designed as if these were three separate populations. UCSD's psychiatric ward strictly excludes people who need IVs, monitors, or catheters. IMDs and board and cares frequently won't take people in wheelchairs or with colostomy bags. Medical hospitals, for their part, don't like psychiatric cases. It's partly stigma. It's partly that medical teams are not as equipped to restrain and contain difficult behavior. And psychiatric patients provide fewer opportunities to bill for the expensive tests and procedures that are hospitals' financial lifeblood.

Sam, the hospital psychologist, rounded out this sad picture by commenting on the last of the three systems supposed to be serving tri-morbid cases. Substance use facilities running voluntary self-improvement recovery programs "require some fairly decent cognitive function to engage appropriately." Chronic alcoholism, the primary diagnosis of many of RAP's clients, leads to behavioral problems, potentially fatal medical complications, and dementia; it can rule someone out for every program but jail. "The patients needing the most help and the ones who are the hardest to serve are the ones needing help from multiple systems," a paramedic from RAP told me. So the first reason the public guardian might deny these applications was that they were rightly worried about where the subjects of Operation Dignity were actually going to go.

The second reason to refuse a petition is concern about what would happen when a conservatee got into a placement. Courts usually grant public guardians blanket authority to consent to noninvasive medical treatment on the conservatee's behalf. For anything more serious—such as amputating a limb for a diabetic—they need to return to court and then find a medical team willing to act on that court order. Joseph DeVico, who worked as a deputy conservator in San Diego, told me a sad story about one of many conservatees "who lost their right to refuse medical treatment . . . [and] died from untreated severe illness anyway." The woman was "gruff, super intelligent, crazy creative, heart of gold, came off like a hard chick standing in a saloon. She was amazing." She also had cancer and believed she could cure it with a mixture of seawater and vinegar. DeVico did his due diligence, talking to her doctors about whether she had the capacity to refuse chemotherapy. He concluded that she didn't. But, he pointed out, "there is no medical team anywhere, certainly not in San Diego . . . [that] is going to dogpile the patient and hold them down [to give them chemotherapy]," whatever authority a court has granted. This is, in fact, a key part of why the

California Hospital Association opposed AB 1971 (the bill to add unmet physical health needs to grave disability): because it would potentially lead to more people being brought to the hospital for conditions that the hospital legally couldn't, or ethically wouldn't, forcibly treat.[25]

Despite the bureaucratic barriers, Dr. Meyer was undaunted. He filed an application for Jesus, a seventy-one-year-old who had been homeless for a decade. Jesus visited the ER four hundred times in one year, sometimes because he called 911 trying to get food, but once because EMS brought him in after being hit by a car, causing a brain bleed that necessitated emergency surgery. Dr. Meyer found somewhere in Jesus's medical record that he had once been diagnosed with schizophrenia. This was enough to apply for an LPS conservatorship (even though Dr. Meyer thinks his problem was really prolonged meth use, alcoholism, and dementia).

As in several other cases, the public conservator told the Operation Dignity team that Jesus's application needed to go the public guardian, the agency that does probate conservatorships. The public guardian then told them he should go to the public conservator, responsible for LPS conservatorships. Dr. Meyer, rightly, found this absurd. Alcoholism and dementia can be the basis for an LPS conservatorship or a probate one.[26] Although the public conservator and the public guardian in San Diego are supposedly separate entities, they have the same address and phone number.[27] ("It seems there's zero communication" between them, Sam assured me.) Dr. Meyer was facing a bureaucratic runaround for trying to get stabilizing treatment for the person who, at least measured in 911 calls, might have been the neediest person in San Diego County.

In Jesus's case, the agency-on-agency battle got even more heated. The San Diego city attorney's Public Nuisance Abatement Unit (really) realized that while public conservators have absolute discretion over whether to file for an LPS conservatorship, the court can order them to file for a probate conservatorship.[28] So the city took the county to probate court. In the hearing, the judge declared that probate conservatorships were really for little old ladies (I saw the court transcript). They berated the public conservator into conducting an LPS investigation. The happy ending to this story, I guess, is that as of September 2022, Jesus was on an LPS conservatorship. He had been waiting for more than a year and a half to step down to a neuropsychiatric nursing home. San Diego only contracts with one such facility, and his wait is typical to get into it.[29] On the plus side, the city attorney donated a PlayStation and Xbox to help entertain these conservatees, for whom the hospital was now home.

There's an essential point here: the LPS criteria were never really the issue. That's why Dr. Meyer thinks the reforms are "garbage." Courts didn't deny a single one of his petitions. In fact, raising someone's decrepit physical state is his trump card when testifying in LPS hearings: "all I have to do is show a picture of their wound, any kind of abnormal lab value, it's almost game over, the judges will rule it's grave disability," he told me. He once had an LPS hold upheld for a homeless person whose main problem was a lice infestation, leading to exceptionally low hemoglobin. LPS criteria are vague, regulations on how to define them are minimal, and oversight is limited. But as Dr. Meyer summarized, "Laws and paper don't matter when there's no buildings. . . . If you don't have places for people to go, no nimble teams [to apply those criteria], no law is going to be successful."

The end of Dr. Meyer's story is a different cautionary tale about trying to force disparate institutions into caring for inconvenient people. After Operation Dignity's "crusade" of conservatorship petitions, UCSD announced the formation of a "conservatorship committee." Matt, a psychiatry resident, described his own hospital's committee as existing to "deny everything." Hospital administration admonished Dr. Meyer to stop putting holds on substance users who would occupy their beds for an indeterminant length of time. They transferred Dr. Meyer temporarily to another hospital that was not formally designated to take LPS patients.

If there's that much resistance throughout the continuum to conserving someone already coming to the ER four hundred times in a year, imagine what it would look like if, after LPS is loosened, someone tried to get the silent, huddled masses of Skid Row inpatient care.

OUTPATIENT CONSERVATORSHIP FOR INPATIENT CARE

One consequence of abdicated authority is that there are multiple tools within LPS law that could be used to push more people onto conservatorship, even absent legislative changes, but that have been lying dormant for lack of government strategy or initiative. Some enterprising actors are changing that. Public defenders have been figuring out a variety of ways for courts and jails to divert people onto LPS conservatorships, for example. San Francisco has begun using the dormant provisions that allow for a determination of grave disability based on chronic alcoholism. This section turns to another such mechanism: a long-ignored statute that allows counties to file a conservatorship petition for someone living on the streets without passing through the whole series of veto points—5150s, ERs, and inpatient units—that people-process most people off the conservatorship continuum.[30]

Most LPS reforms seek to cram more people through existing pathways. I'm intrigued by LA's outpatient conservatorship program because, in contrast, it used this dormant authority as part of a deliberate, government-led reflection to better identify who specifically benefits from conservatorship. Jon Sherin, a former VA psychiatrist appointed to run the three-billion-dollar-a-year DMH in 2016, explained to me that the typical circuit of waiting for someone to be in acute crisis, taking them to a hospital, and only applying for conservatorship if they fail to stabilize, is a "waste of time." People dying on the street, he said, "have a chronic problem . . . and we throw them into an acute [hospital], at great expense to the taxpayer, into beds that are already log-jammed, in an environment that is toxic."

His idea, instead, was for the Homeless Outreach and Mobile Engagement team, which works with those unhoused persons in the county most struggling to survive on the streets, to approach targeted individuals with a "platter" of services. "Guaranteed housing" was a key part of that platter. It could be "a shelter bed, a board and care bed, any type of bed that we will make available to that person in real time from the street." He insisted, "You don't mess with someone's autonomy, unless you offer them resources up front."

As someone who still worked as a street psychiatrist, Sherin knew that most people have been "burned" by the system before, so "99 percent of the time, they say, 'get lost.'" When the team "reach[es] the point where that relentless engagement with dedicated, committed resources up front is not effective . . . then we have to think about compelling engagement." That might start with court-ordered outpatient treatment (AOT) but could ultimately graduate to a conservatorship application—made by an outpatient clinician while that person was still on the street. The point was that HOME would only pursue conservatorship when a full range of resources had been offered and a placement for a newly conserved client was already lined up.

Starting in August 2020, a committee for this outpatient conservatorship pilot brought HOME and the public guardian together weekly to discuss potential cases. I watched a training by Dr. Elizabeth Bromley, a psychiatrist involved with the pilot, that gave a window into the clientele they envisioned. In contrast to Dr. Partovi's approach, Bromley said that "grave disability, it's conceptual, there are criteria, but there's not a checklist where you can have four out of eight, and it's some kind of line or threshold." She gave a range of examples showing the nexus between an inability to provide for one's needs and psychosis: someone convinced they had a "solar powered heart" that they needed to be outside to charge, a person who believed they would be executed by the CIA if they left a street corner, or an individual refusing a board and care because staff were in a cult torturing residents.[31] An absence of hospitalizations, arrests, or ER visits might make their grave disability less visible to a judge. It was thus crucial for street-level clinicians to gradually build up a case for conservatorship over repeated encounters.

In February 2022, the team released the first results of the pilot. The committee discussed forty-three individuals and filed a petition on thirty. The judge ruled to conserve twenty-six.[32] The pandemic, surprisingly, facilitated the process. Rather than having to drag someone to their hearing, clinicians could have them attend virtually, from the street. Judges got to see them in their "natural" environment (where they might be starving, naked, and exposed) and not the artificial space of a hospital (where food, clothing, and shelter were provided). The people they conserved were "highly vulnerable" individuals who, in addition to schizophrenia or substance use, frequently had "physical health conditions" like "HIV, extremity infections, atrial fibrillation, wheelchair-dependence, traumatic brain injury, [or] pulmonary embolism."

The outpatient conservatorship team had hoped that many people could short-circuit an acute hospitalization and go directly to long-term care facilities. And 27 percent did make it to an unlocked facility, like a board and care. One person involved in the pilot told me, enthusiastically, that "at the beginning, I would have told you that the only way this is going to be effective is that they all would have needed to go into some locked setting. I thought maybe the drive to be back out on the streets would result in individuals eloping from their facilities." Happily, they found that "some of the clients, not all, [have] been able to go into an open setting, and they're staying, they're not giving any hint that they want to go back on the streets."

But the others did need an acute hospitalization. Moreover, according to the first results submitted, "medical problems uncovered after referral for conservatorship led to long placement delays" in stepping down from hospitals into

IMDs. Even this coordinated government effort struggled against both the complex needs of conservatees—accumulated thanks to decades of prior government indifference—and a delegated system that still gave private providers ample discretion to turn down those cases of most concern to public authorities.

Jon Sherin's vision was much broader than a fifty-person program. His 2018 pitch for the pilot anticipated "1,000 additional referrals per year [in LA] . . . on an outpatient basis."[33] For that, he's convinced, he would need more than just adding "physical health" to grave disability. In his reading, the original idea behind grave disability "was based on 'living safely in the community,' but it got whittled down to food, clothing, and shelter." He was hoping to bring back that early conception: "There are many indicators [of not living safely]. Not being able to access medical care when you've got gangrene. Allowing yourself to be preyed upon and sexually assaulted, daily. . . . Pushing people into traffic. Having an infectious disease and throwing feces at people." But, as the inpatient placements used by the outpatient conservatorship pilot showed, to treat the people meeting those criteria, you're going to need hospital beds. That's where we turn now.

BREAKING GROUND

December 21, 2021 was a milestone for California's mental health system—and an omen of profound change in the conservatorship continuum. That day, the Sacramento Behavioral Health Facility, a new 117-bed hospital, accepted its first patient. It was the first psychiatric hospital built from the ground up in California in thirty years.[34] (A representative of the hospital industry told me it had been so long that no one in state government knew the procedure to license such a facility anymore, causing significant delays.)

The Sacramento hospital was one of many initiatives to expand capacity in locked, acute-care psychiatric facilities. In 2018, for example, rural Shasta County announced twenty new mental health beds in its Regional Medical Center. "Countless area residents" thanked the board of supervisors for taking action.[35] The response was a far cry from the opprobrium typically heaped on plans to bring people living with mental illness into the neighborhood. A few other notable examples include approval of an eighty-bed facility in Indio, the addition of sixty-six beds to a hospital in San Jose, groundbreaking for two sixteen-bed stand-alone units in Bakersfield, and the opening of a new sixteen-bed facility on the campus of a county Recovery Center in the Central Valley.[36] I was struck by the near-universal welcoming of this expansion of the most restrictive end of the placement continuum. A nurse with an intensive outpatient treatment team for unsheltered homeless people in San Francisco put it pithily: "100 percent of our people need a higher level of care."

Graphs and statistics showing that California has fewer acute psychiatric beds than the national average and most developed countries circulate end-lessly in PowerPoints, hearings, and planning reports around the state. The gap is less dramatic if you include state hospitals and locked settings like IMDs (figure 12.3). Multiple analyses have concluded that California would have enough inpatient beds if there were sufficient crisis intervention services up front and people were not lingering inappropriately waiting to step down to lower levels of care.[37] Yet the conviction that California needs more beds is

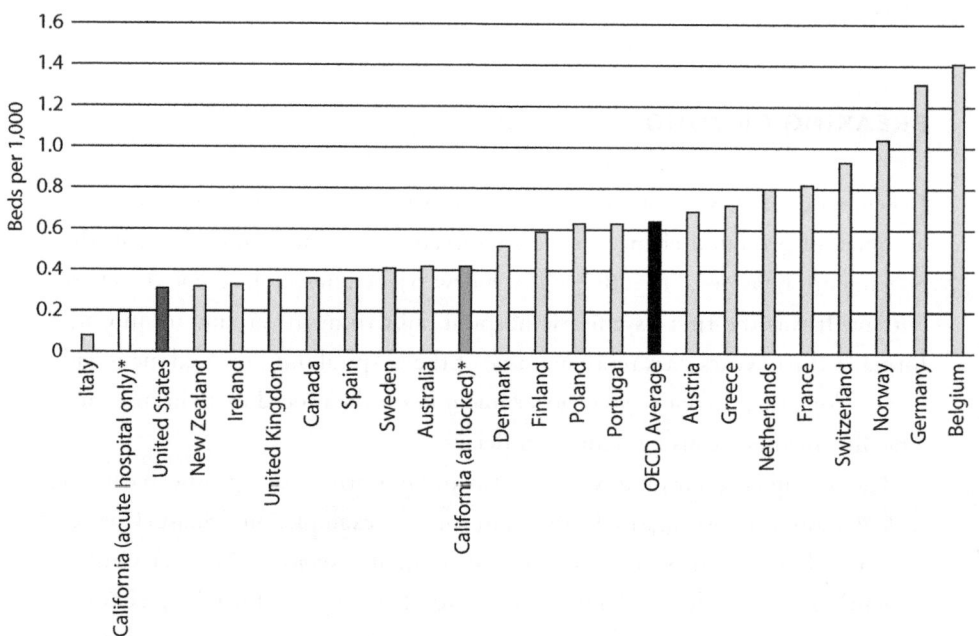

12.3 Psychiatric beds in California and select countries, 2021

Source: OECD, RAND

* Data for California include only adult beds

pervasive. A representative of the hospital industry celebrated, "We've seen the pendulum shift too far to the side that says, 'no involuntary care, all care should be recovery, voluntarily-based.' . . . But in the last three years, except for the hardcore naysayers, we have seen a significant shift back into acknowledging that we have a shortage of beds."

The impetus for the Sacramento hospital came from a private company, Signature Healthcare Services, which operates nineteen hospitals across four states. This mirrors a national trend toward more beds owned by for-profit chains.[38] Jerry Seelig, a financing guru in Los Angeles to whom I turned any time I couldn't figure out how someone in health care was making money, explained, "There's just such a crisis that you can get insurance plans and the government to pay enough for you [a private hospital] to make it work." Tightening financial screws elsewhere in the health care industry, he told me, meant that hospitals had empty beds that could be cheaply converted to psychiatric ones. Meanwhile, insurers, tired of bidding for overpriced beds far away, were willing to invest in increasing capacity locally.

State government is also taking an increasingly aggressive role. In his 2020 State of the State speech, Governor Newsom linked conservatorship reform and investment in new facilities, stating that legislative change would be an "empty promise" without "creating more placements."[39] This was not hollow rhetoric. In 2021, the governor allocated $750 million for 5,000 new treatment beds;[40] after the state found itself with an unexpected budget surplus during the pandemic, the governor added another $2.2 billion for a promised twenty-two thousand housing slots.[41] For Jon Sherin, formerly director of Los Angeles's DMH, the new funds added to a commitment the county supervisors made in 2019 to build one thousand new placements: "We're in the process of a massive expansion of beds— I'm talking about locked beds, subacute beds, open residential beds, and board and cares that have a lot of bells and whistles."

He was nonetheless wary of a "one-time" state investment, since tending to the people in those beds will cost tens of millions of dollars per year. To pay for that, he explained, "we need the IMD exclusion to go away." He was referring to the 1965 rule that Medicaid funds cannot go to a facility with sixteen or more beds if more than half of residents have a primary psychiatric disorder. The late D. J. Jaffe wrote that "eliminat[ing] the IMD exclusion" is the "single most important change" that could be made to the mental health system, since it would allow psychiatric hospitals to tap into a nearly $700-billion-per-year funding stream.[42]

Starting in 2015, the federal government began allowing states to apply for a partial "waiver" from this prohibition.[43] An anonymous source with knowledge of the policy-making process told me that an eventual request from California for these federal funds had unstoppable momentum: "Obviously, given the shortage of beds there is now—consensus might be too strong of a word, but growing support for expanding the capacity of facilities, so that they can take in more folks . . . I haven't heard any debate about it [the waiver]. It is 'the thing that is happening.'"[44]

New interest from private investors, a windfall of funds from state government, and a potential spigot of federal Medicaid money—what does this all add up to? For critics: time travel back a few generations. A lobbyist for a civil rights group lambasted the efforts by the governor as "going back to that course that we've been through [institutionalization], that we know was pretty cruel, caused pretty outstanding problems." Another advocate expressed to me her "deep fear that there are politicians who want to go back to state hospitals, only privately run. [They're thinking], 'We just need to get these homeless people off the streets, lock them up, make money off of them . . .'"

A surprising number of people I interviewed hoped, precisely, that these investments were a down payment on something bigger: bringing back the asylum.[45] Lieutenant Reid from LAPD described to me a vision for a "healthcare campus": "We have this idea of 'we're going to scoop you up on a hold and it'll get better' . . . [but people need] lifetime maintenance . . . a place to live, something like a senior center, with nice parks and green space." (Many people from law enforcement, for whatever reason, seemed to have the same idea.) Others were harsher: a columnist in Marin articulated his totalitarian vision of "promptly abolishing Lanterman-Petris-Short and properly funding twenty-first-century residential state hospitals . . . [providing] life-time mandatory psychiatric care."[46] Deinstitutionalization, it seems, is over. The question is how far to turn back the clock.

CONCLUSION: PESSIMISM AND INSTITUTIONALIZATION

As you saw in the previous chapter, at least rhetorically, the policy makers and government officials behind SB 1045 framed housing conservatorships as oriented toward recovery and independence. And, at least theoretically, that made sense for people whose problematic behaviors could be ameliorated with a period of forced abstinence from methamphetamine.

The initiatives profiled in this chapter—from the push to redefine grave disability to Operation Dignity to LA's outpatient conservatorship pilot—are at once more pessimistic and paternalistic. They are focused on protecting people who are assumed to need ongoing conservatorship and institutional care. This seems less cruel when you look harder at California's streets and focus less on the person shouting in the center of an intersection and more on the person wasting away at the bus stop behind them.

Does meeting the needs of people dying of neglected medical conditions on the streets or overdosing in supported housing require reforming LPS? There's one thing I am sure of: new beds will not lie empty. The definition of grave disability will expand to fill them, regardless of legislators' success in overcoming entrenched opposition to LPS reform. Whether that expansion will catch the individuals who most need care and provide the type of care they actually need is a different question.

This momentum behind rebuilding the asylum makes the question asked by the next chapter even more urgent: are there alternatives that could convince the public and policy makers that ramping up forced inpatient treatment to save those dying and disruptive on the streets is unnecessary?

CHAPTER 13

SHARING AUTHORITY, RESTORING AUTONOMY

I first met Eric Henriques at a "toxic conservatorship" forum (like many similarly titled events on conservatorship in 2021, it nodded to the 2003 Britney Spears song) hosted by Senior Disability Action and the Mad Mob, two San Francisco–based groups at the forefront of opposition to SB 1045. At the event, a lawyer from the ACLU lamented how conservatorship discriminated against people, like her, with psychiatric disabilities. A woman representing the group Depressed While Black decried how African Americans were at the "bottom of the psychiatric hospital ladder," frequently forced into low-quality care. A patients' rights advocate inveighed that "medication is not the answer" and denounced how "people get caught up in conservatorship, and they never learn how to take care of themselves. They have no community. . . . They lose any skills they have. They have to obey." Another speaker blasted California's program of forced sterilizations in state hospitals, which only wound down in the 1970s.[1]

For his part, Eric introduced himself as a "peer in recovery living with mental health challenges." More specifically, he identifies as having schizoaffective disorder. He's circumspect about that label: although he acknowledged that "some people have challenges with those terms," for him the diagnosis is a "useful framework that helps me understand and manage the symptoms of that disorder" (neither a purely objective biological reality nor a manufactured category intended to control deviant or inconvenient people[2]). He had a similar take on medication: "I do realize psychiatric medications are torture, but the right combination—I've been on two antipsychotics for fifteen years—put me in a better place." He even told me in an interview after the event, "I'm not one of those people who think [conservatorship] should be completely eliminated," even though "a lot of additional thought should be put into [its use]."

That's generous, because when he says he knows "how horrific conservatorship is," he's speaking with authority. He grew up in Colorado. When he was seventeen, he attempted suicide; he went to an adolescent hospital unit for two weeks but continued to engage in self-injury. His parents agreed with his doctor that he belonged in a state hospital. Eric says he was flown to the facility on a small sheriff's plane, shackled at the legs. This was 1981, but his experiences speak to the dystopian conditions that persisted even after laws like LPS went into effect nationwide. He recalls, "I saw folks who were physically restrained and taken to the showers. They had leather masks because they were biters and spitters. . . . Much of the time was spent in mindless activities. . . . I experienced sexual assault and sexual coercion by patients and staff." He stayed a year and a half.

When he was discharged, he went back to his hometown to live in a halfway house. He grew frustrated with the program and took a bus to Denver, where he was gripped by worsening psychotic symptoms. He wandered the streets, homeless, until he was hospitalized and sent to a nursing home. It was a "pretty, pretty depressing, horrific place to be as a nineteen-year-old." He decompensated and wound up again in a state hospital. After a year and a half, he got a day pass to leave the facility and hopped a plane to San Francisco. There, too, he was hospitalized. His psychiatrist told him he needed electroconvulsive therapy (ECT). He had four treatments; after each, he'd wake up with "no idea where I was." When he started refusing further ECTs, the county conserved him and sent him to Napa State Hospital.

Eric's story, he said at the forum, was one of both "trauma and hope," because eventually Eric found a therapist and a psychiatrist he liked, started taking medications that worked, and built up a support network anchored by his husband (now of twenty-five years). After going back to school, he discovered that there is a "viable alternative to conservatorship": peer support. "Peers" are people with "expertise from lived experience" who provide "social and/or emotional support . . . delivered with mutual agreement . . . to service users sharing similar challenges."[3]

In 2014, Eric interviewed for a position with the Mental Health Association of San Francisco (MHA-SF) as a "warm-line" counselor, providing a nonjudgmental ear to people who couldn't find one among psychiatrists or therapists. Eric then moved into crisis work in Marin County. He'd accompany clinicians conducting 5150 evaluations, providing "comfort" and "emotional support" to people as they were being transferred to the hospital.

By 2021, Eric had been promoted to the director of peer services for MHA-SF.[4] He oversees a whole continuum of services, including the warm-line and community support groups. Across these settings, he says, peers provide a "personalized, humane approach . . . based on equality not hierarchy." Sometimes, they help with "get[ting] folks connected to very healing, supportive, appropriate services." At other moments, they aid people who don't want to work with a clinician at all but still would like skills to, for example, reduce harm from substance use.

When we spoke, he was starting a new peer program in St. Francis Hospital, where he'd been given ECT back in the 1980s. Unlike virtually every other professional patients encounter in an acute hospital, the MHA peers they meet as they near discharge stay with them as they reenter the community, helping them get into housing or make it to follow-up appointments. The ultimate goal is to "reduce future hospitalizations," which is an urgent task. Nationally, 20 percent of people with schizophrenia discharged from acute psychiatric hospitals are readmitted within thirty days.[5] The St. Francis program had been going for only four months, but Eric already has some success stories: one person was "refusing to communicate with staff" and at risk of being either conserved or discharged without outpatient care. The peer, though, was able to "develop trust and rapport . . . with a little bit of self-disclosure." That person, he said, "is now actually thriving in the community." MHA is developing a similar program for people living with mental illness being released from the county jail.

As the 2021 forum I attended articulated, at heart conservatorship is about taking away choices. More precisely, conservatorship is a mechanism for *substituted* decision making, in which a third party makes choices on behalf of a person deemed incompetent or incapable of doing so. Disability rights advocates have clamored, instead, for the expansion of *supported* decision making. In such arrangements, a person with disabilities relies on a trusted network of friends, family, and professionals to help them make choices that are, ultimately, their own.[6] On September 30, 2022, Governor Newsom signed legislation obligating judges to consider supported decision making in lieu of conservatorship. He trumpeted how the law would ensure that people with disabilities "maintain control over their lives to the greatest extent possible."[7]

That legislation, however, applies only to probate conservatorship. The governor, after all, had long pushed to ramp up the use of substituted decision making for people with mental illness through the expansion of LPS conservatorships. Nationwide, the vast majority of supported-decision-making arrangements are for people with developmental disabilities.[8] Experts working in the developmental disabilities system raised doubts to me about how well these models could translate into the mental health system. They grounded those concerns in the observation that people with severe mental illness might have disruptive crises, refuse needed care, have lost the ability to survive independently (sometimes as a result of prolonged institutionalization or substance use), and have frayed links to their erstwhile supporters such as family or friends.

In this chapter, I sketch out a *continuum of collaboration* (figure 13.1): a series of interlinked interventions that could address the specific challenges posed

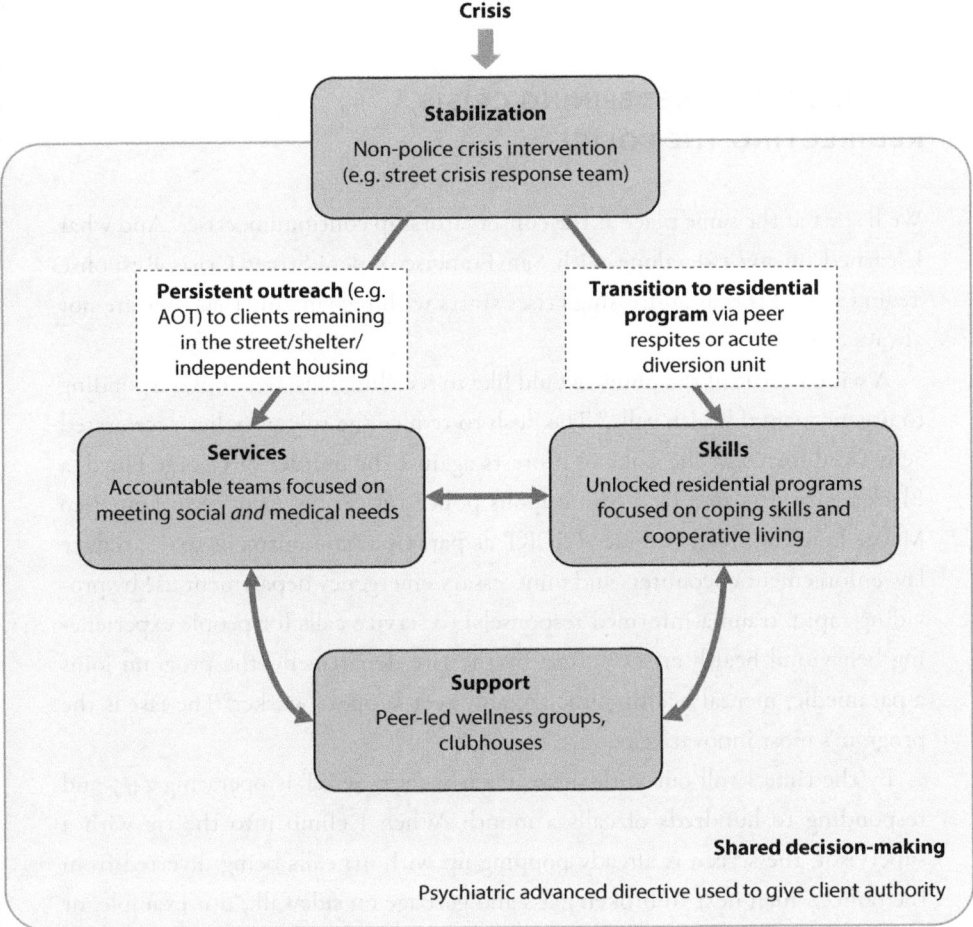

13.1 The continuum of collaboration

by mental illness while enacting the principles of autonomy and choice at the heart of supported decision making. I draw on the example of programs, like the peer supports described by Eric, that already exist, albeit not at scale, in California. This continuum must provide five things, each of which requires building a relationship based on respect and cooperation: *stabilization* that protects people from coercion; patient and persistent *services* that address their medical and social needs in tandem; programs that help them develop *skills* to survive interdependently in the community; *supports* that offer hope, human connection, and purpose; and, ultimately, tools for *shared* decision making that transfer authority for organizing the mental health system to the people it is supposed to serve.

STABILIZATION: REDEFINING CRISIS, REDIRECTING THE POLICE

We'll start at the same place as the conservatorship continuum: crises. And what I learned on my ride-along with San Francisco's new Street Crisis Response Team (SCRT) is that addressing crises starts with recognizing that they are not always crises.

A wide swathe of the public would like to see clinicians, not cops, responding to urgent mental health calls.[9] The push to reduce the role of police accelerated across California in the wake of protests against the murder of George Floyd, a Black man suffocated by a Minneapolis police officer, in 2020.[10] San Francisco Mayor London Breed embraced SCRT as part of a "commitment to . . . reduce law enforcement encounters and unnecessary emergency department use by providing rapid, trauma-informed response[s] to service calls for people experiencing behavioral health crises."[11] Run by the fire department, the program joins a paramedic, mental health clinician, and peer support worker. The last is the program's most innovative feature.

By the time I roll out with them in early 2022, SCRT is operating 24/7 and responding to hundreds of calls a month. When I climb into the rig with a supervisor, the screen is already popping up with 911 calls being diverted from the police: "man next to broken glass and garbage on sidewalk," for example, or "woman in street, writhing on the ground, with headphones." Most calls that go to SCRT are made by third parties about someone they don't know. The majority are flagged as "impulsive or disruptive behavior," with a smaller number classi-fied as "poor self-care or suspected grave disability."[12]

Our first case falls, on first blush, into both camps. According to the caller, the man has "three shopping carts" and "yells and screams all day." We find him sitting outside the door of a café, rocking back and forth, wearing sweatpants rolled up so we can see a peeling, chafed leg. We buy him a coffee. He asks for some lotion, which we don't have. The supervisor is confident he's already on the radar of the city's longer-term homeless outreach team, which is a better fit for his not-very-acute state. Call cleared.

The next call is for a woman reported as "throwing things and waving a crack pipe." When we show up, she's doing exactly that (also dancing to a blaring speaker next to her). A peer from another SCRT team and an outreach worker are talking to her. The worker comes up to our window and tells us, 'she's just using [substances] and being rude. It doesn't even look like she's having a bad day. She's not going anywhere.' We're in the Tenderloin, a neighborhood with a hyper-concentration of unsheltered homeless. It's hard to know why this behav-ior stood out enough to merit a 911 call.

We head to a leafy residential neighborhood, quiet save for an old man curled up on a side street, having a loud conversation with himself. There's already a paramedic here, and he tells the supervisor the man is alert, oriented, appropri-ately dressed for the climate, and accepting food. (SCRT vans have preprepared meals they can heat and hand out.) The supervisor encourages me to go talk to him. "Alert and oriented" seems to be defined expansively. He can't remember how long he's been homeless and says he doesn't want to go to a shelter because he has a friend who is going to give him an apartment at an unspecified date in the future. We head back to the rig. The man goes back to talking. The super-visor thinks he's just hard of hearing and doesn't realize how much noise he's making. The neighbors who called presumably do.

The first evaluation report on SCRT confirmed what I saw on my ride-along: that, "in line with the harm-reduction philosophy underpinning SCRT," 68 per-cent of SCRT clients are left in place where "they feel most comfortable and pre-fer to be." Chief Simon Pang, who heads the community paramedicine team at the fire department, outlined the typical intervention: "Someone is in crisis, they [community members] call us, we go. We de-escalate them, by giving them time, by listening to them, by giving them food. They're no longer shouting. Maybe they're no longer naked, because we gave them clothes. And now we ask them,

'What do you need to improve your situation? Can we take you somewhere, to shelter, treatment, a safe place to rest?' And they say 'no.'"

Pang wishes SCRT could put individuals on a pathway to a broader set of services. In practice, although SCRT makes referrals to the city's outpatient treatment programs, few wind up connecting in an enduring way.[13] Jennifer Friedenbach, from the city's Coalition on Homelessness, pointed out that SCRT "is in the end going to be as effective as the system that's behind them, and whether they have an ability to place people in beds . . . otherwise, it's just going to be the revolving door where [SCRT] is going out to the person, they're de-escalating the crises of the moment, maybe get them access to meds. . . . But the person is still on the streets and their meds get stolen or confiscated by the city [during a homeless encampment sweep]."

The most important feature of SCRT is what it doesn't do. Only 7 percent of SCRT contacts lead to 5150s.[14] This is a sharp difference between SCRT (and other nonpolice crisis interventions) and law enforcement: they hospitalize people less.[15] There are tensions here. In many cases, the public is calling 911 because they want emergency responders to remove homeless people who are out of place, wandering in public transit stations or into higher-income neighborhoods. Mobile crisis programs focus, instead, on stabilizing people in place. One mobile crisis clinician told me, 'We are always looking for a way to walk away and have it not be totally unethical.' One first responder's success in avoiding forced treatment is another's failure. A San Francisco Police Department officer fumed, "I had [a call for] a gentleman with no pants and underwear, he was very psychotic and very embarrassed about it. Filthy, dirty . . . I called [SCRT], but when they come, they give them a sandwich and say they're not holdable when they are holdable. They [SCRT] 'didn't want to stigmatize him.'"

SCRT's low-key interventions might seem ill suited to the intensity of the crises perceived by the community members soliciting them. But they make sense in a system of abdicated authority where forced treatment rarely leads to enduring change. Although there are some exceptions—people hitting rock bottom, getting hospitalized, finally accepting treatment, moving into housing—the best that most 5150s achieve is temporarily removing someone from a dangerous situation. For people with a long-running grave disability, 5150s are often completely pointless. Stabilizing someone on the scene with a hot meal and a calm check-in might accomplish just as much as a few hours in an ER, minus the potential restraints and resultant trauma. Given that 31 percent of SCRT contacts are with Black people, simply not having these calls go to the police is a risk-reducing victory in itself.[16]

There's a more vexing limit to nonpolice responses like SCRT. The program, Chief Pang told me, is aiming to respond to 100 percent of B-level 911 police calls, for "mentally disturbed persons" who are not violent and have no report of a weapon. They're not, for the moment, heading to A-level calls, which are for "mentally disturbed persons" who are armed or deemed potentially dangerous. People with severe mental illness are overwhelmingly not violent and far more likely to be victims than perpetrators.[17] Yet anyone looking to build a more humane mental health system needs to grapple with the fact that psychosis, particularly when coupled with substance use, can be associated with an elevated risk of committing violent acts.[18]

Mental health professionals are understandably reluctant to respond to crises that seem to pose a real threat. When I shadowed Officers Briggs and Harden in Alameda County, I listened to them plead unsuccessfully for a clinician to join them in responding to a person waving knives to protect himself from the demons in his head. During my visit to Devon's supported housing complex, she had been persistently pleading for a mobile crisis team to come out and help with a resident whose paranoia drove him to barricade himself in his unit with a crossbow. As much as commentators would like to take cops out of the equation entirely, it still seems, as one sheriff told me, that "for some of these calls, you could send out Sigmund Freud and he'd need police back-up."

There are two points to make here. One is that not all problematic behaviors are best dealt with by police or clinicians (even Sigmund Freud). Some might be better addressed by skilled "violence interrupters" (piloted in Chicago in the 1990s) or community-led organizations focused on collective disorder, not individual pathology.[19] Second, there are individuals with undeniable mental health challenges who are so vulnerable that teams like SCRT cannot ethically walk away, even after giving a hot meal and a list of (declined) resources. For those individuals, short-term stabilization that avoids forced treatment is the first step to building a collaborative relationship. But it can't stop there: these individuals need to be convinced to accept services.

SERVICES: SNACKS, CIGARETTES, AND PSYCHOTROPIC MEDICATIONS

Becca seems like an unlikely candidate to be a clinician in an involuntary program. She grew up in Marin County and moved to Portland for college, where she was an avowed anarchist and community organizer. Then again, San Francisco's Assisted Outpatient Treatment (AOT) team, where she now works, is not quite involuntary. It instead operates in a gray area between forcing people into care and accepting their choice to refuse it. Without any real coercive "teeth," all her team has available to pressure people to engage are cigarettes and snacks. And with enough persistence, people who take snacks might eventually accept medication, case management, and therapy.

The AOT model, some version of which exists in forty-seven states, is simple: a judge orders a person to accept treatment on an outpatient basis, with failure to comply potentially leading to being picked up by police for an ER evaluation.[20] Proponents of AOT celebrate it as a "less-restrictive/less-intrusive" alternative to inpatient hospitalization; opponents view it as a "social control mechanism in the guise of benevolent coercion" that risks endlessly widening psychiatry's net.[21] In California, policy makers inaugurated AOT in 2001 as Laura's Law, after Laura Wilcox, a clinic volunteer killed by a mental health client who was not taking medication. To assuage civil liberties advocates, California's bill included no enforcement mechanism, allowed judges to order people to see clinicians but not to take medications, and permitted counties to decide, individually, if they wanted to opt into the program.[22] It offered no new funds for doing so. One prominent psychiatrist characterized it as a "sham system."[23]

San Francisco implemented AOT in 2014 only at the insistence of Mayor Lee, who said he "refuse[d] to let people die on the streets any longer" (this was before he declared conservatorship was the solution to the same concern).[24] The city has a dedicated team that serves clients referred to AOT, but it rarely places them under a court order.[25] Most of San Francisco's AOT clients, then, never get berated by a judge telling them to comply with treatment and are thus not even subjected to the much-disputed "black robe" effect (which is applied more consistently in the city's Community Conservatorship program).

People are sent to AOT when they've been hospitalized multiple times as a result of noncompliance with treatment. For some, it's the last community-based way station before conservatorship. Becca told me that often the team's psychiatrist will pop into the inpatient unit while the new referral is still there to see if they're interested in medication. "We have a really, really amazing psychiatrist," she explained, before adding, "but most of the time they [clients] say, 'Fuck you, once I get out of here, I'm not taking medication.'" So when Becca meets them, she avoids talking about mental health altogether. Her strategy, she quipped, starts with "snacks and cigarettes." Her clients have "years and years and years of being in the system, and they don't see any benefit from it." So she grasps at anything: "Let me take you to Target, listen to a song, a YouTube video. . . . Do you want to get reconnected to a primary care doctor?"

Some of these attempts to "meet clients where they're at" sound like the approach of a regular Full-Service Partnership team. It's true that AOT operates on essentially the same model (albeit with lower caseloads—Becca has only eleven clients). There's a key difference, though. As I saw in my observations at the UMH clinic, an FSP will close someone's file once they've said "no" to treatment a few times (three seems to be the standard number). There's no way around it: you can't bill Medi-Cal for medical services you can't provide. But to serve the very small number of clients on AOT, counties have put up their own funds (via MHSA or realignment), which allows teams to press on. Becca recounted, "Some teams will close them [our clients] as soon as they say 'fuck you.' [But we know] the client is going to tell you to fuck off, maybe threaten you. Move on. Figure out how to get through it. . . . It's not a justification to put your hands up and not have responsibility." To be clear, AOT teams can't give someone medication or therapy unless that person says "yes" to them. It's just that they don't take "no" for an answer. "I call us stalkers, we're going to come find you in the community and buy you coffee. We're nice stalkers, but we're going to keep going," admitted another AOT clinician.

This relentless, persistent outreach has shown results. State data show that participants in California's Laura's Law programs exhibit substantial decreases in hospitalization, homelessness, and encounters with law enforcement (although academic studies are more equivocal on AOT's effectiveness).[26] Veronica Kelly, the director of San Bernardino's Behavioral Health Department, reported that their AOT program achieved 90 percent "voluntary" engagement with its clients—albeit after a unyielding barrage of forty face-to-face outreach visits.[27] Despite AOT's arm-twisting approach, I found some surprising converts. "We've been asking the county to expand the program," a public defender in San Francisco told me. "For our clients, it means complete wraparound services and help with housing. The court might say you have to go the clinic, but there's no hammer of 'If you don't take meds, we'll hold you down and inject you.' We like that." Sometimes this murky area between "forced" and "voluntary" is the right place to meet clients who are understandably hostile to the system but whose refusal is putting them at risk of hospitalization or conservatorship.

Clinicians like Becca know that sometimes help should include medication. But she's well aware that "we'll get you a refill of the antipsychotics you were obligated to take in the hospital" is a bad opening offer. I was struck in my interviews how many people who had lived through forced treatment described finally connecting with clinicians once they provided them seemingly banal things, like help getting an ID or a ride to the dentist. Sometimes, though, connecting with clients means relinquishing any aspiration to provide anything akin to services, at least for a while. Becca isn't billing Medi-Cal by the minute, which means "I can spend two months with a client not pursuing any traditional case management goals, just sitting with them on a sidewalk, smoking a cigarette, for a couple hours a week, doing nothing." Then, at some point, "you can tell them, 'I think it's time to try an antipsychotic' and have that conversation with them, and because of that connection, that relational work, then they're open to doing that. It can be really beautiful."

AOT has proven basically useless for several characters in this book. But its emphasis on persistence and providing the services people want (IDs and apartments over meds and therapy) as the first step in building a collaborative relationship should be incorporated everywhere in the continuum. It helps ensure that, when coercion is used, it's short and more likely to be the last time.

Logan, a social worker who oversees an AOT team, offered such an example: "He was a big guy, tattoos, often without a shirt, poorly dressed, threatening people, sometimes exposing himself, just really erratic. He would trespass in a construction site . . . and vandalize it." He had "definitely not the worst behaviors I've seen"—Logan had worked with individuals "who killed people, done really awful things"—but he nonetheless "inspired this outsized angst" in the affluent area he frequented. Locals even started a Twitter account to document his behavior and put pressure on the city.

With Logan's encouragement, the Department of Public Health "greased the wheels" to convince SF General Hospital to admit him on a 5150. Within a day, the hospital declared that his main problem was meth, not mental illness, so he would be released. Logan and his team "went that day [and] offered him services. He was kind of ambivalent but agreed to sign up." They put him in a Single Room Occupancy hotel in the Tenderloin. "Having that place led us to be able to find him," he elaborated, "We'd go out every day with gift-cards [and] peer supports. He had some criminal cases where he had to do community service, and we made a plan where he'd do it by cooking lunch in the clinic." He was still using meth, though, and his behavior got him kicked out of his SRO. Being connected with Logan's team meant that he was a high priority for access to a Navigation Center (one of San Francisco's nicer shelters). Eventually, they coaxed him onto an injectable antipsychotic and got him into more long-term housing. "We saw a real turnaround," Logan said, cheerfully.

I commented that this sounded like an encouraging success story. Logan paused, and added, "We had the best outcome we could hope for, and then, tragically, like eight hundred San Franciscans in the last year, he died of fentanyl. . . . We can't prevent someone from doing that." I think Logan is right to be humble about the power of mental health services, whether forced, voluntary, or somewhere in between. Indeed, the heartbreaking cases of formerly homeless individuals who win the golden ticket of supported housing and then die shortly thereafter suggest that they need something other than services: new skills to help them survive.[28]

SKILLS: LEARNING TO SURVIVE, TOGETHER

There's a gap in the placement continuum. On the one hand, there are hospitals, IMDs, and board and cares. These environments feed, clothe, and shelter individuals presumed incapable of doing it themselves. On the other hand, there's independent housing, whose residents are assumed to be able to take care of these basic needs on their own. Sometimes they can't. Every case manager who provides the supports in supported independent housing has stories of units overrun with cockroaches and smeared in feces.[29] I've gagged in the doorway of a unit where someone covered in bedsores and ulcers was unable to move from a pee-soaked mattress for days. Images like these have become grist for claims that Housing First, which rapidly places individuals into apartments and follows up with voluntary services, is flawed and should be replaced with forced meds and hospital beds.[30] But what if there were something in between: giving people skills that help them transition away from hospitals and IMDs, or shelters and the street, to survive and thrive in community housing?

Steve Fields was witness to this chasm in the heady days of deinstitutionalization. He grew up in a "political, activist family" and, during the Vietnam War, applied for status as a conscientious objector. He assumed the application would be rejected and he'd wind up in prison. Instead, he was assigned to two years of "alternative service" in a halfway house in San Francisco. It was 1969, and a wave of patients from Napa State Hospital were being discharged with little more than a paper bag of possessions and the address of the house where Steve, who had "no background or training in behavioral health," was working. From where he was standing, the mental health system assumed that these refugees from institutions would fail to adapt to life outside them: "We [the mental health system] weren't investing in vocational services, we weren't investing in housing integrated into the community, [and] we weren't looking at rehabilitation as a goal. . . . We had already decided they were going nowhere, so we parked them in a board and care home and overmedicated them, and waited twenty years until we were proven right, when they're still stuck there."[31]

Since then he, as the head of Progress Foundation—which operated that first halfway house—has been trying to build the kind of program that would prove the pessimists wrong. It starts with keeping people out of the hospital, an environment toxic to self-sufficiency. Progress operates Dore Crisis Clinic, at which the new Street Crisis Response Team frequently drops off clients.[32] The space is pretty basic: just a dozen reclining armchairs, with staff offering hot meals and short-term meds. But Kimberly Taylor, Progress's director of crisis services, points out how different it is from an ER: "Clients there are coming asking for help, not feeling coerced to be there. We don't have any police presence, we don't have a security guard, there's nobody there that feels like we're watching you or scared of you." As a result, clients take "ownership of the energy of the space." Like all Progress programs, Dore presumes that the environment in which care is delivered matters as much as the care itself.

If Dore's clinicians assess someone as unable to return to the community once their maximum twenty-four-hour stay is up, they can go to one of Progress's Acute Diversion Units (ADU). ADUs can also take people brought into the ER on a 5150, although they have to come voluntarily. It's easy to see why they might agree, especially when the alternative is a ward in SF General. The ADU I visit, La Posada, is in the same building where Steve Fields started in 1969, a jauntily painted Victorian on a quiet side street in the Mission. The inside is quintessentially Northern California: dark wood-paneled walls, dim light, and somewhat shabby furniture. I'm struck by the schedule posted on the wall. Days in La Posada are packed with community meetings, chores, and groups focused on coping skills.

An ADU is a place of respite but not isolation. Clients keep their phones and can invite family members and friends over for dinner (if the group agrees). This means they might continue interacting with the very people who were precipi-tating an emotional crisis or offering them substances outside. "We're trying to create real life, with extra support," Taylor, the director of crisis services, tells me, "so we want them to be able to practice what they're going to be doing when they're not here anymore." Some of these habits are around treatment. When it comes to medication, she tells me, "They're the ones opening the bottles, tak-ing the correct dose. We're not putting it into a cup and handing it to them." She adds, "We're helping them develop advocacy skills around medication," such as negotiating with a psychiatrist to try a new drug when one isn't working or is causing intolerable side effects. Other habits are around collective life, since many Progress residents, by dint of poverty, are likely to live in congregate set-tings (like SROs or shelters) in the future.

Ultimately, the test of a fourteen-day stay in an ADU is whether it can rein in whatever behavior was putting someone on a pathway to hospitalization.[33] Steve Fields, again, articulates the theory behind the model: "I learned [working at the halfway house] that [disruptive] behavior wasn't unalterable if you offered an environment in which it wasn't inevitable. I'd see people be in a thought-disorder situation in the morning and then cook dinner at night, if you stayed with them [and] you didn't panic and have them pulled out of the house." On the day of my visit, one La Posada resident was hearing the voice of her boyfriend in her head and loudly arguing with him. Staff found a way to divert her: she was assigned to cook dinner that night and didn't want to let her housemates down. "Looking forward to that curry!" Kimberly says when we pop into her room, adding, "I'm glad to see the bed made."

I next walk over to La Amistad, a ninety-day program for people who need more residential care after an ADU. My guide is Jim Roberts, who started his career doing drama therapy in the UK before moving to San Francisco. The build-ing is a maze of narrow hallways and shared bedrooms, quiet until I reach a kitchen in the back. A couple of residents are cooking while reggaeton blares. Someone has left a burner on, but Jim sneaks behind a client scooping eggs onto another client's plate to turn it off. We go to the back patio, fully set up for a barbeque (which, I am told, is a frequent activity). This scene is a stark contrast to a board and care, where by regulation operators are supposed to provide three meals and two snacks, and residents aren't supposed to provide anything but their check.

Jim tells me that when he first came to La Amistad, "I could not under-stand what was going on," since so little time is spent on one-on-one therapy or medication management. The real impact of being in residential treatment comes, he thinks, from just being there. Especially for clients who have been living on the streets, "we're raising people's bar. People think that where they're at is all there is for them. . . . For many, it's a long time since they last had their own bathroom, had the ability to cook a meal for themselves, or had access to a refrigerator." Jim also runs a yearlong program that takes conservatees who have been languishing in nursing homes for years and seeks to recultivate their capabilities. Progress has always accepted clients on conservatorship. Two of ten clients at La Amistad are conserved. But for Steve Fields, it's a "red herring," because "we don't operate any differently with them." You can't compel people to collaborate in a program designed to cultivate self-respect and community; you have to convince them it's worth the sweat and struggle.

When I ask how a stay at La Amistad can change someone's trajectory, a staff counselor—with a half-shaved head and a flannel shirt, the unofficial uniform of Bay Area counterculture—describes an undocumented immigrant from El Salvador who recently passed through. He came, she said, in a "deep despair," tied to the trauma of fleeing his home country, the economic precarity created by the pandemic, and the substances he used to cope with both. When she went to meet him at an ADU, his downward slide had stabilized, but still he "could barely get out of bed to fix breakfast. It was the kind of depression where everything aches, it lives in your bones, everything is painful."

Both La Amistad and La Posada are oriented toward the Hispanic/Latinx community, which the counselor thinks is crucial: "Culturally, for us Latinos, it [mental health] is something you don't talk about. The stigma, it deprives." But over time, "you could hear him expanding his emotional vocabulary, talking about coping skills, learning his meds, internalizing it because he started to care about himself." Because he was undocumented, treatment options in the community were limited (until a 2022 reform, he couldn't get Medi-Cal). So the team focused on connecting him with peer-led support groups. "He left here, drove away in his car, went back to work," she tells me, "but came back to drop off some treats for his friends."

Progress's approach was almost a template for California's entire twenty-four-hour treatment system. In 1978, Steve Fields helped pass the Community Residential Treatment Act, which in its preamble declared that the "current mental health system provides insufficient alternatives to institutionalization and hospitalization."[34] The Act offered grants to counties to start residential programs with a "rehabilitation focus which encourages the client to develop the skills to become self-sufficient." Steve claims that the Act didn't fail for lack of money. "We were rolling in money," he insists, with the 90–10 state match for county programs offered by LPS, federal grants, and the budget for the Act itself. What California lacked, he posits, was "political will and imagination." Counties had to actively apply for these new funds and show how their programs would meet the Act's rehabilitative mandate. They instead relied on board and cares and IMDs, the private sector's ready-made "solution" to cases they assumed were hopelessly chronic.

As a result, Progress's continuum of crisis clinics like Dore, ADUs like La Posada, and residential treatment programs like La Amistad serve only as temporary oases. The skills people learn there, though, are supposed to stay with them. Progress would like to see clients go into cooperative housing: shared apartments scattered in the community. There, residents could collectively decide to be sober or, alternatively, to use drugs together, with Narcan on hand to revive a housemate from an overdose. Progress implicitly operates on the assumption that the opposite of dependence on hospitals is not independence but, as disability theorists argue, *interdependence*.[35]

In practice, most people discharge from Progress's programs into SROs. They are awash in fentanyl and overcrowded. Yet residents, cut off from the friends they had on the street or in treatment, are very much alone. Interdependence, then, requires building new networks of support, to which we now turn.

SUPPORT: THE POWER OF PEERS

There are two ways to think about the power of peers in the continuum of collaboration. First, people with lived experience of being treated (and mistreated) by the mental health system make interventions to provide stability, services, and skills more compassionate and effective. Second, peers can provide something those interventions don't: connection and purpose.

Start with stabilization. Chief Pang, from San Francisco's Street Crisis Response Team, had found that adding a peer alongside a paramedic and a mental health clinician upped the odds that someone would engage: "When we go up to that individual in need, they choose who they want to speak with. . . . That could be the person in uniform [the paramedic], someone who seems to be an official, who's safe. . . . Sometimes it might be the behavioral clinician. Sometimes it's the peer. And sometimes it has nothing to do with what our respective roles are, but who looks the most pleasing to them. . . . If we're having someone who's just distrusting and we have someone who can sit next to them and say, 'I have been through what you've been through,' that's very powerful." A peer also serves as a skeptical third party who might resist other professionals' desire to call the police or impose a 5150.

There's a role for peers in getting people into services, too. Chad Costello, the executive director of the California Association of Social Rehabilitation Agencies, argued that we need a new interpretation of why people refuse care: "We have to stop blaming the customer for our inability to make the sale." By incorporating people with lived experience into clinical teams, "we may actually get the product line . . . and the sales force that we need."[36] Eric Henriques, from the Mental Health Association, described how he could augment the efforts of more traditional clinicians: "Say a participant is prescribed new antipsychotics, and they're having bad reactions to that. . . . A peer isn't there to promote or discourage medication, but we can talk about our experiences. . . . I'm good at working with individuals with schizoaffective disorder, and I've had some trial and error, but also success [with medications], through the decades. I can share my lived experience, whereas a psychiatrist or social worker can't do that, shouldn't do that."

Peers help staff residential programs like those of Progress. In some cases, they just take them over. "Peer respites" are a bit like Acute Division Units, minus the clinicians. Guyton Colantuono, from LA's Project Return Peer Support Network, critiqued "sterile mental health environments [like ERs] that discount everything that you're sharing, feeling, experiencing. They put it all into this . . . mental health lens that whatever you're seeing or experiencing, it's symptoms."[37] Peer respites, by contrast, serve as a "bed and breakfast for people experiencing psychiatric distress," offering "radical hospitality" that says, "You're welcome here, as you are." Hacienda of Hope, a ten-bed residence in Long Beach, has no locked doors, no buzzers, and no mandatory groups (although offerings include meditation or art)—just peer staff available 24/7 for a stay of up to one month. Since respites divert people who might otherwise be hospitalized, Colantuono is frequently asked how they handle crises. He counters, "We almost never have a crisis. Why would people threaten us or act out, when we're giving them love?"[38] Yet there are only five peer respites in California, despite billions of unspent dollars from the Mental Health Services Act that could pay for them.[39]

California is on the precipice of a massive expansion in the role of peers. In 2020, the governor signed SB 803, which allows trained peer specialists to be certified by the state and to bill Medi-Cal. California was the forty-ninth state to do so: previous iterations of the bill had been vetoed because of opposition from clinicians who feared competition from peers (who are generally not unionized and paid much less).[40] As a source in state government told me, with those traditional clinicians retiring in droves and increasingly unable to meet the rising demand for care, certifying peers was the state's "big workforce play" to fill the gap. Not everyone is sure this is an unadulterated positive. Peer supports started within "survivor" and "ex-patient" movements that wanted interventions that were both "caring and . . . defiant" toward mainstream psychiatry.[41] Guyton Colantuono, from Project Return, fears that billing Medi-Cal could "destroy all of us" by forcing peers to fit what they do into the same narrow, symptom-focused boxes as other reimbursable services.[42]

This is why it's important to look at what peers can do that clinical services, whether delivered by peers or others, cannot. I visited the California Clubhouse, in a strip mall in San Mateo, just south of San Francisco, in March 2022. My guide, Dave, a white man who looks to be in his sixties, introduces himself by saying he was married and worked as a machinist until he had a 'psychotic break,' which, he observes after a pause, 'I guess happens to all of us at some point.'

Whether or not that statement is really true, the power of a Clubhouse is that it's a space where you might be able to believe it is. The Clubhouse movement started in 1943 with a patient club at Rockland State Hospital, an asylum in New York that at its height interned nine thousand people.[43] The group incorporated in 1949 as Fountain House, which inhabits a five-story mansion in Manhattan. It is the epicenter of a movement that has spread to thirty countries and has 320 adherents, including ten in California.[44]

Clubhouse participants, as Dave emphasizes on my tour, are members, not patients, clients, or consumers. Activity in the Clubhouse is organized around something other than treatment: the vibrant life of the Clubhouse itself. I sit in on one community meeting where, during a discussion of whether to give receipts for purchases in the Clubhouse's small café, one member cuts in to sheepishly describe having missed a recent meeting because he was in the hospital. Another member offers her condolences and starts talking about a medication change that left her unable to sleep. The meeting's facilitator lets the conversation play out for a few minutes, before gently guiding the group back to a busy agenda that includes planning an upcoming birthday party and producing next month's newsletter. The unconditional acceptance of experiences that the rest of society deems abnormal, while refocusing on the normal minutiae (sometimes painfully normal, to anyone accustomed to the frustration of getting anything done via committee in any voluntary organization), is what makes Clubhouses so distinctive.

One of the busiest units of the California Clubhouse is the one focused on employment. Work, according to Fountain House, is a "generative and reintegrative force" which should "underlie, pervade, and inform all the activities that make up the lifeblood of the clubhouse."[45] A bulletin board is covered in twenty-or-so job postings. An adjacent whiteboard lists five members who have found jobs as library aides, peer specialists, and administrative assistants. America's decrepit welfare state, anthropologist Sue Estroff observed in 1981, requires mental health clients to highlight their own "disabilities, diagnoses, and deficits" in order to get the social security disability income they need to survive.[46] Clubhouses have found some clever ways to help members escape this trap. Clubhouses can organize "transitional employment" whereby staff guarantee employers that they'll step in if a member misses a shift because they're sick or in the hospital. Given its location in Silicon Valley, I'm not surprised that the California Clubhouse organizes events via Slack and uses Square to process payments at the café, both of which give members vocational skills.

For others, Clubhouses offer meaningful activity even if getting a paycheck is unattainable or undesirable. Beverly tells me she's been in the mental health system for forty years, since she had a delusion that she was getting married to a wealthy man and her parents organized a 5150 that was "so traumatic and so awful." When she got out, all the mental health system proposed was a day treatment program where, in her view, staff spoke to her like a child. "I was so severely depressed. . . . It was impossible to make a friend. There was no community," she mourns. Then, five years ago, she discovered the Clubhouse. She loved that members had the authority to decide whom they would hire and that everyone treated her as a "whole person," not a mental health client. For the first time in her adult life, she stopped feeling suicidal.

When I ask Beverly about the Clubhouses' employment programs, she admits, "I'm not interested in employment. I don't like how I'm treated in the regular community. My work is coming to the Clubhouse and being part of what happens there." The Clubhouse is organized around a "work-ordered day": the essential, but for members purely voluntary, tasks necessarily to keep the Club-house going. Erica, the executive director of the Clubhouse, takes me to visit the "business unit" in one corner of the Clubhouse's open floor plan: they're engaged in an endless production of materials on club policies (ranging from emergency preparedness to leaving dirty dishes in the sink) and advertisements to recruit new members when tabling at community events. 'What do you get from making a form?' Erica muses, before answering, 'It restores dignity, it gives people a sense of accomplishment, it takes away patienthood and restores personhood.'

Beverly tells me that part of the vital work of the Clubhouse is throwing a lifeline to members when they drift away: "We are aware of our peers and who's having a hard time and who's not. So that's part of our task board: reaching out to those people." One of her friends has "the most horrible voices . . . telling him to kill himself, telling him terrible things." If all he had was the county day treatment program, she insists, "I don't think he'd still be here. But with the Clubhouse, I'm not worried about losing him. We won't let him fall through the cracks." While the Clubhouse is only open during the day, they're really a 24/7 operation because of the constant stream of telephone calls, letters, and visits by members to other members. Beverly observes, "The two times I've veered away from the Clubhouse, my psychotic symptoms started to return." But her friends reached out to her and brought her back. The symptoms went away.

The research on peer supports is inconclusive. Some studies show that peer-led interventions contribute to modest improvements in symptoms, function-ing, and self-efficacy while others identify very limited impacts.[47] Then again, research on the effectiveness of long-term involuntary care, to which peers are supposed to be the alternative, is almost nonexistent. To build a continuum of collaboration, you need to take seriously the voices of the people with whom you're collaborating. And in dozens of interviews, I heard the same refrain: peer supports work, not just because they make treatment more humane and recovery oriented but because they provide something difficult to measure: companion-ship and purpose.

SHARED DECISION MAKING: A CLIENT-DIRECTED SYSTEM

People with lived experience of mental illness are not just making their way onto treatment teams in California but gradually penetrating the policy-making and planning process. State regulations mandate that their views be taken into account in the distribution of MHSA money. Peers sit on key oversight bodies like county behavioral health boards. But it's hard to translate advisory roles into real authority to shape what happens on the ground. There are the grand principles of autonomy and respect animating the alternatives discussed in this chapter. Then there are the fraught moments when these values are thrown out the window in the name of addressing urgent decompensation or impending death.

Laurie Hallmark has a vision for how we can make the principles of supported decision making meaningful in micro-level interactions, where street-level bureaucrats wield sovereign power over their clients. A California transplant who was previously an attorney with Texas RioGrande Legal Aid, Laurie begins our interview with a leading question: "So, I'm assuming that your philosophical approach is beginning with support for people maintaining autonomy and being able to make as many decisions as possible over their own lives?" If you want her to explain how Psychiatric Advanced Directives (PADs) can become a vehicle for giving people living with mental illnesses authority over the system treating them, the answer, of course, has to be "yes."

Traditionally, a PAD is a document filled out by a mental health client and put in their medical file. PADs authorize certain treatments (like specific hospitals or medications) while refusing others. Wes, a peer who worked with Laurie making PADs in Texas, described his own as "like a parachute": "it rescues you in case of an emergency. The document comes into effect when you've lost control . . . and it keeps you in control somewhat." The majority of people Wes works with use PADs to specify nonmedication coping strategies that help them in a crisis (for him, apparently, it's very loud music; for others, coffee and cigarettes). It turns out that most of what people put into PADs is consistent with clinical best practices, coupled with frequent pleas for "understanding, empathy, and respect."[48] A PAD can push a clinician who might endorse all these things in principle to adhere to them in practice, even in a moment of crisis when a client is not able to advocate on their own behalf. PADs have proven to be among the most effective interventions available to reduce coercion in the mental health system.[49]

When Laurie began to use PADs for her clients at Legal Aid, she started to see them as having much broader potential. A PAD could take a person's preferences and turn them into a binding, organizing framework for all the institutions touching on their life: "I realized that the underlying problem was an absence of accountability to the human beings, to provide services that are based on what each individual wanted and needed, rather than a standardized 'here's what we're going to do, this either works for you or it doesn't . . . and if it doesn't, it's your fault and we'll do more of the same.'" She expanded the PAD template to include housing, financial management, reproduction, and contact with first responders like law enforcement.

I asked Laurie to show me the kind of information that might go into the "crisis response" section of a PAD. Much of it is basic: requests that police explain who they are or why they're there, stay in front of a person, or speak in a soft voice. Others are more personal: a sexual assault victim might prefer to interact with a person of a different gender from their assailant. Some people want to be addressed by a professional wearing civilian clothes using their first name, while others feel dignified by a "sir" or "madam" from a uniformed officer. Laurie observes, "That's what's so interesting. It's the tiniest little thing that can send someone in one direction or another"—back home newly calm or in deepening crisis while being transported in a police cruiser to jail or a hospital—"and when they fall, it's so hard to get them back."

When I talked to her, Laurie was serving as an expert adviser for a Mental Health Services Act–funded project across five counties to expand the use of PADs.[50] Ahmadreza Bahrani, from the Fresno Behavioral Health Department, explained that the county embraced the pilot as a way to "keep people out of hospitals, keep them out of jails, reduce crises and escalations . . . really keep them in the community." In particular, Bahrani believed that PADs could help reengage people who had been estranged by past experiences of coercion: "They'll be empowered to say, 'Now I have this legal document, and I get to control how my care is done. So I'll go talk to them [clinicians].'" The assumption is that people are more likely to do something not because there's a threat that they'll be forced to, but precisely because there is no such threat: "Someone we're outreaching on the street who might say, 'Go away, I don't want to be told, "take your meds,"' might, with a PAD, go like, 'Okay, I have a right to refuse medication. So I'll just take it.'"

Counties are prioritizing different populations for their PADs pilots.[51] Many are interested in diverting people from the criminal-legal system; others are focused on transition-age youth (young adults, between sixteen and twenty-five, moving out of children's services like foster care). Fresno is looking to use PADs with its conservatees. Allowing conservatees—people in a court-imposed substituted decision-making arrangement—to share in decision making requires a philosophical leap of faith. Stacy Vanbruggen, head of Adult Behavioral Health Services in Fresno, explained that it entails accepting that "grave disability isn't like a light switch," with someone's capacity of decision making entirely snuffed out. For her, "there are decisions that people on conservatorship can be making for themselves, and they absolutely should be making for themselves."

In Fresno, the idea of making PADs with conservatees is closely tied to previous reforms to their LPS programs. A few years ago, the county realized that many people already on conservatorship were still frequently hospitalized, unstable, and disconnected from treatment. Rather than responding by further tightening the grip of conservatorship, they loosened it. The protocols for Fresno's Recovery with Inspiration, Support, and Empowerment (RISE) Program, according to Vanbruggen, took out references to "non-compliance" among conservatees and replaced it with "strengths-based, client-centered language." They had clinicians and deputy conservators work side by side so they could identify when a client's seemingly odd behavior (one was walking nearly fifty miles a day from city to city) or refusal of lifesaving treatment was driven by illness and when it was just a human being making conscious choices that others might not agree with.

It was "scary for staff," Vanbruggen admitted, to "allow people to make natural mistakes." But it was also "part of their [clients'] learning process." Letting people take risks (for example, by insisting, via a PAD, on a medication that a clinician might not think is the most effective) could paradoxically help save them. During the coronavirus pandemic, public guardians statewide saw a wave of suicides among conservatees. That people relegated to the social death of conservatorship would try to escape via physical death is, sadly, predictable: in 1899, sociologist Emile Durkheim showed how suicide could be driven by "excessive regulation . . . futures pitilessly blocked . . . by oppressive discipline."[52] Fresno has not had a conservatee die by suicide in seven years. PADs have proven to be a lifesaving parachute in more ways than one.

One of the indispensable features of California's PADs push is for the documents to be filled in with the help of peers, not psychiatrists. For Laurie, this is fairly intuitive: "if you are from the system that involuntarily hospitalized me, violated my rights, treated me poorly—why would I create a self-determination-based document with someone who has had power over me in a situation of force?" Claudia Vargas started helping people create PADs when she heard a presentation by Laurie on patients' rights: "I was like, 'what, you mean you have rights when you go to the hospital? They [the hospital] didn't tell me anything about that!'" She knows at gut level that "people can experience hearing voices . . . and that doesn't mean they have any less insight of what works for them and what doesn't."[53] Sharing her own story helps put clients at ease who otherwise hear "psychiatric" and "legal document" and think immediately "forced treatment." Her personal struggles also mean that she knows what questions to ask. Many clients will say, "'I don't have any wellness tools for this and that,' but after you ask the right questions, it's like, 'okay, you do have these things, maybe you just didn't have a language for it before.'" Research shows that PADs created with peers are more effective in reducing forced treatment than those without.[54]

In attempting to get a large proportion of public mental health clients to fill them out, having peers help them do it, and covering multiple domains beyond medical treatment, California's PADs project is sweeping in its ambition. One consultant told me, "Other states have the Toyota or Dodge of PADs, while we're shooting for the Tesla, the Mercedes . . . taking that advanced directive one step further." But there are open questions about how to actually transform PADs into an "external authority" that can direct interventions in sites as diverse as shelters, clinics, apartments, jails, and hospitals.[55] The logistics of using PADs are complicated, but California is dreaming big: counties are considering storing PADs in wearable bracelets, a QR code, or a cloud-accessible database across institutions. The state will eventually need to pass legislation giving PADs legal weight, setting rules for if and when clinicians can override them, and deciding what consequences professionals will pay for ignoring them.

I am closing this chapter with PADs because of how profoundly they could shift the balance of power in the mental health system. As Laurie put it, "If you think about it from a consumer perspective, if Wal-Mart is putting out one type of green beans, consumers hate it, then saying that green beans are just a terrible product, it's not true. You're just providing a type of green bean that nobody wants." The LPS Act, in theory if not always in practice, was supposed to give people the right to refuse the green beans they didn't want. PADs, to horribly strain the analogy, are about obligating Wal-Mart to finally provide the green beans that its shoppers do want.

CONCLUSION: CONSTRUCTING COLLABORATION

Steve Fields, from Progress Foundation, has an alternative explanation for why deinstitutionalization did not succeed in creating the "self-reliant, autonomous citizens" advocates originally promised.[56] Steve recalls, "I spent many long hours learning from people who had been in hospitals for a long time." What they taught him, he says, was that it was a "fundamental flaw" to assume "that these folks, when they were finally let loose, would voluntarily come to programs they didn't think helped them any." When they voted with their feet against these programs, some of them wound up conserved while others wound up cycling in and out of hospitals, jails, and shelters.

A common thread through all of the alternatives across this chapter is that they radically deemphasize "anosognosia" (lack of insight). A truly collaborative relationship starts with recognizing that people's refusals of services are not random ravings but often reflect real and often traumatic experiences with the mental health system. Building an alternative to conservatorship isn't just renouncing the use of coercion; it is also relinquishing authority, which, as the political scientist Hannah Arendt observed, "always demands obedience," in favor of "persuasion, which presupposes equality."[57] A system based on persuasion could be relentless, even intrusive, but the only threat behind it would be of more, and more creative, attempts at persuasion.

Admittedly, as I investigated these alternatives, I found tensions among them. A few of Becca's AOT clients have been banned for misbehavior from Progress's facilities. One mother brought her son to visit the Clubhouse; he took one look and left, because he didn't want to be identified with "those people." SCRT runs into individuals who would be too impaired to put anything about their preferred crisis response in a PAD. The accumulated consequences of decades of not having a continuum of collaboration mean that some people could not collaborate with such a continuum even if it were built up across the state.

It is not a surprise, then, that many people I interviewed for this chapter still see a role for conservatorship. Eric Henriques, from San Francisco's Mental Health Association, told me, "a few of the folks I've worked with—just a few—if they are not required to have some type of support, they will be victimized or just die in the streets in their feces." Others hesitantly backed reforms to expand conservatorship, if only as a temporary stopgap. But even a system that imposes substituted decision making can incorporate principles of supported decision making such as respect, connection, and maximizing choice.

In the end, despite the innovative grassroots initiatives of clinicians, counties, and service users, neither a comprehensive continuum of collaboration nor an effective (if diminished) conservatorship system to catch people falling off it will come into being on its own. It will take engaged government authority, which I will explore in the conclusion.

CONCLUSION

Beyond Miracles

'I'm hoping you have a miracle.'

I'm sitting in the cab alongside a first responder (they're part of a team consistent with the models of CAMP in LA, RAP in San Diego, or SCRT in San Francisco, which work with ultrahigh utilizers of emergency services who are not engaged in any ongoing treatment). We've just received a call from the social worker at a nearby private hospital. She's reaching out about a patient who, at the insistence of hospital administration, is about to get booted from an ER—even though she is fourteen weeks pregnant, using meth, and struggling with schizophrenia. 'They say they're going to discharge, but I'm like, "to where?" I'm wondering if you have any ideas?' the social worker pleads. My guide looks the woman up in the county's database: she has a long history of short hospitalizations that led nowhere, of being revived by the fire department in a pool of vomit on the street, and of outreach workers finding her sleeping in doorways.

We drive to the hospital. Another team member and a nurse from the local Behavioral Health Department are coming out through the ambulance bay. The nurse gives a debrief: Police brought the woman in screaming. The doctor held her hand while a heavy dose of Zyprexa cut through her psychosis. The physician—a regular emergency doctor—called for a psych eval, but, according to the nurse, 'They [the psychiatrists] are just doing [the evaluation] as a favor. They're not going to keep her [on a 5150]. The ER doc is furious. She'd like to see her held, conserved, whatever.' We run through the options and rule them all out. A family shelter won't take her because she doesn't have a kid (yet). A sobering center doesn't want the liability of a pregnant client in a space designed for substance users. She sounds too behaviorally dysregulated for an unlocked crisis clinic. It's a Sunday night in a state with the fifth largest economy in the world, and we can't find a bed for a sick, homeless, and pregnant woman.

The team brainstorms three options. The first is to plead with the doctor to keep her as a social admission (i.e., someone who doesn't really meet criteria for a hospitalization and whose care will thus go unreimbursed), with the promise that we'll pick her up at 6 a.m. the next morning. The second is let her be released, leave her to wander a bit, 5150 her again, and hope that she's far enough from this hospital that paramedics will transport her instead to a county facility more willing to keep her. It's not a safe bet. She's on a heavy cocktail of sedatives and might not even make it off hospital grounds. The third is to pass the hat among the team members and pay for a hotel room. That's the closest thing to a miracle the discharge social worker at a wealthy private hospital can hope for.

On ride-alongs like these, I saw clinicians, paramedics, social workers, and police officers crisscrossing counties with the frenetic urgency of a war zone. Team meetings involved a gruesome triage: who was sick enough to merit an extra effort to convince other providers to give them scarce beds? When we dropped into shelters, detox centers, or urgent care clinics, we learned that the people we were looking for had disappeared—or, shockingly frequently, died. Victory was ephemeral. The triumphs of getting clients into hospitals, onto conservatorships, or back home to supported housing were rapidly dashed when they popped up again in arrest records or 911 calls.

I ask Lieutenant Howland, who oversees the team, how an ER psychiatrist could possibly let someone like this young woman stagger out through the ER doors alone. "Severe burnout," he tells me, adding, "There's just so many people, one after the other, a tidal wave of need. It's like a trench mentality." He, much like scholars I cited in the introduction, sees medicine and law as locked in intractable conflict, with laws like LPS having put too much emphasis on rights over care: "I think the pendulum has gone too far. There's so much reacting to the sins of the past when people were conserved and put away in an insane asylum and mistreated. Now people are just allowed to die on the street." Like the majority of frontline workers I interviewed, he'd like to see LPS reformed to expand conservatorships—whatever makes the dying stop.

Psychiatric coercion is on the march. In recent years, many states have introduced or passed laws to expand involuntary treatment.[1] Rates of involuntary holds are increasing nationwide (and internationally).[2] Some of this stems from opportunistic politicians looking to distract from their failure to address the root causes of homelessness or gun violence, exploiting a public increasingly fearful of people with mental illness.[3] Much more revealing are other sources of support for expanding forced treatment: the paramedic picking up the same person at the ER exit the three-hundredth time this year; the Housing First case manager whose building is often a once homeless person's last stop before death; the mother who fought to get her child into every voluntary program that exists, only to see them refuse to go; the public defender who sees conservatorship as the only way to keep her clients out of jail; the recovering patient who wishes he'd been obligated to take medication sooner.

This book has documented the truth of these experiences. Laws like LPS and criteria like grave disability are being interpreted so strictly that people are truly being left to die. But it has also catalogued another, incongruent reality. That same law is failing to protect people from abusive institutionalization and unhelpful—and sometimes incompetent—treatment. We learned about that from the most important witnesses, service users themselves. We also heard from doctors who would rather discharge someone than subject them to the trauma of living in their hospital or public guardians who truly believe you're better off free in a tent than stuck in an IMD.

To explain how California can both have an excess of forced treatment and a dearth of lifesaving coercive interventions, I have introduced the concept of *abdicated authority*. At heart, it refers to how governments fail to coordinate and regulate the exercise of their own power. In so doing, they avoid the costs and difficult choices that the accountable exercise of that power entails. Abdication starts at the top, as legislators and state agencies have created pathways for stripping fundamental rights (freedom and bodily integrity) away from people in the name of even more fundamental aims (survival and safety) but done little to fund and monitor how those pathways get used. It's visible at the county level, as long-neglected agencies like the public guardians battle with behavioral health departments or the courts over not taking responsibility for individuals—such as aging, homeless substance users—who probably need interventions from all three of them.

Abdicated authority reaches ground through delegation and discretion. Delegation without accountability has given nonprofit clinics carte blanche to pick and choose their clients, defaulted to for-profit hospitals' more financial than clinical reasons for (not) applying for conservatorship, and left private board and cares to silently disappear at great cost to their invisible residents. Abdicated authority grants uncoordinated discretion, freeing police to use 5150s as a tool for disorder management, ER physicians to rapidly people process people out of needed care, and bureaucrats to define grave disability to exclude someone who can eat roadkill or make their way to a bus stop. The key problem in California is neither a lack of coercion nor a complete absence of compassionate care. It is the absence of overarching strategy and leadership to make either have a meaningful impact.

In this conclusion, I revisit this explanation in light of the most recent legislative initiatives in California, consider other domains where the concept of abdicated authority might offer some analytical insights, suggest how to replace abdication with accountability, and take us back to the bus stop where we started.

THE END OF ABDICATION?

While I was writing this book, there were moments where it seemed as though legislators were on the verge of diagnosing something like abdicated authority and taking steps to reclaim the state's responsibilities. A December 15, 2021 hearing by the legislature's health and judiciary committees on "The Lanterman-Petris-Short Act: How Can It Be Improved?" was one such moment.[4]

Since most of the suggestions for "improvement" in the past five years have hinged on rewriting grave disability, I expected the dozens of speakers to spend the day rehashing arguments about the trade-offs between civil liberties and compassionate care. Indeed, some of the arguments felt familiar—if no less heart-wrenching. Teresa Pasquini, a mother whose son wound up in solitary confinement after many mental health services refused to care for him, lamented how overly strict commitment standards intended to "protect [her son] . . . made him fail over and over again [before getting help]. And there is no dignity in continuous failure." Assemblymember Miguel Santiago, who sponsored numerous reforms to grave disability, challenged listeners to walk Skid Row and "argue that it is more humane to leave somebody on the street than . . . bring them in to give them the help that they need and deserve as human beings." Keris Myrick, a survivor of forced treatment, decried how California was "compel[ling] people to broken systems," countering that the solution was "to compel systems to meet the needs of people in the least restrictive way possible."

The hearing took a different turn, though, when an official from the Department of Health Care Services (DHCS) discussed her agency's role in the LPS system, which included "collecting statistical data and making the data publicly available."

Assemblymember Eloise Reyes observed, "more than 50 percent of the counties do not provide accurate information about their LPS detentions. . . . I am sure that you understand that it would be very difficult for policymakers to determine what our communities need, and whether our efforts to address these needs are actually working [without data]."

The DHCS representative defended, "We don't have any authority for any consequences." That is, she claimed the state had no capacity to make counties provide that most basic element of accountability for involuntary treatment, a *count* of how many people are receiving it.

Assemblymember Jim Wood seemed even more irritated. Observing the money the state was funneling into locked beds, he opined: "Nobody knows what the hell is going on. Is that a fair characterization, or did I not have enough coffee this morning?"

He turned to the representative of DHCS, and asked directly, "Who is strategizing and planning and coordinating these things? . . . How do we know that this ship [LPS] is going anywhere but in a circle?" I don't think his annoyance was just about a lack of caffeine.

The representative took a long pause: "Right, I mean, I think I agree that part of what we need to do is really increase our data."

Wood was unsatisfied: "Who is going to use that data? . . . Who's going to be in charge of making changes? . . . Could there be somebody in charge?" He paused. "Somebody?"

The DHCS division chief offered a last defense: "DHCS is committed to making changes in the areas that we have authority over," but there are "gaps" where "DHCS does not have the ability to oversee," like courts or public guardians.

Wood closed, "I'm begging for, some person or entity . . . to assess where the heck we are going."

The hearing left me hopeful for reforms that would address abdicated authority. In the end, though, 2022 was a pretty mixed bag. Susan Eggman, a Democrat from Stockton (who, notably, was introduced to the issue working at a Crestwood IMD distributing meds and lighting cigarettes while still a high schooler) introduced a package of eight bills to both expand and better regulate conservatorships.[5] The governor ultimately signed two bills in 2022 that addressed the execrable state of data and clarifying LPS law to ban some counties' blatantly illegal practice of placing individuals on back-to-back 5150s to hold them without going to a hearing.[6] Other proposals to beef up oversight and evaluation and to create a statewide database of bed availability went nowhere.[7] Two reforms to allow more testimony into conservatorship hearings and expand grave disability to include "personal or medical care or self-protection and safety" were stopped in their tracks by the head of the Assembly Judiciary Committee.[8] Advocates for more forced treatment largely did not get the deep changes to LPS they wanted.[9]

Instead, they got CARE courts. Recall that in early 2022 the governor had said he would be "leaning into conservatorships"; on March 3rd he announced that, instead, he'd be working around them.[10] CARE (Community Assistance, Recovery, and Empowerment) courts would serve an estimated seven to twelve thousand people with psychotic disorders who were not stabilized in voluntary treatment and were "unlikely to survive safely in the community." Families, first responders, roommates, or outpatient clinicians could refer people for an evaluation; if found eligible, a person would be ordered onto a twelve-month "care plan" and "housing plan" (although CARE court "participants" did not have to be homeless, homeless people were the obvious targets of the bill). The bill passed with only two votes in opposition.[11] According to Governor Newsom, CARE courts showed that the state was finally "tak[ing] some damn responsibility for implementing our ideals."[12]

The proposal is difficult to characterize. The governor tried to thread the proverbial needle by claiming that the program, despite the apparent coercion of compelling people to appear before a court, embraced principles of "supported decision-making."[13] Participants would be offered a "supporter" in the court process and be asked to fill in a psychiatric advance directive. It would ensure relentless and persistent attempts to engage a resistant person for a year (with a possible one-year renewal). The governor hyped the "real accountability" created by the proposal, since a judge could fine a county up to a thousand dollars a day for failing to deliver the services in the care plan. CARE courts, it seemed, would reclaim some of the authority for organizing treatment that otherwise had been delegated so much that authority seemed to disappear altogether. As Sacramento mayor Darrell Steinberg celebrated, "The most important compelled action in CARE Court is the government's obligation to provide the care, not the individual's obligation to accept it."[14]

There were also warning signs that the proposal would fall into some well-worn ruts. Direct funding for the courts was limited.[15] While CARE court participants would jump to the front of the line for housing created by the governor's $15 billion investment in homelessness, there was still no guarantee that the services envisioned in an individual care plan would collectively exist. Moreover, although the pressure to participate in CARE courts came from the threat of a conservatorship for not participating, the governor spurned a request by county public guardians for state funding. There is no mechanism to force counties to conserve individuals "failing" CARE courts, and my guess is that, without more resources, they won't. In short, when State Senator Thomas Umberg (the bill's sponsor) said they were doing something "new and revolutionary in California," he wasn't just inadvertently echoing the rhetoric that had been used to celebrate LPS five decades earlier.[16] He was describing a program that was founded on a similar model of smashing law and medicine, coercion and care, together and hoping for good outcomes on the other side.

The endurance of abdicated authority in California is unsurprising given how deeply embedded it is in the organization of mental health services nationwide. In the mid-twentieth century, the federal government, in the words of the psychiatrist E. Fuller Torrey, "destroyed" a "coherent, if flawed" state hospital system.[17] This happened partly deliberately, through President Kennedy's 1963 Community Mental Health Act, and partly unintentionally, because federal Medicaid and Social Security (available only to people outside state hospitals) made deinstitutionalization fiscally irresistible. The federal government never exercised real authority to create a system in the asylums' place. Notably, it did not mandate that community clinics serve former state hospital patients, and they often didn't.[18] A 1977 report found 135 federal programs touching on the lives of people with serious mental illness, but beneficiaries were "inadvertently victimized" by a "lack of consistent national policies" to create a "coherent system of care."[19] In the early 1980s, President Reagan eviscerated funding for community care, as he had in California. As Torrey put it, the system was virtually "decapitated" and "all authority and responsibility for the mental illness treatment . . . essentially disappeared."[20]

Today, federal programs pay for half of mental health care.[21] Federal laws like the Affordable Care Act have ensured that a steadily expanding number of Americans receive some kind of psychiatric treatment.[22] Yet the federal government's abdication of leadership on the question of involuntary treatment is stark.

The last year for which it conducted a national count of people subject to forced treatment was 1980.[23] Although the government occasionally publishes reports offering a blueprint for reforming the mental health system, the most recent one (in 2003) makes no mention of civil commitments or involuntary care.[24] Federal courts have played a key role in setting limits around the legal criteria and procedures of involuntary treatment, but within those limits, states have free reign. States like California, as I've shown in this book, have left implementation up to the counties, which have granted discretion to individual bureaucrats, who have ultimately produced a nonsystem of care as chaotic at the bottom as at the top.

EXTENDING ABDICATION

This book has focused on showing that the concept of abdicated authority provides a stronger explanation for the functioning and failings of involuntary treatment than the frameworks of medical-legal conflict and control. But the concept is a theoretical tool that can be applied more broadly to analyze public policy, street-level bureaucracy, and state power.

Abdication is a way of resolving complex policy dilemmas by abandoning government's responsibility for resolving them. The pre-LPS commitment system reflected a general consensus that people with various kinds of mental or psychiatric disabilities were state responsibilities. LPS law set guidelines for when clinicians could continue to hospitalize some in this population, but regulators never really clarified when they should do so. Various programs gave counties the option to create programs to serve individuals, but never comprehensively planned—or budgeted—for their collective needs.

We can see a similar process of abdication in the steadily feebler federal response to the coronavirus, which had killed more than a million Americans by the time I wrote this (in late 2022). On September 18, 2022, President Joe Biden told CBS News, "The pandemic is over. We still have a problem with COVID. We're still doing a lotta work on it. But the pandemic is over."[25] Critics howled that the statement was "irresponsible and flat-out wrong," coming in a week that more than three thousand Americans died of the disease.[26] But in an important way Biden's statement was correct: the state would no longer be treating coronavirus as a crisis to be decisively resolved and would cease using the many levers still at the government's disposal in a concerted way.

Abdicating authority avoided answering a question with no easy answers. Once it was clear that vaccines were only partially effective, truly eradicating the virus was no longer possible (even in a totalitarian country like China). But neither was it politically or ethically feasible to do nothing to mitigate its impact. A deliberate policy response would thus require, at least implicitly, deciding how many deaths are acceptable and calibrating mitigation measures to match. It's obvious why setting no objective at all is easier. After all, without goals, there can be no accountability for failing to meet them. That's the essence of abdicated authority: not an absence of government action (the federal government is still distributing vaccines, tracking virus levels, and approving treatments) but a void of purpose and direction.

The downsizing of California's carceral system is another example. California shrank its brutally overstuffed prison system by 26 percent from 2006 to 2018, in no small part by delegating responsibility for many prisoners to county jails.[27] True decarceration, however, requires a delicate balancing of public safety with individual well-being and a clear strategy to address both outside of the criminal justice system. Advocates for abolishing mass incarceration universally recognize that many incarcerated people have complex needs (including around mental health) that will need to be addressed for them to thrive in the community.

It's much cheaper, however, to abdicate. In 2019, the Los Angeles Board of Supervisors announced a plan to replace Men's Central Jail with a four-thou-sand-bed hospital.[28] Although initially celebrated as a move toward replacing coercion with care, advocates riposted that "a jail is a jail is a jail"—whether or not it is labeled a hospital—and defeated the proposal.[29] But the available community-based, noncarceral programs to which courts could divert erstwhile inmates had nowhere near four thousand beds, so many people were diverted to nothing.[30] Not expanding alternative services dissolved a crisis of prison and jail overcrowding by merging it into the crisis of homelessness and disorder on the streets.[31] The likely result of abdicated authority is rarely a libertarian paradise; instead, it's short-term government interventions (whether via 5150s or arrests) that are arbitrary and sometimes violent, oriented toward only the most intoler-able, complaint-generating cases.

In analyzing these interventions, this book has drawn on a rich body of studies on how legal, medical, and welfare agencies *govern*, *discipline*, or *regulate* margin-alized people.[32] Like other researchers in this vein, I have focused on street-level bureaucrats: petty potentates who have significant discretion over whether and how to mete out punishment, provide care, and grant benefits.[33] Recently, Josh Seim, in his study of ambulance workers, argued that this line of research needs to pay greater attention to the relations among street-level bureaucrats, using the example of how police, paramedics, and triage nurses burden shuffle undesirable suffering bodies.[34] Similarly, Armando Lara-Millán analyzed a process of redistributing the poor as institutions address their own funding and legal constraints by moving people back and forth.[35]

Abdicated authority helps us more carefully specify what individual street-level bureaucrats can and cannot do in these horizontal relationships. As government programs become ever more complex, individualized, and targeted (witness the extraordinarily convoluted process for homeless individuals to qualify for permanent supported housing), actually providing care or control requires the alignment of a series of bureaucratic decisions. Yet delegation to a mix of public, nonprofit, and for-profit agencies subjects discretion to divergent financial incentives and disparate professional ethos. It virtually guarantees that bureaucrats will define key eligibility criteria (like grave disability) in inconsistent ways. In systems with myriad veto points, bureaucratic discretion is really only negative discretion—the ability to remove or block someone from receiving services. And when everyone has only negative discretion, the result is not necessarily the burden shuffling of individuals onto other agencies that Seim documents, but their complete abandonment.

The importance of authority becomes more visible if we shift our analytic focus. Previous studies on "hyper-marginalized populations" have critiqued how agencies "hamper, discourage, or oppress individuals" who are deemed morally unworthy of help.[36] Perhaps the most revealing cases, though, are those in which many bureaucrats and agencies claim a genuine desire to assist but fail to do so effectively. A transitional-age youth leaving the foster care system, for example, or a pregnant woman whose substance use leads to incarceration might have a half-dozen case managers and social workers from multiple agencies; not all of them are looking to burden shuffle or redistribute them elsewhere.[37] What is missing in these cases is not bureaucratic compassion but authority, in the sense of a "device to achieve, more reliably and successfully, independently given and agreed objectives that would otherwise be less easy or impossible to attain."[38] Explaining such cases requires attention to how decision-making criteria are defined and regulated, how information flows between agencies, and who has leadership authority over other professionals.

This framework also encourages us to draw insights from different historical moments than previous studies. Lara-Millàn's analysis of redistributing the poor emphasizes periods of austerity, when agencies must rapidly find ways to cut rolls. This forces them to deliberate and define eligibility criteria (the 1991 "realignment" in California, for example, was one of the few times the state clearly articulated who should be served by the public mental health system). But the very concept of austerity presupposes moments of largesse, when abdicating authority may be both easier and more consequential. For example, opponents of expanding conservatorships have pointed to huge new investments in mental health and supported housing as a reason to defer reforming LPS. Yet this conveniently allows the state to put off questions of how to use its authority to ensure that new mental health and housing services actually serve the people who need them, much less whether its sovereign power should be used to force people into accepting them when they don't want to.

Finally, abdicated authority has relevance for how we understand psychiatry and other tools of social control. A long lineage of social scientists have developed the idea that the psychiatric profession seeks to endlessly expand its power by claiming jurisdiction over all sorts of deviance, disorder, and disability.[39] Scholars also claim that the form of psychiatric power has changed: unlike in the era of open-ended internments in asylums policed by physical force, in "modern psychiatric practice . . . overt use of coercion has likely been replaced by more subtle forms of social control."[40]

This book challenges this portrayal. Even as attention has moved to the management of people with mental illness in the community or their incarceration in prisons and jails, hospitals and civil commitment remain at the core of the trajectories of people with serious mental illness. More subtle forms of psychiatric control—like judges encouraging patients to take their medication while living independently or clinicians making access to housing contingent on compliance[41]—are shadowed by the threat of being forcibly interned in settings where control includes being placed in mechanical restraints and injected with medication. It is too frequently overlooked that attempts to divert people from the criminal justice system into treatment often siphon people into *involuntary* treatment. Our inattention to civil commitments, for both mental illness and substance use, may lead us to overlook that, as the criminal-legal system recedes, coercive health care could be taking its place.[42]

While legally imposed psychiatric care may be more widespread than usually depicted, its ambitions are easily overstated. Theorists of medical-legal control portray psychiatric interventions as aiming to produce "productive, responsible, and self-governing individuals."[43] It is easy to confuse aspirational rhetoric for reality. The public mental health system in California, as sociologist Neil Gong argues, is increasingly focused on "tolerant containment": not correcting problematic behaviors, but keeping them out of sight.[44] The contemporary use of conservatorship is reflective of this limited horizon. A person who can pitch a tent, fish for food in a dumpster, or beg for spare change is far enough away from imminent death to be allowed to refuse treatment, even if their untreated mental illness is causing nearly unbearable suffering.

Is this residual role for psychiatry a sign that anti-psychiatry critiques are starting to bite or that the shaky foundations of psychiatric expertise are increasingly exposed?[45] I don't think so. Contrary to depictions of medical-legal conflict, I find that the objective of social control of the mad is widely endorsed. But legal, medical, and government actors are profoundly cynical about their collective capacity to enforce discipline and self-regulation.[46] My differentiation of forms of power helps capture this divergence. Although the movement to expand civil commitments will increase the sovereign power wielded over those labeled as seriously mentally ill, governments have shown little appetite to assume greater authority to ensure that coercion has any enduring impact. This divergence is partly a product of delegation: while private entities (be they prisons or IMDs) can assume the crown and exercise the coercive power of the state, they cannot fill its coordinating role.

As in the case of the anemic coronavirus pandemic response, abdicated authority speaks to how power is exerted in an era of diminished aspiration. "Harm reduction" drug programs, such as "safe consumption" sites where people use illicit substances under supervision, reveal a kind of "palliative governance," whereby society hopes to keep users alive without seeking to make them sober.[47] In international development and global public health, past interventions geared toward building up modern health systems modeled on Western ones have been replaced by programs to distribute bed nets or deworming medication. They measure success purely in lives saved.[48]

In a historical moment when society is skeptical of psychiatry's ability to restore mad people to full citizenship and is reluctant to finance even an attempt, preventing death may be the only consensus goal. But conservatorship is a reminder that palliative interventions can be forceful ones. In fact, our public authorities' failure to do anything more than keep people slightly above the dividing line between life and death may, in practice, destine us to use force over and over again, until the most marginal people in society fall, irretrievably, below that line.

MOVING PAST THE MYTHS

If abdicated authority offers an alternative interpretation for the failings of our mental health system, it also offers a distinctive set of prescriptions. The opposite of abdicated authority is *engaged authority*: active, intentional, and accountable use of the unique coordinating and regulatory authority of government. Such authority should be directed toward, first, creating a mental health system organized as an entitlement; second, incentivizing persistent care that addresses social as well as medical needs; third, constructing a full continuum of residential treatment with a public backstop; and fourth, reducing conservatorship to an evidence-based, targeted intervention.

To get there, we need to challenge two shibboleths stoking the conflagration over reforming LPS. First is the "myth of the criteria." It goes something like this: there is an objectively identifiable group of gravely disabled people who are not able to provide for their own survival; that inability is caused by severe mental illness and, especially, anosognosia; LPS defined grave disability so narrowly that it fails to capture many in that population; redefining grave disability will get that group into lifesaving involuntary care.[49] Opponents of conservatorship are at times stuck in a second myth, the "myth of Reagan." From this perspective, had Governor Reagan not gutted the community care system—and later, as president, funding for both mental health and housing[50]—the replacement of institutional warehousing with voluntary community-based services would have worked out.[51] A generous welfare state and a universal health system, not an expansion of medical-legal control, are the antidote to the crisis on California's streets.

The hard truth for adherents to the myth of the criteria is that, even bracketing concerns about civil rights, expanding grave disability is unlikely to extend coercive care to the people who advocates think need it.[52] There are three pieces of evidence for this. First, past reforms to commitment criteria in other states have generally failed to produce significant changes in involuntary admissions.[53] Second, internationally, rates of involuntary treatment do not vary with laws; countries with loose need-for-treatment standards do not systematically hospitalize people more than countries with tight dangerousness-based ones.[54] This suggests a third claim: as I've argued throughout this book, the criteria are defined not by legal statutes and legislation but by financial incentives, resource availability, and local bureaucratic imperatives.[55] The myth of the criteria falsely assumes that California is short on coerced psychiatric care, whereas I have argued that the problem is a failure to integrate coercion, which is actually quite frequent, into any concerted and coordinated system.

There are certainly tweaks to LPS procedures that could streamline the process without gutting protections.[56] But the myth of the criteria has led advocates to pour too much effort into seeking LPS reforms that have proven, time and time again, to be a bad use of political capital. Governor Newsom acknowledged as much when his team declared that attempts to expand conservatorship had created "many decades of battle scars, hurt feelings, and entrenched opinions," to little effect.[57] Yet the immediate dismissal of Newsom's alternative proposal, CARE courts, was a reminder that many civil liberties advocates, service users, and community treatment providers see expansions of forced treatment as an existential threat impervious to compromise.[58] Alienating these groups in a knock-down, drag-out fight over LPS criteria is a problem because those groups are essential to reforming the mental health system. Anosognosia itself is not a myth. But the myth of the criteria suggests that the response to anosognosia has to be forced treatment rather than the alternatives—which these groups can help develop—that can bring many people deemed lacking in insight into care.

The other side of the debate needs to confront the myth of Reagan. Looking at sixty-plus years of fiscal feast and famine in California, I'm comfortable saying that properly funding the voluntary outpatient mental health services that Reagan eviscerated would be good for people with mental illness. But it isn't quite so simple to throw things into reverse: some people are so alienated that just funding services that should have existed, and that they would have accepted, decades ago won't ensure they get the care they need, but are refusing, today.

When I asked Toby Ewing, the executive director of the Mental Health Services Oversight and Accountability Commission (which oversees the use of MHSA money), to describe the state of the "system" for people with serious mental illness, he rejected the premise of the question itself: "We don't have a mental health system, we have 5,000-odd programs. This is a mosaic of programs, and a mosaic could be beautiful, but in this case, it isn't." With ten thousand programs, it could still be true that none of them in a given county would accept a person with a chronic substance abuse problem, cognitive impairments, and history of violent behavior. The myth of Reagan, so focused on increasing government funding, sidesteps the need for government authority to ensure that providers actually serve the particularly challenging, and occasionally even unpleasant or hostile, people at risk of going onto conservatorship.

The first principle for reform, then, is to construct a mental health system, not just a smorgasbord of services. Fortunately, there is already a model of what that might look like: California's system for people with developmental disabilities. The 1969 Lanterman Mental Retardation Act (yes, it's the same Frank Lanterman) declared that "the state of California accepts a responsibility for its mentally retarded [sic] citizens and an obligation to them which it must discharge."[59] The state is not a direct service provider. Instead, it organizes Regional Centers that are responsible for evaluating anyone in a geographic catchment area, designing a personalized care plan, and contracting for those specific services.

People with developmental disabilities were also once left to rot in state facilities. Unlike in the case of people with mental illness, though, few people are calling to undo their deinstitutionalization.[60] Indeed, it is revealing that many interviewees cited success stories of people exiting homelessness or a cycle of hospitalizations thanks to the discovery of a developmental disability that got them linked to Regional Centers (or military service that qualified them for the Veterans Affairs health care system, which makes a similarly open-ended commitment).

California's provisioning for people with developmental disabilities is an imperfect system marked by, among other things, underfunded services, overly restrictive eligibility criteria,[61] and, yes, imbrication with the abuse and overuse of probate conservatorships.[62] But it's based on the right principle: individualized services that are provided as part of an entitlement, not "to the extent resources are available" (as in the public mental health system). Governor Newsom has frequently touted the billions he is pumping into mental health care and housing, supplemented by a new federal windfall for crisis services (from the 2022 Protecting Our Kids gun control bill). But periods of abundance have too often been followed by brutal belt-tightening. A legal entitlement, enforceable by the courts, is one tool to ensure an enduring commitment.

Second, the mental health system needs services that are accountable for overcoming a very real problem: people refusing care that clinicians, or society writ large, are convinced they need. Partisans for purely voluntary services should give some ground and accept a model of dogged, persistent outreach that doesn't take "no" for an answer and works relentlessly to get to "yes." Engagement should lead with what people actually want, which is often social supports rather than psychiatric care. Although, in principle, this is what Full-Service Partnerships, Assisted Outpatient Treatment, or Early Intervention in Psychosis programs are already doing, a lack of statewide authority has meant that these models are implemented haphazardly. They too often don't adhere to the evidence-based models identified in the literature.[63]

Identifying a more robust approach is not hard. More than a dozen clinicians I interviewed had trained in New York. Every single one saw it as having a superior public mental health system. The state's Office of Mental Health closely oversees Assertive Community Treatment (ACT) and AOT teams to ensure they hew closely to the proven models on which they are based, such as providing truly team-based care.[64] New York fully reimburses ACT teams only if they successfully contact clients six times per month.[65] California relies instead on a "soul-killing" system of minute-by-minute Medi-Cal billing that prioritizes medication management and medical services over building relationships and meeting basic needs.[66] A better approach would give teams clear objectives, a defined budget, and flexibility in how to spend it to meet those goals, even if it means paying a psychiatrist to take someone to the dentist.[67]

A third recommendation is to fund—and rethink—California's placement continuum. Calling to "fund more beds" is easy; just about everyone I talk to agrees with the sentiment. But a "bed" is just a mattress; figuring out where to put it is harder.[68] The myth of Reagan suggests we should reverse the former president's defunding of public housing and focus on supported, independent apartments. Yet this book has documented how a one-size-fits-all approach fails some individuals, who will overdose, get evicted, or die in supported housing. A dogmatic refusal to embrace more structured housing options for a minority of formerly homeless individuals may be undermining public support for Housing First more broadly; polls showing massive endorsement of the governor's CARE courts proposal, for example, speak to a rising desire for a more forceful response to homelessness.[69] It thus inadvertently reinforces the preferred solution implied by the myth of the criteria: locked hospital and IMD beds.

In truth, an all-of-the-above approach to building beds seems right, given the scale of California's crisis (albeit with an emphasis on up-front crisis services to keep people out of hospitals and unlocked residential treatment programs to step them into). But the state should reconceptualize how those placements function. For one thing, it should decouple legal status from level of care. No one should be obligated to have a gamut of rights stripped away via conservatorship to access highly structured or intensive care if they want it. Evidence from other countries suggests that, if there were more inpatient beds, clinicians could propose a hospitalization earlier in someone's downward trajectory and promise that they could stay long enough to actually stabilize. As a result, more people go voluntarily (and, as consumers free to leave, are better positioned to demand improved care and nicer conditions).[70] On the other hand, models like San Francisco's community conservatorship or LA's outpatient conservatorship programs demonstrate that some people do need an authoritative push to stay medication compliant but don't need to be in a locked setting. No level of care (such as an FSP or a residential treatment program) should require, as many de facto do, that someone pass through an acute hospitalization to access them.

This residential care system needs to be organized, not just funded, by engaged public authority. Whether county hospitals or city-run clinics actually deliver better care than their private counterparts is an open question.[71] Certainly, the LPS Act stemmed from the revelation that the state, when it was a direct provider of services, was not doing swimmingly. But if the state continues to delegate care to the private sector, it needs to ensure that providers that take public money operate as public services. This will require putting an end to practices of creaming, blacklisting, and cherry-picking that allocate clients and the resources attached to them based on profit-driven proclivities. There should be a statewide system with transparent criteria for rationing scarce beds in facilities like IMDs. An engaged state will also be one that does some things itself: state hospitals should continue to be a place of last resort for people who are too stigmatized, too isolated, or too complex to be cared for elsewhere.

Fourth and finally, an engaged authority will transform conservatorship into a narrowly targeted, evidence-based intervention. The state needs to set outcome metrics for conservatorship along multiple dimensions (including clinical stability, functioning, and, yes, client satisfaction) and then test which models achieve them. Experiments like Fresno's RISE program (focused on respecting client choice and using combined clinical-conservator teams) should be studied and, if the results are positive, scaled up. We need to know if conservatorship works for substance users or people diverted from the criminal justice system before more individuals facing these difficulties are crammed into an already overwhelmed system. All of this will take, at a bare minimum, a state office responsible for gathering and publishing data, establishing best practices, and channeling badly needed state funds to public guardians, which counties have too long overlooked.

Those adhering to the myth of the criteria should accept that a more robust conservatorship system is only politically and ethically acceptable if coupled with more robust protections from it. There are real and valid concerns about conservatorships' overuse (as highlighted by none other than Britney Spears). The state should specify which alternatives to conservatorship, such as AOT or PADs, must be tried (or ruled out) before a judge can impose a conservatorship. A more careful analysis of someone's need for conservatorship will require ensuring input from family members, outpatient providers, and peers in conservatorship hearings. The state should ensure effective representation for conservatees through a specialized body of trained lawyers, modeled after New York's Mental Hygiene Legal Services.[72]

It would be easy to eliminate conservatorship. The state created this legal tool; it could abolish it. It is usually cheaper, after all, to grant people civil liberties than to care for them. The right way to drive down forced treatment, though, is by reducing the need for it, which previous research has shown can be done through investment in a full continuum of care.[73] Once that continuum is in place, the alternative to conservatorship will no longer be a mix of abandonment and short-term, purposeless coercion. At that point, decreasing the number of people on conservatorship ought to be a goal both sides of a never-ending, acrimonious debate can get behind.

"Every day [in California]," one clinician put it, mental health professionals "work . . . with incredibly sick patients and incredibly limited resources. And every day, they make miracles happen." But "so many of these outcomes that have grown to feel like miracles—someone held for a placement, provided with medication, or referred to a program—in an appropriately resourced world would really just be standard of care." An accountable mental health system does not hope for miracles. Instead, it relies on engaged authority to guarantee fundamental rights for the most vulnerable—not just to food, clothing, and shelter but also to support, care, and dignity.

CODA: BACK TO THE BUS STOP

I went into my 2021 research trip to Los Angeles having already lived years in the Bay Area and conducted hundreds of interviews. I still left deeply distressed about what I had seen. I drove home to Flagstaff, Arizona, where I grew up. I recounted my day conducting outreach to Wally with Dr. Partovi and my visit to Skid Row with Dr. Bollom to my father. "Where do you think those people are in Europe?" he asked. My initial thought was "in a hospital." A more compassionate society with a robust welfare state, I thought, would not hide behind a smokescreen of respect for autonomy and would provide care for such vulnerable individuals.

And then I realized: in a compassionate society with a robust welfare state, these individuals would not exist.

California is not just facing the consequences of an underfunded and disorganized mental health system. It is reaping suffering sown by the highest real poverty rate in the nation,[74] a housing crisis that has made it home to half the nation's unsheltered homeless,[75] and a system of mass incarceration that locked up Black and brown people at rates that would make the worst autocracies of the world blush.[76] There are people with schizophrenia in every country, but in the United States they are at the epicenter of a particularly harsh maelstrom of "systematic and unrelenting structural violence."[77] This has created a distinctively American population, condemned to early death or consigned to "bare life"—the most minimal standard of existence that comes from a beating heart and not much more.[78]

At the end of a book critiquing public authorities' failure to take responsibility for these individuals, it's time for me to assume my own obligations. My uncomfortable conclusion after years of research is that, on balance, there are more people in California who desperately need an LPS conservatorship than are receiving it. It's a deeply unfair consequence of our colossal, collective failures as a society that, without forced treatment, some individuals won't survive long enough to benefit from the reforms I have proposed. (Mark Rippee, profiled in chapter 5, died just as this book went to press. He remained blind, psychotic, and frequently victimized on the streets of Vacaville after Solano County refused to conserve him and went into sepsis from an untreated urinary tract infection for which he refused basic medical care.) To say otherwise, I've realized, would be to abdicate my own accumulated expertise.

With that said, I want to go beyond debates over how widely or narrowly to define grave disability with a call to be bold, to be humble, and to be hopeful. Bold, because expanding conservatorship won't come close to addressing the scale of the problem. The real moonshot, instead, lies in reforms outside the mental health system entirely. As the American Psychiatric Association itself recognized in a recent report, "poverty and associated variables (i.e., unemployment, income, education) have the most robust effect on inpatient admission"—and, by extension, the need for involuntary care—"and should be prioritized."[79]

There are already efforts afoot to address these social determinants, which mental health advocates would be wise to support. California's Advancing and Innovating Medi-Cal (CalAIM) proposal, for example, would shift federal Medicaid dollars away from paying for medical treatment and toward covering apartment security deposits, respite services for caregivers, or healthy meals; for the first time, Medi-Cal will also cover undocumented immigrants, too long an underclass excluded from public services. In 2022, the legislature also made moves to compel localities to make it easier to build housing, a shortage of which (and not mental illness or drug use) is unquestionably the root cause of mass homelessness.[80] The state's moves to decarcerate and ongoing discussions of reparations to Black residents are crucial steps toward chipping away at the structural racism that oppresses the 65 percent of Californians who are nonwhite.

Yet we should be humble, too. Debates around mental illness policy are so stubborn, in part, because we still lack even a basic consensus around what mental illness actually is. Some advocates and clinicians paint it as a brain disease rooted in genes and neurotransmitters; radical psychiatrists and sociologists in the 1960s saw it as a rebellion against capitalism and stifling social norms; disability activists have reframed it as a form of "neurodiversity" or a "dangerous gift." For my part, I've come to see conditions like schizophrenia as potentially all of those things but, at least for the people profiled in this book, also as a source of profound suffering and loss—above all for those afflicted but also for their friends and families.

Thomas Insel, formerly head of the National Institute of Mental Health, recently released a book that sounded the optimistic note that "treatments work," concluding that "solving the care crisis requires nothing more than a wider application of the best care we can offer."[81] Yet behind the walls of IMDs, on the back patios of board and cares, and in the case files of public guardians, we can see where this narrative breaks down. There are painful limits to how well treatments work for some people, a therapeutic impotence that creates suffering for those providing care, too.

I often feel that, in America, we struggle to find a language for the disquieting reality of chronicity and suffering. So I'll offer a quote from a French psychiatrist I interviewed in 2016, a veteran doctor who had spent years working in public psychiatric hospitals for long-term patients: "With psychosis, it's a combat that is often very difficult. It's stronger than we are. We know that a patient could do well today, and tomorrow fall apart. . . . So the goal is not for them to be adapted to society, not to be 'normalized.' But to be as happy as possible. To suffer less." To be humble means accepting that sometimes the most important thing clinicians can offer is neither care nor coercion but compassion and solidarity: a willingness to fight an open-ended, and sometimes losing, battle against conditions that can be both mysterious and so, so cruel.

Yet, in the end, we should be hopeful too. Because once we relinquish the idea that we can care, coerce, or conserve everyone into recovery and independence, we can recognize that people can still live more dignified lives without either.

In spring 2022, Dr. Partovi sent me a picture of herself next to Wally, whom I had met the year before at that bus stop, stripped of all his possession except a winter coat covering him on a sweltering day. In the photo, he was not just cleaned up, thanks to the nursing home where he was now living, but beaming.

It wasn't an easy road to get there. A few months after I visited Wally, Dr. Partovi convinced him to go to a shelter. When she brought him, they said it was too late in the day for an intake, but he could come back tomorrow. But tomorrow, he didn't want to come back. So Partovi tried the forceful route: she called the HOME team (which leads LA's outpatient conservatorship program) and said, "This guy is going to die, he needs to be 5150ed." This time they agreed and took him to the county hospital. He was on track to be conserved.

Except he wasn't. The county transferred him to a private hospital. When Dr. Partovi called them to say she could offer testimony at a conservatorship hearing, the physician's assistant told her, "Oh, no, our administration doesn't like that [conservatorship]." She harangued the social worker, too, who told her, "We have two people who need to be conserved, but we can only do one." So they sent Wally to a nursing home.

And, for whatever reason, he stayed. When Partovi went to visit him, he was "bright eyed and alert." This time he said he remembered Dr. Partovi.

"Do you like it here?" she asked.

"Yeah!" he replied.

"What do you like?"

"Good food!" he enthused.

It looked like the perfect outcome: the persistence of a raft of professionals meant that Wally was getting care, no coercion required. And then, when Partovi was moving to leave, he asked a disquieting question: "Are you taking me with you?"

"Where do you want to go?" she queried.

"Back to my spot," he replied. Back to his bus stop.

"Oh Wally, you're so silly," a staff member interjected.

But without a conservatorship, if he wanted to, he was legally free to go.

As for the young pregnant woman from the start of this chapter, there really was a miracle, of sorts: the ER physician convinced hospital administration to let her stay the night. The first responder I was shadowing went in to get a look at her so we could identify her back out on the streets after she was discharged. When we peeked in, she was sleeping soundly. Over the course of a few hours that evening, she had seen the police officers who put her on a hold, the paramedics who transported her, the ER physician and psychiatrist who evaluated her, a host of techs and nurses who offered her care and comfort, and the discharge social worker who was pleading for help finding a shelter. Thanks to them, she had a tray of half-eaten food by her bed, a hospital gown, and a roof over her head. Food, clothing, and shelter.

In the morning, she'd be gone, and back to being gravely disabled.

METHODOLOGICAL APPENDIX

INTERVIEWING ACROSS
THE CONSERVATORSHIP CONTINUUM

In 2018, I was a graduate student at Berkeley interested in the state and mental health care, and a human being residing in the Bay Area, which meant I was aware of how both government and medicine seemed to be failing many people I saw on my bike ride to campus. I was intrigued when I learned about a government bureaucracy, public guardians, on which almost nothing was written but who policy makers thought ought to be doing more. With a group of research assistants, we began contacting and interviewing the public guardians and public defenders representing conservatees in as many counties as possible. We faced a great deal of skepticism and struggled even to find contact information in many smaller counties, but we ultimately spoke to seven public defenders and nine public guardians in larger counties (those with more than a million people), six and nine in medium counties (between two hundred thousand and one million), and two and four in smaller counties (less than two hundred thousand).

These interviews provided a far from complete survey of how these agencies operated across fifty-eight counties, but consistent patterns quickly emerged. It became clear that decisions about conservatorship that I assumed were taken by courts and public guardians had been largely decided far earlier in the conservatorship continuum by police officers writing 5150s, ER psychiatrists making admissions decisions, or inpatient clinicians filling out conservatorship applications. I reached out to these other professional groups through a range of strategies, including directly contacting clinicians who were quoted in the media or had published research on the topic and relying on referrals from previous interviewees. Following the precepts of "theoretical sampling," my focus was not on identifying a representative sample from each set of institutions but rather enough examples to "reveal the practices, mechanisms, and relationships" shaping each point of the continuum.[1]

In 2020, my research was given an unlikely boost by two "Moms on a Mission," Teresa Pasquini and Lauren Rettagliata. They sent me a copy of a "Heart Paper" they had written based on visits to various providers of *Housing That Heals*— residential care that could have helped their sons avoid years locked in institutions or decompensating in supported housing (for lack of sufficient supports). They clued me in to what should be obvious: those with firsthand experience navigating the system have unique and irreplaceable insights into it. They generously circulated a request for interviews among communities of families of people with mental illness. In 2021, I added another group that I had been hesitant to include (since my original research design was focused on professional decisions) but whose inclusion at this point seemed absolutely essential: people who had experienced forced treatment themselves.

Interviews with professionals generally lasted about an hour, those with families and service users sometimes two, or up to five. Most of them were conducted remotely: even when I lived in the Bay Area, many interviewees were a six-hour drive away. A reader might notice that few interviewees are introduced with a physical description or characterization of the scene, which reflects both my desire to preserve anonymity and the fact that I spoke to many people over the phone. The dawn of the Zoom era during the pandemic in 2020 allowed me to add a welcome video component to the interviews. I adapted my questionnaire to the particular practices and pressures of people working at each point in the system. However, to create some comparability, I ended each interview with a common battery of questions about interviewees' views of LPS reform, vision for improving the mental health system, and understanding of the goals of conservatorship.

All told, I conducted 268 interviews across thirty-four counties; interviewees' roles are summarized in table A.1. While the raw number of interviewees is above the norm for most sociological studies, the numbers within some key groups— say, mobile crisis clinicians (twelve)—are small.[2] I have no doubt I could conduct hundreds more interviews across dozens of counties and learn still more, but the sample is large enough that I am reasonably certain I have identified most of the main trends in the conservatorship system.

TABLE A.1 Interviewee fields

Law enforcement / First responder	25
Outpatient clinician	23
ER / Hospital	26
Public guardian	26
Court / Public defender	28
Housing provider	23
Government	28
Advocacy group	19
Family	29
Person receiving involuntary treatment	30
Professional organization	11
Total	268

It would be easy to see the interview data on which this book is based as a second-best alternative to the kind of vivid and firsthand descriptions that longer-term ethnographic observations would provide. Nonetheless, such an approach would not have allowed me to make this book's most distinctive contribution. There are fantastic ethnographies of outpatient clinics, hospitals, and commitment courts[3] but fewer studies that look at the host of disparate institutions that make up the public mental health system simultaneously. Getting a portrait of each step in the conservatorship continuum required sacrificing depth for breadth. Showing how conservatorship operates in not one but dozens of counties entailed a similar trade-off.

FACT CHECKING

It's both popular wisdom and, to some sociologists, a methodological precept that "talk is cheap."[4] Relying on interviews means this book rests on what people say they do. The artificial setting of an interview creates all sorts of opportunities for doctors to sugarcoat how they treat patients, families to exaggerate the system's failings, or public guardians to shift blame onto others. Even the best-intentioned interviewees can have faulty recollections.

I have adopted four strategies to increase my, and hopefully the reader's, confidence in my interview data. The first is the approach to interviews themselves. Rather than asking general questions ("How do you define grave disability?"), I focused on having decision makers walk me through specific cases. These kinds of questions elicited narratives whose coherence and consistency I could evaluate. While I never solicited documents with identifiable or private information (such as health records), many interviewees had a paper trail to back up what they told me. This included, for example, parents who had collected emails from county public guardians or inpatient psychiatrists who could show memos directing them to reduce conservatorship applications.

Second, I cross-checked interviewees against one another and persistently found that even people with sharply diverging views on what should be done to change the conservatorship system largely concurred on what was happening within in. It might be self-serving for public guardians to report that they almost always were successful with conservatorship petitions they filed with the court. The claim became more credible when I spoke to public defenders who admitted, in more self-deprecating fashion, that they usually lost. In some cases, multiple interviewees were talking about the same cases or programs (such as community conservatorship in the Bay Area), creating additional opportunities for me to challenge or confirm my findings.

Third, I have created ample opportunities for the people with the most knowledge of and stakes in the system I am studying to evaluate my conclusion about it. In late 2020, I posted a preliminary report with findings about the conservatorship continuum onto Google Drive and circulated it to a few people I had interviewed. Their feedback was enthusiastic—but critical. More importantly, they forwarded it to many other stakeholders. I ultimately gave eight public presentations in 2021 and 2022 attended by more than four hundred people. I faced pointed questions in all of them. The more public my research went (as I published newspaper op-eds and was quoted in media stories), the more unsolicited criticism and corrections I had to address.

Fourth, I have followed a growing movement among qualitative researchers in giving my sources the opportunity to be identified by name (this is, of course, a long-established way to increase credibility in journalism).[5] Many government officials could speak only if their county was not identified, and some service users were understandably reticent to be named. But the willingness of at least some interviewees to go public does create a new avenue for fact checking. If you don't believe my account of Operation Dignity, go ask Dr. Meyer about it.

In the end, these last two tactics for increasing the study's credibility have pulled me away from a purely academic approach to accuracy and truth. It's one thing to convince a sociological reviewer with little direct knowledge of California's public mental health system that abdicated authority is a useful concept. It was a different challenge to demonstrate to Dr. Rod Shaner, the former medical director of LA's Department of Mental Health, who graciously read this manuscript, that I accurately understood Medi-Cal contracting with private hospitals. I hope this book is compelling to both academic and nonacademic audiences, but it's the latter that has pushed me the hardest to get the story straight.

TRIANGULATING DATA

I am, in any case, not presenting the reader with data from interviews alone. I have instead *triangulated* my findings with other sources.

One is observational. Although much of this research was conducted remotely (after I moved to New York University), it is informed by observations of a year and a half of weekly triage meetings at the clinic I identify in chapter 1 as Urban Mental Health. In 2018 and 2019, I also attended more than a dozen hearings and public events on SB 1045 in San Francisco as well as statewide working groups on conservatorship and board and cares. In 2021 and 2022, I conducted two-week visits to Southern California and the Bay Area that included five first-responder ride-alongs, five days spent shadowing outreach teams, five tours of locked facilities, and ten visits to residential care settings, supported housing complexes, and shelters. I also attended six days of conservatorship hearings in two different counties.

My visits and ride-alongs provided some surprising confirmations of what I had heard about in interviews. Police officers I spoke to often bemoaned how hard it was to get substance users into treatment in the brief moments they're willing to go. Two hours into one ride-along (recounted in chapter 2), I saw someone agree to treatment and then be turned away because no clinician was available. The number of treatment teams or care providers I visited who had had a client die in the weeks before I visited was heartbreaking. Either I had a

Forrest Gump–like ability to stumble into field sites on momentous occasions, or these things were happening frequently, just as the interviewees said.

This book draws on a separate study that focused specifically on newspapers' representations of involuntary mental health care in California.[6] Using the LexisUni, ProQuest, and Access World News databases, I collected 1,615 newspaper articles on conservatorship, LPS, psychiatric facilities, and mental health policy. These databases included the *Los Angeles Times*, the *San Francisco Chronicle*, and the *San Diego Union* from the 1950s to the present, the *Orange County Register* and the *Sacramento Bee* from 1985 on, and dozens of local papers more recently. These articles provided hundreds of small confirmations that the processes my interviewees were describing had been documented elsewhere, often for decades.

I have also been methodically compiling documents on the LPS and conservatorship system. I mined fifty reports on the state mental health system for their (often quite limited) comments about LPS. I scoured grand jury investigations, public guardian program documents, and board of supervisors resolutions at the county level. I have also tracked down transcripts of legislative hearings on the original LPS legislation, attempted reforms in the 1980s and 2000s, and more recent proposals to change grave disability. I base some of my broad claims about transformations in the system from compilations of quantitative data on hospital beds, lengths of stay, involuntary holds, and conservatorship from all these sources, compared with international data from the World Health Organization and Organization for Economic Cooperation and Development. My claims about California's legislative push to increase forced treatment are contextualized by an ongoing project that has catalogued over 1,000 proposed laws on involuntary care nationwide since 2011.

This book is also informed by three months of research on involuntary treatment I conducted in New York in 2016 and 2017. During this time, I interviewed sixty clinicians, lawyers, judges, and administrators and observed more than two hundred hearings on involuntary medication and civil commitments. These observations provide some evidence that the basic contours of abdicated authority are present elsewhere in the U.S. mental health system. That interviewees in both California and New York saw the New York system as superior, however, is revealing. New York's more robust system of public hospitals, greater fiscal accountability for outpatient teams, and stronger mandates on both providers and patients to adhere to court-ordered treatment plans all point to how that state's Office of Mental Health, a dedicated agency now missing in California, has curbed discretion and delegation to a much greater degree.

I analyzed these data through the qualitative software *Dedoose*. There is no way to automate or delegate the analysis of a mass of disparate transcripts, field notes, and reports. Instead, I manually coded the data by applying to different units of texts one of six hundred different labels. All told, I coded more than 17,000 separate units of text. This allowed me to quickly pull up, for example, every time a media article, interviewee, or report discussed how inpatient psychiatrists defined grave disability, or look side by side at the views of public guardians, public defenders, and county officials on specific reform legislation.

I've written this book, as much as possible, as a string of personal narratives— the stories of individual professionals, family members, and people subjected to forced treatment. But I have chosen these narratives because they are representative of broader trends that emerged in data analysis. I thus interviewed many, many people whose voices I have ultimately not included directly but who provided the vital evidence that the cases I do highlight are not isolated anecdotes.

ETHICS, EXCLUSIONS, REFLEXIVITY

Every research project has its limits. Early on, I decided to focus my research on adults, even though children are also subjected to involuntary treatment. There are many topics orbiting LPS, such as privacy laws (HIPAA), *Riese* hearings for involuntary medication, the shortage of mental health workers, forced treatment in prisons and jails, and California's parallel substance use treatment system, that I have nodded to in the manuscript but ultimately given short shrift. I have no better reason than an attempt to keep this book a manageable size.

This book is a story *about* conservatees but is not always told *by* conservatees. There are many studies in which researchers have managed to interview large samples of people with serious mental illness, but this is not one of them.[7] There are a number of reasons for this limitation. I started trying to interview conservatees late in the process, since the project was initially about professional decision making. By that time, I had moved to New York and thus could not follow strategies, such as posting flyers in drop-in centers or clinics, that might have helped me access this population. My efforts were also constrained by a decision not to recruit potential participants through service providers, for fear of undue influence.

Nonetheless, I made significant efforts to reach people subjected to forced treatment. With the help of research assistants, we circulated the study to dozens of organizations and across social media. We offered compensation of forty dollars for an hour-and-a-half interview. Uptake was limited. A more effective strategy might have been to collaborate directly with community-based or advocacy organizations, actively engaging them in the research project design and execution. I also wonder if, in an era when scholars have an increasingly visible online presence, some potential interviewees looked at some of my writings, concluded that I was overly sympathetic to forced treatment, and opted not to participate.[8]

The fact that much of this book leans heavily on the perspectives of people other than conservatees themselves creates ethical as well as intellectual dilemmas. To wit: I was constantly debating how much detail to give about individuals who had contact with my interviewees but no contact with me (and thus had not given their consent to be included). A book in which professionals speak only in vague generalities, without walking the reader through specific cases, would not just be boring; it would fail to capture the concrete dilemmas stakeholders face or the human side of conservatorship. But including such details makes for a more problematic product.

In general, I have withheld, changed slightly, or kept vague specific demographic information about people who have not directly consented to be in this book. For cases discussed by professionals, I have focused on dimensions of clients' state (like homelessness or psychosis) that are common, while leaving out more specific aspects of their histories (which, in any case, professionals usually did not give me out of respect for clients' privacy). My interviews with parents or siblings of people receiving forced treatment presented an even trickier dilemma. It would be virtually impossible to capture their experiences without giving personal details about their family members. Here, I have focused on keeping the presentation fuzzy enough that, even if that person read the book and might identify themselves in it, an external person could not.

Researchers' own identities shape their research. In my case, some of those impacts are obvious: being a white man opens doors with powerful institutions and offers an unmerited halo of credibility (although you'd be surprised how many psychiatrists wished me "good luck with my final paper," assuming I was a twenty-something undergrad, at the end of our interviews). Perhaps, on the other hand, my difficulties recruiting people subjected to conservatorship reflect the distrust created when highly marginalized people are approached by a researcher who sits on the privileged side of every axis of identity.

Or almost every axis. Over the course of researching this book, I visited several psychiatric hospitals. Multiple times, it was to visit my brother, who struggles heroically with psychiatric and developmental disabilities. As his (likely) future guardian, my personal experience makes me wary of some of the most broad-brush claims about the inherent abusiveness of conservatorships and the universal applicability of alternatives to them. If that suggests a certain bias around forced treatment, here's another factor to consider. I've also been to one of the same hospitals that features in this book, on a 5150. Involuntary treatment is terrifying and also might have saved my life. I hope this book reflects that profound ambivalence.

CHRONOLOGY OF
"ABDICATED AUTHORITY"

1955   Short-Doyle Act provides matching state funds for county inpatient and outpatient mental health programs, many of which counties contract out to private entities. The state begins shutting its own directly operated clinics for released state hospital patients.

1963   The scandalous conditions at Fairview State Hospital spark an inquiry by the legislature, which produces a report, *Dilemma of Mental Commitments* (published in 1966), that becomes the basis for LPS.

1963   Aid to the Totally Disabled becomes available to people with mental illness. This minimum income helps pay for people's basic needs outside of state hospitals and provides a new financial incentive for deinstitutionalization.

1965   The federal government creates Medicaid (called Medi-Cal in California), which provides health insurance for the indigent. The "IMD exclusion" bars Medicaid funds from going to psychiatric hospitals with more than sixteen beds, creating further incentive for states to empty public hospitals.

1967   The Lanterman-Petris-Short Act grants new legal protections aimed to end the "inappropriate, indefinite, and involuntary commitment of mentally disordered persons." The state increases Short-Doyle to cover 90 percent of local program costs. Governor Reagan announces his intention to close state hospitals and turn all responsibilities over to the counties.

1969   LPS goes into effect. Short-term holds (5150s) increase dramatically while lengths of stay (especially in state hospitals) decrease.

1969   The Lanterman Mental Retardation Act creates an entitlement to services for people with developmental disabilities, organized by a network of regional centers. No similar commitment is ever made for people with mental illness.

1970s   Nursing homes paid for with federal Medicaid dollars and board and care homes paid with Social Security Disability Income expand to receive people released from state hospitals. The state begins licensing board and care homes in 1971 but eventually closes the Bureau of Social Work, which actively worked to develop programs and place clients.

1971   A report by the ENKI institute finds that the conservatorship system is "functioning smoothly" and keeping gravely disabled individuals in treatment and institutions. This is the last official statewide evaluation of the LPS conservatorship system.

1978   The Community Residential Treatment Act provides grants to create a continuum of unlocked, rehabilitation-focused facilities throughout the state. Many counties ultimately rely instead on private, locked facilities to provide twenty-four-hour care.

1980s   Governor Deukmejian cuts 25 percent from state allocations for mental health care. Private psychiatric hospitals expand, taking advantage of greater coverage and more limited cost controls from private insurance.

1981   President Reagan limits federal funding that had been offered through the Community Mental Health Centers Act. Federal leadership around mental health is, according to psychiatrist E. Fuller Torrey, "decapitated."

1987   A major attempt to reform LPS by lengthening commitments and expanding the definition of grave disability fails. Opponents argue it would unsustainably increase costs for inpatient care.

1990s   Private "managed care" insurance companies and county mental health departments tighten payment criteria for acute care hospitals, leading to a decline in lengths of stay and in the number of psychiatric beds statewide.

1991   Realignment assigns counties the responsibility for paying for all outpatient, inpatient, and long-term care (including in state hospitals) for people with "severe and disabling" impairments. The law creates a dedicated funding stream but states that services will be provided only "to the extent resources are available."

1992   For the first time, a majority of people in state hospitals are forensic admissions (e.g., incompetent to stand trial or not guilty by reason of insanity) rather than LPS conservatees. By 2002, 90 percent of patients are forensic.

1995 Regulations rechristen IMDs as Mental Health Rehabilitation Centers. Crestwood and Telecare, two private companies, ultimately control two-thirds of MHRC beds.

2000 A set of bills to amend LPS to streamline the process for involuntary medication and make it easier to impose conservatorships is unsuccessful.

2001 Laura's Law authorizes Assisted Outpatient Treatment as a program that counties could opt into (it became "opt out" in 2021). The law contains no new funding for implementation and no enforcement mechanism.

2004 The Mental Health Services Act is passed by voters. It levies a 1 percent tax on incomes above one million dollars. MHSA pays for FSP teams, prevention and early intervention services, and AOT in some counties but cannot be used for inpatient treatment.

2006 The state passes significant reforms to probate conservatorships, including new restrictions on private guardians. LPS conservatorships are not included in reform.

2009 Budget cuts during the Great Recession force as many as one-third of clients out of the public mental health system. MHSA funds, intended to expand the system, are repurposed to maintain existing county mental health services.

2012 The state Department of Mental Health is rolled into the Department of Health Care Services. The office responsible for LPS and conservatorship is closed.

2013 Legislation amends LPS to expand the range of facilities and professionals that can carry out 5150 holds and receive people subject to them.

2014 The implementation of the Affordable Care Act creates a bifurcated system in which people on Medi-Cal with "mild" or "moderate" impairment are served by private managed care plans and those with "significant" impairments by county "mental health plans."

2017 From 2017 to 2022, yearly bills to modify grave disability (including AB 1971, which would have created a pilot program in Los Angeles to conserve any person "unable to provide for his or her medical treatment" if it would lead to death within six months) are unsuccessful.

2018 SB 1045 creates "housing conservatorships" for people with co-occurring substance use and mental health disorders who have been 5150ed eight times in the previous year. The bill allows for pilot programs in San

Francisco, Los Angeles, and San Diego but is implemented only in San Francisco and conserves only three people.

2020   A state audit finds "no evidence to justify . . . expanding or revising the LPS Act's criteria." The audit is limited to three counties and largely ignores the role of public guardians.

2021   Governor Newsom proposes closing state hospitals to LPS conservatees in order to make more space for people found incompetent to stand trial. Resistance, especially from county behavioral health departments, blocks the plan.

2022   Governor Newsom seeks to avoid a fight over LPS reform by introducing CARE courts, a program to compel individuals to follow a court-ordered care and housing plan. People "failing" CARE courts can be referred to conservatorship, but no new funds are allocated to public guardians' offices.

GLOSSARY OF TERMS, PROCEDURES, AND FACILITIES

- 5150 HOLD: Involuntary detention that can be imposed by a peace officer or clinician based on a danger to self, danger to others, or grave disability caused by a mental disorder. Under Welfare and Institutions Code Section 5150, an individual can be held for up to seventy-two hours in a designated facility without any right to judicial review.
- 5250 CERTIFICATION: Fourteen-day involuntary hospitalization that can be imposed at the end of a 5150 on the basis of a danger to self, danger to others, or grave disability and an inability or unwillingness to accept treatment voluntarily. A person on a 5250 must have a probable cause hearing within four days and can ask for a writ to be released.
- ACUTE DIVERSION UNIT (ADU): Voluntary alternative to inpatient hospitalization for individuals in crisis. Provides help to develop coping skills and a therapeutic milieu for a period of up to two weeks.
- ADULT RESIDENTIAL FACILITY (ARF): Nonmedical congregate living facility, commonly referred to as a board and care home.
- ASSISTED OUTPATIENT TREATMENT (AOT): System of compulsory outpatient treatment for people who have been hospitalized multiple times while medication noncompliant. Clients on AOT are expected to report regularly to a court and a treatment provider, but California's law does not allow for forced medication or for enforcement of the treatment plan.
- BOARD AND CARE HOME: Unlocked facility that provides meals, housing, activities, and medication dispensing. Typically paid for through individuals' SSI income. Usually licensed by state Community Care Licensing as Adult Residential Facilities, although some are unlicensed (sometimes known as "room and boards").

- CALIFORNIA ASSOCIATION OF PUBLIC ADMINISTRATORS, PUBLIC GUARDIANS, AND PUBLIC CONSERVATORS (CAPAPGPC): Professional organization representing county departments that serve as LPS and probate conservators. Receives funding from the state.
- CIVIL COMMITMENT: Procedure allowing the state to involuntarily hospitalize a person without accusing them of a crime. Commitments can be based on *parens patriae*—the state's obligation to protect vulnerable citizens—or its police power (duty to prevent harm).
- CONSERVATOR: Person designated by the court to make decisions on behalf of a person who is deemed gravely disabled. Could be a family member or a private professional but for LPS conservatorships is typically a public guardian.
- DEPARTMENT OF MENTAL HEALTH (DMH): California state agency that ran the state hospital system and provided oversight for county programs. It closed in 2012 and was merged into the Department of Health Care Services (DHCS). DMH can also refer to the agency in Los Angeles County (many other counties call their agency a Department of Behavioral Health).
- FULL-SERVICE PARTNERSHIP (FSP): Highest level of voluntary public mental health care in California (called Assertive Community Treatment [ACT] in other states). FSPs have low client-staff ratios, can meet clients "in the field," and have resources to pay for housing and other social needs. They are financed through the Mental Health Services Act and Medi-Cal.
- GRAVE DISABILITY: Inability to provide for food, clothing, or shelter as a result of a mental disorder (or chronic alcoholism). Grave disability is one criterion for a 5150 or 5250 hospitalization (alongside danger to self and danger to others). It is the only criterion for an LPS conservatorship.
- INCOMPETENT TO STAND TRIAL (IST): Finding that a defendant is unable to participate in their own defense or understand the nature of the proceedings against them. IST defendants receive treatment to restore them to competency in state hospitals or jails and can be referred to conservatorship after two years if found "unrestorable."
- INSTITUTION FOR MENTAL DISEASE (IMD): Locked facility providing sub-acute care for people under conservatorship. The "IMD exclusion" refers to a rule that bars Medicaid funds from going to facilities with more than sixteen beds in which more than half the patients have a primary diagnosis of a mental disorder.

- LANTERMAN-PETRIS-SHORT ACT (LPS): Law enacted in 1967 and effective in 1969. Introduced new criteria for involuntary hospitalizations, strengthened patients' rights, and provided state funding for local community services.
- LPS DESIGNATION: Authorization given by a county Behavioral Health Department to clinicians allowing them to place individuals on 5150 holds, or authorization to hospitals allowing them to serve individuals held through LPS procedures.
- MEDI-CAL: California's Medicaid program, which provides public health insurance for low-income individuals and people receiving SSI.
- MENTAL HEALTH REHABILITATION CENTER (MHRC): Formal, regulatory name for an IMD.
- MOBILE CRISIS TEAM (MCT): Clinical teams that respond to mental health crises and conduct 5150 evaluations. Called Psychiatric Emergency Response Teams (PERT) in San Diego and Psychiatric Mobile Response Teams (PMRT) in Los Angeles.
- MOBILE EVALUATION UNIT (MEU): Mental health unit of the Los Angeles Police Department. Manages both Systemwide Mental Assessment Response Teams (SMART) and the Case Assessment Management Program (CAMP) program.
- PATIENTS' RIGHTS ADVOCATE: Professionals who advise people detained under LPS about their rights, represent them in probable cause and *Riese* hearings, and respond to complaints.
- PAYEE: Person designated to receive the social security check of another person who is deemed unable to manage their money. Could be a family member, a social service provider, or a public guardian.
- PERMANENT SUPPORTED HOUSING: Independent apartments with services (such as mental health counseling or case management) attached. Often associated with the Housing First approach, offering unhoused individuals unconditional housing and voluntary services.
- PROBABLE CAUSE HEARING: Hearing held automatically after four days of a 5250 hospitalization to determine if there is "probable cause" to continue detention. Patients are represented by a patients' rights advocate and hearings are held before a hearing officer (not a judge).
- PROBATE CONSERVATORSHIP: Conservatorship (called a guardianship in other states) for adults lacking the capacity to manage their health or finances.

Generally for older adults with dementia or people with developmental disabilities (sometimes called a limited conservatorship). People with mental illness can also go on a probate conservatorship, but a probate conservator cannot place someone in a locked facility or require them to take psychiatric medication.

- PSYCHIATRIC ADVANCE DIRECTIVE (PAD): Legal document that can refuse or authorize certain treatments, hospitals, or crisis interventions in a moment when a person is not able to express those preferences themselves.
- PSYCHIATRIC EMERGENCY SERVICES (PES): Emergency department serving only psychiatric patients. To go to PES, patients typically have to be "medically cleared" by a regular ER, since PES are equipped only to handle mental health and substance use problems.
- PSYCHIATRIC HEALTH FACILITY (PHF): Stand-alone psychiatric facility serving people in acute crisis (compared to a subacute IMD). PHFs provide hospital-like psychiatric care but usually cost less to operate.
- PUBLIC GUARDIAN / PUBLIC CONSERVATOR: County department responsible for probate and LPS conservatorships. Can be attached to the Department of Behavioral Health, Social Services, Aging and Adult Services, or a stand-alone department.
- RIESE HEARING: Legal procedure to determine if a person who has been hospitalized has the "capacity" to refuse medication and, if not, to authorize involuntarily medicating a patient.
- SKILLED NURSING FACILITY (SNF): Locked or unlocked facility providing medical and psychiatric care for people with comorbid health and psychiatric issues.
- STATE HOSPITAL—Psychiatric hospital that is run directly by the state. Ninety percent of California's state hospital patients are forensic admissions such as people deemed incompetent to stand trial or not guilty by reason of insanity. The remainder are individuals under LPS conservatorship, usually with comorbid medical issues or a history of violence.
- STREET CRISIS RESPONSE TEAM (SCRT): San Francisco's alternative to police response to mental health crises, implemented in 2020. Team includes a paramedic, a clinician, and a peer. Initial evaluation shows that SCRT reduces 5150s but connects few people to ongoing treatment.
- SUPPLEMENTAL SECURITY INCOME (SSI)—Combined federal/state program providing monthly income to individuals not able to work as a result of a

disability. Unlike Social Security Disability Income (SSDI), SSI payments are not based on someone's previous payments into the system.

• WRIT OF HABEAS CORPUS—Filing by an involuntarily hospitalized patient, usually with the aid of a public defender, requesting release. Writ hearings can happen during a 5250 or temporary conservatorship.

ACKNOWLEDGMENTS

I first learned about conservatorship thanks to Dan Lewis, and for that—as well as his invaluable mentorship and guidance—my thank-yous start with him. My academic career would not have gotten far without Marion Fourcade. Her encouragement and advice were instrumental in getting this project off the ground. Jordan Bubin, Michelle Cera, David Garland, Neil Gong, Chris Herring, Carly Knight, Jenny Leigh, Marie Mourad, Nick Rekenthaler, Josh Seim, and Rod Shaner read parts or all of this manuscript and offered sharp comments. I am deeply grateful to Eric Schwartz at Columbia University Press for his enthusiasm for a radically different book than the one I initially promised him, as well as his guidance in completing it.

Before I started this project, I had convinced myself that doing sociological research was both isolating and irrelevant. Yoshi Cohn, Michael Long, Sebastien Le Moing, Kimberly Nielsen, Amritha Somasekar, Sierra Timmons, and Didi Wu, my undergraduate "apprentices" at Berkeley, taught me to love research again. Their dogged pursuit of interviews and their excitement when we heard back from a public guardian in the California hinterlands were infectious. Anaja Ferrell, Rachel Goulston, Xander Menor, and Jamie Tang provided research assistance at NYU. This book would not have been possible—or, at the very least, would have been much worse—without the interviews with service users conducted by Jenny Leigh. Her skills as an interviewer and the empathy that comes through even in a transcript are inspiring.

Regrettably, I cannot individually thank many of the (anonymous) individuals who shared so much time and expertise with me. However, I would be remiss if I did not mention Elizabeth Bromley, Joseph DeVico, Melinda Henning, Lucille Lyon, Aaron Meyer, Kerry Morrison, Jill Nielsen, Simon Pang, Susan Partovi,

Teresa Pasquini, David Pugh, Jerry Seelig, Morgan Smythe, Sandra Texeira, and Barbara Wilson as individuals who went above and beyond at various times in support of this book (they are, of course, not responsible for its contents). Lynda Kaufmann, thank you for answering so, so many emails. I am further grateful for the chance to refine my conclusions through presentations of this work to the California Behavioral Health Planning Council, the Semel Institute at UCLA, the Grave Disability Working Group, California Advocates, and the Coalition for Elder Justice.

I was fortunate to welcome into the world two children, Elias and Lydia, while I was writing this book. I am grateful to my partner, Marie Mourad, for taking on double-duty parenting so that I could conduct field research away from home. I hope that I will always love Elias and Lydia with the same unquestioning devotion of many of the parents I interviewed for this book, and that they will have the strength in the face of adversity I saw from many of their children.

I dedicate this book to the many moms I have met who never gave up, above all my own.

NOTES

PREFACE

1. Denis Robilard, "Sur la proposition de loi relative aux soins sans consentement en psychiatrie," *Rapport d'Information* (Paris: Assemblée Nationale, July 17, 2013); Marion Leboyer and Pierre-Michel Llorca, *Psychiatrie: L'État d'Urgence* (Paris: Fayard, 2018).

2. Tami L. Mark et al., "Insurance Financing Increased for Mental Health Conditions but Not for Substance Use Disorders, 1986–2014," *Health Affairs* 35, no. 6 (2016): 958–65.

3. Substance Abuse and Mental Health Services Administration, "National Mental Health Services Survey (N-MHSS) 2020: Data on Mental Health Treatment Facilities" (Washington, DC: Department of Health and Human Services, December 2021), 49, https://samhsa.gov/data/sites/default/files/2016_National_Mental_Health_Services_Survey.pdf.

4. Megan Comfort et al., "How Institutions Deprive: Ethnography, Social Work, and Interventionist Ethics Among the Hypermarginalized," *RSF: The Russell Sage Foundation Journal of the Social Sciences* 1, no. 1 (2015): 100–119.

5. D. J. Jaffe, *Insane Consequences: How the Mental Health Industry Fails the Mentally Ill* (Amherst, NY: Prometheus, 2017), 140.

6. S. P. Sashidharan, Roberto Mezzina, and Dainius Puras, "Reducing Coercion in Mental Healthcare," *Epidemiology and Psychiatric Sciences* 28, no. 6 (2019): 606. Another review concurs that expanding coercive care "does not follow the evidence." Andrew Molodynski, Yasser Khazaal, and Felicity Callard, "Coercion in Mental Healthcare: Time for a Change in Direction," *BJPsych International* 13, no. 1 (2016): 1. Others highlight the lack of clear evidence either way. Nathaniel P. Morris and Robert A. Kleinman, "Taking an Evidence-Based Approach to Involuntary Psychiatric Hospitalization," *Psychiatric Services* 74, no. 4 (2023): 431–433.

7. E. Bainbridge et al., "A Three-Month Follow-Up Study Evaluating Changes in Clinical Profile and Attitudes Towards Involuntary Admission," *European Psychiatry* 33, no. S1 (2016): S477–78; Thomas W. Kallert et al., "Coerced Hospital Admission and Symptom Change—a Prospective Observational Multi-Centre Study," *PLOS ONE* 6, no. 11 (November 30, 2011): e28191; C. Katsakou and S. Priebe, "Outcomes of Involuntary Hospital Admission—a Review," *Acta Psychiatrica Scandinavica* 114, no. 4 (2006): 232–41.

8. Multiple studies find that 40 percent or more of involuntary patients ultimately see their hospitalization as justified or beneficial. Florian Hotzy and Matthias Jaeger, "Clinical Relevance of Informal Coercion in Psychiatric Treatment—a Systematic Review," *Frontiers in Psychiatry* 7 (2016): 197; Gareth S. Owen et al., "Retrospective Views of Psychiatric In-Patients Regaining Mental Capacity," *British Journal of Psychiatry* 195, no. 5 (2009): 403–7; Stefan Priebe et al., "Patients' Views and Readmissions One Year After Involuntary Hospitalisation," *British Journal of Psychiatry* 194, no. 1 (2009): 49–54.

9. Diana Paksarian et al., "Perceived Trauma During Hospitalization and Treatment Participation Among Individuals with Psychotic Disorders," *Psychiatric Services* 65, no. 2 (2014): 266–69; cf. Harriet Meyer et al., "Posttraumatic Stress Disorder Symptoms Related to Psychosis and Acute Involuntary Hospitalization in Schizophrenic and Delusional Patients," *Journal of Nervous and Mental Disease* 187, no. 6 (1999): 343–52.

10. Joshua T. Jordan and Dale E. McNiel, "Perceived Coercion During Admission Into Psychiatric Hospitalization Increases Risk of Suicide Attempts After Discharge," *Suicide and Life-Threatening Behavior* 50, no. 1 (2020): 180–88; M. Large et al., "Systematic Review and Meta-Analysis of the Clinical Factors Associated with the Suicide of Psychiatric In-Patients," *Acta Psychiatrica Scandinavica* 124, no. 1 (2011): 18–19,; Anders Ledberg and Therese Reitana, "Increased Risk of Death Immediately After Discharge from Compulsory Care for Substance Abuse," *Drug and Alcohol Dependence* 236 (2022): 109492; Erin F. Ward-Ciesielski and Shireen L. Rizvi, "The Potential Iatrogenic Effects of Psychiatric Hospitalization for Suicidal Behavior: A Critical Review and Recommendations for Research," *Clinical Psychology: Science and Practice* 28, no. 1 (2021): 60–71.

11. Some studies report that involuntary treatment dissuades people from seeking treatment subsequently. Nev Jones et al., "Investigating the Impact of Involuntary Psychiatric Hospitalization on Youth and Young Adult Trust and Help-Seeking in Pathways to Care," *Social Psychiatry and Psychiatric Epidemiology* 56 (2021): 2017–27; Marvin S. Swartz, Jeffrey W. Swanson, and Michael J. Hannon, "Does Fear of Coercion Keep People Away from Mental Health Treatment? Evidence from a Survey of Persons with Schizophrenia and Mental Health Professionals," *Behavioral Sciences & the Law* 21, no. 4 (2003): 459–72. Others have found no impact of perceptions of coercion or an involuntary legal status on subsequent adherence. Jonathan Bindman et al., "Perceived Coercion at Admission to Psychiatric Hospital and Engagement with Follow-Up," *Social Psychiatry and Psychiatric Epidemiology* 40, no. 2 (2005): 160–66; Susanne Jaeger et al., "Long-Term Effects of Involuntary Hospitalization on Medication Adherence, Treatment Engagement and Perception of Coercion," *Social Psychiatry and Psychiatric Epidemiology* 48, no. 11 (2013): 1787–96; B. O'Donoghue et al., "Physical Coercion, Perceived Pressures and Procedural Justice in the Involuntary Admission and Future Engagement with Mental Health Services," *European Psychiatry* 26, no. 4 (2011): 208–14; S. Opjordsmoen et al., "A Two-Year Follow-up of Involuntary Admission's Influence Upon Adherence and Outcome in First-Episode Psychosis," *Acta Psychiatrica Scandinavica* 121, no. 5 (2010): 371–76; Sarah D. Rain et al., "Perceived Coercion at Hospital Admission and Adherence to Mental Health Treatment After Discharge," *Psychiatric Services* 54, no. 1 (2003): 103–5; Tilman Steinert and Peter Schmid, "Effect of Voluntariness of Participation in Treatment on Short-Term Outcome of Inpatients with Schizophrenia," *Psychiatric Services* 55, no. 7 (2004): 786–91.

12. Jennifer L. Wright, "Guardianship for Your Own Good: Improving the Well-Being of Respondents and Wards in the USA," *International Journal of Law and Psychiatry* 33, no. 5 (2010): 350–68.

13. Arnold Barnes, "Race and Hospital Diagnoses of Schizophrenia and Mood Disorders," *Social Work* 53, no. 1 (2008): 77–83; Frederic C. Blow et al., "Ethnicity and Diagnostic Patterns in Veterans with Psychoses," *Social Psychiatry and Psychiatric Epidemiology* 39, no. 10 (2004): 841–51; Jonathan Metzl, *The Protest Psychosis: How Schizophrenia Became a Black Disease* (Boston: Beacon, 2009).

14. Kimberlyn Gray Houston, Marco Mariotto, and J. Ray Hays, "Outcomes for Psychiatric Patients Following First Admission: Relationships with Voluntary and Involuntary Treatment and Ethnicity," *Psychological Reports* 88 (2001): 1012–14; Sommer Knight et al., "Ethnoracial Differences in Coercive Referral and Intervention Among Patients with First-Episode Psychosis," *Psychiatric Services* 73, no. 1 (2022): 2–8; Timothy Shea et al., "Racial and Ethnic Inequities in Inpatient Psychiatric Civil Commitment," *Psychiatric Services* 73, no. 12 (2022): 1322–29.

15. Morgan C. Shields, "Patient Characteristics Associated with Admission to Low-Safety Inpatient Psychiatric Facilities: Evidence for Racial Inequities," *Psychiatric Services* 72, no. 10 (2021): 1151–59.

16. Colin M. Smith et al., "Association of Black Race with Physical and Chemical Restraint Use Among Patients Undergoing Emergency Psychiatric Evaluation," *Psychiatric Services* 73, no. 7 (2022): 730–36; Tina E. Thomas et al., "Race, History of Abuse, and Homelessness Are Associated with Forced Medication Administration During Psychiatric Inpatient Care," *Journal of Psychiatric Practice* 26, no. 4 (2020): 294–304.

17. Paige L. Sweet, *The Politics of Surviving: How Women Navigate Domestic Violence and Its Aftermath* (Berkeley: University of California Press, 2021).

18. Thomas R. Insel, "Rethinking Schizophrenia," *Nature* 468, no. 7321 (2010): 187–93; Gavin Newsom, "Getting Serious About Mental Health," *Medium*, January 20, 2018, https://medium.com/@GavinNewsom/getting-serious-about-mental-health-8c09ad95a5ae.

19. Matthew S. Lebowitz and Woo-kyoung Ahn, "Effects of Biological Explanations for Mental Disorders on Clinicians' Empathy," *Proceedings of the National Academy of Sciences* 111, no. 50 (2014): 17786–90; B. A. Pescosolido et al., "'A Disease Like Any Other'? A Decade of Change in Public Reactions to Schizophrenia, Depression, and Alcohol Dependence," *American Journal of Psychiatry* 167, no. 11 (2010): 1321–30; G. Schomerus et al., "Evolution of Public Attitudes About Mental Illness: A Systematic Review and Meta-Analysis," *Acta Psychiatrica Scandinavica* 125, no. 6 (2012): 440–52.

20. Athena McLean, "Empowerment and the Psychiatric Consumer/Ex-Patient Movement in the United States: Contradictions, Crisis and Change," *Social Science & Medicine* 40, no. 8 (1995): 1053–71.

21. The debate about "mental" versus "behavioral" health is a little less lively but also merits discussion. I appreciate that "behavioral health" attempts to link together the treatment of substance use and more classic mental illnesses under one roof. In practice, this book shows that these conditions are classified, interpreted, and treated quite differently. At a philosophical level, I believe that people with mental illness have thoughts and emotions

that should be considered in treatment; a focus purely on behaviors seems to treat this inner life as irrelevant. Hence, I mostly speak of mental health.

22. Darcy Haag Granello and Sean R. Gorby, "It's Time for Counselors to Modify Our Language: It Matters When We Call Our Clients Schizophrenics Versus People with Schizophrenia," *Journal of Counseling & Development* 99, no. 4 (2021): 452–61.

23. Substance Abuse and Mental Health Services Administration, "Behavioral Health Barometer United States, Volume 5" (Rockville, MD: U.S. Department of Health and Human Services, 2019), 58.

24. Sukanta Saha et al., "A Systematic Review of the Prevalence of Schizophrenia," *PLoS Med* 2, no. 5 (May 31, 2005): e141.

25. Andrew Scull, *Madness in Civilization* (London: Thames & Hudson, 2015), 11.

26. For an elaboration, see T. M. Luhrmann, *Of Two Minds: The Growing Disorder in American Psychiatry* (New York: Knopf, 2000).

INTRODUCTION: THE OTHER MAGNA CARTA

1. Gwynedd Stuart, "The Renegade Doctor of Skid Row Is Caring for Homeless Addicts in Revolutionary Ways," *Los Angeles Magazine*, March 28, 2019, https://www.lamag.com/citythink blog/the-renegade-doctor-of-skid-row-is-caring-for-homeless-addicts-in-revolutionary -ways/.

2. Following convention in sociological work, single quotation marks indicate dialog that has been reconstructed from notes while double quotations marks reflect direct transcriptions from recordings. The latter are presumably more precise, but I only quote unrecorded conversations when I am confident that they capture speakers' intended meaning.

3. California Welfare and Institutions Code, Section 5008, leginfo.legislature.ca.gov/faces /codes_displaySection.xhtml?lawCode=WIC&sectionNum=5008.

4. Los Angeles Homeless Services Authority, "2022 Greater Los Angeles Homeless Count Results," September 12, 2022, https://www.lahsa.org/news?article=726-2020-greater-los -angeles-homeless-count-results; Department of Mental Health, "Homeless Outreach and Mobile Engagement Program," accessed October 10, 2022, https://dmh.lacounty.gov /our-services/countywide-services/home/.

5. This statement was made when Newsom was mayor of San Francisco. C. W. Nevius, "Finding Help for Homeless Who Won't Help Themselves," *San Francisco Chronicle*, March 11, 2008.

6. I heard this characterization at a forum on conservatorship in San Francisco on November 28, 2018. A similar claim was made by Representative Claude Pepper in 1978, who stated, "The typical [person subject to conservatorship] has fewer rights than the typical convicted felon. . . . It is the most punitive civil penalty that can be levied against an American citizen, with the exception, of course, of the death penalty." Quoted in National Council on Disability, "Beyond Guardianship: Toward Alternatives That Promote Greater Self-Determination," March 22, 2018, 26, https://ncd.gov/publications/2018 /beyond-guardianship-toward-alternatives.

7. Michael Lipsky, *Street-Level Bureaucracy: Dilemmas of the Individual in Public Service*, thirtieth anniversary ed. (New York: Russell Sage Foundation, 2010).

8. I am grateful to Teresa Pasquini for this phrasing.

9. The head of the professional association of California's Public Guardians estimates there are 120,000 conservatees in the state. It is unknown how many are conserved for mental illness versus other conditions or how many are in the public system. Scarlet Hughes, "Opinion: Britney Spears' Conservatorship Was Atypical. Most Lack Funds," *Mercury News*, January 18, 2022, https://www.mercurynews.com/2022/01/18/opinion-britney-spears -conservatorship-was-atypical-most-lack-funds/.

10. See, for example, Carolyn Anspacher, "What's Best for Mental Patients?," *San Francisco Chronicle*, September 10, 1975; Patt Morrison, "Opinion: Skid Row's PR Problem," *Los Angeles Times*, October 13, 2006; "Senate Passes Mental Health 'Bill of Rights,'" *San Diego Union*, August 2, 1967.

11. Eugene Bardach, *The Skill Factor in Politics: Repealing the Mental Commitment Laws in California* (Berkeley: University of California Press, 1972).

12. ENKI Research Institute, "A Study of California's New Mental Health Law" (Chatsworth, CA, 1972), 10.

13. Don Neff, "Fairview Visit Triggers Probe: Massive Inquiry at Southland Mental Facility Follows Tour," *Los Angeles Times*, April 7, 1963.

14. Nicolas Petris, State Government Oral History Program, December 20, 1988, California State Archives, https://archives.cdn.sos.ca.gov/oral-history/pdf/oh-petris-nicholas.pdf.

15. Constance M. McGovern, *Masters of Madness: Social Origins of the American Psychiatric Profession* (Hanover, NH: Vermont, 1985); Owen Whooley, *On the Heels of Ignorance: Psychiatry and the Politics of Not Knowing* (Chicago: University of Chicago Press, 2019).

16. Subcommittee on Mental Health, "The Dilemma of Mental Commitments in California" (Sacramento: California State Legislature, 1966), 12.

17. Subcommittee on Mental Health, "The Dilemma," 19.

18. Art Bolton, the legislative aide who prepared the report, believed that findings about commitment courts were the "most disturbing" part of the investigation. Phyllis Vine, *Fighting for Recovery: An Activists' History of Mental Health Reform* (Boston, Beacon, 2022), 23.

19. Bill Boyarsky, "Changing Policies Affect Care of Sick," *Los Angeles Times*, August 8, 1982.

20. Erving Goffman, *Asylums: Essays on the Social Situation of Mental Patients and Other Inmates* (New York: Anchor, 1961), 135.

21. Subcommittee on Mental Health, "The Dilemma," 46.

22. Harry Nelson, "'Civil Rights' Bill on Mental Health Sets High Goals," *Los Angeles Times*, June 11, 1967. This statement has also been attributed to Maurice Rodgers of the Cal State Psychological Association. Bardach, *The Skill Factor*, 126.

23. Bardach, *The Skill Factor*, 103.

24. Many contemporary portrayals falsely depict LPS as only a civil rights bill. Susannah Cahalan, *The Great Pretender: The Undercover Mission That Changed Our Understanding of Madness* (New York: Grand Central, 2019); Michael Shellenberger, *San Fransicko: Why Progressives Ruin Cities* (New York: Harper, 2021), 85. Early media coverage of the bill actually paid more attention to its proposals to expand local treatment programs. Alex V. Barnard, "From the 'Magna Carta' to 'Dying in the Streets': Media Framings of Mental Health Law in California," *Society and Mental Health* 12, no. 2 (2022): 155–73.

25. "Mental Health Parley to Discuss Home Centers," *Los Angeles Times*, June 11, 1968.

26. Jerry Gillam, "Assembly Group OKs Mental Hospital Bill," *Los Angeles Times*, June 15, 1967.

27. Eugene Bardach, *The Implementation Game: What Happens After a Bill Becomes a Law* (Cambridge, MA: MIT Press, 1977), 34.

28. Ernesto Flores, "State Mental Health Gains Cited Here," *San Diego Union*, August 13, 1970.

29. Paul S. Appelbaum, "Ambivalence Codified: California's New Outpatient Commitment Statute," *Psychiatric Services* 54, no. 1 (2003): 26.

30. Uri Aviram, "Care or Convenience? On the Medical-Bureaucratic Model of Commitment of the Mentally Ill," *International Journal of Law and Psychiatry* 13, no. 3 (1990): 164.

31. Anna Saya et al., "Criteria, Procedures, and Future Prospects of Involuntary Treatment in Psychiatry Around the World: A Narrative Review," *Frontiers in Psychiatry* 10 (2019): 2.

32. Heather Knight, "SF Looks to Change Law That Lets Mentally Ill Choose to Stay on Streets," *San Francisco Chronicle*, December 12, 2017, https://www.sfchronicle.com/news/article/SF-looks-to-change-law-that-lets-mentally-ill-12422969.php.

33. David Garrick, "Gloria Focuses on Infrastructure, Homelessness in Second 'State of City' Speech," *San Diego Union-Tribune*, January 12, 2022, https://www.sandiegouniontribune.com/news/politics/story/2022-01-12/gloria-focuses-on-infrastructure-homelessness-in-second-state-of-city-speech; Alyssa Jeong Perry, "LA County Gets More Power to Force Severely Mentally Ill Homeless Into Treatment," *LAist*, October 2, 2018, https://laist.com/news/la-county-gets-more-power-to-force-severely-mentally-ill-homeless-into-treatment; Jonathan Sherin and Darrell Steinberg, "If People Reject Care, Then What?," *Los Angeles Times*, August 20, 2020, https://www.latimes.com/opinion/story/2020-08-20/op-ed-mentally-ill-people-often-dont-get-treatment-because-of-antiquated-law.

34. This statement was reported in a letter to the editor from his longtime administrative assistant. Ellen Dewees, "Letter: Legislation for the Mentally Ill," *Los Angeles Times*, December 5, 1987.

35. Gavin Newsom, "State of the State—Annotated," *CalMatters*, February 19, 2020, https://calmatters.org/projects/newsoms-state-of-the-state-2020-annotated/.

36. See Treatment Advocacy Center, "Active Legislation," accessed October 22, 2022, https://www.treatmentadvocacycenter.org/fixing-the-system/active-legislation.

37. Dominic A. Sisti, Andrea G. Segal, and Ezekiel J. Emanuel, "Improving Long-Term Psychiatric Care: Bring Back the Asylum," *JAMA* 313, no. 3 (2015): 243–44.

38. In 1969, Judge David Bazelon of the D.C. Circulate of Appeals lauded that LPS "promises virtually to eliminate involuntary hospitalization except for short term crisis situations." David L. Bazelon, "Implementing the Right to Treatment," *University of Chicago Law Review* 36, no. 4 (1969): 753.

39. For example: "Current law makes it nearly impossible for doctors or judges to compel treatment." Editorial Board, "Help from Without," *San Diego Union-Tribune*, June 6, 2001. "California's 40-year-old mental-health law makes it all but impossible for authorities to confine and treat an unstable person." Editorial Board, "Use Confinement," *Riverside Press-Enterprise*, April 29, 2007. With LPS, "involuntary commitments were ended." Garrick, "Gloria Focuses on Infrastructure."

40.   For an excellent exception, see Dinah Miller and Annette Hanson, *Committed: The Battle Over Involuntary Psychiatric Care* (Baltimore: Johns Hopkins University Press, 2016).

41.   See, for example, Paul Brodwin, *Everyday Ethics* (Berkeley: University of California Press, 2012); Kerry Michael Dobransky, *Managing Madness in the Community: The Challenge of Contemporary Mental Health Care* (New Brunswick, NJ: Rutgers University Press, 2014); Jerry Floersch, *Meds, Money, and Manners: The Case Management of Severe Mental Illness* (New York: Columbia University Press, 2002); Neil Gong, "Between Tolerant Containment and Concerted Constraint: Managing Madness for the City and the Privileged Family," *American Sociological Review* 84, no. 4 (2019): 664–89.

42.   Carol Warren, *The Court of Last Resort* (Chicago: University of Chicago Press, 1982), 23–24.

43.   These criteria were later imposed across the United States by the Supreme Court, which in 1975 ruled that the state cannot detain a "non-dangerous" mentally ill person who "is capable of surviving safely in freedom." *O'Connor v. Donaldson*, 422 U.S. 563 (1975).

44.   Paul S. Appelbaum, *Almost a Revolution: Mental Health Law and the Limits of Change* (Oxford: Oxford University Press, 1994), 37; see also Sarah Cleveland et al., "Do Dangerousness-Oriented Commitment Laws Restrict Hospitalization of Patients Who Need Treatment? A Test," *Psychiatric Services* 40, no. 3 (1989): 266–71; Mary L. Durham, "Implications of Need-for-Treatment Laws: A Study of Washington State's Involuntary Treatment Act," *Psychiatric Services* 36, no. 9 (1985): 977; John Monahan, "Empirical Analyses of Civil Commitment: Critique and Context," *Law & Society Review* 11, no. 4 (1977): 619–28.

45.   Someone who is deemed a danger to self or others can be placed on a three-day hold (called a 5150) and fourteen-day hospitalization (5250). Someone who is suicidal can be held for another fourteen days (5264), and a person deemed "imminently dangerous" can be held for additional periods of 180 days. Some counties allow a supplemental thirty-day hold for grave disability (5270). The provisions for danger to self and others are rarely used. Ultimately, most people must either be conserved on the basis of grave disability or be released.

46.   Commentators favorable to forced treatment described conservatorship as the "provision [of LPS] that became the key to keeping the system functional." Rael Jean Isaac and Virginia Armat, *Madness in the Streets: How Psychiatry and the Law Abandoned the Mentally* (New York: Free Press, 1990), 123.

47.   John A. Talbott, "Deinstitutionalization: Avoiding the Disasters of the Past," *Psychiatric Services* 30, no. 9 (1979): 621–24; Julia Schon, "Why Are California's Prisons and Streets Filled with More Mentally Ill Than Its Hospitals: California's Deinstitutionalization Movement," *Santa Clara Law Review* 59 (2019): 269.

48.   This call to pay attention to those left behind from deinstitutionalization echoes that made by Jonathan Metzl, *The Protest Psychosis: How Schizophrenia Became a Black Disease* (Boston: Beacon, 2009).

49.   Ronan Farrow and Jia Tolentino, "Britney Spears' Conservatorship Nightmare," *New Yorker*, July 3, 2021, https://www.newyorker.com/news/american-chronicles/britney-spears -conservatorship-nightmare.

50.   American Civil Liberties Union, "Why Britney Can't Get Out of Her Conservatorship," *At Liberty* (Podcast), accessed August 27, 2021, https://www.aclu.org/podcast/why-britney -cant-get-out-her-conservatorship-ep-164.

51. Madison Hirneisen, "California's Conservatorship Program Proposes Changes After Spears Saga and New Investigation," *Center Square*, August 21, 2022, https://www.the centersquare.com/california/californias-conservatorship-program-proposes-changes -after-spears-saga-and-new-investigation/article_02baa7fa-200a-11ed-87d9-c3836a33f4dc .html.

52. Dan Thompson, "Spears Case Drives California Bid to Limit Conservatorships," Associated Press, January 19, 2022, https://apnews.com/article/britney-spears-entertainment -business-health-california-9bbf21583f7e42b59eef32754d79a620.

53. For an early discussion of the limits of civil liberties protections under LPS, see Henry L. Fuller, "Civil Commitment of the Mentally Ill in California: 1969 Style," *Santa Clara Lawyer* 10, no. 1 (1970 1969): 74–98.

54. Two exceptions are Kristen R. Choi et al., "Mental Health Conservatorship Among Homeless People with Serious Mental Illness," *Psychiatric Services* 73, no. 6 (2022): 613–19; and Grant H. Morris, "Let's Do the Time Warp Again: Assessing the Competence of Counsel in Mental Health Conservatorship Proceedings," *San Diego Law Review* 46 (2009): 283–342.

55. A recent state audit of LPS concluded that professionals were applying the law correctly in cases where someone was conserved. It skirted the question of whether there were people who were not being conserved who needed to be. It provided few data on who conservatees were or where they went. Based on only three counties and containing no analysis of the functioning of public guardians' offices, it is far from a sufficient evaluation. California State Auditor, "Lanterman-Petris-Short Act: California Has Not Ensured That Individuals with Serious Mental Illnesses Receive Adequate Ongoing Care" (Sacramento, CA, July 2020).

56. Nathaniel P. Morris, "Detention Without Data: Public Tracking of Civil Commitment," *Psychiatric Services* 71, no. 7 (2020): 741–44; Elizabeth Warren and Bob Casey, "Letter to Secretary Becerra and Attorney General Garland," July 1, 2021, https://www.warren .senate.gov/imo/media/doc/2021.07.01%20Letter%20to%20DOJ%20and%20HHS%20re%20 Conservatorship.pdf.

57. Andrew Abbott, *The System of Professions: An Essay on the Division of Expert Labor* (Chicago: University of Chicago Press, 1988); Jan Goldstein, *Console and Classify: The French Psychiatric Profession in the Nineteenth Century* (Cambridge: Cambridge University Press, 1987).

58. James A. Holstein, *Court-Ordered Insanity: Interpretive Practice and Involuntary Commitment* (New York: Transaction, 1993), 41; see also Warren, *The Court of Last Resort*.

59. Dennis L. Wenger and C. Richard Fletcher, "The Effect of Legal Counsel on Admissions to a State Mental Hospital: A Confrontation of Professions," *Journal of Health and Social Behavior* 10, no. 1 (1969): 66.

60. For examples of ethical and philosophical fights over forced treatment, see Elizabeth Bennion, "A Right to Remain Psychotic: A New Standard for Involuntary Treatment in Light of Current Science," *Loyola Law Review* 47 (2013): 251; Clarissa Karasch, "Where Involuntary Commitment, Civil Liberties, and the Right to Mental Health Care Collide: An Overview of California's Mental Illness System," *Hastings Law Journal* 54 (2003): 493–523; Stephen J. Morse, "A Preference for Liberty: The Case Against Involuntary

Commitment of the Mentally Disordered," *California Law Review* 70, no. 1 (1982): 54–106; Johnathan Simon and Stephen A. Rosenbaum, "Defying Madness: Rethinking Commitment Law in an Age of Mass Incarceration," *University of Miami Law Review* 70 (2015): 1–52.

61. Brodwin, *Everyday Ethics*; Dobransky, *Managing Madness*; Gong, "Tolerant Containment."

62. D. J. Jaffe, *Insane Consequences: How the Mental Health Industry Fails the Mentally Ill* (Amherst, NY: Prometheus, 2017), 117. Other books make this same argument: LPS set a "gold standard for clueless, destructive government interference" in the treatment of people with mental illness. Ron Powers, *No One Cares About Crazy People: The Chaos and Heartbreak of Mental Health in America* (New York: Hachette, 2017). LPS "expanded . . . the personal freedom of the mentally ill . . . at the expense of government's ability to . . . provide treatment." Stephen Eide, *Homelessness in America: The History and Tragedy of an Intractable Social Problem* (Lanham, MD: Rowman & Littlefield, 2022), 29. LPS "made rational treatment of the mentally ill increasingly difficult." E. Fuller Torrey, *Out of the Shadows: Confronting America's Mental Illness Crisis* (New York: Wiley, 1997), 143. "Passage of the LPS Act created a national disgrace, the homeless mentally ill." Stephen Seager, *Street Crazy: America's Mental Health Tragedy* (Redondo Beach, CA: Westcom, 2000), 27.

63. LPS Reform Task Force II, "The Case for Updating California's Mental Health Treatment Law" (Tustin, CA, March 2012), 11.

64. For a perspective critiquing how medicine continues to trample law, making it so "the very last human right[s] to be recognized" are those of the "mentally disabled," see Geoffrey Robertson, foreword to *Mental Health and Human Rights: Vision, Praxis, and Courage*, ed. Michael Dudley, Derrick Silove, and Fran Gale (Oxford: Oxford University Press, 2012), vii.

65. Michel Foucault, *Abnormal: Lectures at the Collège de France, 1974–1975* (New York: Palgrave Macmillan, 2007), 32.

66. Miller and Hanson give a more precise rendering of this point: "In other areas of medicine, patients can be treated against their will only when they have been deemed incompetent to make decisions for themselves because they cannot understand the treatment options. Psychiatry is the only field where someone may understand what is being offered and still be denied the right to refuse treatment." *Committed*, xxii.

67. Michel Foucault, *Madness and Civilization: A History of Insanity in the Age of Reason*, trans. Richard Howard (London: Routledge, 1964).

68. Chris Chapman, "Five Centuries' Material Reforms and Ethical Reformulations of Social Elimination," in *Disability Incarcerated*, ed. Liat Ben-Moshe, Chris Chapman, and Allison C. Carey (New York: Palgrave Macmillan, 2014), 39.

69. Castel et al. argue that deinstitutionalization was a "myth." Françoise Castel, Robert Castel, and Anne Lovell, *The Psychiatric Society*, trans. Arthur Goldhammer (New York: Columbia University Press, 1982), 298. Scull similarly claims that California "shut down 'superfluous' institutions" and shifted to "non-institutional controls." Andrew T. Scull, *Decarceration: Community Treatment and the Deviant*, 2nd ed. (Englewood Cliffs, NJ: Polity, 1984), 73.

70. Forrest Stuart, *Down, Out, and Under Arrest: Policing and Everyday Life in Skid Row* (Chicago: University of Chicago Press, 2016).

71.   Josh Seim, *Bandage, Sort, and Hustle: Ambulance Crews on the Frontlines of Urban Suffering* (Berkeley: University of California Press, 2019).

72.   Armando Lara-Millán, *Redistributing the Poor: Jails, Hospitals, and the Crisis of Law and Fiscal Austerity* (Oxford: Oxford University Press, 2021); Ji Seon Song, "Policing the Emergency Room," *Harvard Law Review* 134, no. 8 (2021): 2646–2720.

73.   Kerwin Kaye, "Rehabilitating the 'Drugs Lifestyle': Criminal Justice, Social Control, and the Cultivation of Agency," *Ethnography* 14, no. 2 (2013): 207–32; Chad Michael McPherson and Michael Sauder, "Logics in Action: Managing Institutional Complexity in a Drug Court," *Administrative Science Quarterly* 58, no. 2 (2013): 165–96; Rebecca Tiger, "Drug Courts and the Logic of Coerced Treatment," *Sociological Forum* 26, no. 1 (2011): 169–82.

74.   Nikolas Rose, "Governing Risky Individuals: The Role of Psychiatry in New Regimes of Control," *Psychiatry, Psychology and Law* 5, no. 2 (1998): 179.

75.   Katherine Warburton and Stephen M. Stahl, "Balancing the Pendulum: Rethinking the Role of Institutionalization in the Treatment of Serious Mental Illness," *CNS Spectrums* 25, no. 2 (2020): 115–18.

76.   Disability Rights California, "Voluntary Services as Alternative to Involuntary Detention Under LPS Act," March 2010, http://www.disabilityrightsca.org/pubs/548701.pdf.

77.   Mental Health and Substance Use Disorder Services Division, "California Involuntary Detention Reports (FY 2017–2018)" (Sacramento, CA: Department of Health Care Services, 2018), https://www.dhcs.ca.gov/Documents/CSD_YV/MHSA/IDR/FY17-18-IDR-Report .pdf; Gi Lee and David Cohen, "Incidences of Involuntary Psychiatric Detentions in 25 U.S. States," *Psychiatric Services* 71, no. 1 (2021): 61–68. The California figure is almost certainly an undercount. Thirty-two of fifty-eight counties did not report data to the state in 2015–2016. A representative of the hospital industry suggested that the real rate of 5150 holds may be more than twice as high.

78.   Luke Sheridan Rains et al., "Variations in Patterns of Involuntary Hospitalisation and in Legal Frameworks: An International Comparative Study," *Lancet Psychiatry* 6, no. 5 (2019): 403–17.

79.   Michel Foucault, *The History of Sexuality*, vol. 1: *An Introduction*, trans. Robert Hurley, reissue ed. (New York: Vintage, 1990), 135.

80.   Orlando Patterson, *Slavery and Social Death: A Comparative Study* (Cambridge, MA: Harvard University Press, 1982), 41.

81.   Robert Embry, "The Ordeal of Total Power," *Los Angeles Times*, September 3, 1972.

82.   Heidi Blake and Katie Baker, "Beyond Britney: Abuse, Exploitation, and Death Inside America's Guardianship Industry," *BuzzFeed News*, September 17, 2021, https://www .buzzfeednews.com/article/heidiblake/conservatorship-investigation-free-britney-spears.

83.   Max Weber, *Economy and Society*, ed. Guenther Roth and Claus Wittich (Berkeley: University of California Press, 1978), 2:943. For a sharp elaboration of Weber's theory of authority, see Jeffrey Guhin, *Agents of God: Boundaries and Authority in Muslim and Christian Schools* (New York: Oxford University Press, 2021), 12.

84.   Hannah Arendt, *Between Past and Future*, ed. Jerome Kohn (New York: Penguin, 2006), 93.

85.   Daniel A. Menchik, *Managing Medical Authority* (Princeton, NJ: Princeton University Press, 2021); Paul Starr, *The Social Transformation of American Medicine: The Rise of a Sovereign*

Profession and the Making of a Vast Industry (New York: Basic Books, 1982); Stefan Timmermans, "Suicide Determination and the Professional Authority of Medical Examiners," *American Sociological Review* 70, no. 2 (2005): 311–33.

86. In an ethnography of an emergency psychiatric unit, Rhodes also emphasizes that patients and staff are subjects of power. But while she presents both as tangled up in the same Foucaultian disciplinary power, I differentiate the types of power to which patients and professionals are exposed. Lorna A. Rhodes, *Emptying Beds: The Work of an Emergency Psychiatric Unit* (Berkeley: University of California Press, 1991).

87. Joseph Raz, *The Authority of Law: Essays on Law and Morality* (Oxford: Oxford University Press, 1979).

88. Richard Friedman, quoted in Steven Lukes, "Perspectives on Authority Part I: Concepts, Perspectives, and Justifications: Section 4," *NOMOS: American Society for Political and Legal Philosophy* 29 (1987): 65.

89. "Forced treatment by psychiatric and other health and medical professionals is a violation of the right to equal recognition before the law and an infringement of the rights to personal integrity (art. 17); freedom from torture (art. 15); and freedom from violence, exploitation and abuse (art. 16)." Committee on the Rights of Persons with Disabilities, "General Comment No. 1" (United Nations, April 11, 2014), 11.

90. This idea that a core power of government is to define key categories—like "grave disability"—and coordinate a range of social actors is developed in Pierre Bourdieu, *On the State* (Cambridge: Polity, 2015); Matthew Norton, "Classification and Coercion: The Destruction of Piracy in the English Maritime System," *American Journal of Sociology* 119, no. 6 (2014): 1537–75.

91. Embry, "The Ordeal of Total Power."

92. As two doctors put it, grave disability "has been eroded as a justification for inpatient care." Joel T. Braslow and Luke Messac, "Medicalization and Demedicalization: A Gravely Disabled Homeless Man with Psychiatric Illness," *New England Journal of Medicine* 379, no. 20 (2018): 1886.

93. Little Hoover Commission, "Being There: Making a Commitment to Mental Health" (Sacramento, CA, November 2000); California Mental Health Planning Council, "California Mental Health Master Plan: A Vision for California" (Sacramento, CA, March 2003).

94. Behavioral Health Action, "Answering the Call to Action: A Vision for All Californians' Behavioral Health," 2021, 31, https://www.behavioralhealthaction.org/.

95. Kimberly J. Morgan and Andrea Louise Campbell, *The Delegated Welfare State: Medicare, Markets, and the Governance of Social Policy* (New York: Oxford University Press, 2011); Joe Soss, Richard C. Fording, and Sanford F. Schram, *Disciplining the Poor: Neoliberal Paternalism and the Persistent Power of Race* (Champagne, IL: University of Chicago Press, 2011); Paige L. Sweet, *The Politics of Surviving: How Women Navigate Domestic Violence and Its Aftermath* (Berkeley: University of California Press, 2021).

96. Gerald N. Grob, *From Asylum to Community: Mental Health Policy in Modern America* (Princeton, NJ: Princeton University Press, 1991), 3; Gerald N. Grob and Howard H. Goldman, *The Dilemma of Federal Mental Health Policy: Radical Reform or Incremental Change?* (New Brunswick, NJ: Rutgers University Press, 2006), 14.

97. Doris A. Fuller et al., "Going, Going, Gone: Trends and Consequences of Eliminating State Psychiatric Beds, 2016" (Treatment Advocacy Center, June 2016).

98. Richard G. Frank and Sherry A. Glied, *Better but Not Well: Mental Health Policy in the United States Since 1950* (Baltimore: Johns Hopkins University Press, 2006), 48.

99. Yeheskel Hasenfeld, "Community Mental Health Centers as Human Service Organizations," *American Behavioral Scientist* 28, no. 5 (1985): 655–68; H. Brinton Milward and Keith G. Provan, "Governing the Hollow State," *Journal of Public Administration Research and Theory* 10, no. 2 (2000): 359–80.

100. Robert M. Emerson, E. Burke Rochford, and Linda L. Shaw, "Economics and Enterprise in Board and Care Homes for the Mentally Ill," *American Behavioral Scientist* 24, no. 6 (1981): 771–85; Andrew Scull, "A New Trade in Lunacy: The Recommodification of the Mental Patient," *American Behavioral Scientist* 24, no. 6 (1981): 741–54.

101. The way deinstitutionalization has shifted responsibility to families is documented across the Western world by Simon Goodwin, *Comparative Mental Health Policy: From Institutional to Community Care* (London: Sage, 1997).

102. Morgan and Campbell, *The Delegated Welfare State*, 4.

103. Lipsky, *Street-Level Bureaucracy*, 3.

104. Lipsky, *Street-Level Bureaucracy*, 3.

105. Ellen M. Immergut, *Health Politics: Interests and Institutions in Western Europe* (New York: Columbia University Press, 1992).

106. Lara-Millán, *Redistributing the Poor*; Seim, *Bandage, Sort, and Hustle*; Celeste Watkins-Hayes, *The New Welfare Bureaucrats: Entanglements of Race, Class, and Policy Reform* (Chicago: University of Chicago Press, 2009).

107. California WIC, Section 5400(a), leginfo.legislature.ca.gov/faces/codes_displaySection .xhtml?lawCode=WIC&sectionNum=5400.

108. This depiction comes from both right-leaning commentators portraying an ineffectual nonprofit industry feeding at the government trough (Eide, Shellenberger) and left-leaning ones assailing potentially well-meaning charities that nonetheless normalize and depoliticize homelessness (Gowan, Willse). Eide, *Homelessness in America*; Shellenberger, *San Fransicko*; Teresa Gowan, *Hobos, Hustlers, and Backsliders: Homeless in San Francisco* (Minneapolis: University of Minnesota Press, 2010); Craig Willse, *The Value of Homelessness: Managing Surplus Life in the United States* (Minneapolis: University of Minnesota Press, 2015).

109. Starr, *The Social Transformation of American Medicine*, 10.

110. Kimberly J. Morgan and Ann Shola Orloff, eds., "Introduction," in *The Many Hands of the State: Theorizing Political Authority and Social Control* (Cambridge: Cambridge University Press, 2017), 1–32.

111. Milward and Provan, "Governing the Hollow State."

1. OUTPATIENT

1. See also, Timothy Tyler Brown et al., "The Impact of California's Full-Service Partnership Program on Mental Health-Related Emergency Department Visits," *Psychiatric Services* 63, no. 8 (2012): 802–7; Timothy Tyler Brown, Juliette S. Hong, and Richard M.

Scheffler, "Evaluating the Impact of California's Full Service Partnership Program Using a Multidimensional Measure of Outcomes," *Administration and Policy in Mental Health and Mental Health Services Research* 41, no. 3 (2014): 390; Sarah L. Starks et al., "System Transformation Under the California Mental Health Services Act: Implementation of Full-Service Partnerships in L.A. County," *Psychiatric Services* 68, no. 6 (2017): 587–95.

2. California Health Care Foundation, "California Health Care Almanac," June 2022, 3, https://www.chcf.org/wp-content/uploads/2022/06/HealthInsurersAlmanac2022.pdf.

3. Tara F. Bishop et al., "Acceptance of Insurance by Psychiatrists and the Implications for Access to Mental Health Care," *JAMA Psychiatry* 71, no. 2 (2014): 176–81.

4. As Lewis et al. put it, in the community treatment system that replaced asylums, "care is a matter of personal choice for the patient and the provider." Dan A. Lewis et al., *Worlds of the Mentally Ill: How Deinstitutionalization Works in the City* (Carbondale: Southern Illinois University Press, 1991), 93.

5. Janet Coffman et al., "California's Current and Future Behavioral Health Workforce" (San Francisco: Healthforce Center at UCSF, February 12, 2018), 22, https://healthforce.ucsf.edu/.

6. California requires that residential therapeutic programs for children be "organized and operated on a nonprofit basis," so many adolescents are sent out of state where a for-profit industry is flourishing. Proposals to regulate the industry at the federal level have repeatedly failed. Cameron Evans, "State Laws Aim to Regulate 'Troubled Teen Industry,' but Loopholes Remain," *Kaiser Health News*, January 22, 2022, https://khn.org/news/article/state-laws-aim-to-regulate-troubled-teen-industry-but-loopholes-remain/.

7. Chad Terhune, "Report: Kaiser Tops State Health Insurance Market with 40 Percent Share," *Los Angeles Times*, January 29, 2013, https://www.latimes.com/business/la-xpm-2013-jan-29-la-fi-mo-health-insure-market-20130129-story.html.

8. Jocelyn Wiener, "For Families Across California, a Desperate Struggle to Get Mental Health Care," *CALmatters*, March 10, 2019, https://calmatters.org/articles/californians-struggle-to-get-mental-health-care/; Jocelyn Wiener, "Mental Health Care Outcry Targets Kaiser—and State Regulators," *CalMatters*, December 18, 2019, https://calmatters.org/projects/mental-health-care-outcry-targets-kaiser-california-parity-regulators/.

9. Martin Espinoza, "Mental Health Workers' Union Claims Kaiser Permanente Not Providing Psychiatric Crisis Care in Emergency Room," *Santa Rosa Press Democrat*, September 27, 2022, https://www.pressdemocrat.com/article/news/mental-health-workers-union-claims-kaiser-permanente-not-providing-psychia/.

10. Nanette Asimov, "Kaiser Made $8 Billion in Profits Last Year. So Why Are Patients Struggling to Get Mental Health Care?" *San Francisco Chronicle*, September 28, 2022, https://www.sfchronicle.com/bayarea/article/Who-is-going-to-hold-Kaiser-accountable-17474027.php.

11. Michael McGough, "Kaiser Settled 2014 Patient-Dumping Class-Action," *Sacramento Bee*, December 20, 2018, https://www.sacbee.com/news/local/health-and-medicine/article223368950.html.

12. Note that the study does not compare these elevated death rates among young people with psychosis on private insurance to young people on public insurance. Michael Schoenbaum et al., "Twelve-Month Health Care Use and Mortality in Commercially

Insured Young People with Incident Psychosis in the United States," *Schizophrenia Bulletin* 43, no. 6 (2017): 1262–72.

13. Jocelyn Wiener, "'Go on Medi-Cal to Get That': Why Californians with Mental Illness Are Dropping Private Insurance to Get Taxpayer-Funded Treatment," *CalMatters*, July 30, 2020, https://calmatters.org/projects/california-mental-health-private-insurance-medi-cal/.

14. See also Howard Padwa et al., "A Mental Health System in Recovery: The Era of Deinstitutionalisation in California," in *Deinstitutionalisation and After: Post-War Psychiatry in the Western World*, ed. Despo Kritsotaki, Vicky Long, and Matthew Smith (Cham, Switzerland: Palgrave Macmillan, 2016), 241–65.

15. One review found that police were involved in accessing care for 29 percent for people with serious mental illness in the United States. The average in other Western countries was 11 percent. James D. Livingston, "Contact Between Police and People with Mental Disorders: A Review of Rates," *Psychiatric Services* 67, no. 8 (2016): 850–57.

16. Southern Poverty Law Center, "Costly and Cruel: How Misuse of the Baker Act Harms 37,000 Florida Children Each Year," 2021, https://splcenter.org/sites/default/files/com_special_report_baker_act_costly_and_cruel.pdf.

17. This practice of only paying for cheaper medications, even if a patient had previous success on a more expensive second-generation antipsychotic, also took place in Florida's jails. Pete Earley, *Crazy: A Father's Search Through America's Mental Health Madness* (New York: Putnam, 2006), 163.

18. Marcia L. Meldrum et al., "Implementation Status of Assisted Outpatient Treatment Programs: A National Survey," *Psychiatric Services* 67, no. 6 (2016): 630–35.

19. Substance Abuse and Mental Health Services Administration, "Funding and Characteristics of Single State Agencies for Substance Abuse Services and State Mental Health Agencies, 2015" (Rockville, MD: U.S. Department of Health and Human Services, 2017), 132, https://store.samhsa.gov/sites/default/files/d7/priv/sma17-5029.pdf.

20. Teknekron Inc., "Improving California's Mental Health System: Policymaking and Management in the Invisible System" (Berkeley: California Assembly Permanent Subcommittee on Mental Health and Developmental Disabilities, December 1978), 9. Subsequent legislation, authored by Frank Lanterman, required that counties contract for some services rather than run them themselves. Eugene Bardach, *The Implementation Game: What Happens After a Bill Becomes a Law* (Cambridge, MA: MIT Press, 1977), 11.

21. Quoted in Eugene Bardach, *The Skill Factor in Politics: Repealing the Mental Commitment Laws in California* (Berkeley: University of California Press, 1972), 83. The programs LPS funded were "contacting a population group that was not reached pre-LPS . . . who were [not] likely to require inpatient services." ENKI Research Institute, *A Study of California's New Mental Health Law (1969–1971)* (Chatsworth, CA: Author, 1972), 196.

22. Nicolas Petris, "State Government Oral History Program," December 20, 1988, California State Archives, https://archives.cdn.sos.ca.gov/oral-history/pdf/oh-petris-nicholas.pdf.

23. John R. Elpers, "Public Mental Health Funding in California, 1959 to 1989," *Psychiatric Services* 40, no. 8 (1989): 799–804.

24. Bill Boyarsky, "Changing Policies Affect Care of Sick," *Los Angeles Times*, August 8, 1982.

25. Deborah Vrana, "California Shifts $2.2 Billion of New Responsibility Onto Its Counties' Shoulders," *Bond Buyer*, July 15, 1991.

26. Linda Roach Monroe, "County Faces Tough Choices on Mental Health," *Los Angeles Times*, August 4, 1988.

27. California WIC, Section 5600(a), https://leginfo.legislature.ca.gov/faces/codes_displayText .xhtml?lawCode=WIC&division=5.&title=&part=2.&chapter=1.

28. Lonnie Snowden, Richard Scheffler, and Amy Zhang, "The Impact of Realignment on the Client Population in California's Public Mental Health System," *Administration and Policy in Mental Health* 29, no. 3 (2002): 229–41.

29. Ben Kane et al., "California County Spending on 24-Hour Behavioral Care" (Berkeley, CA: Goldman School of Public Policy, April 2018); Mac Taylor, "Rethinking the 1991 Realignment" (Sacramento, CA: Legislative Analyst's Office, October 15, 2018).

30. Legislative Analyst's Office, "Realignment Revisited: An Evaluation of the 1991 Experiment in State-County Relations" (Sacramento, CA, February 6, 2001).

31. Little Hoover Commission, "Promises Still to Keep: A Decade of the Mental Health Services Act" (Sacramento, CA, January 2015), 10.

32. Mental Health Services Oversight and Accountability Commission, "Transparency Suite: Full-Service Partnerships," accessed January 12, 2022, https://mhsoac.ca.gov/transparency -suite/full-service-partnership/.

33. An investigation by the *Sacramento Bee* found that only one in ten people with an urgent request for services received an appointment within one week. Michael Finch, "Long Waits and Treatment Shortages Plague Sacramento County's Mental Health Services," *Sacramento Bee*, May 27, 2021, https://www.sacbee.com/news/investigations/the-public -eye/article251683983.html.

34. Karen de Sá, "Mental Health Spending Creating Haves and Have-Nots in California," *Contra Costa Times*, June 26, 2011.

35. This is most visible in the state's mental health workforce crisis: many counties report that 30 to 40 percent of clinical positions are unfilled. Jocelyn Wiener, "Unanswered Cries: Why California Faces a Shortage of Mental Health Workers," *CalMatters*, September 8, 2022, https://calmatters.org/health/2022/09/california-shortage-mental-health-workers/.

36. Thanks to the ACA and MHSA, the number of people receiving county mental health services was back over 627,000 in 2019. Behavioral Health Concepts, Inc., "Medi-Cal Specialty Mental Health External Quality Review, FY 2020-21" (Department of Health Care Services, January 25, 2022), 24, https://caleqro.com/mh-eqro.

37. Department of Health Care Services, "MediCal Managed Care Plan Responsibilities for Outpatient Mental Health Services" (Sacramento, CA, October 27, 2017), https://www .dhcs.ca.gov/formsandpubs/Documents/MMCDAPLsandPolicyLetters/APL2017 /APL17-018.pdf.

38. Benjamin Brown, Eloise O'Donnell, and Lawrence P. Casalino, "Private Equity Investment in Behavioral Health Treatment Centers," *JAMA Psychiatry* 77, no. 3 (2020): 229–30, https://doi.org/10.1001/jamapsychiatry.2019.3880.

39. Kim Lewis and Abbi Coursolle, "Mental Health Services in Medi-Cal" (Los Angeles, CA: National Health Law Program, January 12, 2017), 1, https://healthlaw.org/resource /issue-brief-mental-health-services-in-medi-cal/.

40. Xavier Amador, *I Am Not Sick, I Don't Need Help! How to Help Someone with Mental Illness Accept Treatment* (New York: Vida, 2006).

41. D. J. Jaffe, *Insane Consequences: How the Mental Health Industry Fails the Mentally Ill* (Amherst, NY: Prometheus, 2017), 72.

42. A 2012 report on reforming LPS, for example, called it the "Magna Carta" for "those individuals who are well enough to respond to treatment in a voluntary . . . system." LPS Reform Task Force II, "The Case for Updating California's Mental Health Treatment Law" (Tustin, CA, March 2012), 4.

43. Tara A. Niendam et al., "The Rise of Early Psychosis Care in California: An Overview of Community and University-Based Services," *Psychiatric Services* 70, no. 6 (2019): 480–87.

44. Iruma Bello et al., "OnTrackNY: The Development of a Coordinated Specialty Care Program for Individuals Experiencing Early Psychosis," *Psychiatric Services* 68, no. 4 (2016): 318–20.

45. Henry A. Nasrallah, "For First-Episode Psychosis, Psychiatrists Should Behave Like Cardiologists," *Current Psychiatry* 16, no. 8 (2017): 4–7.

46. Elaine Stasiulis et al., "The Disjuncture Between Medication Adherence and Recovery-Centered Principles in Early Psychosis Intervention: An Institutional Ethnography," *Society and Mental Health* 12, no. 1 (2022): 32–48.

47. Franco Mascayano et al., "Disengagement from Early Intervention Services for Psychosis: A Systematic Review," *Psychiatric Services* 72, no. 1 (2021): 49–60.

48. As one psychiatrist put it in 1972, when "the entry of persons exhibiting mentally disordered behavior into the mental health system of social control is impeded . . . [they will be] force[d] into the criminal justice system of social control." Marc F. Abramson, "The Criminalization of Mentally Disordered Behavior," *Psychiatric Services* 23, no. 4 (1972): 15.

49. E. Fuller Torrey, the psychiatrist at the helm of the Treatment Advocacy Center (which militates for more forced treatment), insists that "Anosognosia . . . separates involuntary treatment from being a civil rights issue and makes it a biological one." Quoted in Dinah Miller and Annette Hanson, *Committed: The Battle Over Involuntary Psychiatric Care* (Baltimore: Johns Hopkins University Press, 2016), 21.

50. Neil Gong, "'That Proves You Mad, Because You Know It Not': Impaired Insight and the Dilemma of Governing Psychiatric Patients as Legal Subjects," *Theory and Society* 46, no. 3 (2017): 220.

51. California State Auditor, "Lanterman-Petris-Short Act: California Has Not Ensured That Individuals with Serious Mental Illnesses Receive Adequate Ongoing Care" (Sacramento, CA, July 2020), 90.

52. A survey found that three hundred was the average caseload of public outpatient clients in California. Hunter L. McQuistion and Rachel Zinns, "Workloads in Clinical Psychiatry: Another Way," *Psychiatric Services* 70, no. 10 (2019): 963–66.

53. This critique of a mental health system that "all too often opts for pharmaceutical over therapeutic interventions" also emerged in a study of homeless women in Los Angeles. Rose Ricciardelli and Laura Huey, *Adding Insult to Injury: (Mis)Treating Homeless Women in Our Mental Health System* (Boulder, CO: Lynne Rienner, 2016), 3.

54. Behavioral Health Action, "Answering the Call to Action: A Vision for All Californians' Behavioral Health," 2021, https://www.behavioralhealthaction.org/.

55. Coffman et al., "California's Behavioral Health Workforce," 27.

56. I am grateful to Jenny Leigh for making this point.

57. One review concluded, "Mental health services that integrate elements addressing an individual's immediate needs may enhance engagement." Lisa B. Dixon, Yael Holoshitz, and Ilana Nossel, "Treatment Engagement of Individuals Experiencing Mental Illness: Review and Update," *World Psychiatry* 15, no. 1 (2016): 14.

58. Thomas E. Smith et al., "Disengagement from Care: Perspectives of Individuals with Serious Mental Illness and of Service Providers," *Psychiatric Services* 64, no. 8 (2013): 772.

59. This statement was made at a December 15, 2021 hearing in the state legislature.

60. Isabel M. Perera and Alex V. Barnard, "Myths of Mental Health: Revelations from the French System for the United States," *Perspectives in Biology and Medicine* 64, no. 1 (2021): 103–18.

2. CRISIS

1.   A recent investigation in San Francisco found that nearly 20 percent of permanent supported housing residents received eviction notices in a given year; although only a small number were ultimately evicted by the courts, many left to avoid legal proceedings. Joaquin Palomino and Trisha Thadani, "The Breed Administration Offered Them Homes. Then It Spent Millions to Kick Them Out," *San Francisco Chronicle*, August 22, 2022, https://www.sfchronicle.com/projects/2022/sf-sro-evictions/. In a survey by the Coalition on Homelessness, 18 percent of individuals currently experiencing homelessness in San Francisco had previously been in supported housing. Coalition on Homelessness, "Stop the Revolving Door: A Street-Level Framework for a New System," September 2020, 19, https://www.cohsf.org/wp-content/uploads/2020/11/Stop-the-Revolving-1.pdf. These statistics do not identify eviction rates for people with serious mental illness specifically.

2.   Mental Health and Substance Use Disorder Services Division, "California Involuntary Detention Reports (FY 2017–2018)" (Sacramento, CA: Department of Health Care Services, 2018), https://www.dhcs.ca.gov/Documents/CSD_YV/MHSA/IDR/FY17-18-IDR -Report.pdf.

3.   In San Francisco, from 2013 to 2017, the number of 911 calls about homelessness nearly doubled, while "homeless concerns" reported to the city's 311 number grew almost tenfold. Chris Herring, "Complaint-Oriented Policing: Regulating Homelessness in Public Space," *American Sociological Review* 84, no. 5 (2019): 769–800.

4.   A review of records in San Francisco found that half of police 5150s were initiated by strangers with no relationship to the person being held; 34 percent were from friends or acquaintances, 10 percent clinicians or case workers, and only 5 percent directly from law enforcement. San Francisco Housing Conservatorship Working Group, "SFPD Incident Report Data," November 16, 2020, https://sfdph.org/dph/files/housingconserv/Housing _Conservatorhip_Meeting_11.16_Combined_updated.pdf.

5.   Department of Housing and Urban Development, "2020 AHAR: PIT Estimates of Homelessness in the U.S.," March 2021, https://www.hudexchange.info/resource/6291 /2020-ahar-part-1-pit-estimates-of-homelessness-in-the-us/.

6.   Everyone Home, "Point-in-Time Count" (Alameda County, 2022), https://everyonehome .org/main/continuum-of-care/everyone-counts/.

7. From 2009 to 2014, mental health–related calls to Oakland police went up 50 percent, while Berkeley's police department reported a 43 percent increase in calls leading to an involuntary hold. Holly McDede, "Mental Health 911," *East Bay Express*, April 6, 2016, https://eastbayexpress.com/mental-health-911-2-1/.

8. A 2019 *Los Angeles Times* analysis claimed 67 percent of unsheltered homeless had a mental illness or substance use disorder, which tracks with a survey in San Francisco that identified 50 percent of the city's homeless as having both conditions. Doug Smith and Benjamin Oreskes, "Are Many Homeless People in L.A. Mentally Ill? New Findings Back the Public's Perception," *Los Angeles Times*, October 7, 2019, https://www.latimes.com /california/story/2019-10-07/homeless-population-mental-illness-disability; Dominic Fracassa and Trisha Thadani, "SF Counts 4,000 Homeless, Addicted and Mentally Ill, but Timeline for Help Still Unclear," *San Francisco Chronicle*, December 31, 2019, https://www .sfchronicle.com/bayarea/article/SF-counts-4-000-homeless-addicted-and-mentally -14412061.php. The federal government, however, estimates that only 20.8 percent of homeless people had severe mental illness and 17.0 percent chronic substance use in 2020, although the proportion among unsheltered homeless is higher. U.S. Department of Housing and Urban Development, "Continuum of Care Homeless Assistance Programs Homeless Populations and Subpopulations," December 15, 2020, https://files .hudexchange.info/reports/published/CoC_PopSub_NatlTerrDC_2020.pdf. Social scientists have long argued that claims of a very high prevalence of mental illness among homeless people conflate severe pathologies that contributed to causing homelessness with less severe conditions that are a consequence of homelessness. Gregg Colburn and Clayton Page Aldern, *Homelessness Is a Housing Problem: How Structural Factors Explain U.S. Patterns* (Berkeley: University of California Press, 2022); David Snow et al., "The Myth of Pervasive Mental Illness Among the Homeless," *Social Problems* 33, no. 5 (1986): 407–23.

9. Elizabeth Sinclair Hancq, Kelli South, and Molly Vencel, "Dual Diagnosis: Serious Mental Illness and Co-Occurring Substance Use Disorders" (Arlington, VA: Treatment Advocacy Center, March 2021), 12.

10. Beth Han et al., "Methamphetamine Use, Methamphetamine Use Disorder, and Associated Overdose Deaths Among U.S. Adults," *JAMA Psychiatry* 78, no. 12 (2021): 1329–42.

11. April Dembosky, "Meth Vs. Opioids: America Has Two Drug Epidemics, but Focuses on One," *California Healthline*, May 8, 2019, https://californiahealthline.org/news/meth-vs -opioids-america-has-two-drug-epidemics-but-focuses-on-one/.

12. While many officers were critical of Prop 47, research so far suggests it has not led to an increase in violent crimes, although larceny and vehicle theft rose after its passage. Bradley J. Bartos and Charis E. Kubrin, "Can We Downsize Our Prisons and Jails Without Compromising Public Safety?," *Criminology & Public Policy* 17, no. 3 (2018): 693–715.

13. Susan Anthony, Rebecca Catterson, and Suzanne Campanella, "In Their Own Words: How Fragmented Care Harms People with Both Mental Illness and Substance Use Disorder" (California Health Care Foundation, August 2021).

14. A recent grand jury report in Alameda observed that, since the county ACCESS line closes at 5 p.m., "There is no place for law enforcement or others to call for mental health referral support during evening hours, so psychiatric emergency services or jail become the only option for law enforcement by default." Alameda County Grand Jury, "Final

Report," 2021–2022, 18, https://grandjury.acgov.org/grandjury-assets/docs/2021-2022 /Grand.Jury.Report.2022.for.ITD.Web.pdf.

15. Department of Health Care Services, *Assessing the Continuum of Care for Behavioral Health Services in California Data, Stakeholder Perspectives, and Implications* (Sacramento, January 10, 2022), 154.

16. Ed Connolly, "Emergency Call," *East Bay Express*, February 29, 2012, https://m.eastbayexpress .com/oakland/emergency-call/.

17. Tarak K. Trivedi et al., "Emergency Medical Services Use Among Patients Receiving Involuntary Psychiatric Holds and the Safety of an Out-of-Hospital Screening Protocol to 'Medically Clear' Psychiatric Emergencies in the Field, 2011 to 2016," *Annals of Emergency Medicine* 73, no. 1 (2019): 42–51.

18. Los Angeles County made this same point: multiple 5150s do "not necessarily correlate to the need for specialty mental health services or services designed for higher acuity clients [like FSPs or AOT]" because "individuals are at times placed on numerous 5150 holds for reasons other than a primary mental health disorder." California State Auditor, "Lanterman-Petris-Short Act: California Has Not Ensured That Individuals with Serious Mental Illnesses Receive Adequate Ongoing Care" (Sacramento, CA, July 2020), 87.

19. California State Auditor, "Lanterman-Petris-Short Act," 40.

20. In Alameda County, 55 percent of people with ten or more holds at John George Hospital in 2018–2020 were Black. The county is 11 percent Black. Disability Rights California, "Complaint for Declaratory and Injunctive Relief" (United States District Court— Northern District of California, July 30, 2020), 20, https://www.disabilityrightsca.org /system/files/file-attachments/ECF-1-Complaint.pdf.

21. According to data from the National Suicide Prevention Lifeline, around 2 percent of such hotline calls lead to a police welfare check. Ron Wipond, *Your Consent Is Not Required: The Rise in Psychiatric Detentions, Forced Treatment, and Abusive Guardianships* (Dallas, TX: BenBella, 2023), 110.

22. People subjected to involuntary holds feel "trapped," "ambushed," or "surrounded," especially when police are involved. Rebecca Murphy et al., "Service Users' Experiences of Involuntary Hospital Admission Under the Mental Health Act 2001 in the Republic of Ireland," *Psychiatric Services* 68, no. 11 (2017): 1127–35.

23. Scholars have characterized this as "epistemic injustice": by merit of their disabilities, people with mental illness are blocked from "contesting distorted understandings of their social experiences." Karen Newbigging and Julie Ridley, "Epistemic Struggles: The Role of Advocacy in Promoting Epistemic Justice and Rights in Mental Health," *Social Science & Medicine* 219 (2018): 37.

24. Giorgio Agamben, *Homo Sacer: Sovereign Power and Bare Life*, trans. Daniel Heller-Roazen (Stanford, CA: Stanford University Press, 1998).

25. One way the authors of LPS gained support for the reform among clinicians was by abolishing the "commitment courts" that had to authorize all hospitalizations, making legal review into something that patients had to actively request via a writ. Eugene Bardach, *The Skill Factor in Politics: Repealing the Mental Commitment Laws in California* (Berkeley: University of California Press, 1972), 185. This changed in *Doe v. Gallinot*, discussed in chapter 4.

26. Esmé Weijun Wang, *The Collected Schizophrenias* (Minneapolis, MN: Graywolf, 2019), 109.

27. Erving Goffman, "The Moral Career of the Mental Patient," *Psychiatry* 22 (1959): 127.

28. Such filings dropped 99 percent in the years after LPS went into effect. Albert H. Urmer, "Implications of California's New Mental Health Law," *American Journal of Psychiatry* 132, no. 3 (1975): 251.

29. When Mobile Crisis came to Sonoma County, for example, the team only operated in a narrow corridor around Highway 101. Jason Walsh, "Shock Corridor," *Sonoma Index-Tribune*, May 29, 2018.

30. Molly Hennessy-Fiske, "Mental Health Staff Relying on Police," *Los Angeles Times*, November 21, 2008.

31. Rod Shaner, the former medical director for LA County's Department of Mental Health, explained this to me: "In the hands of law enforcement, [a 5150] is a passport to scarce resources. . . . Those who believe that alternative crisis response teams would be more useful often appear to misunderstand the reason for police presence. It isn't to control dangerous situations, it's to assure access into evaluation and treatment."

32. The original LPS Act required that the determination of dangerousness or disability for a 5150 hold be based on an evaluator's "personal observations." This imposed "unique limitations on the application of clinical judgment as justification for commitments" as compared to other states. Urmer, "Implications of California's New Mental Health Law," 251. Later amendments allowed police or clinicians to consider "information about the historical course of the person's mental disorder" from third parties (WIC 5150.05) and clarified that "danger" is not limited to "imminent harm" (WIC 5150(b)). The extent to which these amendments are taken into account by the police seems variable.

33. Nationwide, the use of "tactical disengagement" from suicidal individuals is expanding in response to concerns about law enforcement killing people with mental illness. Caren Chesler, "On Calls When a Person Is Suicidal, Some Police Try a New Approach," *Washington Post*, September 23, 2022, https://www.washingtonpost.com/national-security/2022/09/23/calls-when-person-is-suicidal-some-police-try-a-new-approach/.

34. Amam Z. Saleh et al., "Deaths of People with Mental Illness During Interactions with Law Enforcement," *International Journal of Law and Psychiatry* 58 (2018): 114.

35. Los Angeles Police Department, "LAPD's Mental Evaluation Unit Is Selected as a National Law Enforcement/Mental Health Learning Site," November 9, 2010, https://www.lapdonline.org/newsroom/news_view/46481.

36. Malcolm Gladwell, "Million-Dollar Murray," *New Yorker*, February 13, 2006.

37. Paul S. Appelbaum and Thomas G. Gutheil, "'Rotting with Their Rights On': Constitutional Theory and Clinical Reality in Drug Refusal by Psychiatric Patients," *Journal of the American Academy of Psychiatry and the Law* 7, no. 3 (1979): 306–15.

38. Egon Bittner, "Police Discretion in Emergency Apprehension of Mentally Ill Persons," *Social Problems* 14, no. 3 (1967): 287.

39. I'm grateful to Nick Rekenthaler for this turn of phrase.

40. This observation is backed up by other sources. The review of 5150 records in San Francisco cited above (note 4) found that 61 percent of police 5150s were for "danger to self," 38 percent "danger to others," and 12 percent "grave disability." The state auditor found

that in only nine of sixty 5150s they reviewed were based solely on grave disability. California State Auditor, "Lanterman-Petris-Short Act," 20.

3. EMERGENCY ROOM

1. According to many interviewees, California's public mental health system used to conduct relatively little outreach to homeless individuals. Today, someone in his situation might have more frequent contacts.

2. David Garland, *The Culture of Control* (Chicago: University of Chicago Press, 2001), 170; Chris Herring, "Complaint-Oriented Policing: Regulating Homelessness in Public Space," *American Sociological Review* 84, no. 5 (2019): 780; Forrest Stuart, *Down, Out, and Under Arrest: Policing and Everyday Life in Skid Row* (Chicago: University of Chicago Press, 2016), 166.

3. Centers for Medicare and Medicaid Services, "Emergency Medical Treatment and Labor Act," August 25, 2022, https://www.cms.gov/Regulations-and-Guidance/Legislation/EMTALA.

4. Ruth E. Malone, "Whither the Almshouse? Overutilization and the Role of the Emergency Department," *Journal of Health Politics, Policy and Law* 23, no. 5 (1998): 795–832.

5. Janet R. Cummings et al., "The Changing Landscape of Community Mental Health Care: Availability of Treatment Services in National Data, 2010–2017," *Psychiatric Services* 72, no. 2 (2021): 204–8; Luther G. Kalb et al., "Trends and Geographic Availability of Emergency Psychiatric Walk-In and Crisis Services in the United States," *Psychiatric Services* 73, no. 1 (2022): 26–31.

6. California Hospital Association, "California Overview: Behavioral Health Emergency Department Growth," n.d., https://calhealth.org/sites/main/files/file-attachments/11_-_stratasan_ed_data.pdf.

7. See Josh Seim, *Bandage, Sort, and Hustle: Ambulance Crews on the Frontlines of Urban Suffering* (Berkeley: University of California Press, 2019).

8. Seim, *Bandage, Sort, and Hustle*, 124.

9. Clinicians assess as much of one-third of psychiatric ER patients as malingering. These suspicions are strongly predictive of discharge. Sean M. Rumschik and Jacob M. Appel, "Malingering in the Psychiatric Emergency Department: Prevalence, Predictors, and Outcomes," *Psychiatric Services* 70, no. 2 (2018): 115–22.

10. U.S. Department of Justice, "Investigation of Alameda County, John George Psychiatric Hospital, and Santa Rita Jail" (Washington, DC: Civil Rights Division, April 22, 2021), 2; Aaron J. Fischer, Rebecca Cervenak, and Kim Swain, "Suicides in San Diego County Jail: A System Failing People with Mental Illness" (Disability Rights California, April 2018), https://www.disabilityrightsca.org/system/files/file-attachments/SDsuicideReport.pdf.

11. One study, which found that 50 percent of people seen in an ER for a psychiatric issue did not make it to their follow-up appointment, concluded that "transportation and financial difficulties were the main barriers to transitions and engagement." Elizabeth Reisinger Walker et al., "A Qualitative Study of Barriers and Facilitators to Transitions from the Emergency Department to Outpatient Mental Health Care," *Psychiatric Services* 72, no. 11 (2021): 1316.

12.   Yeheskel Hasenfeld, "People Processing Organizations: An Exchange Approach," *American Sociological Review* 37, no. 3 (1972): 256–63; Jeffrey Prottas, *People Processing: The Street-Level Bureaucrat in Public-Service Bureaucracies* (Lexington, MA: Lexington, 1979).

13.   One 2012 survey of 123 emergency department directors in California reported that many psychiatric evaluation teams would not even come to general hospital emergency rooms to evaluate patients if there were no inpatient beds available. Ashley Stone et al., "Impact of the Mental Healthcare Delivery System on California Emergency Departments," *Western Journal of Emergency Medicine* 13, no. 1 (2012): 54.

14.   Bret Nicks and David Manthey, "The Impact of Psychiatric Patient Boarding in Emergency Departments," *Emergency Medicine International* 2012 (2012): 360308.

15.   This statement was made by Alex Hawthorne at a December 15, 2021 hearing before the legislature. This corresponds with reported figures from Alameda and Shasta counties as well as most of my interviews with ER psychiatrists. Scott Zeller, Nicole Calma, and Ashley Stone, "Effects of a Dedicated Regional Psychiatric Emergency Service on Boarding of Psychiatric Patients in Area Emergency Departments," *WestJEM* 15, no. 1 (2014): 1–6; Alayna Shulman, "Untreated, Severe Mental Illness at Root of Other Problems," *Redding Record*, November 7, 2015.

16.   Hemal K. Kanzaria et al., "Frequent Emergency Department Users: Focusing Solely on Medical Utilization Misses the Whole Person," *Health Affairs* 38, no. 11 (2019): 1866–75.

17.   Heather Knight, "Mentally Ill People in S.F. Are Cycling in and out of Emergency Rooms," *San Francisco Chronicle*, March 9, 2022, https://www.sfchronicle.com/sf/bayarea/heatherknight/article/Mentally-ill-people-in-S-F-are-cycling-in-and-16987694.php.

18.   For many such examples—and an explanation of why psychiatrists choose to discharge them—see Paul Linde, *Danger to Self: On the Front Line with an ER Psychiatrist* (Berkeley: University of California Press, 2012).

19.   Trisha Thadani and Dominic Fracassa, "SF General Relaxes Policy That Tries to Keep Psychiatric ER Patients Awake to Shorten Visits," *San Francisco Chronicle*, August 28, 2019, https://www.sfchronicle.com/bayarea/article/SF-General-relaxes-policy-that-tries-to-keep-14383111.php.

20.   "Sleep, Its Importance in Preventing Insanity," *American Journal of Psychiatry* 1, no. 4 (1845): 319–23.

21.   One older study estimated that hospital emergency departments lose $2,200 per psychiatric patient as a result of their extended length of stay and low reimbursement rates. Nicks and Manthey, "Psychiatric Patient Boarding."

22.   Ish P. Bhalla et al., "Involuntary Psychiatric Hospitalization: How Patient Characteristics Affect Decision-Making," *Psychiatric Quarterly* 93, no. 1 (2021): 297–310; George J. Unick et al., "Factors Affecting Psychiatric Inpatient Hospitalization from a Psychiatric Emergency Service," *General Hospital Psychiatry* 33, no. 6 (2011): 618–25.

23.   Christopher G. Hudson, "Behavioral Mental Health: An Emerging Field of Service or an Oxymoron?" *Social Work* 63, no. 1 (2018): 27–36. California's 2021 proposal for reforming Medi-Cal, CalAIM, plans to integrate substance and mental health services into a single system. Department of Health Care Services, "California Advancing and Innovating Medi-Cal (CalAIM) Proposal" (Sacramento, CA, January 2021).

24. San Francisco Budget and Legislative Analyst, "Performance Audit of the Department of Public Health Behavioral Health Services" (San Francisco, CA, April 19, 2018), v.

25. A 2019 survey by the Department of Public Health claimed that 95 percent of dual-diagnosis homeless individuals in San Francisco had chronic alcoholism. Dominic Fracassa and Trisha Thadani, "SF Counts 4,000 Homeless, Addicted and Mentally Ill, but Timeline for Help Still Unclear," *San Francisco Chronicle*, December 31, 2019, https://www.sfchronicle.com/bayarea/article/SF-counts-4-000-homeless-addicted-and-mentally-14412061.php.

26. Mallory Moench, "Five Patients Cost $4 Million in Ambulance Rides," *San Francisco Chronicle*, July 28, 2022, https://www.sfchronicle.com/sf/article/5-patients-cost-S-F-4-million-in-ambulance-17336870.php.

27. California WIC, Sections 5170 and 5343, https://leginfo.legislature.ca.gov/faces/codes_displaySection.xhtml?lawCode=WIC&sectionNum=5170.

28. A 2020 report from Los Angeles said that commitments for substance users under 5343 were "not . . . utilized." Jon Sherin, "Disrupting the Cycle of Chronic Homelessness in Los Angeles County" (Los Angeles: Department of Mental Health, January 22, 2020), 2, http://file.lacounty.gov/SDSInter/bos/supdocs/140390.pdf. While thirty-one states have statutes for commitment for substance use, they are invoked very rarely. Paul P. Christopher et al., "Nature and Utilization of Civil Commitment for Substance Abuse in the United States," *Journal of the American Academy of Psychiatry and the Law Online* 43, no. 3 (2015): 313–20.

29. Moench, "Five Patients Cost."

30. The failure to provide true dual-diagnosis treatment is systemic: nationwide in 2019, only 12.7 percent of people with a serious mental illness and substance use disorder received treatment for both; 52 percent received only mental health services and 1.9 percent only substance use services. Elizabeth Sinclair Hancq, Kelli South, and Molly Vencel, "Dual Diagnosis: Serious Mental Illness and Co-Occurring Substance Use Disorders" (Arlington, VA: Treatment Advocacy Center, March 2021), 25.

31. In one case study, the fact that a chronically psychotic person came to the ER asking for shelter showed that he was "capable of making plans" to meet his basic needs, and he was therefore released. Joel T. Braslow and Luke Messac, "Medicalization and Demedicalization: A Gravely Disabled Homeless Man with Psychiatric Illness," *New England Journal of Medicine* 379, no. 20 (2018): 1885.

32. Edward W. Lempinen, "Debate Rages Over Locking Up the Mentally Troubled," *San Francisco Chronicle*, June 3, 1987.

33. Research consistently finds that dangerousness—particularly suicide risk—is a stronger prediction of involuntary admission than grave disability. Alisa Lincoln, "Psychiatric Emergency Room Decision-Making, Social Control and the 'Undeserving Sick,'" *Sociology of Health & Illness* 28, no. 1 (2006): 54–75; Steven P. Segal, Theresa A. Laurie, and Matthew J. Segal, "Factors in the Use of Coercive Retention in Civil Commitment Evaluations in Psychiatric Emergency Services," *Psychiatric Services* 52, no. 4 (2001): 514–20; B. B. Way and S. Banks, "Clinical Factors Related to Admission and Release Decisions in Psychiatric Emergency Services," *Psychiatric Services* 52, no. 2 (2011): 214–18.

34. For fragmented but consistent data on the overrepresentation of men on conservatorship, see Kristen R. Choi et al., "Mental Health Conservatorship Among Homeless People with Serious Mental Illness," *Psychiatric Services* 73, no. 6 (2022): 613–19; Richard H. Lamb and Linda E. Weinberger, "Conservatorship for Gravely Disabled Psychiatric Patients: A Four-Year Follow-Up Study," *American Journal of Psychiatry*, no. 149 (1992): 909–13; M. Susan Ridgely, Randy Borum, and John Petrila, "The Effectiveness of Involuntary Outpatient Treatment: Empirical Evidence and the Experience of Eight States" (Santa Monica, CA: Rand Corporation, 2001), 90. On differences in how men and women express mental illnesses, see Terrence D. Hill and Belinda L. Needham, "Rethinking Gender and Mental Health: A Critical Analysis of Three Propositions," *Social Science & Medicine* 92 (2013): 83–91.

35. Two iterations of this claim can be found in Dinah Miller and Annette Hanson, *Committed: The Battle Over Involuntary Psychiatric Care* (Baltimore: Johns Hopkins University Press, 2016), 64; and D. J. Jaffe, *Insane Consequences: How the Mental Health Industry Fails the Mentally Ill* (Amherst, NY: Prometheus, 2017), 22.

36. Julie Holland, *Weekends at Bellevue: Nine Years on the Night Shift at the Psych ER* (New York: Bantam, 2009), 10.

37. Seim, *Bandage, Sort, and Hustle*, 53.

4. INPATIENT

1. I would like to acknowledge the assistance of Jenny Leigh, who conducted this thorough and thoughtful interview (as well as interviews with Lola, Florence, Lorraine, and Thatcher).

2. Olufemi Babalola et al., "Length of Hospitalisation for People with Severe Mental Illness," *Cochrane Database of Systematic Reviews*, no. 1 (2014).

3. Someone who is involuntarily hospitalized can still be forced to pay whatever costs insurance companies pass on to them. Nathaniel P. Morris and Robert A. Kleinman, "Involuntary Commitments: Billing Patients for Forced Psychiatric Care," *American Journal of Psychiatry* 177, no. 12 (2020): 1115–16.

4. Based on the state's (spotty) data, in fiscal year 2017–2018 there were 52,069 5250s. Only 5,645 patients (or 10.8 percent) stayed for a subsequent hold (which includes temporary conservatorships). Mental Health and Substance Use Disorder Services Division, "California Involuntary Detention Reports (FY 2017–2018)" (Sacramento, CA: Department of Health Care Services, 2018), https://www.dhcs.ca.gov/Documents/CSD_YV/MHSA/IDR/FY17-18-IDR-Report.pdf.

5. Harry Nelson, "Mental Patient Pile Up Blamed on Bureaucracy," *Los Angeles Times*, August 13, 1967.

6. Sarah Linsley Starks and Joel T. Braslow, "The Making of Contemporary American Psychiatry, Part 1: Patients, Treatments, and Therapeutic Rationales Before and After World War II," *History of Psychology* 8, no. 2 (2005): 176.

7. Albert H. Urmer, "Implications of California's New Mental Health Law," *American Journal of Psychiatry* 132, no. 3 (1975): 252.

8. Phil Brown and Elizabeth Cooksey, "Mental Health Monopoly: Corporate Trends in Mental Health Services," *Social Science & Medicine* 28, no. 11 (1989): 1129–38.

9. Howard Seelye, "Owner Claims Hospital Boycotted by Doctors," *Los Angeles Times*, December 12, 1969. Private hospitals "warmly endorsed" LPS because they "perceiv[ed] an opening for private hospitals to gain access to more paying patients." Eugene Bardach, *The Skill Factor in Politics: Repealing the Mental Commitment Laws in California* (Berkeley: University of California Press, 1972), 133.

10. See LPS Reform Task Force, "A New Vision for Mental Health Treatment Laws" (Long Beach, CA, February 1999); Susan Moffat, "Healing Patients, or Profits?" *Los Angeles Times*, February 2, 1992. These practices of leveraging involuntary holds to maximize insurance reimbursements have not disappeared. A 2019 *Seattle Times* investigation found that a private hospital owned by Universal Health Services, which manages 188 facilities nationwide, frequently placed voluntary patients on involuntary holds if they asked to be released, especially if their insurance company had authorized additional days of treatment. County evaluators ultimately found two-thirds of these holds to be unjustified. Daniel Gilbert, "Free to Check In, but Not to Leave," *Seattle Times*, October 6, 2019, https://www.seattletimes.com/seattle-news/times-watchdog/public-crisis -private-toll-free-to-check-in-but-not-to-leave-washington-mental-health-care/.

11. T. M. Luhrmann, *Of Two Minds: The Growing Disorder in American Psychiatry* (New York: Knopf, 2000), 243.

12. California Hospital Association, "California's Acute Psychiatric Bed Loss" (Sacramento, CA, February 2019), https://www.calhospital.org/sites/main/files/file-attachments/6 _-_psychbeddata.pdf.

13. For more on the techniques of managed care in mental health systems, see Teresa L. Scheid, *Tie a Knot and Hang On: Providing Mental Health Care in a Turbulent Environment* (Hawthorne, NY: Transaction, 2004).

14. The average stay in a California psychiatric hospital was 8.3 days in 2018, but this is inflated by a small number of people remaining for long periods of time. California Health Care Foundation, "Mental Health in California: Waiting for Care," July 2022, 44, https://www.chcf.org/wp-content/uploads/2022/07/MentalHealthAlmanac2022.pdf.

15. Other scholars have documented a more wholesale embrace of a single-minded focus on shortening length of stay. One psychiatrist told an anthropologist, "Here everyone is an inappropriate admission. I don't admit patients. I discharge them." Lorna A. Rhodes, *Emptying Beds: The Work of an Emergency Psychiatric Unit* (Berkeley: University of California Press, 1991), 41.

16. In 2020, 89 percent of people in public psychiatric hospitals were involuntary. Substance Abuse and Mental Health Services Administration, "National Mental Health Services Survey (N-MHSS) 2020: Data on Mental Health Treatment Facilities" (Washington, DC: Department of Health and Human Services, December 2021), 254, https://samhsa.gov /data/sites/default/files/2016_National_Mental_Health_Services_Survey.pdf.

17. One study from a county hospital in Southern California found that patients were "almost exclusively" involuntary. Ish P. Bhalla et al., "Involuntary Psychiatric Hospitalization: How Patient Characteristics Affect Decision-Making," *Psychiatric Quarterly* 93, no. 1 (2021): 299.

18. California WIC, Section 5250, https://leginfo.legislature.ca.gov/faces/codes_displaySection .xhtml?lawCode=WIC&sectionNum=5250.

19. San Francisco Department of Public Health, "Behavioral Health Bed Optimization Project: Analysis and Recommendations for Improving Patient Flow" (San Francisco, June 2020).

20. Owen Whooley, *On the Heels of Ignorance: Psychiatry and the Politics of Not Knowing* (Chicago: University of Chicago Press, 2019), 50.

21. During the Great Recession, for example, San Francisco cut the number of acute psychiatric beds in SF General from eighty-seven to twenty-one. C. W. Nevius, "SF Hospital Services for Mentally Ill Suffer Drastic Cuts," *San Francisco Chronicle*, March 3, 2016, https://www.sfchronicle.com/bayarea/nevius/article/SF-hospital-services-for-mentally-ill-suffer-6866700.php.

22. In 2021 the San Diego city attorney filed suit against Scripps Health for discharging a sixty-eight-year-old man back to an independent living facility where he was found "disheveled and living in filthy conditions . . . naked and delusional, thinking the year was 1992." "Scripps Health Denies City Attorney Office's Accusation of Patient Dumping," *NBC 7*, August 30, 2021, https://www.nbcsandiego.com/news/local/scripps-health-denies-city-attorney-offices-accusation-of-patient-dumping/2706104/.

23. California Health and Safety Code, Section 1262.5(n)(3) and 1262.5(n)(4)(a), https://leginfo.legislature.ca.gov/faces/codes_displayText.xhtml?lawCode=HSC&division=2.&title=&part=&chapter=2.&article=1. The law contains an astonishing loophole, however: Psychiatric Health Facilities, which are specialized hospital-like facilities (which also take LPS patients and can apply for conservatorship) are not bound by these discharge-planning requirements. See Sara Kassabian, "'What Was He Going to Do with My Kid?': Woman from Paso Robles Was Released Early from a Psychiatric Facility," *San Luis Obispo Tribune*, October 2, 2022.

24. Kristen R. Choi et al., "Mental Health Conservatorship Among Homeless People with Serious Mental Illness," *Psychiatric Services* 73, no. 6 (2022): 615.

25. *Doe v. Gallinot* (C.D.Cal. 1979) 486 F.Supp. 983, 991–992, aff'd, (9th Cir. 1981) 657 F2.d 1017.

26. Mike Phillips, who oversees Patients' Rights Advocates in San Diego, told me in 2022 that hearing officers ruled in favor of keeping patients in the hospital around 85 or 90 percent of the time.

27. Previous research also found that psychiatrists in LPS hearings (in this case, when a patient filed a writ) sometimes delivered testimony in favor of their release. This was particularly common for private hospitals. Carol Warren, *The Court of Last Resort* (Chicago: University of Chicago Press, 1982), 14.

28. As evidence of the backlog, the number of days adults in San Diego on Medi-Cal spent waiting in hospitals for step-down beds increased 48 percent from 2020 to 2021. Lisa Halverstadt, "New Mandate Could Further Stress San Diego's Clogged Behavioral Health System," *Voice of San Diego*, September 21, 2022, https://voiceofsandiego.org/2022/09/21/new-mandate-could-further-stress-san-diegos-clogged-behavioral-health-system/.

29. Department of Health Care Services, "California Code of Regulations: 1820.205. Medical Necessity Criteria for Reimbursement of Psychiatric Inpatient Hospital Services," accessed November 8, 2022, https://www.dhcs.ca.gov/formsandpubs/MHArchives/InfoNotice01-attachment.pdf.

30. The average statewide rate for acute psychiatric hospitalization for Medi-Cal patients is $888 a day, going up to $1575 in the Bay Area. Department of Health Care Services, "Medi-Cal Psychiatric Inpatient Hospital Services Non-Negotiated Rates," July 1, 2021, https://www.dhcs.ca.gov/formsandpubs/Documents/BHIN-21-064-Regional-Rates-Enclosure.pdf. The administrative rate, increased significantly in the pandemic, is $693. Department of Health Care Services, "Administrative Day Rate Level 1," accessed November 8, 2022, https://www.dhcs.ca.gov/services/medi-cal/Pages/Administrative-Day-Rate-Level-1.aspx.

31. Department of Health Care Services, "California Designated LPS Facilities," May 2020, https://www.dhcs.ca.gov/Documents/LPS-24hr.pdf.

32. Los Angeles County Department of Mental Health, "Annual Report to the Board for Expanding LPS Conservatorship," January 26, 2021.

33. For example, nearly 40 percent of adults discharged from private hospitals in Los Angeles returned to the hospital within thirty days, versus 20 percent in county hospitals. Mercer Health and Benefits LLC, "Countywide Mental Health and Substance Use Disorder Needs Assessment" (Los Angeles: Los Angeles County Health Agency, August 15, 2019), 6, https://file.lacounty.gov/SDSInter/bos/supdocs/142264.pdf.

34. San Francisco Budget and Legislative Analyst, "Review of Lanterman-Petris-Short (LPS) Conservatorship in San Francisco" (San Francisco, July 30, 2019), A-15. The figures from Los Angeles are similar: 75 percent of bed-days in county hospitals were not being paid the full acute rate. LA DMH, "Report Response to Addressing the Shortage of Mental Health Hospital Beds" (Los Angeles, October 29, 2019), 17–18.

35. This is evident in the greater length of stay at county hospitals, which in Los Angeles was twenty-two days versus seven for private fee-for-service hospitals. Mercer, "Countywide Needs Assessment," 61.

36. Private doctors who bill for each patient they see might also be less willing to spend a half-day in court waiting to testify, vis-à-vis salaried county physicians who testify full-time. Julie Marquis and Dan Morain, "The Broken Contract: Rights of Mentally Ill Pitted Against Public, Patient Safety," *Los Angeles Times*, November 23, 1999.

37. Research shows that having more private psychiatric hospitals is associated with homelessness and incarceration in the areas they serve, unlike public hospitals. Jangho Yoon, "Effect of Increased Private Share of Inpatient Psychiatric Resources on Jail Population Growth: Evidence from the United States," *Social Science & Medicine* 72, no. 4 (2011): 448; Fred E. Markowitz, "Psychiatric Hospital Capacity, Homelessness, and Crime and Arrest Rates," *Criminology* 44, no. 1 (2006): 45–72.

38. Over time, counties have threatened to remove LPS designation for other reasons. Los Angeles went after one hospital that discharged people to unlicensed board and care facilities where five people died, while San Diego threatened a hospital that left people in physical restraints for days at a time. Rex Dalton, "Tri-City Hospital Cited for Psychiatric Violations," *San Diego Union-Tribune*, August 29, 1993; Charles Ornstein, "Five Residents Die at Unlicensed Care Home That County Tried to Close," *Los Angeles Times*, August 29, 2002.

39. Inland Valley Daily Bulletin, "Psychiatric Center Stops Adolescent Program," April 6, 2004; Cindy Carcamo, "Fewer Beds for Mentally Ill," *Orange County Register*, August 12, 2008.

40. Jeffrey Guhin, *Agents of God: Boundaries and Authority in Muslim and Christian Schools* (New York: Oxford University Press, 2021).

41. Gail Evanguelidi, a family member and advocate in Los Angeles, told me in 2020 that Los Angeles used to require that a person have at least three inpatient hospitalizations.

42. Michael Oliver, *The Politics of Disablement: A Sociological Approach* (London: Palgrave Macmillan, 1990).

43. LA DMH, "Report Response," 12.

44. LA DMH, "Report Response," 22.

45. LA DMH, "Report Response," 14.

46. LA DMH, "Report Response," 10. A recent report out of San Diego similarly concluded that 40 percent of inpatient admissions could be avoided with an appropriate array of alternative crisis responses. Behavioral Health Services, "Optimal Care Pathways Model" (San Diego County, CA: Board of Supervisors, September 27, 2022), https://bosagenda .sandiegocounty.gov/cob/cosd/cob/doc?id=0901127e80f13b6a.

5. PUBLIC GUARDIAN

1. California Hospital Association, "California's Acute Psychiatric Bed Loss" (Sacramento, CA, February 2019), https://www.calhospital.org/sites/main/files/file-attachments/6 _-_psychbeddata.pdf, 6.

2. Robert Castel, *La gestion des risques: de l'anti-psychiatrie à l'après-psychanalyse* (Paris: Minuit, 1981); Michel Foucault, "L'évolution de la notion d''individu dangereux' dans la psychiatrie légale," *Déviance et société* 5, no. 4 (1981): 403–22; Nikolas Rose, "Governing Risky Individuals: The Role of Psychiatry in New Regimes of Control," *Psychiatry, Psychology and Law* 5, no. 2 (1998): 177–95.

3. Subcommittee on Mental Health, "The Dilemma of Mental Commitments in California" (Sacramento: California State Legislature, 1966), 20.

4. Subcommittee on Mental Health, "The Dilemma of Mental Commitments," 138.

5. ENKI Research Institute, *A Study of California's New Mental Health Law (1969–1971)* (Chatsworth, CA: Author, 1972), 166.

6. Grant H. Morris, "Conservatorship for the 'Gravely Disabled': California's Nondeclaration of Nonindependence," *International Journal of Law and Psychiatry* 1 (1978): 405; Mental Health and Substance Use Disorder Services Division, "California Involuntary Detention Report Summary (FY 1990–2000)" (Sacramento, CA: Department of Health Care Services, 2001).

7. Richard H. Lamb and Linda E. Weinberger, "Conservatorship for Gravely Disabled Psychiatric Patients: A Four-Year Follow-Up Study," *American Journal of Psychiatry*, no. 149 (1992): 909–13; S. L. Reynolds and K. H. Wilber, "Protecting Persons with Severe Cognitive and Mental Disorders: An Analysis of Public Conservatorship in Los Angeles County, California," *Aging & Mental Health* 1, no. 1 (1997): 87–98; John L. Young, Mark J. Mills, and Robert L. Sack, "Civil Commitment by Conservatorship: The Workings of California's Law," *Bulletin of the American Academy of Psychiatry and the Law* 15, no. 2 (1987): 127–39.

8. Lamb and Weinberger, "Conservatorship," 909.

9. Morris, "Conservatorship for the 'Gravely Disabled,'" 406.
10. Robert Embry, "The Ordeal of Total Power," *Los Angeles Times*, September 3, 1972.
11. Legislative Analyst's Office, "Overview of Funding for the Lanterman-Petris-Short Act" (Sacramento, CA, December 15, 2021), 5. The state does provide one million dollars per year for the CAPAPGPC to train and certify guardians.
12. This characterization was made to me by Kim Lewis of the National Health Law Project. A 2008 audit, for example, described DMH's review of county plans under MHSA as "inefficient" and "ineffective." It had "not provided adequate or consistent guidance to counties, which reflects poorly on the competency of DMH staff." Office of State Audits and Evaluations, "Final Report: California Department of Mental Health, Mental Health Services Act Performance Audit" (Sacramento, CA: Department of Finance, June 2008), 10.
13. It is also frustrating for providers, who face different rules around the release of information, consent to medical procedures, or contact with families based on the county from which a conservatee comes. See Psynergy, "LPS Hearing Comments," December 14, 2021, https://ajud.assembly.ca.gov/sites/ajud.assembly.ca.gov/files/Psynergy%20Programs.pdf.
14. This point has been made in myriad grand jury reports on the functioning of guardians' offices statewide. Alameda County Grand Jury, "Final Report," 2021–2022, 18, https://grandjury.acgov.org/grandjury-assets/docs/2021-2022/Grand.Jury.Report.2022.for.ITD.Web.pdf; Contra Costa County Grand Jury, "Caring for Those Who Can No Longer Care for Themselves" (Martinez, CA, May 26, 2015); Humboldt County Grand Jury, "BeHOLD: The Department of Mental Health's Management of the Public Guardian Office and Patients' Rights Advocate" (Humboldt, CA, 2020), https://humboldtgov.org/DocumentCenter/View/87426/BeHOLD---The-Dept-of-Mental-Healths-Mgmt-of-the-Public-Guardian-Office-and-Patients-Rights-Advocate; Orange County Grand Jury, "Changing of the Guardian: Life After the Reorganization of the PA and PG Offices" (Orange County, CA, 2016), https://www.ocgrandjury.org/pdfs/2015_2016_GJreport/2016-05-23_Website_Report.pdf.
15. Mike A'Dair, "More County Service Cuts on the Way," *Willits News*, March 17, 2004.
16. This tenfold variation is only between larger counties. San Francisco Budget and Legislative Analyst, "Review of Lanterman-Petris-Short (LPS) Conservatorship in San Francisco" (San Francisco, CA, January 10, 2022), 31, http://file.lacounty.gov/SDSInter/bos/supdocs/116143.pdf. An analysis from Humboldt County of small-to-medium counties found eightfold differences. Humboldt County Grand Jury, "BeHOLD."
17. In Santa Clara County (which contains San Jose), the average stay in LPS conservatorship is eight to ten years. Public Administrator-Guardian-Conservator, "Annual Report" (Santa Clara County, CA: Department of Aging and Adult Services, 2021), 11, https://socialservices.sccgov.org/sites/g/files/exjcpb701/files/documents/PAGC-Annual-Report-2021.pdf.
18. Some counties have implemented a thirty-day 5270 hold after a 5250; in those counties, a temporary conservatorship would start after forty-seven days of hospitalization.
19. Some counties call the agency overseeing LPS conservatorships the Office of the Public Conservator, to differentiate them from the Office of the Public Guardian (overseeing probate conservatorships). For simplicity, I typically use Office of the Public Guardian for both.

20. Although I did not ask for Rippee's consent, his case has been so extensively reported that protecting his anonymity is not possible. As for Mark's own perspective, he told reporter Jocelyn Wiener, "I don't need to be in a locked-up facility. It was like I was a hostage." Jocelyn Wiener, "'We've Lost Our Compass.' For California's Most Visible Mentally Ill, Is a Return to Forced Treatment a Solution—or a False Promise?," *CalMatters*, December 30, 2019, https://calmatters.org/projects/mentally-ill-forced-treatment -conservatorship-california-debate/.

21. There are other technicalities that can justify a denial of conservatorship for people with a Mark Rippee–level of vulnerability. Ashlynn Miles had been hospitalized fifty times, been raped twelve times, attempted suicide eight times, and been stabbed and beaten over the course of four years before being admitted to a psychiatric health facility in San Luis Obispo. The hospital applied for a conservatorship, but the public guardian denied the application claiming they lacked records from a hospitalization in Nevada, where Ashlynn had attempted to kidnap a child thinking it was her own. She was discharged to a homeless shelter, despite having been previously banned by shelters for violence. Within seventy-two hours, she was found in the back of a truck driven by a registered sex offender in Arizona. The hospital in California would not accept a transfer, so she would be released to the streets. Sara Kassabian, "Paso Woman Picked Up by Sex Offender Has Been Hospitalized More than 50 Times in 4 Years," *San Luis Obispo Tribune*, September 30, 2022, https://www.sanluisobispo.com/news/local/article265797411.html.

22. For a discussion of the debates over when dementia qualifies for LPS, see Department of Auditor-Controller, "Management Audit of the Department of Mental Health—Office of the Public Guardian" (Los Angeles: County of Los Angeles, May 11, 2005), 44.

23. In another high-profile case, Abraham Siliezar was found dead in a San Francisco park after his family spent years trying to get him conserved for a combination of PTSD, alcoholism, and a traumatic brain injury. Mallory Moench, "A Struggling Veteran Was Found Dead in an S.F. Park Ravine. Could Conservatorship Have Helped Prevent His Death?," *San Francisco Chronicle*, October 21, 2021, https://www.sfchronicle.com/bayarea /article/A-struggling-veteran-was-found-in-a-Lands-End-16546952.php.

24. A RAND study also found that facilities reported a consistent inability to place individuals with dementia or traumatic brain injuries. Ryan McBain et al., "Adult Psychiatric Bed Capacity, Need, and Shortage Estimates in California—2021" (Santa Monica, CA: Rand Corporation, 2022), 4, https://www.rand.org/pubs/research_reports/RRA1824-1-v2.html.

25. Solano's head of Social Services gave precisely this explanation when asked about Mark's case. Wiener, "'We've Lost Our Compass.'"

26. California WIC, Section 5350(e)(1), https://leginfo.legislature.ca.gov/faces/codes_display Section.xhtml?sectionNum=5350.

27. Deborah A. Stone, *The Disabled State* (Philadelphia: Temple University Press, 1984), 4.

28. California WIC, Section 5352, https://leginfo.legislature.ca.gov/faces/codes_displaySection .xhtml?lawCode=WIC&sectionNum=5352.

29. See, also, Nathaniel P. Morris and Renée L. Binder, "Grave Disability in U.S. Jails and Prisons," *Psychiatric Services* 73, no. 5 (2022): 577–79.

30. David Sjostedt, "In SF and Across California, People with Severe Mental Illness Languish Untreated in Jails, Hospitals," *SF Standard*, October 4, 2022, https://sfstandard

.com/public-health/under-conservatorships-sf-mental-health-patients-languish-in-jails
-hospitals-awaiting-care/.

31. California Assembly Bill 1810, Chapter 2.8A: Diversion of Individuals with Mental Disorders,
https://leginfo.legislature.ca.gov/faces/billTextClient.xhtml?bill_id=201720180AB1810.
Such individuals can also be offered voluntary diversion programs or assisted outpatient
treatment.

32. See also Katherine Warburton et al., "A Survey of National Trends in Psychiatric
Patients Found Incompetent to Stand Trial: Reasons for the Reinstitutionalization of
People with Serious Mental Illness in the United States," *CNS Spectrums* 25, no. 2 (2020):
245–51.

33. Another pathway, called a Murphy conservatorship, applies to people who are not
gravely disabled but are charged with violent felonies for which they cannot stand trial.
Joseph R. Simpson, "When Restoration Fails: One State's Answer to the Dilemma of
Permanent Incompetence," *Journal of the American Academy of Psychiatry and the Law* 44,
no. 2 (2016): 171–79.

34. California Senate Bill 317, Competence to Stand Trial, https://leginfo.legislature.ca.gov
/faces/billNavClient.xhtml?bill_id=202120220SB317.

35. Armando Lara-Millán, "States as a Series of People Exchanges," in *The Many Hands of the
State: Theorizing Political Authority and Social Control*, ed. Kimberly J. Morgan and Ann
Shola Orloff (New York: Cambridge University Press, 2017), 82.

36. California WIC, 5358(a)(1)(A), https://leginfo.legislature.ca.gov/faces/codes_displaySection
.xhtml?lawCode=WIC&sectionNum=5358.

37. Gøsta Esping-Andersen, *The Three Worlds of Welfare Capitalism* (Princeton, NJ: Princeton
University Press, 1990), 61.

38. SF BLA, "Review of LPS Conservatorship," July 30, 2019; Abby Sewell, "The Ordeal of
His Illness," *Los Angeles Times*, April 13, 2015; Los Angeles County Department of Mental Health, "Annual Report to the Board for Expanding Lanterman-Petris-Short and
Probate Conservatorship Capacity" (Los Angeles, January 26, 2021). San Diego appears
to be a large-county exception, filing on 53 percent of referrals in fiscal year 2020–2021.
Jennifer Bowman, "More San Diegans Could Enter Mental Health Conservatorships. But
the System Is Already Struggling," *INewSource*, September 19, 2022, https://inewsource
.org/2022/09/19/california-lps-conservatorships-mental-illness-homeless-crisis/.

6. COURT

1. Paul Starr, *The Social Transformation of American Medicine: The Rise of a Sovereign Profession
and the Making of a Vast Industry* (New York: Basic Books, 1982), 13.

2. *People v. Sanchez* (2016), 63 Cal. 4th 665.

3. Prior to LPS, California's commitment standard was that a person be "of such mental
condition that they are in need of supervision, treatment, care or restraint." Subcommittee on Mental Health, "The Dilemma of Mental Commitments in California" (Sacramento: California State Legislature, 1966), 6.

4. Robert A. Kagan, *Adversarial Legalism: The American Way of Law* (Cambridge, MA: Harvard University Press, 2003).

5. Meta S. David, "Legal Guardianship of Individuals Incapacitated by Mental Illness: Where Do We Draw the Line?," *Suffolk University Law Review* 45, no. 2 (2012): 482.

6. My understanding of LPS hearings has benefited significantly from the assistance of Morgan Smythe, whose website is a wealth of information on case law and legal procedures. See https://www.lpsconservatorship.com/.

7. "Hearing: Dilemma of Mental Commitments in California" (Sacramento, CA, January 18, 1966), 14–15.

8. Disability theorists, for their part, have argued that different forms of incarceration are all common "manifestations of a centuries' old process of segregating and isolating those individuals deemed unworthy and incapable of full participation in society." Michael Rembis, "The New Asylums: Madness and Mass Incarceration in the Neoliberal Era," in *Disability Incarcerated*, ed. Liat Ben-Moshe, Chris Chapman, and Allison C. Carey (New York: Palgrave Macmillan, 2014), 144.

9. *Doe v. Gallinot* (C.D.Cal. 1979) 486 F.Supp. 983, 991–992, aff'd (9th Cir. 1981) 657 F2.d 1017.

10. Hannah Arendt, *The Origins of Totalitarianism* (San Diego, CA: Harcourt, Brace, Jovanovich, 1973), 296.

11. This point has been made specifically in the case of people with disabilities by Allison C. Carey, *On the Margins of Citizenship: Intellectual Disability and Civil Rights in Twentieth-Century America* (Philadelphia: Temple University Press, 2009); David M. Engel and Frank W. Munger, *Rights of Inclusion: Law and Identity in the Life Stories of Americans with Disabilities* (Chicago: University of Chicago Press, 2003).

12. Sheila Shea, "The Mental Hygiene Legal Service at 50: A Retrospective and Prospective Examination of Advocacy for People with Mental Disabilities," *Government, Law, and Policy Journal* 14, no. 2 (2012): 35–41.

13. The Treatment Advocacy Center, which advocates for expanding involuntary treatment, gives New York's laws a grade of "C" while California gets a "D-," suggesting that patients have more protections from forced treatment in the latter. Treatment Advocacy Center, "Grading the States: An Analysis of Involuntary Psychiatric Treatment Laws" (Arlington, VA, September 2020), 5, https://www.treatmentadvocacycenter.org/storage/documents/grading-the-states.pdf.

14. A review of the available literature concluded, "Empirical surveys are consistent. The quality of counsel remains the single most important factor in the disposition of cases in involuntary civil commitment." Michael L. Perlin, "Fatal Assumption: A Critical Evaluation of the Role of Counsel in Mental Disability Cases," *Law and Human Behavior* 16, no. 1 (1992): 49.

15. Sheryl Stolberg, "Where Patients Fight for Dignity," *Los Angeles Times*, August 24, 1992.

16. Natalie Wolf, "The Ethical Dilemmas Faced by Attorneys Representing the Mentally Ill in Civil Commitment Proceedings," *Georgetown Journal of Legal Ethics* 6 (1992): 175.

17. James A. Holstein, *Court-Ordered Insanity: Interpretive Practice and Involuntary Commitment* (New York: Transaction, 1993), 48.

18. Morgan Smythe, an expert in LPS law, said that these "submittals" affect a patient's right to have rights because they may lose their opportunity to later appeal the case.

19. Grant H. Morris, "Let's Do the Time Warp Again: Assessing the Competence of Counsel in Mental Health Conservatorship Proceedings," *San Diego Law Review* 46 (2009): 317.

Statistics from other states also show that between 10 and 20 percent of involuntary patients affirmatively file for their release. Dinah Miller and Annette Hanson, *Committed: The Battle Over Involuntary Psychiatric Care* (Baltimore: Johns Hopkins University Press, 2016), 64; Shea, "MHLS at 50," 38.

20.   The techniques lawyers use to pressure clients to agree to involuntary treatment is well documented in Dan A. Lewis et al., "The Negotiation of Involuntary Civil Commitment," *Law & Society Review* 18, no. 4 (1984): 629–49.

21.   *Conservatorship of Benevuto* (1986) 180 Cal.App.3d 1030.

22.   *Conservatorship of Chambers* (1977) 71 Cal.App.3d 277, 284 [139 Cal.Rptr. 357].

23.   Data from San Diego show that 85 percent of petitions are granted by the court. Jennifer Bowman, "More San Diegans Could Enter Mental Health Conservatorships. But the System Is Already Struggling," *INewSource*, September 19, 2022, https://inewsource .org/2022/09/19/california-lps-conservatorships-mental-illness-homeless-crisis/.

24.   Harold Garfinkel, "Conditions of Successful Degradation Ceremonies," *American Journal of Sociology* 61, no. 5 (1956): 421.

25.   In Los Angeles, 20 percent of conservatorships were dropped because of doctor no-shows at hearings. California State Auditor, "Lanterman-Petris-Short Act: California Has Not Ensured That Individuals with Serious Mental Illnesses Receive Adequate Ongoing Care" (Sacramento, CA, July 2020), 31.

7. LOCKED IN

1.   In one MHRC in Los Angeles, 86 percent of residents had "past serious violence against persons." Richard H. Lamb and Linda E. Weinberger, "One-Year Follow-Up of Persons Discharged from a Locked Intermediate Care Facility," *Psychiatric Services* 56, no. 2 (2005): 198–201.

2.   Kristen R. Choi et al., "Mental Health Conservatorship Among Homeless People with Serious Mental Illness," *Psychiatric Services* 73, no. 6 (2022): 613–19.

3.   *Conservatorship of Roulet* (1979) 23 Cal.3d 219, 223.

4.   Department of State Hospitals, "2021–22 May Revision Budget Estimate" (Sacramento, CA, May 14, 2021), https://www.dsh.ca.gov/About_Us/docs/FY_2020-21_DSH_May_Revision _Estimate.pdf.

5.   Internal data provided to the author by the Department of State Hospitals.

6.   Doris A. Fuller et al., "Going, Going, Gone: Trends and Consequences of Eliminating State Psychiatric Beds, 2016" (Treatment Advocacy Center, June 2016), 14. Although Fuller puts California as having the fourteenth-most beds per capita in 2016, the state's reported number of patients in 2022 is significantly larger and would put it in fourth place, assuming the number of patients in other states has not increased.

7.   Fuller et al., "Going, Going, Gone," 19.

8.   Some large counties, such as San Diego, now have no LPS patients in state hospitals (although as of 2022 they had thirty-six clients awaiting a bed). Behavioral Health Services, "Optimal Care Pathways Model" (San Diego County, CA: Board of Supervisors, September 27, 2022), 13, https://bosagenda.sandiegocounty.gov/cob/cosd/cob/doc?id =0901127e80f13b6a.

9. Until recently, state hospitals were the only place where "restoration" treatment was possible. Local jails can now provide this treatment, while misdemeanor IST cases are now being referred to diversion programs, AOT, or conservatorship (see chapter 5).

10. Incompetent to Stand Trial Workgroup, "Report of Recommended Solutions" (Department of Health and Human Services, November 2021), 9, https://www.chhs.ca.gov/wp-content/uploads/2021/12/IST_Solutions_Report_Final_v2.pdf.

11. Katherine Warburton et al., "A Survey of National Trends in Psychiatric Patients Found Incompetent to Stand Trial: Reasons for the Reinstitutionalization of People with Serious Mental Illness in the United States," *CNS Spectrums* 25, no. 2 (2020): 248.

12. County Behavioral Health Directors' Association, "RE: May Revision Proposal to Discontinue Lanterman-Petris-Short Department of State Hospital Contracts with Counties—OPPOSE," May 25, 2021, http://64.166.146.245/docs/2021/MXCAB/20210714_1853/46329_LPS%20State%20Hospital%20Contract%20Discontinuation_%20Oppose_%205.25.21_Final%20%281%29.pdf.

13. *Stiavetti v. Clendenin* (June 15, 2021, A157553). Cal.App.5th.

14. California State Auditor, "Lanterman-Petris-Short Act: California Has Not Ensured That Individuals with Serious Mental Illnesses Receive Adequate Ongoing Care" (Sacramento, CA, July 2020), 22.

15. This vision was most thoroughly fleshed out in a "master plan" devised by stakeholders in the mental health system in the late 1970s. Areta Crowell, "A Model for California: Community Mental Health Programs" (Sacramento, CA: Mental Health Association of California, 1981).

16. U.S. Code, 42 U.S.C. §1396d, uscode.house.gov/view.xhtml?req=(title:42%20section:1396d%20edition:prelim.

17. Stephen Eide and Carolyn D. Gorman, "Medicaid's IMD Exclusion: The Case for Repeal" (Manhattan Institute, February 2021), https://www.manhattan-institute.org/medicaids-imd-exclusion-case-repeal.

18. Isabel M Perera, "States of Mind: A Comparative and Historical Study on the Political Economy of Mental Health" (Philadelphia: University of Pennsylvania, 2018), https://repository.upenn.edu/dissertations/AAI10978250.

19. I am grateful to Steve Fields from the Progress Foundation and Lucille Lyon from the LA Office of the Public Guardian for recounting this (seemingly unwritten) history to me.

20. As a 1980 federal report observed, the IMD exclusion "has led to younger persons being misdiagnosed in order to be admitted to traditional nursing homes, where there are little or no mental health services." Steering Committee on the Chronically Mentally Ill, "Toward a National Plan for the Chronically Mentally Ill" (Rockville, MD: U.S. Department of Health and Human Services, December 1980), 1–5.

21. Legislative Analyst's Office, "Reforming California's Mental Health System" (Sacramento, CA, March 26, 1991), 5.

22. Dan Morain, "Leaving State Hospitals Sent Many Into Psychotic Abyss," *Los Angeles Times*, November 22, 1999.

23. Ben Kane et al., "California County Spending on 24-Hour Behavioral Care" (Berkeley, CA: Goldman School of Public Policy, April 2018).

24. Department of Health Care Services. "Facilities and Programs Defined as Institutions for Mental Disease—2022 Q4." https://www.dhcs.ca.gov/services/MH/Documents/Qtr -4-2022-IMD.pdf; CHHS Open Data, data.chhs.ca.gov/dataset/licensed-mental-health -rehabilitation-centers-mhrc-and-psychiatric-health-facilities-phf.

25. In 1996, San Francisco opened an MHRC but wouldn't staff it because unionized public employees would cost two million dollars a year more than private ones. Clarence Johnson, "S.F. Supervisor Unhappy with Empty Hospital," *San Francisco Chronicle*, February 2, 1996. In 2001, an MHRC in Fresno that had been successful in returning patients to the community closed because its operating costs were "two to three times more than similar private programs." Jim Davis, "Rehab Center's Future Unsure," *Fresno Bee*, September 9, 2001.

26. "Mental Health Misers," *Mercury News*, July 3, 1985.

27. Internal data provided to the author in January 2021.

28. Mercer Health and Benefits LLC, "Countywide Mental Health and Substance Use Disorder Needs Assessment" (Los Angeles: Los Angeles County Health Agency, August 15, 2019), 16, https://file.lacounty.gov/SDSInter/bos/supdocs/142264.pdf.

29. San Francisco Board of Supervisors Budget and Legislative Analyst (SF BLA), "Review of LPS Conservatorship," January 10, 2022, iv; Los Angeles County Department of Mental Health, "Annual Report to the Board for Expanding Lanterman-Petris-Short and Probate Conservatorship Capacity" (Los Angeles, February 14, 2022), 4.

30. San Francisco Department of Public Health, "Behavioral Health Bed Optimization Project: Analysis and Recommendations for Improving Patient Flow" (San Francisco, June 2020), 6; see also Mercer, "Countywide Needs Assessment," 109.

31. This term is from Teresa Pasquini and Lauren Rettagliata, "Housing That Heals: A Search for a Place Like Home for Families Like Ours," May 2020, https://hth.ttinet.com /Housing_That_Heals_2020.pdf.

32. For example, in 2021 one-third of California's patients at the subacute level met criteria for discharge but were waiting for step-down to a lower level of care. Ryan McBain et al., "Adult Psychiatric Bed Capacity, Need, and Shortage Estimates in California—2021" (Santa Monica, CA: Rand Corporation, 2022), 17, https://www.rand.org/pubs/research _reports/RRA1824-1-v2.html.

33. There are at least some cases on which this legal advocacy seems to have had an impact. In September 2019, a San Francisco public defender quizzed the placement coordinator from the Department of Public Health as to why his client had skipped ten places on the waitlist to get from jail into an IMD. "To get him out before this hearing, so we wouldn't have to appear," the coordinator replied. Joe Eskenazi, "Breaking: SF Health Dept. Allowed Mental Patient to Skip Waitlist for Psych Facility—Solely to Avoid Legal Scrutiny," *Mission Local*, September 25, 2019, https://missionlocal.org/2019/09/breaking -sf-health-dept-allowed-mental-patient-to-skip-waitlist-for-psych-facility-solely-to -avoid-legal-scrutiny/.

34. SF BLA, "Review of LPS Conservatorship," July 30, 2019, 7.

35. Los Angeles County Department of Mental Health, "Report Response to Addressing the Shortage of Mental Health Hospital Beds" (Los Angeles, October 29, 2019), 19–20.

36.   The only evaluation study I could find reported that, in the year after discharge from an IMD, more than half of individuals spent at least ninety days in a hospital, jail, or another IMD, suggesting that the stabilizing effects of an IMD stay were not enduring. Lamb and Weinberger, "One-Year Follow-Up."

8. STEPPED DOWN

1.   Eide argues that the declining availability of "low-quality" housing like SROs or board and cares is a key driver of the contemporary crisis of chronic homelessness. Stephen Eide, *Homelessness in America: The History and Tragedy of an Intractable Social Problem* (Lanham, MD: Rowman & Littlefield, 2022), 25.

2.   A journalist recently uncovered one revealing example of how some operators view their clients: five residential facilities in Southern California are owned by Meshuga Operations Holdings LLC. "Meshuga" is the Yiddish word for "crazy." Thomas Curwen, "A World Gone Mad: Schizophrenia and a Journey through California's Failed Mental Health System," *Los Angeles Times*, December 8, 2022, https://www.latimes.com/california/story/2022-12-08/young-mans-life-with-schizophrenia.

3.   Richard H. Lamb and Linda E. Weinberger, "Conservatorship for Gravely Disabled Psychiatric Patients: A Four-Year Follow-Up Study," *American Journal of Psychiatry*, no. 149 (1992): 909.

4.   After LPS, "tens of thousands of patients from the big asylums streamed out across the state, overwhelming the unprepared county and private treatment agencies and flooding the streets and the criminal justice system." Ron Powers, *No One Cares About Crazy People: The Chaos and Heartbreak of Mental Health in America* (New York: Hachette, 2017), 194. Deinstitutionalization was an "unplanned social disaster." Pete Earley, *Crazy: A Father's Search Through America's Mental Health Madness* (New York: Putnam, 2006), 71. The "most massive movement of medical care in twentieth-century America" had "no master plan, no coordination, no corrective mechanism, no authority, no one in charge." E. Fuller Torrey, *American Psychosis: How the Federal Government Destroyed the Mental Illness Treatment System* (Oxford: Oxford University Press, 2013), 94.

5.   James T. Barter, "California: Transformation of Mental Health Care: 1957–1982," *New Directions for Mental Health Services* 1983, no. 18 (1983): 10,.

6.   "Dozens of Children and Adults Looking for 'Half-Way' Homes," *Los Angeles Times*, October 20, 1968.

7.   Eugene Bardach, *The Implementation Game: What Happens After a Bill Becomes a Law* (Cambridge, MA: MIT Press, 1977), 161.

8.   Andrew Scull, "A New Trade in Lunacy: The Recommodification of the Mental Patient," *American Behavioral Scientist* 24, no. 6 (1981): 747.

9.   Steven P. Segal, Jim Baumohl, and Edwin W. Moyles, "Neighborhood Types and Community Reaction to the Mentally Ill: A Paradox of Intensity," *Journal of Health and Social Behavior* 21, no. 4 (1980): 345–59.

10.   Robert M. Emerson, E. Burke Rochford, and Linda L. Shaw, "Economics and Enterprise in Board and Care Homes for the Mentally Ill," *American Behavioral Scientist* 24, no. 6 (1981): 771–85.

11. Doug Shuit, "Board and Care: A New Approach to Mental Illness," *Los Angeles Times*, May 13, 1972.

12. Andrew Scull, *The Insanity of Place / The Place of Insanity: Essays on the History of Psychiatry* (London: Routledge, 2006), 93.

13. Legislative Analyst, "Overview of the Public Mental Health System in California" (Sacramento, CA, 1984). Other figures put it at 64,000. Teknekron Inc., "Improving California's Mental Health System: Policymaking and Management in the Invisible System" (Berkeley: California Assembly Permanent Subcommittee on Mental Health and Developmental Disabilities, December 1978), 3. The federal government in 1980 estimated that there were at least 300,000 people in such facilities nationally, most of them "substandard, isolating, and a form of 'trans-institutionalization' and continued neglect." Steering Committee on the Chronically Mentally Ill, "Toward a National Plan for the Chronically Mentally Ill" (Rockville, MD: U.S. Department of Health and Human Services, December 1980)," 2–20.

14. Richard H. Lamb and Marjorie B. Edelson, "The Carrott and the Stick: Inducing Local Programs to Serve Long-Term Patients," *Community Mental Health Journal* 12, no. 2 (1976): 139.

15. Bardach, *The Implementation Game*, 161.

16. Paul Jacobs, "Mentally Ill: The Way State Fixes Benefits, They're Lucky If They Are Also Retarded," *Los Angeles Times*, May 19, 1985.

17. Lisa O'Neill, "Home for Mentally Ill May Lose Its License," *Los Angeles Times*, February 24, 1995.

18. Jack Leonard, "State to Revoke Board-Care Home's License," *Los Angeles Times*, January 15, 2005.

19. The absence of state policy is documented in Jonathan Wisner, "No Time to Waste: An Imminent Housing Crisis for People with Serious Mental Illness Living in Adult Residential Facilities" (Los Angeles: Heart Forward, October 2021).

20. Caroline Kelly et al., "A Call to Action: The Precarious State of the Board and Care System Serving Residents Living with Mental Illness in Los Angeles County" (Los Angeles: County Mental Health Commission, January 22, 2018), 7; see also California Mental Health Planning Council, "Adult Residential Facilities (ARFs): Highlighting the Critical Need for Adult Residential Facilities for Adults with Serious Mental Illness in California" (October 2017).

21. Los Angeles County Department of Mental Health, "Addressing the Ongoing Board and Care Crisis" (Los Angeles, March 4, 2022), 14, https://file.lacounty.gov/SDSInter /bos/supdocs/141894.pdf. In San Diego, 146 of 781 licensed ARFs have closed since 2017. Behavioral Health Services, "Optimal Care Pathways Model" (San Diego County, CA: Board of Supervisors, September 27, 2022), 16, https://bosagenda.sandiegocounty.gov /cob/cosd/cob/doc?id=0901127e80f13b6a.

22. Jocelyn Wiener, "Overlooked Mental Health 'Catastrophe': Vanishing Board-and-Care-Homes Leave Residents with Few Options," *CalMatters*, April 15, 2019, https://calmatters .org/articles/board-and-care-homes-closing-in-california-mental-health-crisis/.

23. This shift was reported to me by two individuals who worked as ombudspeople with the state Department of Aging. For additional documentation, see Kelly et al., "A Call to

Action," 4; Doug Smith, "To Stop Adults with Mental Illness from Losing Their Housing, L.A. County May Intervene," *Los Angeles Times*, November 6, 2019, https://www.latimes.com /california/story/2019-11-06/homeless-housing-board-and-care-homes-mental-illness.

24. Residential homes for people with developmental disabilities typically receive between $85 and $150 a day but face much greater state oversight through the Regional Center system.

25. Hector Tobar and Jeff Brazil, "Boarding Home Abductions on the Rise," *Los Angeles Times*, September 16, 1996; Jeff Brazil, "Profiting by Preying on the Poor," *Los Angeles Times*, December 22, 1996.

26. Kelly et al., "A Call to Action," 10.

27. Kelly et al., "A Call to Action," 12.

28. The rate of conservatees is higher—like 90 or 95 percent—for "augmented" board and cares like Psynergy in Morgan Hill, which provides much more intensive services that counties have to pay for directly.

29. California WIC, Section 5358.5, https://leginfo.legislature.ca.gov/faces/codes_displaySection .xhtml?sectionNum=5358.5.

30. Overall, people with schizophrenia who take antipsychotic medications have lower mortality rates than those who do not. However, prolonged use of higher doses may ultimately increase mortality. J. Vermeulen et al., "Antipsychotic Medication and Long-Term Mortality Risk in Patients with Schizophrenia: A Systematic Review and Meta-Analysis," *Psychological Medicine* 47, no. 13 (2017): 2217–28.

31. Informants described a growing Wild West of unlicensed board and care homes (sometimes called room and boards) that lure people by promising that, with a lower rent (closer to five hundred dollars a month), residents can keep more of their SSI check.

32. This phrase is borrowed from Cathy Warner, the Deputy Director of Los Angeles DMH. See Marcia Meldrum, "Interview with Cathy Warner," *UCLA Hope Story Project*, accessed October 28l 2022, https://hpmh.semel.ucla.edu/oral-histories/#1614060063588-5e5e4b79 -62de.

33. Sandra R. Levitsky, *Caring for Our Own: Why There Is No Political Demand for New American Social Welfare Rights* (Oxford: Oxford University Press, 2014).

34. Not all the facilities that closed cater to people with mental illness. Yet, given that payments are higher for other populations potentially living in board and cares (people who are elderly, homeless, or living with developmental disabilities), it seems likely that homes serving people with mental illness made up the lion's share of closures.

35. These reforms are detailed in Los Angeles County Department of Mental Health, "Addressing the Ongoing Board and Care Crisis."

9. NEGLECT AND ABUSE

1. Erving Goffman, *Stigma: Notes on the Management of Spoiled Identity* (Englewood Cliffs, NJ: Prentice Hall, 1963), 3.

2. Esmé Weijun Wang, *The Collected Schizophrenias* (Minneapolis, MN: Graywolf, 2019), 104.

3. "Mental Commitment Abuse," *San Francisco Chronicle*, June 27, 1975. As the first major evaluation of LPS concluded, "the 'gravely disabled' category may have been used as a

catchall for patients the hospital felt it could not hold under the stricter definition [of dangerousness]." ENKI Research Institute, "A Study of California's New Mental Health Law" (Chatsworth, CA, 1972), 155.

4. Teknekron Inc., "Improving California's Mental Health System: Policymaking and Management in the Invisible System" (Berkeley: California Assembly Permanent Subcommittee on Mental Health and Developmental Disabilities, December 1978), 167.

5. Erving Goffman, *Asylums: Essays on the Social Situation of Mental Patients and Other Inmates* (New York: Anchor, 1961), 135.

6. Leigh Fenly, "Gravely Disabled? Court May Stop Man's Career," *San Diego Union*, April 28, 1978.

7. A later article suggested there was quite a bit more to the story. Michael P developed psychosis after taking mescaline; he had two passages through the state hospital before the county made a conservatorship application. In any case, at trial, Michael's psychiatrist testified that his schizophrenia was in remission and that he was no longer gravely disabled; the judge denied the petition. Leigh Fenly, "Court Gives Michael P. a New Lease on Life," *San Diego Union*, May 24, 1978.

8. Leigh Fenly, "Patients Lose Rights, Freedom," *San Diego Union*, April 9, 1978.

9. Richard Neugebauer, "Diagnosis, Guardianship, and Residential Care of the Mentally Ill in Medieval and Early Modern England," *American Journal of Psychiatry* 146, no. 12 (1989): 1581. By contrast to the treatment of "idiots," guardians were expected to maintain "lunatics" at their previous standard of living.

10. Gertrude Bonnin, Charles Fabens, and Matthew Sniffen, "Oklahoma's Poor Rich Indians: An Orgy of Graft and Exploitation of the Five Civilized Tribes—Legalized Robbery" (Philadelphia: Indian Rights Association, 1924), 6.

11. Martha Willman, "County Confiscates Property: 'Dirty Sally' Can't Go Home," *Los Angeles Times*, January 15, 1976.

12. Ronan Farrow and Gia Tolentino, "Britney Spears' Conservatorship Nightmare," *New Yorker*, July 3, 2021, https://www.newyorker.com/news/american-chronicles/britney -spears-conservatorship-nightmare.

13. Heidi Blake and Katie Baker, "Beyond Britney: Abuse, Exploitation, and Death Inside America's Guardianship Industry," *BuzzFeed News*, September 17, 2021, https://www .buzzfeednews.com/article/heidiblake/conservatorship-investigation-free-britney-spears.

14. Robin Fields, Evelyn Larrubia, and Jack Leonard, "Guardians for Profit," *Los Angeles Times*, November 13, 2005.

15. Rachel Aviv, "How the Elderly Lose Their Rights," *New Yorker*, October 2, 2017, https:// www.newyorker.com/magazine/2017/10/09/how-the-elderly-lose-their-rights.

16. There may be a different kind of financial exploitation of LPS conservatees, however. Several public defenders reported that, in their counties, the public guardian takes a significant cut of their clients' meager SSI checks to help finance their office.

17. Adrianna Bagnall and Gil Eyal, "Forever Children and Autonomous Citizens: Comparing the Deinstitutionalizations of Psychiatric Patients and Developmentally Disabled Individuals in the United States," in *Fifty Years After Deinstitutionalization: Mental Illness in Contemporary Communities*, ed. Brea L. Perry (Bingley, UK: Emerald, 2016), 27–61; National Council on Disability, "Turning Rights Into Reality: How Guardianship and

Alternatives Impact the Autonomy of People with Intellectual and Developmental Disabilities," June 10, 2019, 29, https://ncd.gov/publications/2019/turning-rights-into-reality.

18. Robert Perske, "The Dignity of Risk and the Mentally Retarded," *Mental Retardation* 10, no. 1 (1972): 24–27.

19. Neil Gong describes this approach of leaving public mental health clients to deal with the consequences of their actions as "tolerant containment."

20. National Council on Disability, "Beyond Guardianship: Toward Alternatives That Promote Greater Self-Determination," March 22, 2018, 98, https://ncd.gov/publications/2018/beyond-guardianship-toward-alternatives.

21. For more on the public guardians' "trouble performing basic services for their clients, such as shopping for clothes or acquiring a cell phone, in a timely fashion" due to growing caseloads, see Humboldt County Grand Jury, "BeHOLD: The Department of Mental Health's Management of the Public Guardian Office and Patients' Rights Advocate" (Humboldt, CA, 2020), 7, https://humboldtgov.org/DocumentCenter/View/87426/BeHOLD---The-Dept-of-Mental-Healths-Mgmt-of-the-Public-Guardian-Office-and-Patients-Rights-Advocate.

22. João Biehl, *Vita: Life in a Zone of Social Abandonment* (Berkeley: University of California Press, 2013), 4.

23. Michael Lipsky, *Street-Level Bureaucracy: Dilemmas of the Individual in Public Service*, thirtieth anniversary ed. (New York: Russell Sage Foundation, 2010), 181.

24. Department of Auditor-Controller, "Management Audit of the Department of Mental Health—Office of the Public Guardian" (Los Angeles: County of Los Angeles, May 11, 2005), 67.

25. Blake and Baker, "Beyond Britney."

26. As usual, this varies among counties: Sacramento reported that one person lost voting rights from 2014 to 2015, whereas 132 did in Los Angeles. These reports do not specify how many of those individuals were on LPS versus probate conservatorships. Dan Morain, "Stepping Toward Full Voting Rights," *East Bay Times*, August 15, 2015, https://www.eastbaytimes.com/2015/08/17/dan-morain-stepping-toward-full-voting-rights/.

27. The actual efficacy of inpatient hospitalization in preventing suicide, given extraordinary rates of suicide right after discharge, is contested. Erin F. Ward-Ciesielski and Shireen L. Rizvi, "The Potential Iatrogenic Effects of Psychiatric Hospitalization for Suicidal Behavior: A Critical Review and Recommendations for Research," *Clinical Psychology: Science and Practice* 28, no. 1 (2021): 60–71.

28. Soumya Karlamangla, "Their Children Died on a Psych Ward. Was It Preventable?" *Los Angeles Times*, December 1, 2019, https://www.latimes.com/california/story/2019-12-01/psychiatric-hospital-deaths-california. More recently, the characteristics of psychiatric facilities—frequent comorbid medical issues among patients, difficulty enforcing social distancing, and an unwillingness of facilities to transfer patients to open settings—made them particularly vulnerable to COVID. The Department of State Hospitals resisted calls to draw down its census (as many prisons and jails had done), even as fifty-six patients died of the disease. "California Argues Mentally Ill Patients Must Stay Put at State Hospital Despite COVID Outbreak," *Mercury News*, January 11, 2021, https://www.sbsun.com/2021/01/10/state-argues-mentally-ill-patients-must-stay-put-at-patton-state-hospital-despite-covid-outbreak/.

29. Rebecca Kimitch, "Safety Questioned at Long Beach Mental Health Facility," *Inland Valley Daily Bulletin*, September 22, 2013, https://www.dailybulletin.com/2013/09/22/safety-questioned-at-long-beach-mental-health-facility/.

30. A *Los Angeles Times* database found multiple incidents of sexual assaults between patients at John George. Soumya Karlamangla and Iris Lee, "Database of Deaths and Assaults at California Psychiatric Facilities," *Los Angeles Times*, December 1, 2019, https://www.latimes.com/projects/psychiatric-hospital-deaths-incidents-database/.

31. Joshua T. Jordan and Dale E. McNiel, "Perceived Coercion During Admission Into Psychiatric Hospitalization Increases Risk of Suicide Attempts After Discharge," *Suicide and Life-Threatening Behavior* 50, no. 1 (2020): 180–88; Diana Paksarian et al., "Perceived Trauma During Hospitalization and Treatment Participation Among Individuals with Psychotic Disorders," *Psychiatric Services* 65, no. 2 (2014): 266–69.

32. Department of State Hospitals, "Violence Report: 2010–2019," September 2020, 14, https://www.dsh.ca.gov/Publications/Reports_and_Data/docs/DSH_ViolenceReport_2010-2019.pdf.

33. Susan Goldsmith, "The Lunatics Have Taken Over the Asylum," *East Bay Express*, February 18, 2004, https://eastbayexpress.com/the-lunatics-have-taken-over-the-asylum-1/.

34. U.S. Bureau of Labor Statistics, "Psychiatric Technicians and Aides," *Occupational Outlook Handbook*, October 4, 2022, https://www.bls.gov/ooh/healthcare/psychiatric-technicians-and-aides.htm#tab-3.

35. Scott Zeller, Nicole Calma, and Ashley Stone, "Effects of a Dedicated Regional Psychiatric Emergency Service on Boarding of Psychiatric Patients in Area Emergency Departments," *WestJEM* 15, no. 1 (2014): 1–6.

36. U.S. Department of Justice, "Investigation of Alameda County, John George Psychiatric Hospital, and Santa Rita Jail" (Washington, DC: Civil Rights Division, April 22, 2021), 8.

37. Wang, *The Collected Schizophrenias*, 110.

38. B. Christopher Frueh et al., "Patients' Reports of Traumatic or Harmful Experiences Within the Psychiatric Setting," *Psychiatric Services* 56, no. 9 (2005): 1123–33.

39. Vern Pierson, "Hard Truths About Deinstitutionalization, Then and Now," *Press Enterprise*, May 13, 2019, http://www.pe.com/hard-truths-about-deinstitutionalization-then-and-now.

40. Robert Embry, "The Ordeal of Total Power," *Los Angeles Times*, September 3, 1972.

41. Goffman, *Asylums*, 14, 43.

42. Goffman, *Asylums*, 305.

43. Goffman, *Asylums*, 189.

44. Margaret Blenkner et al., "Protective Services for Older People—Findings from the Benjamin Rose Institute Study," 1974, 81–83, quoted in Jennifer L. Wright, "Guardianship for Your Own Good: Improving the Well-Being of Respondents and Wards in the USA," *International Journal of Law and Psychiatry* 33, no. 5 (2010): 350–68.

45. Although it's hard to know if there's a link, in 1971 Governor Reagan—in one of the many moments when he showed his deep concern for people living with mental illness—appointed a union boss who believed a "huge dose of vitamins is the best cure for schizophrenia" to the state mental health council. Apparently, this partisan for mineral cures was the only one on the council who could get the governor on the phone. Harry Nelson, "Union Chief DeSilva Named by Reagan to Mental Health Board," *Los Angeles Times*, March 26, 1971.

46. See Héctor Ramírez, "After Thirty Years the ADA Leaves People with Psychiatric Disabilities Behind," *Disability Visibility Project*, July 19, 2020, https://disabilityvisibility project.com/2020/07/19/after-30-years-the-ada-leaves-people-with-psychiatric-disabilities -behind/.

47. Adult residential facilities (i.e., board and cares) are limited to only 25 percent of their residents over sixty and generally cannot accept clients who are nonambulatory or require nursing care (see California Code of Regulations, Title 22, Division 6, Chapter 6, 85068.4(g)). However, residential care facilities for the elderly, which serve as a board and care equivalent for people over sixty, are barred from serving individuals with "an ongoing behavior, caused by a mental disorder, that would upset the general resident group" (see California Code of Regulations, Title 22, Division 6, Chapter 8, 87455(3)(A)). People over sixty with comorbid medical and mental health needs, then, must in effect either go to a nursing home or die.

48. Goffman, *Asylums*, 15.

49. Arboleda-Flórez argues that the primary "challenges currently facing mental patients in many countries are not individual abuses of freedom or autonomy, but structural and systematic neglect that covers all mental patients as an unprotected social underclass." As I have shown in this chapter, conservatees face both individual abuse and collective abandonment. Julio Arboleda-Flórez, "Mental Illness and Human Rights," *Current Opinion in Psychiatry* 21, no. 5 (2008): 481.

10. STABILIZATION AND RECOVERY

1. Robert Embry, "The Ordeal of Total Power," *Los Angeles Times*, September 3, 1972.

2. Quoted in Jane Jenkins, *Extraordinary Conditions* (Berkeley: University of California Press, 2015), 23.

3. Neil Gong, "Between Tolerant Containment and Concerted Constraint: Managing Madness for the City and the Privileged Family," *American Sociological Review* 84, no. 4 (2019): 664–89.

4. Kristen R. Choi et al., "Mental Health Conservatorship Among Homeless People with Serious Mental Illness," *Psychiatric Services* 73, no. 6 (2022): 613–19; Richard H. Lamb and Linda E. Weinberger, "Conservatorship for Gravely Disabled Psychiatric Patients: A Four-Year Follow-Up Study," *American Journal of Psychiatry*, no. 149 (1992): 909–13; John L. Young, Mark J. Mills, and Robert L. Sack, "Civil Commitment by Conservatorship: The Workings of California's Law," *Bulletin of the American Academy of Psychiatry and the Law* 15, no. 2 (1987): 127–39.

5. Ron Wipond, *Your Consent Is Not Required: The Rise in Psychiatric Detentions, Forced Treatment, and Abusive Guardianships* (Dallas, TX: BenBella, 2023), 169.

6. Erica Wood, Pamela Teaster, and Jeneka Cassidy, "Restoration of Rights in Adult Guardianship" (American Bar Association Commission on Law and Aging, 2017), https://www .americanbar.org/content/dam/aba/administrative/law_aging/restoration%20report .authcheckdam.pdf.

7. San Francisco Budget and Legislative Analyst (SF BLA), "Review of LPS Conservatorship," July 30, 2019, A-10.

8. One of the few studies on the impacts of conservatorship suggests it can reduce hospitalization, arrests, and ER visits precisely through improved care coordination. Eliot Levine et al., "Outcomes of a Care Coordination Guardianship Intervention for Adults with Severe Mental Illness: An Interrupted Time Series Analysis," *Administration and Policy in Mental Health and Mental Health Services Research* 47 (2019): 1–7.

9. California State Auditor, "Lanterman-Petris-Short Act: California Has Not Ensured That Individuals with Serious Mental Illnesses Receive Adequate Ongoing Care" (Sacramento, CA, July 2020), 41.

10. Giorgia Agamben, *Homo Sacer: Sovereign Power and Bare Life*, trans. Daniel Heller-Roazen (Stanford, CA: Stanford University Press, 1998).

11. See also Evi Verbeke et al., "Coercion and Power in Psychiatry: A Qualitative Study with Ex-Patients," *Social Science & Medicine* 223 (2019): 89–96.

12. Nev Jones et al., "Investigating the Impact of Involuntary Psychiatric Hospitalization on Youth and Young Adult Trust and Help-Seeking in Pathways to Care," *Social Psychiatry and Psychiatric Epidemiology* 56 (2021): 2017–27; J. Monahan et al., "Coercion and Commitment: Understanding Involuntary Mental Hospital Admission," *International Journal of Law and Psychiatry* 18, no. 3 (1995): 249–63; Stefan Priebe et al., "Patients' Views and Readmissions One Year After Involuntary Hospitalisation," *British Journal of Psychiatry* 194, no. 1 (2009): 49–54.

13. Bruce J. Winick, "A Therapeutic Jurisprudence Approach to Dealing with Coercion in the Mental Health System," *Psychiatry, Psychology and Law* 15, no. 1 (2008): 25–39.

14. Subcommittee on Mental Health, "The Dilemma of Mental Commitments in California" (Sacramento: California State Legislature, 1966), 135.

15. National Council on Disability, "Beyond Guardianship: Toward Alternatives That Promote Greater Self-Determination," March 22, 2018, 88, https://ncd.gov/publications/2018/beyond-guardianship-toward-alternatives."

16. SF BLA, "Review of LPS Conservatorship," January 10, 2022, 27.

17. Note that this cohort is carefully selected and not representative of the broader population of LPS conservatees. Behavioral Health Care Services, "Serving Individuals Who Are Conserved Through Lanterman-Petris-Short (LPS) Conservatorships" (Alameda County Board of Supervisors: Joint Social Services and Public Protection Committee Meeting, November 29, 2021), 12, http://www.acgov.org/board/bos_calendar/documents/DocsAgendaReg_SSPP/GENERAL%20ADMINISTRATION/Regular%20Calendar/Item_2_LPS_Conservator_11_29_21.pdf.

18. Substance Abuse and Mental Health Services Administration, "Recovery and Recovery Support," September 13, 2022, https://www.samhsa.gov/find-help/recovery.

19. A finding of "permanent" disability is required for receipt of Supplemental Security Income, but not an LPS conservatorship. This quote thus reflects one county's decision about how to use conservatorship, not the law itself.

20. Nora Jacobson and Dianne Greenley, "What Is Recovery? A Conceptual Model and Explication," *Psychiatric Services* 52, no. 4 (2001): 482–85.

21. Psynergy is technically licensed as a board and care (adult residential facility), but its programs are "augmented" by a county "patch" of around $150 a day (on top of patients' society security checks).

22.   U.S. Department of Justice, "Investigation of Alameda County, John George Psychiatric Hospital, and Santa Rita Jail" (Washington, DC: Civil Rights Division, April 22, 2021, 13.

23.   U.S. Department of Justice, "Breaking Down Barriers to Employment of People with Disabilities," October 14, 2015, https://www.justice.gov/archives/opa/blog/breaking-down -barriers-employment-individuals-disabilities.

24.   Neely Laurenzo Myers, "Culture, Stress and Recovery from Schizophrenia: Lessons from the Field for Global Mental Health," *Culture, Medicine, and Psychiatry* 34, no. 3 (2010): 515.

25.   Jenkins, *Extraordinary Conditions*, 68; see also Kerry Michael Dobransky, *Managing Madness in the Community: The Challenge of Contemporary Mental Health Care* (New Brunswick, NJ: Rutgers University Press, 2014).

11. PAVING A NEW PATHWAY

1.   Harder & Co. Community Research, "San Francisco Housing Conservatorship: Preliminary Evaluation Report" (San Francisco, CA, January 2022), 2, https://www.sfdph.org/dph /files/housingconserv/SF_Housing_Conservatorship_Local_Report_Updated_01.20.22.pdf.

2.   Senate Bill 1045, "Conservatorship: Serious Mental Illness and Substance Use Disorders," https://leginfo.legislature.ca.gov/faces/billTextClient.xhtml?bill_id=201720180SB1045.

3.   In San Francisco, the number of locked skilled nursing and mental health rehabilitation center beds dropped 29 percent from 2010 to 2016; 37 percent of unlocked board and care beds disappeared during this period. San Francisco Budget and Legislative Analyst (SF BLA), "Performance Audit of the Department of Public Health Behavioral Health Services" (San Francisco, CA, April 19, 2018), 84.

4.   C. W. Nevius, "Finding Help for Homeless Who Won't Help Themselves," *San Francisco Chronicle*, March 11, 2008.

5.   Heather Knight, "SF Looks to Change Law That Lets Mentally Ill Choose to Stay on Streets," *San Francisco Chronicle*, December 12, 2017, https://www.sfchronicle.com/news /article/SF-looks-to-change-law-that-lets-mentally-ill-12422969.php.

6.   Heather Knight, "A Life on the Sidewalk Ends with a Dignified Death," *San Francisco Chronicle*, February 27, 2018.

7.   Scott Wiener, "Press Release: Senators Wiener and Stern Announce Bill to Expand Conservatorships," February 1, 2018, http://sd11.senate.ca.gov.

8.   Rachel Swan, "SF Will Try New Approach for Conservatorships for the Most Troubled," *San Francisco Chronicle*, May 2, 2018, https://www.sfchronicle.com/politics/article/SF-will -move-mental-health-conservatorships-from-12879660.php.

9.   Editorial Board, "Getting Help to the Homeless," *San Francisco Chronicle*, February 14, 2018.

10.   Andrea M. López, "Necropolitics in the 'Compassionate' City: Care/Brutality in San Francisco," *Medical Anthropology* 39, no. 8 (2020): 761.

11.   Senate Judiciary Committee, "SB 1045: Conservatorship: Chronic Homelessness: Mental Illness and Substance Use Disorders" (Sacramento: California State Legislature, April 9, 2018), 18.

12.   Nuala Sawyer, "Mental Health, Homelessness and Civil Rights: S.F.'s Crisis of Conscience," *SF Weekly*, March 20, 2019, http://www.sfweekly.com/news/mental-health-homelessness -and-civil-rights-s-f-s-crisis-of-conscience/.

13. For example, in one 2019 poll, 89 percent of Californians supported "involuntary commitment of homeless individuals who have severe mental/behavioral issues that may be a danger or harm to themselves or others in the community." California Chamber of Commerce, "The People's Voice: CalChamber's Fifth Annual Survey of California Voter Attitudes," 2019, 26, https://advocacy.calchamber.com/wp-content/uploads/2019/10/ThePeoplesVoicePoll2019.pdf.

14. One review concluded that the majority of studies "failed to detect any significant positive impacts" from compulsory drug treatment. D. Werb et al., "The Effectiveness of Compulsory Drug Treatment: A Systematic Review," *International Journal on Drug Policy* 28 (2016): 7; see also Abhishek Jain, Paul Christopher, and Paul S. Appelbaum, "Civil Commitment for Opioid and Other Substance Use Disorders: Does It Work?," *Psychiatric Services* 69, no. 4 (2018): 374–76.

15. Senate Judiciary Committee, "SB 1045," 16.

16. Sawyer, "Mental Health, Homelessness and Civil Rights."

17. Joshua Sabatini, "Impact of Homeless Conservatorship Plan More Limited Than Expected," *San Francisco Examiner*, February 11, 2019, https://www.sfexaminer.com/news/impact-of-homeless-conservatorship-plan-more-limited-than-expected/.

18. Senate Bill 40, "Conservatorship: Serious Mental Illness and Substance Use Disorders," https://leginfo.legislature.ca.gov/faces/billTextClient.xhtml?bill_id=201920200SB40.

19. Senate Judiciary Committee, "SB 40: Conservatorship: Serious Mental Illness and Substance Use Disorders" (Sacramento: California State Legislature, April 4, 2019).

20. California WIC, Section 5450(b)2, https://leginfo.legislature.ca.gov/faces/billTextClient.xhtml?bill_id=201720180SB1045.

21. Alyssa Jeong Perry, "LA County Gets More Power to Force Severely Mentally Ill Homeless Into Treatment," *LAist*, October 2, 2018, https://laist.com/news/la-county-gets-more-power-to-force-severely-mentally-ill-homeless-into-treatment; Gary Warth, "Homeless Conservatorship Tried," *San Diego Union-Tribune*, November 10, 2019.

22. Los Angeles estimated that 150–180 individuals met the eight-5150s criterion but concluded that these documentation requirements were "very challenging" for a county of its size. Los Angeles County Department of Mental Health, "Disrupting the Cycle of Chronic Homelessness in Los Angeles County" (Los Angeles, January 22, 2020), 9, http://file.lacounty.gov/SDSInter/bos/supdocs/140390.pdf. San Diego declined the program by citing a "disproportionate administrative burden" relative to "very few individuals" who would be directly affected. Helen Robbins-Meyer, "Report Back on Housing Conservatorship: A New Tool for Addressing Serious Mental Illness and Substance Use Disorder" (County of San Diego, November 17, 2020), 3, https://bosagenda.sandiegocounty.gov/cob/cosd/cob/doc?id=0901127e80c3ceed.

23. Chris Herring, "Complaint-Oriented 'Services': Shelters as Tools for Criminalizing Homelessness," *Annals of the American Academy of Political and Social Science* 693, no. 1 (2021): 264–83.

24. Heather Knight, "Breed, Wiener Working to Ease Destructive Behavior on Street," *San Francisco Chronicle*, February 10, 2018, https://www.sfchronicle.com/news/article/Breed-Wiener-working-to-ease-destructive-12597752.php.

25. Sabatini, "Impact of Homeless Conservatorship Plan."

26. One audit found that 5 percent of users of the city's urgent care and emergency services accounted for 52 percent of spending; 90 percent of them had a psychiatric diagnosis. SF BLA, "Performance Audit," vii.

27. Tessa Paoli, "Critics Gather in the Mission to Question Upcoming Vote on Conservatorship," *Mission Local*, February 25, 2019, https://missionlocal.org/2019/02/critics-gather-in-the-mission-to-question-upcoming-vote-on-conservatorship/.

28. Coalition on Homelessness, "Stop the Revolving Door: A Street-Level Framework for a New System," September 2020, 19, https://www.cohsf.org/wp-content/uploads/2020/11/Stop-the-Revolving-1.pdf.

29. Jessica Lehman quoted in Joshua Sabatini, "Mayor Prepared to Compel Treatment for Frequently Detailed Homeless," *San Francisco Examiner*, September 28, 2018, https://www.sfexaminer.com/news/mayor-prepared-to-compel-treatment-for-frequently-detained-homeless/.

30. This statement was made in a hearing on SB 40 before the Senate Judiciary Committee on April 18, 2019.

31. Bay City News Service, "City Adds Dozens of Conservatorship Beds to Help Mentally Ill," *SFGate*, March 6, 2018, https://www.sfgate.com/news/bayarea/article/City-Adds-Dozens-Of-Conservatorship-Beds-To-Help-12731188.php.

32. Trisha Thadani, "Supes Reach Deal on Care for Mentally Ill," *San Francisco Chronicle*, June 4, 2019.

33. "At Issue: Housing Crisis / Homeless 'Conservatorship,'" KPIX 5, March 10, 2019.

34. Harder & Co., "San Francisco Housing Conservatorship," 10.

35. Harder & Co., "San Francisco Housing Conservatorship," 7.

36. Trisha Thadani, "Why SF's New Laws to Force More Mentally Ill, Addicted Into Treatment Haven't Been Used Yet," *San Francisco Chronicle*, June 4, 2020, https://www.sfchronicle.com/politics/article/Why-SF-s-new-laws-to-force-more-mentally-ill-15318574.php.

37. Department of Health Care Services, "California Designated LPS Facilities," May 2020, https://www.dhcs.ca.gov/Documents/LPS-24hr.pdf.

38. California State Auditor, "Lanterman-Petris-Short Act: California Has Not Ensured That Individuals with Serious Mental Illnesses Receive Adequate Ongoing Care" (Sacramento, CA, July 2020), 34; San Francisco Housing Conservatorship Working Group, "SFPD Incident Report Data," October 18, 2021.

39. The bad data informing policy making in San Francisco is appalling. In 2019, a report commissioned by Mandelman declared that San Francisco was "below the statewide average" for conservatorship, basing the conclusion on data from the state. SF BLA, "Review of LPS Conservatorship," July 30, 2019, A-9. When the budget and legislative analyst went back in 2022 and relied on internal data from the public conservator, it turned out that San Francisco had the most permanent conservatorships relative to population of twelve large counties. SF BLA, "Review of LPS Conservatorship," January 10, 2022, ii. Needless to say, these data paint contrasting portraits as to whether San Francisco suffers from an overly constricted conservatorship system.

40. Presciently, San Diego had cited this as a reason not to implement SB 1045: many facilities "do not share data regarding detainment and 5150 status [with the county] and are not legally required to do so." Robbins-Meyer, "Report Back on Housing Conservatorship," 3.

41. The Shelter-in-Place program in San Francisco reduced psychiatric emergency services use by 75 percent for previously high-utilizing individuals, relative to people not placed in such hotels. Mark D. Fleming et al., "Association of Shelter-in-Place Hotels with Health Services Use Among People Experiencing Homelessness During the COVID-19 Pandemic," *JAMA Network Open* 5, no. 7 (2022): e2223891.

42. J. D. Morris, "S.F. Planned to Compel More People Into Drug and Mental Health Treatment. So Far, Only Two Have Been Helped," *San Francisco Chronicle*, February 5, 2022, https://www.sfchronicle.com/bayarea/article/S-F-planned-to-compel-more-people -into-drug-and-16833440.php.

12. ASYLUM FOR THE DYING

1. County of Los Angeles Public Health, "Mortality Among People Experiencing Homelessness in Los Angeles County: One Year Before and After the Start of the COVID-19 Pandemic" (Los Angeles, April 2022), http://publichealth.lacounty.gov/chie/reports /Homeless_Mortality_Report_2022.pdf.

2. Chris Herring, "Complaint-Oriented Policing: Regulating Homelessness in Public Space," *American Sociological Review* 84, no. 5 (2019): 769–800.

3. For a portrait from a journalist who had access to some HOME clients, see Doug Smith, "L.A.'s First Street Psychiatrist Makes His Sidewalk Rounds, Transforming Homeless Lives," *Los Angeles Times*, September 7, 2022, https://www.latimes.com/california/story /2022-09-07/l-a-countys-first-street-psychiatrist-treats-patients-where-they.live.

4. According to state statute, "agencies and departments administering state programs" around homelessness "shall . . . incorporate the core components of Housing First." California WIC, Section 8256(b), https://leginfo.legislature.ca.gov/faces/codes_displayText .xhtml?lawCode=WIC&division=8.&title&part&chapter=6.5.

5. Maria C. Raven, Matthew J. Niedzwiecki, and Margot Kushel, "A Randomized Trial of Permanent Supportive Housing for Chronically Homeless Persons with High Use of Publicly Funded Services," *Health Services Research* 55, no. S2 (2020): 797–806.

6. San Francisco Budget and Legislative Analyst, "Impact of Supportive Housing on the Costs of Homelessness" (San Francisco, CA, May 31, 2016), 8.

7. One report from Los Angeles found 418 deaths in shelter-in-place hotels during the pandemic. Of these, 60 percent were attributed to drug or alcohol overdoses, a much higher proportion than deaths on the streets. Ananya Roy and Chloe Rosenstock, "We Do Not Forget: Stolen Lives of LA's Unhoused During the COVID-19 Pandemic" (UCLA Luskin Institute on Inequality and Democracy, December 1, 2021), 6, https://escholarship.org /uc/item/9104j943. In San Francisco, 166 people overdosed in city-financed hotels, comprising 14 percent of all overdose deaths in the city in 2020 and 2021. Joaquin Palomino and Trisha Thadani, "Broken Homes," *San Francisco Chronicle*, April 26, 2022.

8. Yoohyun Jung, "Drug Overdose Deaths in California Are Skyrocketing, as the Fentanyl Crisis Reaches Beyond San Francisco," *San Francisco Chronicle*, October 14, 2022, https:// www.sfchronicle.com/health/article/california-fentanyl-overdose-deaths-17508010.php; Benjamin Schneider, "Fentanyl: The City's Biggest Public Health Crisis," *SF Weekly*, May 6, 2021, https://www.sfweekly.com/news/fentanyl-the-citys-biggest-public-health-crisis/.

9. Revealingly, one of the most cited studies showing the efficacy of Housing First approaches actually logged more deaths among people who were housed through the program than those who were not. Raven, Niedzwiecki, and Kushel, "Randomized Trial of PSH"; see also Jill S. Roncarati et al., "Housing Boston's Chronically Homeless Unsheltered Population: 14 Years Later," *Medical Care* 59 (2021): S170.

10. Eugene Bardach, *The Skill Factor in Politics: Repealing the Mental Commitment Laws in California* (Berkeley: University of California Press, 1972), 126, 130.

11. Susan Partovi, "Hiding Behind 'Free Will,'" *Los Angeles Times*, June 10, 2007.

12. Barbara Mauer, "Morbidity and Mortality in People with Serious Mental Illness" (Alexandria, VA: National Association of State Mental Health Program Directors, October 2006), 5, https://www.nasmhpd.org/content/morbidity-and-mortality-people-serious -mental-illness.

13. Emily Alpert Reyes and Thomas Curwen, "Panel Looks at Policing, Mentally Ill," *Los Angeles Times*, June 14, 2018.

14. Los Angeles County Department of Mental Health, "Assessment of Grave Disability" (Los Angeles, January 10, 2018), 3, http://file.lacounty.gov/SDSInter/bos/supdocs/120790.pdf.

15. LA Public Health, "Mortality Among PEH," 8.

16. Alex V. Barnard, "From the 'Magna Carta' to 'Dying in the Streets': Media Framings of Mental Health Law in California," *Society and Mental Health* 12, no. 2 (2022): 155–73.

17. Senate Judiciary Committee, "AB 1971: Mental Health Services: Involuntary Detention: Gravely Disabled" (Sacramento: California State Legislature, April 12, 2018), https:// leginfo.legislature.ca.gov/faces/billAnalysisClient.xhtml?bill_id=201720180AB1971.

18. Melody Gutierrez, "SF Could Hold More Mentally Ill People for Care," *San Francisco Chronicle*, August 31, 2018, https://www.sfchronicle.com/politics/article/SF-could-hold -more-mentally-ill-people-for-care-13195276.php.

19. Senate Judiciary Committee, "SB 516: Certification for Intensive Treatment: Review Hearing" (Sacramento: California State Legislature, February 17, 2021), 15–16, https:// leginfo.legislature.ca.gov/faces/billAnalysisClient.xhtml?bill_id=202120220SB516#.

20. Paul S. Appelbaum, "Ambivalence Codified: California's New Outpatient Commitment Statute," *Psychiatric Services* 54, no. 1 (2003): 26–28.

21. A narrower attempt to incorporate evidence of "medical conditions" into probable cause hearings (automatically held during a fourteen-day hold) was similarly amended to oblivion in 2020. For an explanation, see Senate Judiciary Committee, "SB 516."

22. California State Auditor, "Lanterman-Petris-Short Act: California Has Not Ensured That Individuals with Serious Mental Illnesses Receive Adequate Ongoing Care" (Sacramento, CA, July 2020), 21.

23. Editorial Board, "Forced Care Is Not the Answer," *Los Angeles Times*, August 7, 2020, https:// www.latimes.com/opinion/story/2020-08-07/improve-mental-health-care-before-forcing -it-on-people.

24. Nicole Nixon, "Pandemic, Climate Change, Homelessness Highlight Newsom's Initial California Budget Proposal," CAPRadio, January 10, 2022, https://www.capradio.org/173161.

25. Jocelyn Wiener, "Why Is It So Hard to Get Mentally Ill Californians Into Treatment?" *CalMatters*, August 30, 2018, https://calmatters.org/articles/california-homeless -mental-illness-conservatorship-law/.

26. The courts confirmed that a dementia diagnosis can be a basis for an LPS conservatorship in *County of Los Angeles v. Superior Court* (2013) 222 Cal.App.4th 434.

27. San Diego Health and Human Services Agency, "Public Guardian," https://www.sandiego county.gov/content/sdc/hhsa/programs/papg/public_guardian.html.

28. California Probate Code, Section 2920(b), https://law.justia.com/codes/california/2005 /prob/2920-2922.html.

29. A recent report quantified the coming avalanche of cases like Jesus's, determining that San Diego needed thirteen times as many neuropsych beds. Behavioral Health Services, "Optimal Care Pathways Model" (San Diego County, CA: Board of Supervisors, September 27, 2022), https://bosagenda.sandiegocounty.gov/cob/cosd/cob/doc?id =0901127e80f13b6a.

30. California WIC, Sections 5200 and 5352, https://leginfo.legislature.ca.gov/faces/codes _displaySection.xhtml?lawCode=WIC&sectionNum=5352.

31. Elizabeth Bromley, "Clinical Assessment and Management of Grave Disability," *PMHP Trainings*, rise.articulate.com/share/l2ftbWBLsYCteV56sVZzcA1blXgyvSYg#/lessons /F65mI9RijBToCaj8M3Uer33K7zs_NKKO.

32. Elizabeth Bromley et al, "Outpatient Conservatorship: Preliminary Results from a Pilot Program Serving Gravely Disabled Adults Experiencing Homelessness in Los Angeles County," unpublished manuscript, February 13, 2022.

33. Los Angeles County Department of Mental Health (LA DMH), "Report Response on Expanding Lanterman-Petris-Short and Probate Conservatorship Capacity" (Los Angeles, July 10, 2018), 10, http://file.lacounty.gov/SDSInter/bos/supdocs/116143.pdf.

34. Cathie Anderson, "New Psychiatric Hospital Opens in Sacramento with 117 Beds Amid Demand for Mental Health," *Sacramento Bee*, January 7, 2022, https://www.sacbee.com /article257098382.html.

35. Trevor Montgomery, "Supervisors Unanimously Vote to Add 20 Mental Health Beds at SRMC," *Shasta County News Service*, September 14, 2018, https://myrcns.com/2018/09/14 /supervisors-unanimously-vote-to-add-20-mental-health-beds-at-srmc/.

36. Ricardo Lopez, "Indio City Council Unanimously Approves Behavioral Health Center Despite Neighborhood Opposition," *Desert Sun*, February 6, 2019, https://www .desertsun.com/story/news/local/indio/2019/02/06/indio-approves-mental-health -facility-despite-resident-objections/2795228002/; Kevin Forestieri, "El Camino Completes New $96M Mental Health Care Facility," *Mountain View Voice*, November 1, 2019, https://mv-voice.com/news/2019/11/01/el-camino-completes-new-96m-mental-health -care-facility; Sam Morgen, "Kern Supervisors Approve Two New Psychiatric Health Facilities," *Bakersfield.Com*, April 27, 2021, https://www.bakersfield.com/news/kern-supervisors -approve-two-new-psychiatric-health-facilities/article_2393399a-a795-11eb-ada1 -aba5e0219dc9.html; Cara Hallam, "Momentum Builds for Psychiatric Facility Opening," *Turlock Journal*, February 14, 2014, https://www.turlockjournal.com/news/government /momentum-builds-for-psychiatric-facility-opening/.

37. This same conclusion was made in reports on the need for beds in San Francisco, Los Angeles, San Diego, and statewide. San Francisco Department of Public Health, "Behavioral Health Bed Optimization Project: Analysis and Recommendations for Improving Patient Flow" (San Francisco, June 2020); LA DMH, "Report Response," October 29,

2019; BHS, "Optimal Care Pathways Model"; Ryan McBain et al., "Adult Psychiatric Bed Capacity, Need, and Shortage Estimates in California—2021" (Santa Monica, CA: Rand Corporation, 2022).

38. Morgan C. Shields et al., "Increases in Inpatient Psychiatry Beds Operated by Systems, For-Profits, and Chains, 2010–2016," *Psychiatric Services* 73, no. 5 (2022): 561–64.

39. Newsom, "State of the State—Annotated."

40. Legislative Analyst's Office, "Behavioral Health: Continuum Infrastructure Funding Proposal," February 2021, https://lao.ca.gov/reports/2021/4379/Behavioral-Health-Continuum-Infrastructure-021721.pdf.

41. McBain et al., "Adult Psychiatric Bed Capacity," 8.

42. D. J. Jaffe, *Insane Consequences: How the Mental Health Industry Fails the Mentally Ill* (Amherst, NY: Prometheus, 2017), 82. The evidence so far does not support Jaffe's claim. A federal pilot project found that allowing IMDs to receive Medicaid funds had little impact on patient outcomes beyond shifting costs from states to the federal government. Mathematica Policy Research, "Medicaid Emergency Psychiatric Services Demonstration Evaluation: Final Report" (Washington, DC: Department of Health and Human Services, August 18, 2016).

43. As of August 2022, ten states had an IMD waiver for mental health while thirty-four (including California) had one for substance use facilities. Kaiser Family Foundation, "Medicaid Waiver Tracker: Approved and Pending 1115 Waivers by State," February 1, 2022, https://www.kff.org/medicaid/issue-brief/medicaid-waiver-tracker-approved-and-pending-section-1115-waivers-by-state/.

44. Actually implementing an IMD waiver is tricky. One condition imposed by the federal government is that the average statewide length of stay be under thirty days; no stay above sixty days will be reimbursed. The state's plan for the waiver, released in 2022, delegated implementation back to counties, who would have to opt in. Whether they do so will, in turn, depend on complex negotiations between counties and for-profit IMD operators over who foots the bill for patients who stay too long (recall that sojourns in IMDs in California are often many months). Department of Health Care Services, "The California Behavioral Health Community-Based Continuum Demonstration," November 2022, https://www.dhcs.ca.gov/CalAIM/Documents/CalBH-CBC-Demonstration-External-Concept-Paper-11-14-22.pdf.

45. Some academics and psychiatrists have echoed this call. Dominic A. Sisti, Andrea G. Segal, and Ezekiel J. Emanuel, "Improving Long-Term Psychiatric Care: Bring Back the Asylum," *JAMA* 313, no. 3 (2015): 243–44.

46. Dick Spotswood, "Opinion: Our Society Needs to Care for the Homeless Mentally Ill," *Marin Independent Journal*, August 1, 2018.

13. SHARING AUTHORITY, RESTORING AUTONOMY

1. California's program conducted twenty thousand forced sterilizations, one-third of the national total. Alexandra Minna Stern, "Sterilized in the Name of Public Health," *American Journal of Public Health* 95, no. 7 (2005): 1128–38.

2. The most famous statement of this perspective is Thomas S. Szasz, "The Myth of Mental Illness," *American Psychologist* 15, no. 2 (1960): 113–18.

3. Karen L. Fortuna, Phyllis Solomon, and Jennifer Rivera, "An Update of Peer Support/ Peer Provided Services Underlying Processes, Benefits, and Critical Ingredients," *Psychiatric Quarterly* 93 (2022): 575.

4. Henriques asked me to specify that his views are his own, not necessarily those of MHA.

5. Kevin Heslin and Audrey Weiss, "Hospital Readmissions Involving Psychiatric Disorders, 2012" (Agency for Healthcare Research and Quality, May 2015), https://www.hcup-us .ahrq.gov/reports/statbriefs/sb189-Hospital-Readmissions-Psychiatric-Disorders -2012.pdf.

6. According to a 2018 report, governments in Canada, Great Britain, Israel, Bulgaria, Israel, India, the Czech Republic, Sweden, Norway, and parts of Germany, New Zealand, and Australia have adopted features of supported decision making. National Council on Disability, "Beyond Guardianship: Toward Alternatives That Promote Greater Self-Determination," March 22, 2018, 61, https://ncd.gov/publications/2018/beyond-guardianship-toward -alternatives.

7. Office of Governor Gavin Newsom, "Governor Newsom Signs Legislation to Protect Civil Rights, Support Community Living for Californians with Disabilities," September 30, 2022, https://www.gov.ca.gov/2022/09/30/governor-newsom-signs-legislation-to-protect -civil-rights-support-community-living-for-californians-with-disabilities/.

8. National Council on Disability, "Turning Rights Into Reality: How Guardianship and Alternatives Impact the Autonomy of People with Intellectual and Developmental Disabilities," June 10, 2019, 27, https://ncd.gov/publications/2019/turning-rights-into-reality.

9. Emma Frankham, Christopher Jacobi, and Brandon Vaidyanathan, "Race, Trust in Police, and Mental Health Crisis Support," *Contexts* 20, no. 3 (2021): 60–62.

10. In San Diego, Supervisor Nathan Fletcher stated that it was "the spirit of reform that followed the death of George Floyd" that helped get the city's nonpolice crisis response "off the ground." Lyndsay Winkley and Tammy Murga, "No Guns, No Badges, No Sirens. County Reimagines Response to Mental Health Calls," *San Diego Union-Tribune*, February 27, 2022, https://www.sandiegouniontribune.com/news/health/story/2022-02-27/a-year-in-the -works-san-diegos-mobile-crisis-response-teams-expand-operations-countywide.

11. Harder & Co. Community Research, "Street Crisis Response Team [SCRT] Pilot: Final Report" (San Francisco, CA, May 2022), 1, https://www.sfdph.org/dph/files/IWG/SCRT _Final_Report_FINAL-1_year.pdf.

12. Harder & Co., "SCRT Pilot," 7.

13. Although the city's "coordinated entry" program contacts 63 percent of SCRT cases referred to them, only 9 percent were seen more than once. Harder & Co., "SCRT Pilot," 16.

14. Harder & Co., "SCRT Pilot," 13.

15. For a review Margaret E. Balfour et al., "Cops, Clinicians, or Both? Collaborative Approaches to Responding to Behavioral Health Emergencies," *Psychiatric Services* 73, no. 6 (2022): 658–69.

16. Harder & Co., "SCRT Pilot," 10.

17.   Sherry Glied and Richard G. Frank, "Mental Illness and Violence: Lessons from the Evidence," *American Journal of Public Health* 104, no. 2 (2014): e5–6.

18.   Daniel Whiting et al., "Association of Schizophrenia Spectrum Disorders and Violence Perpetration in Adults and Adolescents from 15 Countries: A Systematic Review and Meta-Analysis," *JAMA Psychiatry* 79, no. 2 (2022): 120–32.

19.   Patrick Sharkey, Gerard Torrats-Espinosa, and Delaram Takyar, "Community and the Crime Decline: The Causal Effect of Local Nonprofits on Violent Crime," *American Sociological Review* 82, no. 6 (2017): 1214–40.

20.   Marcia L. Meldrum et al., "Implementation Status of Assisted Outpatient Treatment Programs: A National Survey," *Psychiatric Services* 67, no. 6 (2016): 630–35.

21.   Jeffrey Geller, "The Evolution of Outpatient Commitment in the USA: From Conundrum to Quagmire," *International Journal of Law and Psychiatry* 29, no. 3 (2006): 236.

22.   This changed in 2020, when AB 1976 required counties to have an AOT program unless their board of supervisors expressly opted out of it. See https://leginfo.legislature.ca.gov /faces/billNavClient.xhtml?bill_id=201920200AB1976.

23.   Paul S. Appelbaum, "Ambivalence Codified: California's New Outpatient Commitment Statute," *Psychiatric Services* 54, no. 1 (2003): 27.

24.   John Coté and Heather Knight, "New Focus on Law to Help Mentally Ill," *San Francisco Chronicle*, February 10, 2014.

25.   Statewide, only about 25 percent of people referred to AOT and found to qualify are placed on a court order. That totaled 218 individuals in 2018–2019. Department of Health Care Services (DHCS), "Laura's Law: Assisted Outpatient Treatment Demonstration Project Act of 2002" (Community Services Division, May 2021), 10, https://www.dhcs.ca .gov/formsandpubs/Documents/Legislative%20Reports/Lauras-LawLegRpt-July2018 -June2019.pdf.

26.   DHCS, "Laura's Law," 4. A meta-review found there is "little evidence for the effectiveness of compulsory community treatment." Steve R. Kisely and Meredith A. Campbell, "Compulsory Community and Involuntary Outpatient Treatment for People with Severe Mental Disorders," in *Cochrane Database of Systematic Reviews* (Wiley, 2014), 22, http://onlinelibrary.wiley.com/doi/10.1002/14651858.CD004408.pub4/abstract. The evidence is particularly lacking for AOT as a form of violence prevention, even though this has often been billed as its primary justification (as hinted at by the choice to name bills after homicide victims). Marvin S. Swartz et al., "Involuntary Outpatient Commitment and the Elusive Pursuit of Violence Prevention: A View from the United States," *Canadian Journal of Psychiatry* 62, no. 2 (2017): 102–8.

27.   The statement about San Bernardino's program was made at a hearing on LPS in the state legislature on December 15, 2021. In Los Angeles, people referred to AOT receive an average of ten contacts with outreach workers. At the end, three times as many people agree to participate in AOT voluntarily as are placed on a court order. Sarah L. Starks et al., "Client Outreach in Los Angeles County's Assisted Outpatient Treatment Program: Strategies and Barriers to Engagement," *Research on Social Work Practice* 32, no. 7 (2022): 839–54.

28.   Many ethnographers have documented the skills homeless people develop to survive on the streets. My point here is that at least some individuals, whom we might identify as

gravely disabled by mental illness, either lack these skills and are dying or have skills that do not translate to life indoors. Mitch Duneier, *Sidewalk* (New York: Farrar, Straus, and Giroux, 1999); Teresa Gowan, *Hobos, Hustlers, and Backsliders: Homeless in San Francisco* (Minneapolis: University of Minnesota Press, 2010); Tanya Marie Luhrmann, "'The Street Will Drive You Crazy': Why Homeless Psychotic Women in the Institutional Circuit in the United States Often Say No to Offers of Help," *American Journal of Psychiatry* 165, no. 1 (2008): 15–20.

29.   Joaquin Palomino and Trisha Thadani, "Broken Homes," *San Francisco Chronicle*, April 26, 2022.

30.   See Stephen Eide, *Homelessness in America: The History and Tragedy of an Intractable Social Problem* (Lanham, MD: Rowman & Littlefield, 2022); Michael Shellenberger, *San Fransicko: Why Progressives Ruin Cities* (New York: Harper, 2021).

31.   The emergence of the fatalistic categorization of board and care residents as "young chronics" is charted by Martin Fleishman, "Board and Care Homes 1984: Return of the House Call," *Psychiatric Annals* 15, no. 11 (1985): 654–60.

32.   Nineteen percent of clients transported by SCRT are taken to Dore. Harder & Co., "SCRT Pilot," 13.

33.   Research has generally shown that residential crisis services are as effective in improving symptoms and functioning as inpatient stays, with higher user satisfaction and lower costs. Bevin Croft and Nilüfer İsvan, "Impact of the Second Story Peer Respite Program on Use of Inpatient and Emergency Services," *Psychiatric Services* 66, no. 6 (2015): 632–37; Thomas K. Greenfield et al., "A Randomized Trial of a Mental Health Consumer-Managed Alternative to Civil Commitment for Acute Psychiatric Crisis," *American Journal of Community Psychology* 42, no. 1 (2008): 135–44; Kerry A. Thomas and Debra Rickwood, "Clinical and Cost-Effectiveness of Acute and Subacute Residential Mental Health Services: A Systematic Review," *Psychiatric Services* 64, no. 11 (2013): 1140–49.

34.   California State Legislature, "AB 3052: Community Residential Treatment Act," 1978.

35.   Solveig Reindal, "Independence, Dependence, Interdependence: Some Reflections on the Subject and Personal Autonomy," *Disability & Society* 14, no. 3 (1999): 364.

36.   This comment was made in a hearing before the State Assembly Judiciary Committee on LPS reform on December 15, 2021.

37.   Heart Forward, "What Is Peer Respite and Why Don't We Have More Crisis Beds Available?" April 5, 2022, https://www.heartforwardla.org/season-3.

38.   Some studies show that respites help reduce the use of hospitals and ERs while others identify their main impact as improving treatment satisfaction. Croft and İsvan, "Impact of the Second Story Peer Respite Program"; Greenfield et al., "Randomized Trial of a Mental Health Consumer-Managed Alternative."

39.   Sarah Kwon, "These Neighborly Havens Help People Facing Mental Health Crises," *Los Angeles Times*, January 11, 2021, https://www.latimes.com/california/story/2021-01-11/peer-respites-people-facing-mental-health-crises-pandemic.

40.   Jocelyn Wiener, "Unanswered Cries: Why California Faces a Shortage of Mental Health Workers," *CalMatters*, September 25, 2022, https://www.ijpr.org/health-and-medicine/2022-09-25/unanswered-cries-why-california-faces-a-shortage-of-mental-health-workers.

41. Liat Ben-Moshe, "Alternatives to (Disability) Incarceration," in *Disability Incarcerated: Imprisonment and Disability in the United States and Canada*, ed. Liat Ben-Moshe, Chris Chapman, and Allison C. Carey (New York: Palgrave Macmillan, 2014), 262.

42. Heart Forward, "What Is Peer Respite?"

43. Fountain House, "The Wellspring of the Clubhouse Model for Social and Vocational Adjustment of Persons with Serious Mental Illness," *Psychiatric Services* 50 (1999): 1473–76.

44. Clubhouse International, "Clubhouse Directory," accessed October 18, 2022, https://clubhouse-intl.org/what-we-do/international-directory/.

45. John H. Beard, Rudyard N. Propst, and Thomas J. Malamud, "The Fountain House Model of Psychiatric Rehabilitation," *Psychosocial Rehabilitation Journal* 5 (1982): 47.

46. Sue E. Estroff, *Making It Crazy: An Ethnography of Psychiatric Clients in an American Community* (Berkeley: University of California Press, 1981), 119; see also Helena Hansen, Philippe Bourgois, and Ernest Drucker, "Pathologizing Poverty: New Forms of Diagnosis, Disability, and Structural Stigma Under Welfare Reform," *Social Science & Medicine* 103 (2014): 76–83.

47. Fortuna, Solomon, and Rivera, "An Update of Peer Support"; Steve Gillard et al., "Peer Support for Discharge from Inpatient Mental Health Care Versus Care as Usual in England (ENRICH): A Parallel, Two-Group, Individually Randomised Controlled Trial," *Lancet Psychiatry* 9, no. 2 (2022): 125–36; Sarah White et al., "The Effectiveness of One-to-One Peer Support in Mental Health Services: A Systematic Review and Meta-Analysis," *BMC Psychiatry* 20, no. 1 (2020): 534; Cecilie Høgh Egmose, Chalotte Heinsvig Poulsen, Carsten Hjorthøj, Sara Skriver Mundy, Lone Hellström, Mette Nørgaard Nielsen, Lisa Korsbek, Klavs Serup Rasmussen, and Lene Falgaard Eplov, "The Effectiveness of Peer Support in Personal and Clinical Recovery—Systematic Review and Meta-Analysis." *Psychiatric Services* appi.ps.202100138. doi: 10.1176/appi.ps.202100138 (2023).

48. Anne-Sophie Gaillard et al., "The Content of Psychiatric Advance Directives: A Systematic Review," *Psychiatric Services*, August 30, 2022.

49. Mark H. de Jong et al., "Interventions to Reduce Compulsory Psychiatric Admissions: A Systematic Review and Meta-Analysis," *JAMA Psychiatry* 73, no. 7 (2016): 657–64; Emma Molyneaux et al., "Crisis-Planning Interventions for People with Psychotic Illness or Bipolar Disorder: Systematic Review and Meta-Analyses," *BJPsych Open* 5, no. 4 (2019).

50. Christopher Schneiders et al., "Psychiatric Advance Directives and Supported Decision-Making: Preliminary Developments and Pilot Studies in California," in *Mental Health, Legal Capacity, and Human Rights*, ed. Charlene Sunkel et al. (Cambridge: Cambridge University Press, 2021), 300.

51. Concepts Forward, Inc, "Psychiatric Advance Directives Multi-County Collaborative" (Mental Health Services Oversight and Accountability Commission, May 2021), http://www.mhsoac.ca.gov/sites/default/files/Multi%20County_INN_PADs_0.pdf.

52. Emile Durkheim, *Suicide* (New York: Free Press, 1997 [1897]), 276.

53. As one review concluded, "the clinical reality suggests that residual autonomy and decisional freedom exist, even for involuntarily hospitalized patients." Anna Saya et al., "Criteria, Procedures, and Future Prospects of Involuntary Treatment in Psychiatry Around the World: A Narrative Review," *Frontiers in Psychiatry* 10 (2019): 2.

54. Aurélie Tinland et al., "Effect of Psychiatric Advance Directives Facilitated by Peer Workers on Compulsory Admission Among People with Mental Illness: A Randomized Clinical Trial," *JAMA Psychiatry* 79, no. 8 (2022): 752–59.

55. Jeffrey Guhin, *Agents of God: Boundaries and Authority in Muslim and Christian Schools* (New York: Oxford University Press, 2021).

56. Adrianna Bagnall and Gil Eyal, "Forever Children and Autonomous Citizens: Comparing the Deinstitutionalizations of Psychiatric Patients and Developmentally Disabled Individuals in the United States," in *Fifty Years After Deinstitutionalization: Mental Illness in Contemporary Communities*, ed. Brea L. Perry (Bingley, UK: Emerald, 2016), 42.

57. Hannah Arendt, *Between Past and Future*, ed. Jerome Kohn (New York: Penguin, 2006), 92.

CONCLUSION: BEYOND MIRACLES

1. For example, twenty-five states have passed laws expanding forced drug treatment in the past four years. Health in Justice Lab, "Involuntary Commitment for Substance Use," accessed October 17, 2022, https://www.healthinjustice.org/involuntary-commitment-for-substanc.

2. Gi Lee and David Cohen, "Incidences of Involuntary Psychiatric Detentions in 25 U.S. States," *Psychiatric Services* 71, no. 1 (2021): 61–68; Luke Sheridan Rains et al., "Variations in Patterns of Involuntary Hospitalisation and in Legal Frameworks: An International Comparative Study," *Lancet Psychiatry* 6, no. 5 (2019): 403–17.

3. Bernice A. Pescosolido, Bianca Manago, and John Monahan, "Evolving Public Views on the Likelihood of Violence from People with Mental Illness: Stigma and Its Consequences," *Health Affairs* 38, no. 10 (2019): 1735–43.

4. California State Assembly, Committee on Judiciary, https://ajud.assembly.ca.gov/reports.

5. Sigrid Bathen, "Capitol Weekly Interview: Susan Talamantes Eggman," *Capitol Weekly*, September 20, 2021; Susan Eggman, "Modernizing Our Behavioral Health Continuum" (Stockton: California State Senate, April 4, 2022), 2, https://sd05.senate.ca.gov/sites/sd05.senate.ca.gov/files/pdf/Packet%20Modernizing%20Our%20Behavioral%20Health%20Continuum.pdf.

6. This process of serial or stacked 5150s takes place in at least seven counties. In Imperial County, one individual stayed in an ER for forty-four days. Although LPS is unclear about when exactly the seventy-two-hour clock starts—which creates some ambiguity that state regulators had failed to clarify—it's difficult to believe that hospitals think denying someone the hearing they would get if they passed to a 5250 is consistent with the spirit of the law. Jennifer Bowman, "Imperial County's Use of Psychiatric Holds Appears to Violate State Law," *INewSource*, September 22, 2022, https://inewsource.org/2022/09/22/imperial-county-serial-psychiatric-holds/.

7. The laws discussed in this section are, in order, SB 929, Community Mental Health Services: Data Collection; AB 2275, Mental Health: Involuntary Commitment; SB 970, Mental Health Services Act; SB 1154, Facilities for Mental Health or Substance Use Disorder Crisis: Database; SB 965, Conservatorships: Medical Record: Hearsay Rule; SB 1227, Mental Health Services: Gravely Disabled Persons. Information on each bill can be found at leginfo.legislature.ca.gov.

8. Sigrid Bathen, "Capitol Weekly Interview: Randall Hagar and Mental Health Care," *Capitol Weekly*, September 12, 2022, https://capitolweekly.net/capitol-weekly-interview-randall-hagar-and-mental-health-care/.

9. Two potentially significant expansions of forced treatment proposed by Eggman did pass, however. One bill would allow medication to be included in court-ordered AOT plans (SB-1035, Mental Health Services: Assisted Outpatient Treatment). Another would expand the use of 5270s, an alternative to temporary conservatorship that allows hospitals to hold a gravely disabled person for an additional thirty days without going to court. The bill would allow for a second 5270 hold (SB 1227, Involuntary Commitment: Intensive Treatment).

10. Newsom's senior counselor, Jason Elliot, stated, "One of the important and early strategic policy decisions the governor made was not to attempt a significant reform of LPS. . . . Sometimes to make a real policy breakthrough, you need to cut a new path." Sigrid Bathen, "Helping Mentally Ill People: The Debate Over 'Involuntary Treatment,'" *Capitol Weekly*, May 18, 2022, https://capitolweekly.net/helping-mentally-ill-people-the-debate-over-involuntary-treatment/.

11. California Health and Human Services Agency, "CARE Court FAQ" (Sacramento, CA, September 2022), https://www.chhs.ca.gov/wp-content/uploads/2022/09/CARE_FAQ.pdf.

12. Governor Gavin Newsom, "Press Conference: Governor Newsom Unveils Plan for Californians Struggling with Behavioral Health Challenges," March 3, 2022, https://www.youtube.com/watch?v=NGAvQ_YRrPE.

13. A member of the governor's team "disputes widespread criticism that the plan entails 'forced' treatment," stating, "There is a court-ordered care plan [but] . . . not a locked door." Bathen, "Helping Mentally Ill People."

14. Darrell Steinberg, "CARE Court Plan Rightly Targets Government's Responsibilities on Homelessness," *CalMatters*, August 19, 2022, https://calmatters.org/commentary/2022/08/care-court-plan-rightly-targets-states-responsibilities-on-homelessness/.

15. The 2022 budget allocation for CARE courts was $88 million: $57 million for county start-up costs and $31 million to train court staff. Manuela Tobias and Jocelyn Wiener, "California Lawmakers Approved CARE Court. What Comes Next?," *CalMatters*, September 8, 2022, https://calmatters.org/housing/2022/09/california-lawmakers-approved-care-court-what-comes-next/.

16. Officer of Governor Gavin Newsom, "Governor Newsom Signs CARE Court Into Law, Providing a New Path Forward for Californians Struggling with Serious Mental Illness," September 14, 2022, https://www.gov.ca.gov/2022/09/14/governor-newsom-signs-care-court-into-law-providing-a-new-path-forward-for-californians-struggling-with-serious-mental-illness/.

17. E. Fuller Torrey, *American Psychosis: How the Federal Government Destroyed the Mental Illness Treatment System* (Oxford: Oxford University Press, 2013), 88. "The system has become decentralized, so much so that the term 'system' borders on a misnomer." Richard G. Frank and Sherry A. Glied, *Better but Not Well: Mental Health Policy in the United States Since 1950* (Baltimore: Johns Hopkins University Press, 2006), 5.

18. Community mental health centers "attracted a new type of patient who was not very ill and not a candidate for hospitalization in a state institution." Comptroller General of

the United States, "Returning the Mentally Disabled to the Community" (Washington, DC, 1977), 73.

19.   Comptroller General, "Returning the Mentally Disabled to the Community," 5; Steering Committee on the Chronically Mentally Ill, "Toward a National Plan for the Chronically Mentally Ill" (Rockville, MD: U.S. Department of Health and Human Services, December 1980), 1–6.

20.   Torrey, *American Psychosis*, 89.

21.   Substance Abuse and Mental Health Services Administration, "Projections of National Expenditures for Treatment of Mental and Substance Use Disorders, 2010–2020" (Rockville, MD: U.S. Department of Health and Human Services, 2014). Note that part of Medicaid (which provided 30 percent of the budget for mental health in 2020) is paid for by states.

22.   David Mechanic, "More People Than Ever Before Are Receiving Behavioral Health Care in the United States, but Gaps and Challenges Remain," *Health Affairs* 33, no. 8 (2014): 1416–24.

23.   National Institute of Mental Health, "Mental Health United States," DHHS-ADM-85-1378 (Rockville, MD: U.S. Department of Health and Human Services, 1985). The National Mental Health Services Survey provides a point-in-time percentage of hospital inpatients by legal status, but the survey design does not allow us to estimate the total number of people subject to involuntary care. Substance Abuse and Mental Health Services Administration, "National Mental Health Services Survey (N-MHSS) 2020: Data on Mental Health Treatment Facilities" (Washington, DC: Department of Health and Human Services, December 2021), https://samhsa.gov/data/sites/default/files/2016_National_Mental _Health_Services_Survey.pdf

24.   President's New Freedom Commission on Mental Health, "Achieving the Promise: Transforming Mental Health Care in America" (Rockville, MD, 2003). A recently published report on civil commitments reviews the history of commitment statutes and lays out ethical principles, but does not provide any new data on how commitments are being used. Substance Abuse and Mental Health Services Administration, "Civil Commitment and the Mental Health Care Continuum: Historical Trends and Principles for Law and Practice" (Rockville, MD: Department of Health and Human Services, 2019), https://www.samhsa.gov/sites/default/files/civil-commitment-continuum-of-care.pdf.

25.   "President Joe Biden: The 2022 60 Minutes Interview," *60 Minutes* (CBS, September 18, 2022), https://www.cbsnews.com/news/president-joe-biden-60-minutes-interview-transcript -2022-09-18/.

26.   Gregg Gonsalves, "No, Joe Biden, the Pandemic Is Not Over," *Nation*, September 30, 2022, https://www.thenation.com/article/society/biden-pandemic-over-deaths/.

27.   Legislative Analyst Office, "The 2021–22 Budget: State Correctional Population Outlook" (Sacramento, CA, November 2020), https://lao.ca.gov/reports/2020/4304/correctional -population-outlook-111920.pdf.

28.   Maya Lau, "In Landmark Move, L.A. County Will Replace Men's Central Jail with Mental Health Hospital for Inmates," *Los Angeles Times*, February 13, 2019, https://www.latimes .com/local/lanow/la-me-jail-construction-20190212-story.html.

29.   Francisco Aviles Pino, "Los Angeles County Votes to Stop Construction of New Jail-Like Facility, Adding Momentum to National Abolition Movement," *Intercept*, August 22,

2019, https://theintercept.com/2019/08/22/los-angeles-county-mental-health-facility-abolition/.

30.   James Blanco, "Op-Ed: An L.A. Program Helps People Get Mental Health Care Instead of Jail Time. Why Not Expand It?," *Los Angeles Times*, July 18, 2022, https://www.latimes.com/opinion/story/2022-07-18/jails-mental-health-los-angeles-county-diversion.

31.   See also Armando Lara-Millán, "The Administrative Disappearing of State Crisis: The Resolution of Prison Realignment in Los Angeles County," *American Journal of Sociology* 127, no. 5 (2022): 1460–1506.

32.   Frances Fox Piven and Richard Cloward, *Regulating the Poor: The Functions of Public Welfare* (New York: Vintage, 2012); Joe Soss, Richard C. Fording, and Sanford F. Schram, *Disciplining the Poor: Neoliberal Paternalism and the Persistent Power of Race* (Champagne, IL: University of Chicago Press, 2011); Forrest Stuart, *Down, Out, and Under Arrest: Policing and Everyday Life in Skid Row* (Chicago: University of Chicago Press, 2016).

33.   Yeheskel Hasenfeld, "People Processing Organizations: An Exchange Approach," *American Sociological Review* 37, no. 3 (1972): 256–63; Michael Lipsky, *Street-Level Bureaucracy: Dilemmas of the Individual in Public Service*, thirtieth anniversary ed. (New York: Russell Sage Foundation, 2010); Jeffrey Prottas, *People Processing: The Street-Level Bureaucrat in Public-Service Bureaucracies* (Lexington, MA: Lexington, 1979).

34.   Josh Seim, *Bandage, Sort, and Hustle: Ambulance Crews on the Frontlines of Urban Suffering* (Berkeley: University of California Press, 2019).

35.   Armando Lara-Millán, *Redistributing the Poor: Jails, Hospitals, and the Crisis of Law and Fiscal Austerity* (Oxford: Oxford University Press, 2021).

36.   Megan Comfort et al., "How Institutions Deprive: Ethnography, Social Work, and Interventionist Ethics Among the Hypermarginalized," *RSF: The Russell Sage Foundation Journal of the Social Sciences* 1, no. 1 (2015): 101; see also Patricia Fernández-Kelly, *The Hero's Fight: African Americans in West Baltimore and the Shadow of the State* (Princeton, NJ: Princeton University Press, 2015).

37.   Carolyn Sufrin, *Jailcare: Finding the Safety Net for Women Behind Bars* (Berkeley: University of California Press, 2017).

38.   Steven Lukes, "Perspectives on Authority Part I: Concepts, Perspectives, and Justifications: Section 4," *NOMOS: American Society for Political and Legal Philosophy* 29 (1987): 70.

39.   Robert Castel, *La Gestion des risques: de l'anti-psychiatrie à l'après-psychanalyse* (Paris: Minuit, 1981); Michel Foucault, "L'évolution de la notion d'"individu dangereux' dans la psychiatrie légale," *Déviance et société* 5, no. 4 (1981): 403–22; Nikolas Rose, "Governing Risky Individuals: The Role of Psychiatry in New Regimes of Control," *Psychiatry, Psychology and Law* 5, no. 2 (1998): 177–95; Livia Velpry and Benoît Eyraud, "Confinement and Psychiatric Care: A Comparison Between High-Security Units for Prisoners and for Difficult Patients in France," *Culture, Medicine, and Psychiatry* 38, no. 4 (2014): 550–77.

40.   Brea L. Perry, Emma Frieh, and Eric R. Wright, "Therapeutic Social Control of People with Serious Mental Illness: An Empirical Verification and Extension of Theory," *Society and Mental Health* 8, no. 2 (2018): 109.

41.   Studies show that, among public outpatient clients, as many as 40 percent experience "leveraged" treatment that links adherence to benefits like housing. Pamela Clark Robbins et al., "The Use of Housing as Leverage to Increase Adherence to Psychiatric

Treatment in the Community," *Administration and Policy in Mental Health and Mental Health Services Research* 33, no. 2 (2006): 226–36.

42.   Scholars have observed an inverse relationship between declining internment in hospitals and increasing incarceration in jails and prisons in the second half of the twentieth century. Bernard E. Harcourt, "From the Asylum to the Prison: Rethinking the Incarceration Revolution," *Texas Law Review* 84 (2005): 1751–86. There has been little research on whether, as incarcerated populations decline, forced internment in health care institutions is rising in turn.

43.   Forrest Stuart, Amada Armenta, and Melissa Osborne, "Legal Control of Marginal Groups," *Annual Review of Law and Social Science* 11 (2015): 246; see also Kerwin Kaye, "Rehabilitating the 'Drugs Lifestyle': Criminal Justice, Social Control, and the Cultivation of Agency," *Ethnography* 14, no. 2 (2013): 207–32; Allison McKim, "'Getting Gut-Level': Punishment, Gender, and Therapeutic Governance," *Gender & Society* 22, no. 3 (2008): 303–23.

44.   Neil Gong, "Between Tolerant Containment and Concerted Constraint: Managing Madness for the City and the Privileged Family," *American Sociological Review* 84, no. 4 (2019): 664–89.

45.   See, for example, Peter Conrad, *The Medicalization of Society: On the Transformation of Human Conditions Into Treatable Disorders* (Baltimore: Johns Hopkins University Press, 2007); Allan V. Horwitz, *Creating Mental Illness* (Chicago: University of Chicago Press, 2001); Owen Whooley, *On the Heels of Ignorance: Psychiatry and the Politics of Not Knowing* (Chicago: University of Chicago Press, 2019).

46.   This draws inspiration from theories of legal cynicism: the idea that in certain groups, people endorse the aims of controlling deviance through law but doubt that courts or the police can actually do it in ways that are rational, fair, or effective. Robert J. Sampson and Dawn Jeglum Bartusch, "Legal Cynicism and (Subcultural) Tolerance of Deviance: The Neighborhood Context of Racial Difference," *Law & Society Review*, no. 4 (1998): 777–804.

47.   Anthony DiMario, "To Punish, Parent, or Palliate: Governing Urban Poverty Through Institutional Failure," *American Sociological Review* 87, no. 5 (2022): 860–88.

48.   Didier Fassin, "That Obscure Object of Global Health," in *Medical Anthropology at the Intersections*, ed. Marcia C. Inhorn and Emily A. Wentzell (Durham, NC: Duke University Press, 2012), 95–115.

49.   One of the clearest statements of this position is D. J. Jaffe, *Insane Consequences: How the Mental Health Industry Fails the Mentally Ill* (Amherst, NY: Prometheus, 2017).

50.   The extent to which Reagan actually defunded public housing and his contribution to the concomitant rise in homelessness are contested. Stephen Eide, *Homelessness in America: The History and Tragedy of an Intractable Social Problem* (Lanham, MD: Rowman & Littlefield, 2022).

51.   For a recent example, see Editorial Board, "The Solution to America's Mental Health Crisis Already Exists," *New York Times*, October 4, 2022, https://www.nytimes.com/2022/10/04/opinion/us-mental-health-community-centers.html.

52.   A panel of experts recently deemed changing legal criteria one of the least effective strategies for improving the conservatorship system. Amy L. Shearer et al., "Improving

Mental Health Guardianship: From Prevention to Treatment," *Psychiatric Services* 73, no. 6 (2022): 642–49.

53. Paul S. Appelbaum, *Almost a Revolution: Mental Health Law and the Limits of Change* (Oxford: Oxford University Press, 1994); Jonathan I. Marx and Richard M. Levinson, "Statutory Change and 'Street-Level' Implementation of Psychiatric Commitment," *Social Science & Medicine* 27, no. 11 (1988): 1247–56; Robert D. Miller, "Need-for-Treatment Criteria for Involuntary Civil Commitment: Impact in Practice," *American Journal of Psychiatry* 149, no. 10 (1992): 1380–84. For a counterexample from North Carolina, see Mary L. Durham, "Implications of Need-for-Treatment Laws: A Study of Washington State's Involuntary Treatment Act," *Psychiatric Services* 36, no. 9 (1985): 975–77.

54. Rains et al., "Variations in Patterns of Involuntary Hospitalisation."

55. One study found, for example, that whether clinicians perceived beds as available was the primary determinant of involuntary admissions decisions. Nancy B. Engleman, David A. Jobes, Alan L. Berman, and Laura I. Langbein, "Clinicians' Decision Making About Involuntary Commitment," *Psychiatric Services* 49, no.7 (1998): 941–45.

56. Two LPS reform task forces, for example, proposed sensible reforms around combining hearings for detention and involuntary medication, ensuring that family members' views are considered in hearings, and clarifying hospitals' responsibilities before discharge. LPS Reform Task Force, "A New Vision for Mental Health Treatment Laws" (Long Beach, CA, February 1999); LPS Reform Task Force II, "The Case for Updating California's Mental Health Treatment Law" (Tustin, CA, March 2012).

57. Bathen, "Helping Mentally Ill People."

58. Disability Rights California, "Joint Letter in Opposition to CARE Court," June 22, 2022, https://www.disabilityrightsca.org/latest-news/disability-rights-california-advocates -urge-assembly-health-committee-to-vote-no-on-sb; Human Rights Watch, "Opposition to CARE Court (SB 1338) as Amended May 19, 2022," June 14, 2022, https://www.hrw.org /news/2022/06/14/human-rights-watchs-opposition-care-court-sb-1338.

59. Quoted in in Sharon Shueman and Janel Johnson, "Strengthening the Commitment . . . Reinvesting in the System: A Journey of Community Partnership" (Los Angeles: Frank D. Lanterman Regional Center, 2016), 8.

60. Adrianna Bagnall and Gil Eyal, "Forever Children and Autonomous Citizens: Comparing the Deinstitutionalizations of Psychiatric Patients and Developmentally Disabled Individuals in the United States," in *Fifty Years After Deinstitutionalization: Mental Illness in Contemporary Communities*, ed. Brea L. Perry (Bingley, UK: Emerald, 2016).

61. These strict criteria can lead to people with mental illness and developmental disabilities being bounced between the two systems.

62. "Taken by the State," *The Price of Care* (ABC 10, August 18, 2022), https://www.abc10 .com/article/news/local/abc10-originals/conservatorships-price-of-care-taken-by-the -state/103-1e797c90-e530-4beb-8923-0c75d49f420b.

63. Timothy T. Brown et al., "What Predicts Recovery Orientation in County Departments of Mental Health? A Pilot Study," *Administration and Policy in Mental Health and Mental Health Services Research* 37, no. 5 (2010): 388–98; Todd P. Gilmer et al., "Variation in the Implementation of California's Full Service Partnerships for Persons with Serious Mental Illness," *Health Services Research* 48, no. 6pt2 (2013): 2245–67; Tara A. Niendam et

al., "The Rise of Early Psychosis Care in California: An Overview of Community and University-Based Services," *Psychiatric Services* 70, no. 6 (2019): 480–87.

64. Research shows highly involved Departments of Mental Health are crucial for ensuring adherence to best practices. Sushmita Shoma Ghose et al., "State Mental Health Authority Level of Involvement in Coordinated Specialty Care Clinics and Client Outcomes," *Psychiatric Services* 74, no.3 (2023): 250–56.

65. FSPs with "high fidelity" to the ACT model are more effective in increasing the use of outpatient services. Todd P. Gilmer et al., "Fidelity to the Housing First Model and Variation in Health Service Use Within Permanent Supportive Housing," *Psychiatric Services* 66, no. 12 (2015): 1283–89.

66. Department of Mental Health, "The TRIESTE Project: True Recovery Innovation Embraces Systems That Empower" (Los Angeles, April 18, 2019), 19.

67. This was also the approach of The Village in Long Beach in the 1980s, as described to me by Mark Ragins (a psychiatrist who led the program). His team had a fixed budget per client, which they would also have to tap into if someone needed to be hospitalized. The Village's clinical approach became the basis for FSPs, but its funding model was discarded in favor of billing Medi-Cal.

68. I am grateful to Chad Costello, from the California Association of Social Rehabilitation Agencies, for this pithy point.

69. Seventy-six percent of registered voters favored CARE court while only 15 percent were opposed. Hannah Wiley and Phil Willon, "Voters Support Newsom's Mental Health Plan and Back Mandatory Kindergarten, Poll Shows," *Los Angeles Times*, October 6, 2022, https://www.latimes.com/california/story/2022-10-06/voters-strongly-support-newsoms -mental-health-plan.

70. Stephen Allison, Tarun Bastiampillai, and Doris A. Fuller, "Should the Government Change the Mental Health Act or Fund More Psychiatric Beds?," *Lancet Psychiatry* 4, no. 8 (2017): 585–86; Magali Coldefy, Sarah Fernandes, and David Lapalus, "De l'hospitalisation aux soins sans consentement en psychiatrie: premiers résultats de la mise en place de la loi du 5 juillet 2011," *Questions d'économie de La Santé* (Paris: Institut de recherche et documentation en économie de la santé, February 2017); Patrick Keown et al., "Association Between Provision of Mental Illness Beds and Rate of Involuntary Admissions in the NHS in England 1988–2008: Ecological Study," *BMJ* 343 (2011): d3736.

71. For competing evidence, see Pauline Vaillancourt Rosenau and Stephen H. Linder, "A Comparison of the Performance of For-Profit and Nonprofit U.S. Psychiatric Inpatient Care Providers Since 1980," *Psychiatric Services* 54, no. 2 (2003): 183–87; Morgan C. Shields and Meredith B. Rosenthal, "Quality of Inpatient Psychiatric Care at VA, Other Government, Nonprofit, and For-Profit Hospitals: A Comparison," *Psychiatric Services* 68, no. 3 (2016): 225–30.

72. Sheila Shea, "The Mental Hygiene Legal Service at 50: A Retrospective and Prospective Examination of Advocacy for People with Mental Disabilities," *Government, Law, and Policy Journal* 14, no. 2 (2012): 35–41.

73. Previous research has shown how an expansion of community-based services can reduce rates of involuntary treatment, even absent legal reform. Tim A. Bruckner et al., "Involuntary Civil Commitments After the Implementation of California's Mental Health

Services Act," *Psychiatric Services* 61, no. 10 (2010): 1006–11; Coralie Gandré et al., "Involuntary Psychiatric Admissions and Development of Psychiatric Services as an Alternative to Full-Time Hospitalization in France," *Psychiatric Services* 68, no. 9 (2017): 923–30.

74.   Liana Fox and Kalee Burns, "The Supplemental Poverty Measure: 2020" (U.S. Census Bureau, September 2021), https://www.census.gov/content/dam/Census/library/publications /2021/demo/p60-275.pdf.

75.   Office of Community Planning and Development, "The 2020 Annual Homeless Assessment Report (AHAR) to Congress" (U.S. Department of Housing and Urban Development, January 2021), 10, https://www.huduser.gov/portal/sites/default/files/pdf/2020 -AHAR-Part-1.pdf.

76.   For example, in 2010 the Black incarceration rate in California was 3,036 per 100,000; it was 757 for Hispanics. In Cuba, the incarceration rate is 510.

77.   Brendan D. Kelly, "Structural Violence and Schizophrenia," *Social Science & Medicine* 61, no. 3 (2005): 727.

78.   Giorgio Agamben, *Homo Sacer: Sovereign Power and Bare Life*, trans. Daniel Heller-Roazen (Stanford, CA: Stanford University Press, 1998), 4.

79.   American Psychiatric Association, "The Psychiatric Bed Crisis in the US: Understanding the Problem and Moving Toward Solutions" (Washington, DC, May 2022), 39.

80.   Gregg Colburn and Clayton Page Aldern, *Homelessness Is a Housing Problem: How Structural Factors Explain U.S. Patterns* (Berkeley: University of California Press, 2022).

81.   Thomas R. Insel, *Healing: Our Path from Mental Illness to Mental Health* (New York: Penguin, 2022), 42.

METHODOLOGICAL APPENDIX

1.   Kathleen Gerson and Sarah Damaske, *The Science and Art of Interviewing* (Oxford: Oxford University Press, 2021), 46.

2.   See Nicole M. Deterding and Mary C. Waters, "Flexible Coding of In-Depth Interviews: A Twenty-First-Century Approach," *Sociological Methods & Research* 50, no. 2 (2021): 708–39.

3.   See, for example, Paul Brodwin, *Everyday Ethics* (Berkeley: University of California Press, 2012); Kerry Michael Dobransky, *Managing Madness in the Community: The Challenge of Contemporary Mental Health Care* (New Brunswick, NJ: Rutgers University Press, 2014); James A. Holstein, *Court-Ordered Insanity: Interpretive Practice and Involuntary Commitment* (New York: Transaction, 1993); Lorna A. Rhodes, *Emptying Beds: The Work of an Emergency Psychiatric Unit* (Berkeley: University of California Press, 1991); Carol Warren, *The Court of Last Resort* (Chicago: University of Chicago Press, 1982).

4.   Colin Jerolmack and Shamus Khan, "Talk Is Cheap: Ethnography and the Attitudinal Fallacy," *Sociological Methods & Research* 43, no. 2 (2014): 178–209.

5.   Victoria Reyes, "Three Models of Transparency in Ethnographic Research: Naming Places, Naming People, and Sharing Data," *Ethnography* 19, no. 2 (2018): 204–26.

6.   Alex V. Barnard, "From the 'Magna Carta' to 'Dying in the Streets': Media Framings of Mental Health Law in California," *Society and Mental Health* 12, no. 2 (2022): 155–73.

7. See, for example, Dan A. Lewis et al., *Worlds of the Mentally Ill: How Deinstitutionalization Works in the City* (Carbondale: Southern Illinois University Press, 1991); Tanya Marie Luhrmann, "'The Street Will Drive You Crazy': Why Homeless Psychotic Women in the Institutional Circuit in the United States Often Say No to Offers of Help," *American Journal of Psychiatry* 165, no. 1 (2008): 15–20; Rose Ricciardelli and Laura Huey, *Adding Insult to Injury: (Mis)Treating Homeless Women in Our Mental Health System* (Boulder, CO: Lynne Rienner, 2016.

8. See Jennifer A. Reich, "Old Methods and New Technologies: Social Media and Shifts in Power in Qualitative Research," *Ethnography* 16, no. 4 (2015): 394–415.

INDEX

Printed and bound by CPI Group (UK) Ltd, Croydon, CR0 4YY

09/10/2023

08128269-0001